Radical Islam
in the West

ALSO BY BRIAN R. FARMER

*American Political Ideologies: An Introduction to the
Major Systems of Thought in the 21st Century* (McFarland, 2006)

Radical Islam in the West

Ideology and Challenge

BRIAN R. FARMER

McFarland & Company, Inc., Publishers

Jefferson, North Carolina, and London

LIBRARY OF CONGRESS CATALOGUING-IN-PUBLICATION DATA

Farmer, Brian R., 1959–
    Radical Islam in the West : ideology and challenge /
Brian R. Farmer.
        p.   cm.
    Includes bibliographical references and index.

    ISBN 978-0-7864-5953-7
    softcover : 50# alkaline paper ∞

    1. Islam and politics — Europe, Western.   2. Islam and
politics — North America.   3. Islamic fundamentalism —
Europe, Western.   4. Islamic fundamentalism — North
America.   I. Title.
    BP173.7.F368   2011
    297.09182'1— dc22   2010039981

British Library cataloguing data are available

Cover images © 2010 Shutterstock

Manufactured in the United States of America

McFarland & Company, Inc., Publishers
  Box 611, Jefferson, North Carolina 28640
    www.mcfarlandpub.com

Table of Contents

Preface

From the end of World War II until 1989, the predominant security pre-occupation of Western democracies was the Cold War and the containment of communism. The collapse of the communist bloc from 1989 to 1991, however, left in its wake the illusion that the largest threat to security in the geopolitical system had been eliminated and that Western-style capitalist democracy had emerged as the "victor" and represented the "end of history" or at least the end of ideological conflict. Concurrent with this thesis was the idea that the United States occupied a position as a dominant hegemon that no other political entity could seriously challenge. This view, however, proved to be naïve and short-lived. The terrorist attacks of 9/11 shattered these illusions and revealed that the post–Cold War world could be every bit as deadly as the system that preceded it and perhaps even more so. Suddenly, radical Islam had arrived on the scene in shocking fashion to demonstrate that Western capitalism was neither secure nor universally accepted, that ideological conflict had not reached its end, and that the United States, with all its economic and military power, remained vulnerable to attack from political enemies. Furthermore, given that so many of the persons associated with the 9/11 attacks were either residents of the West or were Muslims who were in many ways greatly "Westernized," the 9/11 attacks also demonstrated that the most recent challenge to Western dominance was not isolated in the non–Western realm, but instead in some cases dwelt within the West itself. Seemingly from nowhere, radical Islam, in part spawned within the West itself, had dealt the most powerful Western nation an unprecedented blow and proved that it was a force with which to be reckoned.

Many in the United States in particular and in the West in general were bewildered after 9/11 as they had kept their eyes firmly on the communist threat during the Cold War, but had scarcely noticed the rise of radical Islam. As of 9/11, however, Islam has supplanted communism in the minds of most Westerners as the most pressing global threat. Polls in the United States and Europe now showed that radical Islam and the Global South (where most predominantly Islamic countries are located) were perceived by the Western public as the greatest threats.[1]

French writer Michel Houellebecq was apparently speaking for many Westerners when he proclaimed in the September 2001 issue of *Lire* magazine that "Islam is definitely the most [f**ked up] of all religions."[2] Similarly, the next month the founder of the French newspaper *Le Point* declared himself to be an Islamophobe and denounced the religion as an "inanity of various archaicisms."[3]

Statements of this nature, not to mention acts of horrific violence in Western countries themselves, suggest that radical Islam within Western societies may be among the greatest challenges that Western democracies will face in the coming decades. That being the case, this investigation into the state of radical Islam in the West and its impact on Western societies is warranted.

This book will provide a survey of the major tenets, segments, and developments surrounding the emergence of radical Islam within Western societies. The historical development of radical Islam within Western democracies will be discussed along with the current politics surrounding Islam in the West, and a discussion of the Islamists living in the West themselves. The survey will include discussions of significant terrorist events and activities of Western Islamists, and the policies and reactions of the Western societies regarding Muslims living within their borders. The connections between the authoritarian personality type and radical Islam also will be explored along with the major problems and contradictions of radical Islam as well as the clashes between Islamist ideology and the existing cultures in Western societies, including the clashes over terrorism, headscarves, halal slaughter, and political cartoons. The ways in which Islamists use Western freedoms, such as freedom of speech and religion, to their advantage, along with their use of modern technologies, most notably the Internet, also will be explored.

The connection of radical Islam with the research on authoritarian personality types, which, it will be argued, appears to be what is at the root of radical Islam, opens up a different direction in the approach to understanding radical Islam that hopefully will not only provide greater insight into the questions of why, but also provide more insight into how the problem of radical Islam within Western societies can best be approached.

This investigation into radical Islam in the West will also provide in-depth portraits of a good number of "Westernized" Islamists so as to illuminate common characteristics and similarities among the Islamists that may be contributing factors to their choice of radical Islam as a way of life. Given that some of the most notorious Islamists watched Western television as children, went to Western universities, drank alcohol in ~~rn~~ bars, etc., it appears that immersion of Muslims in Western culture i ~~the perfect solution to~~ the problem of radicalization among Western Mu

It will also be shown that international event ~~ch~~ as thirty years of war and unrest in Afghanistan, sixty years of violence unrest in Palestine, and the American invasion of Iraq, contribute to the r ~~of~~ Islamism within Western societies themselves. The Fort Hood tragedy November 2009, where U.S. Army Major Nidal Malik Hasan is thought to have killed thirteen fellow American soldiers due to his outrage at the idea of Americans killing Muslims in Afghanistan, is a case in point. Although the U.S. military's own investigation into the tragedy at this point is not complete, the early evidence is at least suggestive that Hasan committed his acts of murderous violence for the same reasons that Osama bin Laden once declared war on America. In essence, both acted in reaction to what they perceived as American persecution and murder of Muslims across the globe. As will be demonstrated, the same can be said for the London bombers of 7/7 and the Madrid bombers of 3/11. When these and other events are placed together, a pattern emerges that suggests that if Western societies are serious about thwarting the growth of radical Islam within their societies, they may also need to alter their behavior in international affairs.

Clarification of Terms

Some clarification of a few terms that will be utilized in this book is warranted in an effort to make the discussion more clear for those that might be less familiar with the subject matter. First, a distinction needs to be made between Islam, the religion that some 1.5 billion people on the globe profess, and radical Islam or "Islamism" (radical Islam and Islamism are terms that can be used synonymously), which refers to radical, militant, ideological versions of traditional conservative Islam, where the practitioners typically consider Islamic jihad against infidels to be a primary duty of all Muslims. The practitioners of radical Islam or Islamism are referred to as "Islamists" or "radical Muslims" (two more terms that can be used synonymously).

Islamists

It is the Islamists, rather than Muslims in general, that are the primary concern of this book because it is they, not Muslims in general, who have exhibited a greater tendency to engage in violent acts, including kidnapping,

summary executions, suici̶   ̶nbings, and other forms of terrorism over
the last several decades th̶   ̶ general population.

One does not, how̶   ̶have to engage in violent acts or terrorism in
order to subscribe to th̶   ̶ology of Islamism. In general, those who should
be considered as Islam̶   ̶are those who place Islam at the core of their political
beliefs and practices̶   ̶d use the language of Islam and Islamic metaphors as
a framework throu̶   ̶ which they view reality. Islamists are also those who
justify their radical political activities through religious terminology. It should
be noted, however, that Islamists, like those who subscribe to other ideologies — such as Marxism, for instance — are not all identical in their beliefs and
motives, so the discussion of Islamism is a discussion of general tendencies.
Selected individuals may violate some of the general tendencies of Islamism,
yet still be considered as Islamists. In the words of S. Sayyid, "Islamism is a
discourse that attempts to center Islam within the political order. Islamism
can range from the assertion of a Muslim subjectivity to a full-blooded attempt
to reconstruct society on Islamic principles."[4] In other words, there are
Islamists who simply believe that Islam should be the basis of politics and
society, whereas other Islamists believe that it is necessary to intervene in the
affairs of state and seize control of politics in the name of Islam so that a
global Islamic order can be imposed. Still other Islamists argue that they must
wage a physical war against the enemies of Islam. In all cases Islamism includes
the goal of moral reform of society according to Islamic principles. After all,
if one's ultimate goal is to convert the entire world to a purer form of Islam,
it would do little good to seize control of politics in the name of Islam if the
people are to remain infidels resistant to Islam.[5]

Jihad

Importantly, Islamism includes a call to jihad. The word "jihad" is often
interpreted as meaning holy war against the enemies of Islam, but more literally it means "struggle" and refers to the struggle by every Muslim for the
good Islamic life. In this sense, jihad is widely considered one of the basic
commandments of the faith and an obligation imposed on all Muslims.[6] In
the most widely accepted definition, jihad is largely an affair between the
believer and God, and normally is an act of faith rather than an act of politics;
consequently, most Muslims believe there is no obligation for the jihadists to
commit acts of terrorism or to actually defeat the enemies of God. Instead,
the jihad or struggle is for God; hence, the struggle itself is successful if it
demonstrates one's devotion to God and is therefore pleasing in His sight,
even when a specific action is physically unsuccessful in the temporal world.[7]

Jihad is normally declared by a religious leader and consists not of a war between states, but of the struggle between Muslims and nonbelievers or infidels.[8] In the Islamist interpretation, the focus of global jihad is on the struggle or war of Muslims against infidels and oppressors of Islam, normally represented by Israel and the West, with the United States in particular a popular target as the most powerful supporter of Israel, as the most efficient killer of Muslims, and as the most grievous infidel occupier of Muslim lands. The struggle is ongoing and without limits of time or space, and Islamists believe that they are obligated to continue the jihad until the entire world has either accepted Islam or submitted to the power of a global Islamic state. In the Islamists' conception, until Islam ultimately prevails, the world will remain divided into the House of Islam and the "House of War" that comprises the rest of the world.[9]

The Islamists' justification for warfare and killing in the name of jihad is that the violence is for God and against God's enemies, and in cases where Islam is under attack or the followers of Mohammed are under attack from infidels, the good Muslims need show no mercy.

It is worth reiterating that within the Koranic verses sanctioning war against the enemies of God, believers are also instructed to "aggress not: God loves not aggressors." Consequently, more moderate Muslims do not necessarily agree with the Islamists in their contention that the Koran compels Muslims to wage war against infidels, and moderate Muslims therefore may be expected to condemn Islamic jihad and terrorism in any given circumstance, depending on the importance they give to "aggress not" and their interpretation of its application. In other words, Islam need not be a violent religion in spite of the Koranic sanction of jihad, and Muslims are likely to disagree as to what conditions are necessary to justify jihad in any given situation.

Islam Is Here to Stay

The vitality of the Islamic faith when it is transplanted into Western democracies is obvious. Western democracies are typically characterized by a shift away from the collective and the sacred and toward the individual and the secular. This shift simply has not occurred in Islamic societies, and, as a consequence, literally millions of Muslims living in the West, many of whom were born in the West, generally have not abandoned the sacred and collective of Islam for Western secularism or Christianity. Instead, Western Muslims generally have retained their faith, often both inwardly and outwardly, and in many cases have rejected Western individualism. Given that the main thrust of Islam is submission to God, devout Muslims have conflict with Western individualism because in Islam, the individual ultimately depends on God and there is no right of action without God. The Western Enlightenment is therefore rejected by most Muslims because it does not come from God. Devout Muslims also reject Western moral relativism (as do fundamentalist Christians). As a consequence, many Muslims do not view the Western individualist path as the only path, but instead favor an as-yet-undefined Muslim version of modernity in the West.[10]

This places Muslims in Western societies at odds with many other Westerners who assume that the Muslim worldview can and must change. Thus, there have been clashes within Western societies between Muslims and the society at large over a variety of issues, including headscarves, political cartoons, and halal meat. Most Muslims living in the West have very reliably used Western democratic means in attempts to shape policies in these areas to be more palatable to the general Western Muslim population. Islamists, however, have often resorted to horrific acts of violence and terrorism; consequently, success in meeting the Islamist challenge from within will be a major preoccupation of Western societies for decades to come, and it is certain that the challenge cannot be met without in-depth understanding of the Islamist's mindset. Hopefully, this work can help contribute to that understanding.

CHAPTER 1

The Western Islamist Challenge

Islam (in general, not specifically radical Islam) is now the world's second largest religion, involving more than 1.2 billion people residing on every continent except Antarctica and amounting to approximately 20 percent of the world's population. Furthermore, due to the high birth rates in Islamic countries, Islam is expected to overtake Christianity as the world's largest religion by 2025 and account for approximately 30 percent of the world's population, some two billion people.[1] With such a large global population, Muslims have not remained in the traditionally Islamic realm, but have emigrated in large numbers over the last century until significant Muslim populations now reside in virtually every Western industrialized democracy. In fact, currently more Muslims live as minorities in non–Muslim countries than in the Arab lands of North Africa and the Middle East that many Westerners view as the cradle of Islamic civilization.[2] For example, China now is home to approximately 20 million Muslims, a figure close to the number of Muslims in Saudi Arabia.[3] Economic opportunity in the West is expected to continue to be greater than in the Islamic realm, and, what's more, the combinations of economic stagnation and political instability that have been endemic to the Islamic realm over the last century are expected to continue well into the current century, thus providing push factors for even greater Muslim immigration to the West.

Over 15 million Muslims live in Europe and the United States, and an estimated 12 million more live in Russia, although the exact number is unclear due to a lack of reliable statistics and some confusion over exactly what constitutes a Muslim.[4] Most countries do not include questions on religious affiliation in their censuses, so the number of Muslims present in any country at any given time must be estimated from surnames or immigration statistics. For example, if there are 2.4 million Turkish-origin residents in Germany, and 98 percent of the Turkish population is Muslim, then there should be a bit fewer than 2.4 million Muslims in Germany. This number, however, does not take into account those who have converted to Islam whether by marriage or otherwise, nor does it consider whether someone of Turkish origin has ever even been inside a mosque. The number also does not include the number of illegal immigrants, which cannot be known precisely and may be significant. For example, it is estimated that in Germany there are between 0.6 and 1.5 million illegal immigrants; the percentage of which are Muslim is unknown, but is expected to be the vast majority.[5] Similarly, the number of illegal immigrants from North Africa in Spain may be as high as 4 million, and boats filled with illegal immigrants regularly sink in the Straits of Gibraltar.[6] Some 600,000 Muslims now reside in Italy, and estimates of the number of Muslims in France vary from 2.6 to 5 million. In the UK, however, the 2001 census did ask respondents to state their religion and more than 1.5 million persons, 3 percent of the population of the UK, self-identified as Muslims.[7]

The Western Muslim population is also far from stagnant, but growing both due to immigration and natural increase from birth rates that exceed Western averages. By the early 1990s, two-thirds of all immigrants in Europe were Muslim and Muslims accounted for approximately 10 percent of all births.[8] France, which is now approximately 10 percent Muslim, is expected to be approximately one-fourth Muslim by 2040.[9] In any case, the presence of such vast numbers of Muslims residing in the West, and the prospect that the number will only increase, means that Islam must now be considered a Western religion. Of the world's 1.2 billion Muslims, only approximately one-third now reside in countries where non–Muslims are the majority. Obviously, conservative Muslim juristic discourses that reject the legality in Islamic law of Muslims living in non–Muslim territories have been rendered irrelevant and obsolete as the Muslim peoples have chosen to live in lands dominated by "infidels."[10]

In the United States, the Muslim population remained small until the relaxation of immigration policies in 1965 eliminated strict immigration quotas placed on Muslim countries. As a result, Muslims were arriving in America at a rate of 35,000 per year prior to the terrorist attacks of 9/11.[11]

Muslims living in the West are also concentrated in urban areas. Muslims are currently estimated to compose almost one-fourth of the population of Amsterdam, one-fifth of Marseilles, and 15 percent of Paris, Brussels, and Birmingham. Muslims currently make up approximately 10 percent of the populations in London and Copenhagen. As a result, there are 2,400 mosques in Germany, 2,000 in France, and 1,000 in England, thus changing not only the ethnic and religious makeup of Europe, but the architectural landscape as well.[12]

Western Muslims and Sharia

Undoubtedly, the vast majority of these Western Muslims, whether legal or otherwise, are not Islamic extremists, are not terrorists, do not support the introduction of sharia (Islamic law) into the West, and do not support applying sharia to non–Muslims. Even if they did, they would find that there is simply no way that sharia could be implemented in Western democracies since Koranic traditions of polygamy, wife-beating, beheading and stoning are illegal in every advanced Western democracy.[13] Furthermore, Western courts will not recognize the sharia requirement that the man receive custody of the children in cases of divorce, and the sharia requirement that a specific time period must elapse before one is allowed to remarry will not be recognized by Western courts. Sharia also specifies that sons get twice the inheritance imparted to daughters, but Western courts allow Muslims and non–Muslims alike to structure their wills as they please. Furthermore, the practice of female circumcision is illegal in every Western country.[14]

For most Western Muslims, these Western intrusions into sharia are just fine; it appears that the vast majority of Western Muslims oppose altering Western civil laws to respect Islamic law, and instead prefer to allow Islamic legal scholars to decide on legally binding decisions for Muslims living in the West within the Western legal systems. Survey data in Denmark, Sweden, France, and Germany suggest that over three-fourths of Muslims in these countries oppose any supplanting of Western civil law with sharia.[15] In the United States, Muslims of Middle Eastern or North African origin tend to view themselves as Arab Americans and not fundamentally different from other ethnic groups that may have immigrated decades or centuries prior.[16] As such, there is no significant movement in the U.S. to replace supplant American laws with sharia.

Western governments have stressed the need to demarcate between Islamists, who favor a return to strict sharia, even in Western countries, and other more "moderate" Muslims that have lived in the West as good citizens in many cases for generations. This simple dichotomy, however, fails to consider popular support among Western Muslims for the Islamists' position on numerous issues, most notably the Palestinian question and the question of the morality of Muslim suicide attacks against Israel. Though these are foreign policy questions in the West, rather than domestic issues, the popular support for these more radical policies among Western Muslims tends to blur the border between Islamists and moderate Muslims in the West and make assessment of the dangers posed by Islamism within Western countries more difficult.[17]

The Muslims who favor Western law and reject application of sharia in

Western countries are not the primary subject of this book; however, there does not appear to be complete unanimity among Western Muslims as to what facets of sharia should be applied in the West and to what extent. Clearly, the existence of such a large Muslim diaspora is one of the key elements that enable the spread of global Islamism, especially given the lack of a clear-cut dichotomy between "moderate" and "radical" Islam as radical and moderate Muslims in the West are brought into contact with each other within the dominant Western cultures. Most Muslims living in the West do not feel that they have to jettison their religion in its entirety in order to live comfortably in the Western world; however, many Muslims in the West are finding that there are often unattractive compromises that they must make in the interest of avoiding conflict and prospering in the West. Often, Muslims find that there may be fine lines between retaining religious traditions sufficiently to call themselves Muslim and retaining ancient practices that make Muslims appear ridiculous to the majority in a foreign culture where reason often takes precedence over revelation.

The Emergence of Western Islamism

Many Western Muslims find that they are forced to uncomfortably compromise religious principles in one area or another in order to advance themselves in Western societies, though they do not view Western culture as incompatible with Islam as a whole. For a small minority of more radical Muslims, however, any religious compromise is unpalatable and the West itself, though they live within it, is viewed as an enemy of Islam. Though this clearly is not representative of the vast majority of Western Muslims, there are ominous signs that radical Islam is growing in strength within the Western countries. For example, an estimated 24 percent of British Muslims surveyed in July 2005 stated that they sympathized with the London bombers that attacked the London transport system on July 7, 2005. A 1997 poll of Turkish Germans revealed that approximately a third believed that Islam should come to power in every country in the world (essentially the goal of Osama bin Laden) and that violence against nonbelievers was justified in the interest of the greater Islamic good. In Britain in 2008, a poll revealed that 40 percent of Muslim students at British Universities favored the implementation of sharia and a third thought that killing in the name of Islam was acceptable.[18] To top it all off, there was jubilation in the Muslim quarters of several European cities after the terror attacks of 9/11, including London and Rotterdam.[19] Osama bin Laden himself stated on one of his videotapes released after 9/11 that the 9/11 attacks had led to Islamic conversions in Europe, and in the Netherlands in particular. In the words of bin Laden,

> In Holland, at one of the centers, the number of people who accepted Islam during the days that followed the operations was more than the people who accepted Islam in the last eleven years. I heard someone on Islamic radio who owns a school in America say: "We don't have time to keep up with the demands of those who are asking about Islamic books to learn about Islam." This event made people think (about Islam) which benefited Islam greatly.[20]

The fact that several of the 9/11 terrorists were European, combined with the fact that large numbers of Muslims celebrated across Europe on 9/11, added to the fact that there have also been major terrorist attacks in Madrid and London since 9/11 and political unrest among Muslims across Europe, suggests that radical Islam among Muslims living in the West may be among the most important challenges facing Western societies in the twenty-first century. To complicate matters further, the factors that scholars typically viewed as capable of dampening the radicalism of religion — democracy, the free market, and advanced technology — may be combining to allow a more radicalized version of Islam to thrive, leaving death and destruction in their wake. Tragically, victims of Islamist violence are typically not soldiers, diplomats, legislators, governmental bureaucrats, or heads of state, but everyday citizens engaged in everyday activities such as shopping, working, and commuting. It is the exploration of these challenges to Western society presented by the growing presence of radical Islam in the West that is forcing Western countries to re-examine the role of religion, free speech, and civil rights in general in Western societies. It is possible that the Western paradigm that has been in place since World War II is in the midst of a serious transformation. The role that radical Islam is currently playing in Western societies is the subject matter of this book, with the primary goal being enlightenment without alarmism, while at the same time acknowledging some disturbing Islamist trends in Western Muslim communities.

From Afghanistan to Western Jihad

An increase in radicalization of Muslims in the West after 1990 undoubtedly has been aided by the end of the war against the Soviet Union in Afghanistan and the global dispersion of Afghan jihadists to Western locations throughout the globe. In the United States in particular, anticommunist zeal led to the granting of aid and visas to members of the Afghan mujahadeen, some of whom later had connections with al-Qaeda. The Reagan administration essentially promoted the mujahadeen as "freedom fighters" and provided mujahadeen leaders access to the United States for the purpose of recruiting jihadists for the Afghan war against the Soviet Union. Mujahadeen leaders were similarly romanticized in the American media and even made tours through American churches, where they were applauded for their courage in the fight against godless communism.[21]

Many of the mujahadeen, however, did not view the Afghan war simply as a war against communism, but as part of a global jihad or holy war against infidels with the ultimate goal of converting the world to Islam. In this view, the defeat of the Soviets by the mujahadeen was just the first victory of God's warriors over a Western power. With God's help, more victories would surely follow.[22]

The West as the Battleground for Jihad

Osama bin Laden's mentor, Ayman al-Zawahiri, views the world as in the midst of a clash between Islam and forces hostile to Islam, which include not only secular dictatorships in the Islamic realm, but Western industrialized democracies, most specifically the United States (which Zawahiri terms as the "grand master of evil"), but also Russia.[23] Similarly, Zawahiri views the United Nations; nongovernmental humanitarian organizations, such as Amnesty International and Human Rights Watch; international corporations; and the Western media all to be the enemies of Islam.[24] For Zawahiri and his followers, it is not enough to wage jihad in the Islamic realm, but instead the jihad must be taken to the "far enemy" itself, hence, the necessity of the 9/11 attacks, the Madrid bombings, the London bombings, and the jihad in Chechnya.[25]

In terms of tactics, Zawahiri advocates attacks on the enemies of Islam in the West by small groups, since the military superiority of the West makes it impossible for the jihadists to take confront their adversary head on. In the words of Zawahiri, "It is entirely possible to kill Americans and Jews with a single bullet, a knife, an ordinary explosive device, an iron bar. It is not all difficult to set fire to their property with a Molotov cocktail. With the available means, small groups can pose a threat to Americans and Jews."[26] Zawahiri further argues that the jihadists should inflict "maximum damage" and contends that it is legitimate to kill Western civilians and not just attack Western governments because "Western voters vote freely. Therefore, these are the people who deliberately requested, supported, and encouraged not only the creation but also the perpetuation of the state of Israel."[27]

The Enlightenment, Western Culture, and Islamism

Western culture in its present state diverges from Islamic cultures in that it has been forged by its passage through the Age of Enlightenment, which was described by Immanuel Kant as "man's coming of age, a freeing of the mind from external controls," certainly including religion.[28] The Enlightenment brought a belief in human natural goodness, an optimistic faith in reason and knowledge, and a confidence in empirical research, the enemies of which are political tyranny, ideological enthusiasm, religious fanaticism, moral hypocrisy, and prejudice. The Enlightenment essentially brought unanimity on the requirement of religious toleration, but also on the need for less barbaric criminal law that would be unreliant upon torture and cruel and unusual punishments.[29] Consequently, some of the ideas of criminal punishment contained in the Koran and favored by Islamists, such as stonings and amputations, have been taboo in the West for over 200 years. It should be noted, however, that Western societies also jettisoned many of the draconian criminal codes of the Old Testament, such as the prescriptions of execution for homosexuality and bestiality. Instead, the Western idea is perhaps best summed by Victorian British PM Gladstone, who argued in a letter to his son that the best way to actually bolster the Church of England was to discard its most indefensible aspects.[30]

In contrast, for radical Islamists, the very idea of religious compromise is abominable and one more reason to despise the decadent West. For the radical Islamists, the goal is to Islamize modern Western society as part of their eventual goal of a world under Islam. The very idea of a secular enlightenment based on science and rationalism that is so dear to the West is anathema to the Islamists.[31]

Scottish philosopher David Hume, in his *Natural History of Religion* (1757), argues that religion emerged as a reaction to the chaos of human life. In primitive religions, there were gods for everything and as humans experienced new events, they invented new gods and new supernatural explanations. The explanations were full of contradictions and inconsistencies, but prior to the emergence of written scriptures, the ancient religions could adapt and cope with the inconsistencies and were fundamentally tolerant.[32] For the Islamists, the Koran is timeless and represents God's last word; there can be no deviations from its commands regardless of human experiences and developments (even though Islamists quarrel among themselves over what the Koran actually means).[33] Consequently, the Islamist view of Islam is fundamentally opposed to social change and intolerant by nature. That being the case, Islamism is replete with anti–Western views that have been translated into the violence and terrorism of the present age.

It is this violent anti–Western component of Islamism that has made Islamism the most important concern of Western politics since 9/11. Westerners have proven that they will tolerate cultural differences and will support other nonliberal governments and cultures (such as that of Saudi Arabia), as long as they are not anti–Western in character. After all, the United States and its Western allies in 1991 committed their militaries to defending the perhaps the most fundamentalist of all cultures in the Islamic world when they launched the effort to protect Kuwait and Saudi Arabia against Saddam Hussein's Iraq. Few would dispute that Saddam Hussein's Iraq at the time was more culturally Westernized than Saudi Arabia, but the more fundamentalist Saudi Arabia was also at the time more pro–Western.[34] Given that Islamism in the early twenty-first century has developed a violent anti–Western and particularly anti–American character, Islamists have placed themselves on a collision course with the West.

The Radicalizing Impact of Contact with the West

The rise of Islamism in the West is clearly a product of globalization as religious fundamentalists are thrown into societies with exceedingly different cultural mores. While other immigrants (including most Muslims) adapt to Western culture and assimilate, Islamists find themselves unable to do so and resist Western acculturation. Islamism itself provides an antidote to the pervasive globalization of Westernism that the Islamists abhor.[35]

The reasons for the anti–Western stance of the Islamists are undoubtedly rooted in their strict views of the Koran that command them to keep separate from infidels and to refrain from adopting their ways. Unfortunately, immersion in Western culture in some cases only appears to exacerbate the anti–Western feelings among some fundamentalist-leaning Muslims. In fact, many of the most important Islamists both past and present experienced extensive contact with Western culture only to react with even greater revulsion. One of the most important Islamists to fall into this category is Sayyid Qutb, an Egyptian Islamist "martyred" in the 1960s, who was important in forging the radical anti–Western Muslim political ideology espoused by Islamists in the twenty-first century.

Sayyid Qutb

Qutb came to the United States after World War II after having already become acquainted with the West through French literature and Hollywood movies. Qutb arrived in New York City in 1948 and was shocked by what he viewed as Western moral decadence. Not only did American women dishonor themselves by allowing themselves to be seen in public, Americans engaged in sexual mixing, drunkenness, lewd music, dancing, and premarital sex. To make matters worse, prostitutes in New York City openly shopped their wares in full public view. For Qutb, Western culture was replete with lust and materialism and devoid of morality.[36] In the words of Qutb, although he came from a little village in Egypt, it was in America that he found a "primitiveness that reminds us of the ages of jungles and caves."[37]

Qutb moved to Washington, D.C., where he learned English at Wilson Teachers College. While in Washington, Qutb required a tonsillectomy which led to him being scandalized by an American nurse who itemized for him the qualities she preferred in a lover. It was during his time in Washington that Qutb joined the Islamist group known as the Muslim Brotherhood.[38]

In 1949, Qutb moved to the American heartland to attend college at the Colorado State College of Education at Greeley. Although Greeley lacked the bars, prostitutes, and liquor stores of New York City, Qutb still found Western materialism sufficiently prevalent to detest, and Qutb even condemned Greeley homeowners for tending to their lawns. In the words of Qutb, "Every house is like a flowering plant and the streets are like garden pathways. One observes the owners of these homes toiling away in their leisure time, watering their yards and manicuring their gardens. This is all they appear to do."[39]

In Greeley as in New York, Qutb found himself scandalized by an American woman who was able to speak with him frankly concerning human sexuality. According to Qutb, a woman informed him that the "issue of sexual relations is simply biological" and that "You Orientals complicate this simple matter by introducing a moral element to it."[40] Qutb, with his strict Muslim sensibility, was aghast.

Qutb also experienced racism in America and was once turned away at a Greeley movie theatre when the theater owner mistook him for an African American.[41] Qutb was also exposed to American music in Greeley as he had been in New York City and expressed his disapproval (much as many conservative American parents did during the same time period) thusly,

> Jazz is the American music, created by Negroes to satisfy their primitive instincts — their love of noise and their appetite for sexual arousal.... The American is not satisfied with jazz music unless it is accompanied by noisy singing. As the volume increases, accompanied by unbearable pain to the ears, so does the excitement of the audience, their voices rising, their hands clapping, till one can hear nothing at all.[42]

Finally, Qutb was repulsed by a visit to an American church, where one Sunday evening he experienced a dance, which Qutb found repulsive and decadent. In the words of Qutb, "the room convulsed with the feverish music from the gramophone. Dancing naked legs filled the hall, arms draped around the waists, chests met chests, lips met lips, and the atmosphere was full of love."[43] Scandalized by his experiences, Qutb returned to Egypt convinced that Western culture was the number one enemy of Islam and Muslims should therefore endeavour to destroy it.[44] Qutb's writings later led thousands of Muslim readers to the same conclusions.

Colonialism and Humiliation

Islamists such as Qutb reject the values of the West, but while Qutb argued that it should be destroyed, others seek to reform Western societies to be more in conformity with Islam. The failure of Western societies to fully conform to the tenets of Islam and allow what Islamists view as "decadence" may fuel some Islamist rage, but some of the roots of Islamist rage are clearly also due to a feeling of humiliation that has emerged as a consequence of colonization and military subjugation by the West along with what they view as Western economic exploitation.[45] For example, Ayatollah Khomeini of Iran explained to Germany's foreign minister in 1988 that Iran's rejection of the West and its choice of Islam was because of historic insults suffered by Iran at the hands of the West.[46] Another explanation for Islamist rage is the "envy factor" where Muslims are forced to contrast the attractiveness and accomplishments of Western culture with the deprivation of the Islamic world. In the words of Shireen Hunter, "Many in the Muslim world who have turned against the West have done so because they cannot have access to it and to the benefits that flow from it."[47]

For many other Islamists, however, including Osama bin Laden, Western support for unrepresentative, oppressive, and, in their view, un–Islamic governments in the Muslim world is another cause for concern. In particular, the American support for what he viewed as a corrupt regime in Saudi Arabia was a major reason cited by bin Laden for the attacks of 9/11. Coterminously, the Muslim Brotherhood in Egypt deplores the American support of Egyptian President Hosni Mubarak, who has implemented numerous purges of his Islamist opposition. Thus, Islamists in Egypt view the United States as partially responsible for their oppression at the hands of the Egyptian state. Finally, the most important complaint of the Islamists against Western foreign policy is Western support of Israel. In the minds of the Islamists living both in and outside of the West, Western countries share guilt with Israel for taking Muslim lands and slaying Muslim children in Palestine.[48]

The Muslim Diaspora and Growing
Islamism in the West

The Muslim diaspora in the West allows a diverse population of radical Islamists from all parts of the world to develop contacts and safe havens with each other within the boundaries of the "far enemy" of the West itself, using the very freedoms that the West so cherishes as cover. Exactly what percentage of the 15 million Muslims living in the West are radical Islamists is unknown, but simple math reveals that even if the number were one-tenth of 1 percent, then there are at least 15,000 radical Islamists living in Western countries that may pose threats to society at large, a number that should strike fear into the hearts of officials in charge of domestic security in all Western countries. This is especially true in light of the damage that just nineteen men (with significant financial support from globalized Islamism) were able to bring about on 9/11.

Unfortunately, it is apparent that Islamism has been on the increase among Western Muslims. In the words of French scholar of Islam Olivier Roy, Islamism has

> gained ground among rootless Muslim youth, particularly among second- and third-generation migrants in the West. Even if only a small minority is involved, the phenomenon feeds new forms of radicalization, among them support for al-Qaeda, but also new sectarian communitarian discourse, advocating multiculturalism as a means of rejecting integration into Western society. These Muslims do not identify with any given nations-state, and are more concerned with imposing Islamic norms among Muslim societies and minorities and fighting to reconstruct a universal Muslim community, or ummah. Thus, they occasionally resort to the sort of internationalist and jihadist militancy directed against the Western world that was previously the Islamist trademark.[49]

Roy goes on to argue that the increase in Islamism among Western Muslims has coincided with an increase in the number of radical madrassas and the deterritorialization of the Muslim population that has come with increased immigration.[50] Roy explains that secularism in Muslim societies, such as that of Saddam Hussein, was dictatorial and repressed religion. In contrast, Western secularism sprang from a reaction to oppressive religion. Roy argues that when the religiously repressed Muslims arrive in the West, they can suddenly practice their religion freely and do so with vigor that results from the decades of repression in their countries of origin. Muslims in the West then tend to form closed religious communities, leading to ghettoization and radicalism.[51]

The ghettoization leads to radicalism because Muslims living in secluded Muslim enclaves are likely to feel more social pressure to respect traditional Muslim values, such as the chastity and seclusion of women and arranged marriages.[52] Conversely, a greater dispersion of Muslims throughout the general populations of Western urban centers is likely to subject Muslims to a different set of social pressures that tend to oppose tradition in favor of equality and choice. Thus, while Islamists call for a return to "traditional values," polygamy and fertility rates among Western Muslims are on the decline, while divorce rates and prostitution among Western Muslim women are on the increase.[53] Radicalization and assimilation among Muslims living in the West appear to be on the increase coterminously.

Scholarly estimates vary greatly, however, and there is not unanimity among scholars on how an Islamist "threat" should be measured and in what ways that radical Muslims pose a "threat." Is an individual a "threat" to Western society if that person simply refuses to eat food that is not halal, or must one call for the destruction of the West on a radical Islamic website before he is considered to be a threat? Is terrorism the only threat posed by radical Islam to the West, or is the West also in danger of cultural destruction as it is overwhelmed by vast populations of radical Muslims? For example, Giles Kepel concluded that 24 percent of France's Muslims were "too orthodox to interact with French society," thus suggesting that Muslims constitute a major threat to French culture.[54] Similarly, Archbishop Giuseppe Bernardini, the head of the Izmir archdiocese in Turkey, has denounced Muslim immigration to Europe as "reconquest" and termed ecumenical efforts with Muslims as "a dialogue of the deaf." Bernardini further stated that such terms as freedom, equality, justice, rights of man, and democracy "have a completely different meaning for the Muslims than for us."[55]

Some empirical evidence, however, is in conflict with the Archbishop's conclusions. A French study in 2001, for instance, found that only 10 percent of French Muslims were religiously observant, though 70 percent did the "little things" such as avoiding drinking alcohol or eating pork. In other words, some 10 percent of Muslims in France refused to do such things as eat with non–Muslims, thus seriously hindering integration, while 70 percent could eat with other Frenchmen as long as they avoided pork and a glass of good French wine. In another study of Muslims in the area of Detroit, Michigan, 8 percent of Muslims stated that they adhered to strict, traditionalist interpretations of Islam, thus perhaps hindering the process of integration into the larger American society, but how great of a threat that may pose in terms of political violence by radical Islamists is unclear. In the Netherlands, less than 10 percent belong to any sort of Islamic political organization, thus suggesting that the rates of Islamist political activism are low, yet the Netherlands was also the location of the brutal Van Gogh murder by a radical Islamist that not only shocked the nation, but the entire European continent.[56]

A further challenge for Islamists living in the West involves conflict with devout Western Christians. Conflict between Islamists and Christians in Western countries is perhaps endemic in that both fundamentalist Christians and Islamists desire to make converts and share the goal of eventually unifying all mankind under one God and one religion. For that reason, Cardinal Joseph Ratzinger (now Pope Benedict XVI) in 2004 opposed the acceptance of Turkey to the European Union under the pretense that Muslim Turkey had been opposed to "Christian" Europe throughout history and therefore belonged in an association of Muslim states, rather than Christian.[57]

While conflict between Christianity and Islam is not new and even predates the Crusades, perhaps a bigger question is why religious people, who are supposedly devoted to a higher power, a higher moral code, and all that is good and just, commit actions that the rest of society view as the most immoral of all. This question is the essential subject of the following chapter.

CHAPTER 2

The Authoritarian Personality: Piety and Immorality

Mark Juergensmeyer asks the age-old question of "why bad things are done by people who otherwise appear to be good, or in the cases of religious terrorism, by pious people dedicated to a moral vision of the world."[1] The answer, according to John Shepherd, is that "the religions that engender the piety simultaneously inspire the immorality."[2] In other words, it was religion that led otherwise pious people to the Inquisition and subsequent execution of thousands for witchcraft across Europe over several centuries, the execution of twenty people for witchcraft in Salem Village in 1692, the blowing up of abortion clinics by devout evangelical Protestants in the United States in the last three decades, the 1994 slaughter of 29 Muslims at the Tomb of the Patriarchs by Jewish zealot Baruch Goldstein, Timothy McVeigh's killing of 169 innocent civilians in the bombing of the Federal building in Oklahoma City, as well as the murder of almost 3000 people by the Muslim terrorists of 9/11. Religion was the motivation for the murder of Theo Van Gogh, the bombing of the transit system in Madrid, and the bombing of the transit systems in London. Religion therefore appears to play a role in the most violent acts that have occurred in the West in the post–Cold War era.

Although the religions involved in all of the violence mentioned above, Judaism, Christianity, and Islam, all teach the virtues of peace and non-violence, they also have an ability to sanction violence that gives them potent political power. Other than the state, religion is the only other entity that can provide moral sanction for violence; consequently, it has the potential to spawn widespread violence and even war and revolution.[3] The great twentieth-century philosopher Reinhold Niebuhr expressed concern over the destructive roles that religion can play and stressed that "illusion is dangerous," because it "encourages terrible fanaticisms."[4] For that reason, Niebuhr argued that it must be "brought under the control of reason."[5] Unfortunately, many segments of religion in Western societies at present, whether Jewish, Christian, or Muslim, appear to be outside of the control of reason. Among these is Dominion Theology, a worldview that is shared by the extremist segments of all three.

Dominion Theology

Whether one is discussing the terrorists of 9/11, Timothy McVeigh, or Baruch Goldstein, the terrorists involved wanted to replace what they viewed as a corrupt, secular order with a "moral" order based on religion. In the words of Bernard Lewis concerning Islamic terrorists, in the minds of the Islamists, "the very notion of a secular jurisdiction and authority ... is seen as an impiety, indeed as the ultimate betrayal of Islam" and the "righting of this wrong" is the principal goal of Islamists.[6]

This attitude is well exemplified by Osama bin Laden and his call for global implementation of sharia, but also by Christians in the West that subscribe to Dominion Theology. Dominion Theologists, including popular evangelicals Jerry Falwell and Pat Robertson, maintain that Christianity has to assert the dominion of God over all the earth.[7] In this, the parallel with bin Laden's brand of Islamism is unmistakable. For example, Randall Terry, the founder of the anti-abortion organization Operation Rescue and a writer for the Dominion Theology magazine *Crosswinds,* argued in his "Manifesto for the Christian Church" that America should function as a "Christian nation" opposed to the "social moral evils" of secular society.[8] In this, Terry's theology is clearly in line with that of the Islamists who both want to rid society of "social moral evils" and to establish God's dominion over all the earth. Whether Muslim or Christian, the Dominion Theologists' worldview has proven to have dangerous, violent tendencies.

Reconstruction Theology

Building on the foundation of Dominion Theology in the United States is an even more extreme Christian theological movement known as Reconstruction Theology. The book that essentially established Reconstruction Theology as a movement is Rousas John Rushdoony's *Institutes of Biblical Law* (1973). Rushdoony based his arguments on the teachings of John Calvin, who argued that it was necessary to presuppose the authority of God in all worldly matters, a position that Islamists also support. The Reconstructionists therefore argue that it is necessary to "reconstruct" society by using the Bible as the basis for America's laws. In this, their arguments are no different than the

Islamists' calls for implementation of sharia or Islamic law. To propagate these views, the Reconstructionists established their own think tank, the Institute for Christian Economics, in Tyler, Texas. Similarly, Islamists in the West have created their own nongovernmental organizations to formulate and propagate their views, such as Supporters of Sharia, which will be discussed in greater detail later in this book. The Reconstructionists also publish a journal in Vallecito, California, known as the *Chalcedon Report.* Meanwhile, Islamists counter with their own publications both on the Internet and in print. The most prolific writer of the Reconstructionists, with over twenty books published, is Gary North, who argues that the moral obligation of Christians is to "recapture every institution for Jesus Christ."[9] In other words, the government, schools, laws, etc., must be based on Christianity. The ultimate goal of the Reconstructionists according to North is to eventually win over the whole world for Jesus Christ.[10] The similarity of these arguments with those of Islamists is unmistakeable.

The arguments of the Christian Dominion Theologists and Reconstructionists, however, like those of the Islamists, have proven to be more than just words, and instead often have been transformed into violent action. One person that famously set out to put North's arguments into action is the Reverend Michael Bray of the Reformation Lutheran Church in Bowie, Maryland, who was convicted and served prison time for bombing abortion clinics.[11] Bray argues that America needs a Christian form of government in order to "cleanse its soul." According to Bray, he cannot be satisfied until the legal status of the U.S. Constitution is replaced by the moral codes of the Bible.[12]

In Bray's view, a "Christian revolution" in the United States is needed to bring the changes necessary for the supplanting of the Constitution with biblical law. In his book *A Time to Kill: A Study Considering the Use of Force and Abortion,* Bray argues that violence is an appropriate response to what he views as the secularization of America. For Bray, violence is justified to accomplish what he views as the moral end of establishing God's kingdom on earth.[13] Ironically, Osama bin Laden would make similar statements about the deaths of Muslims as a result of the al-Qaeda bombings in Nairobi and Dar Es Salam in 1998. Similarly, when Islamist El Sayyid Nosair assassinated Jewish activist Meier Kahane in New York City in 1990, Islamist leaders at his Mosque explained that the killing of Kahane did not violate the Koran because Kahane was an enemy of Islam.[14]

An associate of Bray's, Paul Hill, put Bray's ideas into action in Pensacola, Florida, in 1994 when he approached a doctor that performed abortions as he entered a clinic and shot the doctor and his escort, killing them both. Hill explained his reasoning and motivation for the murders on a Christian web site. According to Hill, he found the justification and motivation for committing the acts through reading the Bible, and the verses he read directed him to his actions. Hill was convicted of murder and executed for his crimes by the state of Florida.[15]

The Christian Identity Movement

Religious fundamentalism, when combined with notions of racial supremacy appears to be a particularly potent mix. Wahhabi Islamists, for instance, stress the special place of the Arabian people in God's ordering of things. Their reasoning is that since Mohammed was Arabian and he originally recited the Koran in Arabic (God's language) as given to him in visions from Allah, then the Arabs and the Arabic language are special to God. Furthermore, the Arabs interpret God's promise to Abraham in Genesis as a blessing on his son Ishmael, the father of the Arab peoples, rather than Isaac, the father of the Jewish peoples. In short, the Wahhabi Arabs, like the Orthodox Jews, view themselves as God's chosen people.

Similarly, Christian Identity groups in the United States, such as the Posse Comitatus, The Order, the Aryan Nations, Herbert Armstrong's Worldwide Church of God, the Freeman Compound of Second Amendment advocates in Montana, and the World Church of the Creator, essentially argue that conservative white Protestant fundamentalist Americans are God's chosen people.[16] Perhaps unsurprisingly, members of Christian Identity groups have proven to be prone to violence in a manner sometimes eerily consistent with their Islamist parallels. For instance, Buford Furrow, who attacked a Jewish daycare center in Los Angeles in 1999 and shot three children and a receptionist, once lived in an Aryan Nation compound in Idaho.[17] Similarly, Eric Robert Rudolph, who exploded a bomb at the Atlanta Olympics that killed three people and injured 150, did so because of what he viewed as the pro-gay stance of Olympic organizers. Rudolph also bombed abortion clinics in Birmingham and Atlanta and at a lesbian nightclub in Atlanta.[18]

Perhaps the most important Christian Identity figure, however, is Timothy McVeigh, who was eventually executed for the worst terrorist attack in American history prior to 9/11. McVeigh was associated with a Christian Identity encampment at Elohim City on the Oklahoma-Arkansas border. Elohim City was established by Christian Identity minister Robert Millar and former Nazi Party member Glenn Miller, who stockpiled weapons to prepare themselves for an anticipated Branch Davidian–style raid from the Bureau of Alcohol, Tobacco, and Firearms.[19] McVeigh made several phone calls to the commune at Elohim City, including one two weeks before the Oklahoma City bombing.[20] McVeigh also evidently developed his Christian Identity ideas through reading a Christian Identity newsletter along with his reading of a fictional Christian Identity book from American Nazi Party writer William Pierce, entitled *The Turner Diaries*.[21] Pierce's novel, written under the pseudonym Andrew MacDonald, describes an apocalyptic battle between Christian freedom fighters and a dictatorial American government. In Pierce's book, a guerrilla band known as "The Order" calls for Christians to rise up in revolt and overthrow the U.S. government. One member of "The Order" bombs a federal office building with a truckload of "a little under" 5,000 pounds of ammonium nitrate fertilizer and fuel oil. Timothy McVeigh's actual bomb carried 4,400 pounds in an apparent effort to emulate his heroes in the non-sensical novel.[22] In short, that Timothy McVeigh, the worst terrorist in American history prior to 9/11, was a member of a Christian Identity cult is not accidental.

Similarly, it was not without accident that Osama bin Laden and fifteen of the nineteen 9/11 hijackers are from Saudi Arabia, among the most religiously conservative places in the entire Islamic realm. It is also not without accident that bin Laden was harbored in Afghanistan by the Taliban, who, if possible, were even more conservative than their Wahhabi counterparts in Saudi Arabia and dedicated to imposing God's law on earth. Extreme religious conservatism was also a characteristic of Baruch Goldstein; Jim Jones of Jonestown, Guyana; David Koresh of the Branch Davidians at Waco, Texas; the Madrid bombers of 3/11; the London bombers of 7/7; and the murderer of Theo Van Gogh. A link between religious fundamentalist extremism and political violence is obviously evident, regardless of which religion is involved.

Religion alone, however, appears to be insufficient as an explanation since literally billions of people throughout the world are religious, yet the vast majority do not engage in any form of sacred violence. Furthermore, the atrocities committed by Imperial Japan in China during World War II, the murderous purges of Joseph Stalin and the communists in the Soviet Union, and the Holocaust committed by the Nazis during World War II were not committed in an effort to please God or bring about a global theocracy. In the Soviet Union, religion was even a target of the communist purges. That being the case, religion is not a necessary component of violent extremism and there must be other psychological factors in operation in addition to religion that explain violent and intolerant human behavior. The answer may actually be found in existing psychological research based on World War II and the suggestion here is that the real culprit is the authoritarian personality type, and that the same authoritarian personality types that allowed Nazis to engage in genocide against the Jews during World War II with a clear conscience also allow fundamentalist Christians to kill abortion doctors and radical Muslims to fly planes into buildings and indiscriminately kill thousands of innocent people.

Authoritarian Personality

After World War II, psychologists and social scientists were interested in unravelling the mystery of how large segments of the populations in Germany and Italy could comply with the murderous wishes of the Nazi and fascist leaders of their respective countries. In 1950, T.W. Adorno et al. published their groundbreaking work entitled *The Authoritarian Personality* in response to that question. Adorno et al. essentially argued that there is a personality type, typically characterized by contradictions, such as educated but superstitious, and individualistic but afraid of not being like others, who are inclined to submit blindly to authoritarian leaders or groups. Adorno et al. labeled these people as authoritarian personality types.[23]

Since the introduction of the idea of the authoritarian personality by Adorno et al., other scholars have investigated and refined the research on the concept, most notably Bob Altemeyer (1996) and Stanley Feldman (2003). Both Altemeyer and Feldman found that the authoritarian personality is consistently associated with right-wing ideology.[24] In the case of Islamist terrorism, this makes sense because the Islamists are essentially the religious ultra-conservatives of the Islamic world.

Similarly, John Jost et al. studied the psychology of political conservatism in the United States and found that conservatism was associated with a "heightened psychological need to manage uncertainty and threat." Jost et al. concluded that conservatism was also associated with intolerance of ambiguity, the need for certainty or structure in life, overreaction to threats, and a disposition to dominate others. The similarity with the authoritarian personality types discussed by Adorno et al. is unmistakable.[25]

While all humans surely have some psychological needs to manage uncertainty and threat, and most humans also may have some intolerance of ambiguity, have a need for certainty and structure, overreact to threats, and even have some dispensation to dominate others, these characteristics clearly become dangerous when they are extreme and combined with a cause, such as German nationalism in 1933 or with fundamentalist religion. Mark Juergensmeyer argues that religion is an ideology of order and that movements with a strong religious vision have a tendency toward authoritarian leadership and internal discipline. Islamists, such as Osama bin Laden and Ayatollah Khomeini, are essentially the ultraconservatives and authoritarian personality types of Islamic society and also the religious fundamentalists of Islamic society.[26] As such, they appear to conform well to the psychological characteristics of political conservative authoritarians in the United States as observed by Jost et al.

Robert Altemeyer argues that a factor associated with right-wing authoritarianism is the direct method of teaching. In right-wing authoritarian households, Altemeyer found that children tended to be directly taught social conventions concerning dressing, undressing, eating, playing, speaking, sleeping, praying, and virtually everything that a person does from dawn to dusk, with obedience being a central theme. Children are not taught the reasons behind the commands to "sit up straight" or "keep your elbows off the table," but merely told what to do and what not to do.[27] Unfortunately, this method of teaching is prevalent in Islamic societies where rote memorization of the Koran is stressed and questioning of the validity or wisdom of Koranic teachings is disallowed, much as children of Protestant fundamentalist parents in the United States are told that the Bible is the literal and inerrant Word of God and cannot be questioned. The apostle Thomas, who needed to see and touch Jesus to know that he was resurrected (in other words, he needed factual evidence rather than hearsay), is disparaged as "doubting Thomas" while Apostle Paul proclaims blessings on those who believe without seeing (in other words, those who believe without any concrete evidence).

If the psychological characteristics of Islamists and American Protestant fundamentalist conservatives is similar, however, what factors explain the more aggressive behavior of the Islamists in juxtaposition with their Western counterparts (though one must concede that Timothy McVeigh's actions were as aggressive as the most extreme Islamist)? Albert Bandura argues that aggressive behaviors are instigated by some aversive stimulus, but are acted out only if the innate inhibitions against aggression can be overridden. Though there are numerous stimuli that can cause humans to overcome their inhibitions against aggression, Bandura finds that the most important factors are fear and self-righteousness, both of which appear to be present among Islamists and conservative fundamentalist Protestants. Islamists typically perceive waves of Western infidels, Muslim apostates, corruption, and sin invading their Islamic realm. Similarly, Protestant fundamentalists view waves of secular humanists, liberals, and decadent sinners as invading their realm and destroying their Godly societies. Both groups view their societies as increasingly lawless and depraved and, depending on their situations, must fear government authorities.[28] Right-wing authoritarians in the United States fear that the government is going to come get their guns, thus leading to self-fulfilling prophecies at Ruby Ridge, Idaho, and Waco, Texas, in the 1990s as the government came to get the weapons they had illegally stockpiled. Similarly, Islamists in the United States had proof that the U.S. government after 9/11 was waging a war against Islam, viewed the Islamists as a threat, and devoted tremendous energy during the War on Terror to rooting them out.

Bandura's argument that fear allows humans to override their inhibitions against aggressive behavior, however, may have policy implications for Western decision-makers as Western societies grapple with the Islamist challenge. For example, if fear is the stimulus that induces Islamists to resort to aggression, then it may be prudent for Western leaders to avoid provocative actions such as the indefinite detention of Muslims at Guantanamo Bay, the American invasion of Iraq, and the American-backed Israeli incursions into Lebanon. It is reasonable to expect that such actions would produce fear among the Islamists at whom they are directed and thus induce more Islamists into aggressive behavior. This in fact was the conclusion of America's 2006 National Intelligence Estimate (NIE) that concluded that "the Iraq jihad is shaping a new generation of terrorist leaders and operatives" and had become "a cause celebre for jihadists, breeding deep resentment of U.S. involvement in the Muslim world and cultivating supporters for the global jihadist movement."[29]

Milgram Study

Further insight into the workings of the Islamist mind is present in the work of Stanley Milgram, an American psychologist, who in 1961 conducted a study on obedience to authority. Milgram's experiment involved having an authority figure in a lab coat instruct ordinary persons selected at random to administer what they believed were painful, if not lethal, electric shocks to an actor visibly writhing to the effects of the administered shocks in another room. Milgram found that 65 percent of his subjects were willing to deliver what they believed were extremely painful, if not lethal, doses when told to do so.[30] Milgram's findings may go a long way in explaining the phenomenon of Islamic terror. Not only does Milgram's study suggest that the majority of humans evidently have the capability to inflict extreme pain or death when told to do so by an authority figure, it explains how Islamists can commit horrific acts without remorse since Islamists believe they have been told to do so by God, the ultimate authority figure.

Milgram explained, "Often it is not so much the kind of person a man is as the kind of situation in which he finds himself that determines how he will act."[31] Milgram's problem of "situation" may not only explain Islamist suicide bombers in Palestine and the terrorists of 9/11, but also the actions of Baruch Goldstein, the murders of abortion doctors by fundamentalist Christians, and the behavior of American soldiers involved in prisoner abuse in Iraq at Abu Ghraib. It may also explain the conscience of American political commentator Rush Limbaugh, who applauded the abuses at Abu Ghraib as "a brilliant maneuver."[32]

Milgram argues that the human conscience is the human "inner inhibitory system" that provides a check on destructive impulses. Because of this conscience, Milgram argues that in most situations humans will not harm one another. Milgram explains, however, that the human conscience apparently changes when the individual becomes part of a group, with the individual's conscience often becoming subordinate to that of the group or of its leader. In this group setting, unfortunately, Milgram found that persons who are normally harmless may act with severity and malice against other persons because their conscience or inhibitory system becomes subordinate to the group or the group's leader. Milgram suggests that those who submit to an authoritarian group or leader and adopt the conscience of the group or authority figure who issues an order are in an "agentic state." In other words, such persons have become "agents" of the group or authority figure's conscience.[33]

Milgram's study obviously has explanatory power for understanding how masses of people could have followed Hitler, Lenin, Pol Pot, and a host of other authoritarian ideologues with alternate views of morality. It also may explain how ordinary Muslims, such as 9/11 pilot Mohammed Atta, can adopt an alternative morality and commit mass murder for an Islamist group or authority figure such as Osama bin Laden. In short, when under the spell of such an ideology or authority figure, ordinary people have the ability to set aside their own conscience and obey the will of the group or authority figure. This is not unique to Muslims (as the abuse of prisoners by American soldiers at Abu Ghraib prison so vividly illustrates), but does appear to be a characteristic of the most radical Islamists who engage in terrorism.

Zimbardo Experiment

Another psychologist whose work has provided insight into how ordinary persons can commit the most atrocious acts is Philip Zimbardo, who in 1971 designed an experiment to test the psychological results of incarceration. Zimbardo's intent was to study the psychology of prisoners, but the final result of his experiment explained much more about the psychological effects of prison on the prison guards. Zimbrano set up a mock prison and recruited eighteen young men at random to play the roles of prisoners and guards.

Zimbardo instructed his guards to create "a psychological atmosphere that would capture some of the essential features characteristic of many prisons."[34] Zimbardo instructed his guards that they could not physically harm the prisoners, but he had to abandon the experiment after six days when his future wife, then a psychology Ph.D. student, walked in one evening to see a line of shackled, hooded prisoners being led down the hall by the guards for their bathroom break.

Although the guards in the Zimbardo experiment never physically struck the prisoners, they used every other form of intimidation and humiliation they could think of. Prisoners were forced to sing their fictitious prisoner numbers during roll call and forced to do push-ups for being out of tune. Pointless and redundant chores were invented such as making and remaking perfectly made beds, polishing boots, and picking burrs out of blankets. Prisoners were verbally assaulted, singled out for ridicule, threatened with clubs, stripped, placed in solitary confinement, and left naked all night chained to a bed. On the final evening, prisoners were forced to simulate sodomy with other prisoners bent over in front of them.[35] In just six days, the roles assigned to the participants by Zimbardo had turned the guards to abusive behavior.

Zimbardo noted, however, that among the guards there were essentially three different categories of behavior. There were the leaders that invented the routines and punishments and followers who looked up to the leaders and carried out their actions. There was, however, a third category of guards that neither invented the abusive schemes nor carried them out, but absented themselves from the business when activities were present of which they disapproved.[36]

Clearly, something had gone awry with the reasoning processes of the persons in the studies designed by Milgram and Zimbardo, as well as the reasoning processes of those, whether Islamist or otherwise, who engage in indiscriminate killing. Some of this cognitive disconnect may be due to the fact that psychologists believe that reasoning capacity is centered in parts of the brain that have more recently evolved, while other emotions, such as fear, were present much earlier and appear to be more "hardwired" in the brain. Thus when an emotion, such as one rooted in religion, is particularly strong, it can override the more subtle reasoning processes in the brain. In other words, people have a tendency to make snap judgments based principally on emotions rather than on reasoned consideration of all options.[37] That being the case, insults to revered symbols, whether they be the American flag, the cross, or the prophet Mohammed, should be expected to elicit the kind of violent reactions that the world witnessed over cartoons of Mohammed in Danish newspapers in 2004.

To compound matters further, Bob Altemeyer explains that authoritarian personality types are intolerant of criticism of the authorities they follow because they believe the authority is unassailably correct.[38] Islamists have exhibited this tendency repeatedly as they point to the Koran and sharia as their authority for committing horrific acts without applying any rules of critical thinking to the source. This type of noncritical thinking clearly permeated the Salman Rushdie affair, the violent reaction to Danish cartoons depicting Mohammed with a bomb in his Turbin, and the brutal murder of Dutch filmmaker Theo Van Gogh. Altemeyer also finds that authoritarian personality types are especially submissive to what they view as legitimate authority figures and display aggressiveness toward others when such aggressive behavior is perceived to be sanctioned by the legitimate authority. Hence, when a "legitimate authority" such as Ayatollah Khomeini called for the death of Salman Rushdie, there appeared to be no shortage of individuals ready and willing to commit violence against a fellow human being.

Altemeyer points out, however, that authoritarian personality types do not bow to every authority, but only to those that they view as good and proper. The decision of the authoritarian personality types to submit is generally determined by whether or not a particular authority has views compatible with their own, though Altemeyer finds that right-wing authoritarians are more likely than others to submit to established authorities that they do not like.[39] Once they submit, however, they tend to exhibit what Altemeyer terms as "authoritarian aggression," which he defines as a predisposition to cause harm to others when one believes that such harm is sanctioned by a trusted authority.[40] Unfortunately for Westerners, Osama bin Laden has expressed views with which far too many Muslims, both in the West and outside the West, concur; consequently, he has been able to inspire others to authoritarian aggression.

Altemeyer explains that authoritarian personality types exhibit a number of consistent personality traits, most of which fit the Islamist mindset well, including the terrorists of 9/11.[41] For instance, authoritarian personality types tend to socialize only in tight circles of like-minded people. Islamist groups are legendary for being so tight knit that the CIA is unable to successfully infiltrate it with agents.[42]

Altemeyer also demonstrates that rather than thinking critically, authoritarian personalities tend to think more based on what they are told by authority figures. As a result, the thinking of authoritarians tends to be filled with inconsistencies and they harbor numerous double standards and hypocrisies.[43] For example, Islamists are likely to proclaim that Islam is "peace" while condoning terrorism. Right-wing authoritarians are also typically hostile to anyone outside their group, and they view the world as a dangerous place with their group under attack.[44] In fact, Osama bin Laden has claimed that his war against the United States is in retaliation for America's "crusade" against Islam.

Right-wing authoritarians also appear to be predisposed to control the behavior of others through punishment.[45] Consequently, the Taliban in Afghanistan imposed harsh punishments that included amputations of hands and execution by stoning. Finally, right-wing authoritarians think of themselves as more moral than the rest of society. This sense of morality is boosted by religion, which helps them eliminate guilt knowing that they are working for God. Thus, authoritarian personality types are able to lie, cheat, steal, kill, etc., because they are certain that it is for a moral end that is pleasing to God.[46] Consequently, Mohammed Atta and the 9/11 terrorists were able to fly planes into buildings knowing that they were murdering thousands because they believed that God would be pleased.

Altemeyer argues that right-wing authoritarians exhibit a strong adherence to social conventions and generally believe in "God's law." Right-wing authoritarians therefore adhere to the conventions of society set forth in their holy books in an effort to be consistent with God's law. For these individuals, the source of human conflict is because people do not follow God's law. Their goal then is to impose God's law and thus correct societal problems.[47] Hence, among Islamists is the constant call for a return to strict sharia that they believe will bring perfect justice to human society. For Islamists, this means standard gender roles, traditional clothing, beards, and anything else that was present in the time of Mohammed. Unfortunately, this also means that right-wing authoritarians are hostile to those with whom they disagree and are likely to favor violence against people that they do not like.[48]

Because they must adhere to their holy books or authority figures, right-wing authoritarians, including Islamists, generally cannot support individual rights because those rights will allow people to ignore directives from the authoritative sources.[49] Consequently, right-wing authoritarians will tolerate abuses of power by government or authority figures with whom they agree and they will not favor harsh punishment for individuals with whom they agree. As such, Islamism becomes incompatible with the rule of law, rights and "permissiveness" of Western societies.

Altemeyer's survey data reveal that authoritarian personality types do not view themselves as prejudiced, hostile, or violent. Instead, they are essentially able to compartmentalize things in their minds and thus separate their internal contradictions and hypocrisies so that they are unable to detect them. Thus, in many ways, the authoritarians adhere to high moral standards (devotion to prayer and other pillars of Islam, for instance), but their self-right-eousness and compartmentalized conscience allow them to pray to God one moment and fly planes into buildings another. According to Altemeyer, this self-righteousness appears to be the main factor that unleashes authoritarian aggression. Altemeyer refers to these people as "God's designated hitters" and notes the irony that though they are people who believe they are very good, moral, and so close to God, they end up doing what is viewed as most evil by the rest of society.[50] Unfortunately, this is the mindset with which Western societies must learn to cope in increasing numbers.

CHAPTER 3

The Islamist Influence in
Western Democracies

The presence of such large numbers of Muslims in Western democracies obviously means that the Muslim presence will influence and alter Western democracies much as the concentration of fundamentalist Christians in the American South makes politics in Southern states somewhat different than that in Northern American states. While no Southern politician can ignore the influence of fundamentalist Protestants, many European elected officials are finding that they may ignore Muslims only at their peril. For example, Boris Johnson, mayor of London, in 2008 helped organize a festival in Trafalgar Square to celebrate the end of Ramadan. Johnson, however, is not alone. Across Europe, mayors of European urban centers are frequently concerned with things such as setting up abattoirs to cope with the slaughter of sheep for the Eid al-Adha feast or organizing security and parking around mosques on Fridays.[1] Furthermore, Muslims are now being elected to European parliaments and occupying other positions in government in virtually every Western European country. For instance, Faouzia Hariche, a Muslim, was elected mayor of Brussels and 14 Muslims have been elected members of the Brussels regional parliament. Muslim mayors have also been elected in Rotterdam and Leicester.[2]

This also means, however, that some Muslim politicians in Europe can be expected to cater to the Islamist elements if not entirely adhering to the tenets of Islamism themselves, much as Southern politicians in the United States cater to Protestant fundamentalist positions on issues such as abortion, school prayer, gay marriage, and the teaching of creationism in schools as science. For example, the Belgian Secretary for Public Monuments, Emir Kir, a Muslim, made news recently when he called for the demolition of the Belgian monument commemorating the 1915 Turkish genocide of 1.5 million Armenian Christian civilians. Kir clearly pandered to Islamists when he erroneously referred to the Armenian genocide as a "hoax" concocted by "imperialists."[3]

33

As the Muslim population grows in Western societies, it is only reasonable to expect more of this type of behavior from democratically elected politicians since democracy tends to reflect its people. Much as Southern elected politicians in the United States have often opposed gay marriage and the teaching of evolution, but favored the posting of the Ten Commandments in school, etc., more Western politicians in the future may be expected to emulate the politics of Emir Kir and oppose bans on headscarves, favor the introduction of Halal meat in schools, adopt an anti–Israel posture in foreign policy, and display sympathy for many other measures favored by devout Muslims that once would have been unthinkable in the West.

Muslim Advocacy Organizations

The Muslim diaspora has also led to the growth of Western-based Muslim advocacy organizations, Islamic groups, publications, and all manners of Muslim associational groups. Most of these groups, organizations, and publications are not Islamist in character; however, the sheer numbers of Muslims and the sheer numbers of the groups and publications lead to the probability that some will be supporters of the more dangerous strains of Islamism. This issue emerged after 9/11 when the U.S. government froze the assets of numerous America-based Islamic charities due to accusations that they had supported terrorism.[4] Even ultraconservative Saudi Arabia has taken measures against some of the more radical Islamic charities in recent years after a wave of Islamist terrorist attacks on Saudi soil.[5]

The growth and development of Muslim associational groups across the globe may be partially linked to the Western political party systems which are typically inadequate to meet the needs of Muslims in general, much less the demands of Islamists. For example, in most European countries, the political divide includes a generally "clerical" right, complete with major "Christian Democrat" parties in many countries, including the party systems of France, Italy, and Germany. While Islamists certainly must be considered to be on the far right of the political spectrum, they can hardly be expected to join the existing conservative parties in the West if they include the Christian Democrats in France or Italy that favor a preferred position for Catholicism as the official state religion. In the case of the United States, the conservative Republican Party also includes a very large contingent of the Protestant fundamentalist Christian right, many of whom consider Muslims to be abominations before God. The Christian right in the United States is also predominantly pro-Israel in foreign policy, a position that can only alienate Islamists, the most conservative segment of Islamic society, from any possible participation in the American Republican Party, the conservative Party in American society at large.

Given that the political party systems in the West are so poorly suited to the views of conservative Muslims, it is not surprising that many Muslim associations developing outside of the political party systems would be Islamist in character. Unfortunately, too many of the Islamist Muslim associational groups in the West have also displayed a tendency to ferment dangerous radical Islamic activities. While some scholars argue that these Muslim associational groups are no more dangerous than right-wing Christian religious groups in the West, such as Randal Terry's Operation Rescue that opposes abortions, others, such as noted scholar of Islam Fouad Ajami, have argued that such radical associations pose a threat to Western societies.[6] Ajami warned that the new Muslim associational groups in the West could serve as vehicles for the spread of radical Islamism with violent and dire consequences. In Ajami's view, European Muslim Associational groups are often fronts for Islamists associated with the Muslim Brotherhood and other organizations that are banned in their countries of origin. Ajami argues that Islamists who have been expelled from their countries of origin for their radicalism have exploited European political asylum policies to their advantage. The Islamists then use the Muslim associational groups to shape a radical Islamic agenda in Europe and influence policy in European countries in a way that they were unable to do in their countries of origin.

Similarly, Kepel argues that European Muslim organizations are part of a subversive strategy of the Muslim brotherhood, which has used the associations as part of a Trojan Horse strategy to try to mobilize Europe's Muslim underclasses. For Kepel, the strategy is similar to that taken by Europe's communist parties in the 1980s, whose strategy was to renounce the USSR and Leninism and instead work within the Western systems to achieve communist goals while abandoning the strategy of Leninist revolution.[7] Kepel concludes that the Muslim associations radicalize Europe's directionless Muslim youths for the purpose of advancing an Islamist agenda.[8]

Although it is clear that all European Muslim associations have not been hijacked by Islamists, some specific cases support Kepel and Ajami's conclusions. For example, Sheikh Yousuf Al-Qaradawi, the head of the European Council for Fatwa and Research, stated that the 2005 Indonesian tsunami disaster was due to the decadence of what he termed "sex tourism." In the words of Qaradawi,

> People must ask themselves why this earthquake occurred in this area and not in others. Why did it occur at this time and not another? Why? Whoever exam-

ines these areas discovers that they are tourism areas. Tourism areas are areas where the forbidden acts are widespread, as well as alcohol consumption, drug use, and acts of abomination. Whoever knows about tourism in our age knows this. These areas were notorious because of this type of modern tourism, which has become known as "sex tourism." Don't they deserve punishment from Allah?[9]

Although Qaradawi here may sound at least as much like Jerry Falwell and Pat Robertson (who blamed Hurricane Katrina on the homosexuality of New Orleans native comedienne Ellen DeGeneres) as Osama bin Laden, his views in this case are clearly not moderate, but Islamist in character.

Qaradawi has also stated publicly that he considers the death penalty a reasonable punishment for homosexuality and has publicly led prayers calling for God to destroy the "Jews and their wicked Crusader allies."[10] When al-Qaradawi was invited to London in 2004 by Ken Livingstone, the mayor of London, the invitation caused uproar among Britain's general population. Meanwhile, the Muslim Council of Britain (MCB) and Muslim Association of Britain (MAB) both publicly defended Qaradawi as a "moderate" and a "respected Islamic scholar" in spite of these statements.[11] In the MAB's publication *Inspire*, dated September 28, 2002, the MAB included an article on the organizations' "historical roots and background" that explicitly linked its beginning to the Muslim Brotherhood and stated that the goal of the MAB was "the widespread implementation of Islam as a way of life; no longer to be sidelined as a mere religion."[12]

Other evidence of Islamism among Europe's Muslim associations is in abundant supply. For example, the UK Action Committee on Islamic Affairs, the forerunner of the current British Muslim Association, and the MCB, spearheaded the campaign in Britain against Salman Rushdie. The current leader of the MCB, Iqbal Sacranie, was at the forefront of the effort. In 1989, Sacranie was quoted as saying that "death was perhaps too easy" for Rushdie, a statement that hardly reflects a moderate approach. As late as January 2005, Sacranie was involved in a Muslim boycott of a Holocaust Memorial Day ceremony. Although the MCB is generally considered a "moderate" Muslim association and the organization condemned the London bombings, the MCB has its origin in the Islamist politics of Pakistan and the writings and ideology of the famous Pakistani Islamist, Maulana Maudoodi, best known for formulating the Islamist perspective that became the foundation of the Muslim Brotherhood. The MCB is also alleged to have links to the Pakistani Islamist group, Jamaat-i-Islami (founded by Maudoodi), which is committed to the establishment of an Islamic state in Pakistan ruled by sharia. The MCB's Inayat Bunglawala publicly professed his "deep respect" for Maudoodi and stated his belief that Maudoodi should be considered "a very important Muslim thinker."[13]

It should also be noted, however, that though the MCB may be the most important mouthpiece for Islam in Britain, 45 percent of British Muslims in a 2004 poll stated that the MCB did not generally reflect their views. Secondly, the MCB distributed a letter to more than 1,000 mosque councils after the Madrid bombing urging British Muslims to help the government in identifying radical imams.[14] This position can hardly be labeled as radical or Islamist, so it appears that the MCB follows the political winds in different directions.

Another group associated with the MCB, the Muslim Association of Britain (MAB), is essentially a political action committee for Muslim interests focusing on the Palestinian issue. The MAB was established in 1997 by Kemal el-Hebawy, who at the time was considered to be the London-based spokesman for the Muslim Brotherhood.

Still another British Muslim group, known as the Muslim Parliament, was launched in 1992 following the fervor over the Rushdie affair. The leader and founder of the Muslim Parliament, Kalim Siddiqui (who died in 1996), advocated separatism and the creation of a "nonterritorial" Islamic state in Britain.[15]

Britain, however, does not have an exclusive on European Islamist groups. In Germany, Nadeem Elyas, the head of the Turkish Muslim Association known as the DITIB in Germany, is rumored to be connected to the Muslim Brotherhood (an allegation denied by Elyas). Elyas is also formerly the chair of the Islamische Zentrum Aachen-Bilal Moschee (IZA) which is also alleged to be a group associated with the Muslim Brotherhood.[16]

In France, the Union des Organisations Islamiques de France (OUIF) was formed with support from Saudi Arabia and the other Gulf states. The UOIF was founded by members of the Muslim Brotherhood (MB) and has retained links to the MB for over twenty years. The UOIF also has links to the Federation of Islamic Organizations in Europe (FIOE), another group linked to the Muslim Brotherhood. The OUIF sponsors a conservative mosque that emphasizes Arabic and deference to conservative imams. Politically, the OUIF opposes the French ban on headscarves and favors support for the Palestinian cause in the Middle East.[17]

Another French Muslim association with radical ties is Le Federation nationale des Musulmans de France (FNMF) that was created in 1985 with support from the government of Morocco. The president of the organization, Mohamed Bechari, preaches moderation, but also journeyed to Qatar in 2004 to attempt to negotiate the release of two French journalists held hostage and met with Abassi Madani, the leader of the Algerian Islamist organization Front

Islamique du Salut (FIS). The FIS is notorious in France for a series of terror bombings in Paris in the late 1980s. Bechari is also the head of the Fiqh Council of the Organization of Islamic Conferences based in Morocco that exists for the purpose of formulating Islamic unity against Israel.[18]

Overtly Islamist Groups

In addition to the Muslim Associations discussed above that may have Islamist ties, but claim to be moderate associations, there are numerous groups in the West that are openly Islamist in character. Islamism appears to be very much a group phenomenon and Islamists tend to operate in a world of social networks, some of which are web-based, but some of which also include person-to-person in-the-flesh contact. In either case, Islamist education and information-sharing is a major focus, and constant religious reinforcement is necessary to ensure that all members stay on the right path.

Islamist groups promote a set of values that challenge the dominant cultural codes in the West. In order to effectively promote the alternative set of values, it is necessary that they create a community of true believers who share a radical interpretation of Islam. Group members must know that they are not the only ones who share the radical interpretation, but that there are others who are also on the correct path. In order to show that they are on the correct path, there is a focus on the deviance of Western society and mainstream Islam from God's true teachings. Furthermore, the Omniscient, Omnipotent and Omnipresent God somehow needs human foot soldiers to help him implement what he desires human existence on the earth to be. Thus, what results is a shared meaning that becomes the basis of the common identity among the Islamists as God's servants, commanded by God to act in his name.[19]

The Saviour Sect

One major Islamist group in the West is known as the Saviour Sect (formerly Al-Muhajiroun), led by Anjem Choudry and Sheikh Omar Bakri Mohammed. Omar Bakri Mohammed was granted asylum in the UK in 1985 after he was expelled from Saudi Arabia for his radicalism.[20] The Saviour Sect at one time claimed over 800 members in Britain alone and had connections with other Islamist groups throughout Europe.[21] The name of the group (the Saviour Sect) is a reference to a statement ascribed to Mohammed in the Hadith, where the Prophet stated, "My nation will be divided into 73 sects, all of them will be in the Fire except for one" (the saved sect).[22] During 1998, Bakri Mohammed published the communications of Osama bin Laden, for whom Bakri Mohammed claimed to be a spokesman. Al-Muhajiroun gained global notoriety for its conference after the September 11, 2001, terrorist attacks where they praised the "Magnificent 19" in reference to the nineteen terrorists who flew the jetliners full of passengers into buildings in the United States. Bakri Mohammed also gained notoriety in 2003 for praising the terrorist attacks by British Muslims Asif Mohammed Hanif and Omar Khan Sharif in Tel Aviv as "martyrdom."[23]

After 9/11, the Saviour Sect became a focus of debates in the UK about the balance between free speech and national security due not only to its support of the 9/11 terrorist attacks, but also to its support of violence for the purpose of establishing Islamic states everywhere, including in the UK. Specifically, the Saviour Sect advocated that Western Muslims should join the Taliban against the U.S.-led invasion of Afghanistan. Bakri Mohammed and other leaders of the Saviour Sect have also issued fatwas calling for jihad against India, Russia and Israel, as well as condoning attacks on former British prime ministers John Major and Tony Blair.[24]

Among the items Al-Muhajiroun termed as its "vision" were the categorization of Islam as "a complete system of life" and a call to persuade all Muslims to implement Islam, and to "formulate a fifth column as a community pressure group which is well equipped with the Islamic culture, e.g., ruling, social, economic, judicial, penal, and ritual systems in order to become capable of implementing Islam fully and comprehensively in society."[25] Although the Saviour Sect's unapologetic web site clearly states that they neither engage in nor "condone or incite any type of hatred whatsoever," the group simultaneously posts articles on its web site that teach that Israel, the Jews, and the West in general are evil enemies of Islam and it is the duty of all Muslims to fight them.[26]

While it may be true that the Saviour Sect should not be considered a terrorist organization, and the group has not claimed responsibility for any terrorist acts, as most Islamist terror groups tend to do, the Saviour Sect's propaganda does most certainly serve as a radicalizing agent, and it is fact that members of the Saviour Sect have become radicalized to the point of violence since some have served as suicide bombers in the intifada against Israel.[27] In particular (as mentioned previously), two British members of the Saviour Sect were identified as Hamas suicide bombers who killed three people when they attacked a bar in Tel Aviv in April 2003. Furthermore, in 2004, Saviour Sect members were arrested in London after police seized a warehouse containing 1,200 pounds of ammonium nitrate fertilizer.[28]

The Saviour Sect is also associated with the call for emigration of all Muslims to a true Muslim land (although in their minds, one does not exist since the Taliban were ousted from power). Those in the Saviour Sect evidently adhere to the strict Islamic interpretation that holds that Muslims cannot live as a non-ruling minority in the land of infidels (though the Saviour Sect itself is based in one). One way that the Savoir Sect combats this problem is to call for the conversion of all non–Muslims in Western countries to Islam.[29] Finally, the Saviour Sect was also associated with Richard Reid, the infamous "shoe-bomber," and Hizb ut-Tahrir, an Islamist group whose stated goal is to restore the caliphate.[30]

Hizb ut-Tahrir

The Saviour Sect itself was essentially begun in 1996 as an offshoot of Hizb ut-Tahrir (the Islamic Liberation Party), an international Islamist movement dedicated to the creation of a united Khilafah (Islamic state) and the reestablishment of the caliphate consistent with that of the seventh century. Hizb ut-Tahrir is estimated to have up to two thousand members spread across Europe and it can be found on most university campuses even though it is banned in several countries, including Germany.[31] The head office of Hizb ut-Tahrir is not Afghanistan, Saudi Arabia, or Palestine, but London, from where they provide finance and recruitment to Islamist groups worldwide, including Hamas, Egyptian Islamic Jihad, and Hizbollah. Hizb ut-Tahrir also supports other radical Islamic groups in the West, including the Supporters of Sharia.

Where necessary, Hizb ut-Tahrir calls for jihad against infidels in order to establish the Islamic state. Hizb ut-Tahrir opposes all existing Arab and Muslim states (and all other existing governments, for that matter) as apostates and favors a limitless Islamic state without national boundaries; consequently, Hizb ut-Tahrir has been banned in current Islamic countries.[32] Hizb ut-Tahrir also vehemently opposes the existence of the state of Israel and draws no distinction between the state of Israel and Jews in general; consequently, Hizb ut-Tahrir has opposed all phases of the Palestinian-Israeli peace process. Additionally, Hizb ut-Tahrir is decidedly anti–Hindu, anti–Sikh, antihomosexual, antifeminist, antidemocratic, and anti–Western. In fact, Hizb ut-Tahrir is so anti–Semitic that they deny the Holocaust, arguing that the real holocaust is the killing of Muslims in Palestine by Jews. One leaflet distributed by the group calls for the killing of Jews wherever they are found, and another stated that "the only place to meet Jews is on the battlefield." In spite of these radical statements, Hizb ut-Tahrir also claims that they have "no relationships whatsoever with any violent, terrorist, or sectarian organization, nor does the party engage in violent or sectarian actions," an apparent contradiction with their stated call to kill Jews wherever they are found.[33] Recently, Hizb ut-Tahrir gained notoriety in Denmark where it ran candidates in local Danish elections on a platform calling for the implementation of sharia in Denmark.[34]

Supporters of Sharia

Unlike Hizb ut-Tahrir and the Saviour Sect, the Supporters of Sharia are a Western-based Islamist group involved in more than just Islamist propaganda, with direct ties to terrorism. The Supporters of Sharia are associated with the radical Finsbury Park Mosque in London, the home mosque for Zacarias Moussaoui, the so-called "twentieth hijacker," and Richard Reid, the American "shoe-bomber."[35] Supporters of Sharia also have been linked to the kidnapping of sixteen Western tourists in Yemen in 1998 and a bomb plot in Aden in 1999.[36]

Like Hizb ut-Tahrir, the Supporters of Sharia also wish to re-establish the seventh-century caliphate and replace what they term as "man-made laws" with the sharia. The Supporters of Sharia emphasize jihad as a Muslim obligation and claim to have supported mujahadeen in Afghanistan, Bosnia, and Kashmir. In fact, the leader of the Supporters of Sharia, Abu Hamza, claims to have fought in the Afghan war, and lost both hands and an eye in an "accident."[37]

The focus of the Supporters of Sharia appears to be primarily on what they consider to be apostate Muslim governments, which for all practical purposes includes all Muslim governments in the eyes of Abu Hamza. For example, after the death of King Hussein of Jordan, Abu Hamza's web site had a page dedicated to what Hamza viewed as an apostate ruler under the heading "Another one bites the dust," that showed King Hussein, whom Hamza viewed as an apostate, with demonic horns on his head, surrounded by flames, apparently burning in hell.[38]

Though Abu Hamza's main concerns are the apostate governments in Muslim countries, he also poses a threat to Western governments in his opposition to the introduction of Western culture into Muslim countries, which he views as "polluting" Islam. Abu Hamza focuses on Yemen in particular because he views it as the only Muslim country that "has not surrendered to the United States of America," but he views it on the verge of doing so; hence, Abu Hamza argues that jihad in Yemen is necessary against those who would capitulate to the Western cultural pollution. Abu Hamza argues that Muslims must "explode in the faces of the snake" in Yemen, and in doing so hopefully trigger a jihadist domino effect over the entire Arabian peninsula. Abu Hamza views allowing Western involvement in an Islamic country, whether in the form of Western militaries, humanitarian aid, oil exploration, or tourism, as "surrender," and therefore opposes all contact with the West.[39]

The future of Abu Hamza and his organization is in question at the time of this writing, however, since Hamza was arrested in London in 2005 by British officials for using language construed as a solicitation to murder.[40] When British officials raided his mosque, they found an arsenal of stun guns, tear gas, chemical warfare protection suits, false passports, knives, and radio equipment. The jury in Hamza's case was treated to extracts from speeches and sermons where he railed against adultery, democracy, and alcohol, and declared that jihad was a religious duty, arguing that "Islam will never be dear to your hearts unless you sacrifice for it, until your blood comes out for it."[41] Hamza also was quoted as saying, "Killing a Kaffir (non-believer) for any reason, you can say it is okay, even if there is no reason for it."[42]

Committee for the Defence of Legitimate Rights

The Committee for the Defence of Legitimate Rights in Saudi Arabia (CDLR) was formed in Riyadh in 1993 in reaction to the decision of the Saudi government to allow the United States and other Western troops to defend the kingdom following Iraq's August 1990 invasion of Kuwait. The CDLR publicly questioned the Islamic credentials of the ruling family and championed the revival of puritanical Wahhabi religious principles and a return to strict sharia. CDLR leaders argued that what was happening in the Gulf was part of a larger Western plot to dominate the entire Arab and Muslim world. The CDLR was quickly banned by the Saudi government and its leading members were arrested and fired from their jobs. One member, Abdallah al-Hudhaif, was beheaded following a secret trial; consequently, the group moved its home base to London in 1994. In 1996, the CDLR diminished in importance after a major segment split into the Islamic Reform Movement in Arabia led by Saad al-Fagih, which continues to disseminate propaganda against the Saudi government from London.[43]

Hilafet Devleti

Hilafet Devleti, also known as the Anatolian Federated Islamic State and "Kalifasstaat," is a German-based group founded in 1984 by Turkish native Cemaleddin Kaplan, who fled to Germany from Turkey, after being denounced as an "enemy of the state" in Turkey in 1983, a charge that would have carried the death penalty if he had not fled. Kaplan favored the creation in Turkey of an Islamic state modelled after the Islamic Republic of Iran under Ayatollah Khomeini. Followers of Hilafet Devleti in Germany wear traditional Islamic clothing, men wear full beards and turbans, and women wear full black Islamic coverings. Under Kaplan's son, Metin Kaplan, who took the reins of the group after his father's death in 1995, the group has called for a restoration of the caliphate and the overthrow of Turkey's secular government that they view as a government of apostates.[44] Hilafet Devleti's published statement, entitled "The New World Order," states,

> Our goal is the control of Islam over everyday life. In other words, the Koran should become the constitution, the Islamic system of law should become the law, and Islam should become the state.... Is it possible to combine Islam with democracy and the layman's system on which it is based? For this question only one answer exists, and that is a resounding "NO!"[45]

Hilafet Devleti appears to be more than a mere propaganda organization, however, and is accused by German authorities of having direct ties to violence and terrorism. In particular, Metin Kaplan was suspected in the murder of his rival to power among Muslim extremists in Germany, Ibrahim Sofu, in 1996. Kaplan had publicly stated that "he would like to see Sofu dead," but German prosecutors could not prove that he had ordered the killing. He was, however, convicted of solicitation of murder and spent four years incarcerated for the crime in Germany.[46]

In a separate incident in Turkey in 1998, Turkish security forces claim that Metin Kaplan and the Hilafet Devleti orchestrated a failed plot to bomb the mausoleum of Mustafa Kemal with a plane filled with explosives that they had planned to crash into the mausoleum. Twenty-three members of Hilafet Devleti were arrested in conjunction with the failed terror plot, and forty more were arrested in Germany during a demonstration involving approximately 500 followers of Hilafet Devleti, who were demanding Kaplan's release after his arrest for his part in the plot.[47] In May 2004, German authorities evidently decided that they had had enough, and Kaplan's refugee status in Germany was revoked so that he could be extradited back to Turkey on charges of terrorism. In June 2005, Kaplan faced trial in Turkey and was convicted of plotting terrorist attacks against the Turkish government and sentenced to life imprisonment in Turkey, but his organization continues in his absence.[48]

Jamaat al-Tabligh

The Jamaat al-Tabligh (Society for the Propagation of Islam) is concentrated primarily in Pakistan, but has a mosque in Queens, New York City, that serves as a center for its activity. For example, the Queens mosque hosted a gathering of approximately 200 Jamaat al-Tabligh missionaries in 2003. The Jamaat al-Tabligh, like other Islamist groups, is dedicated to the purification of Islam and the return to the practices of Mohammed in the seventh century. Jamaat al-Tabligh rejects modernism, advocates segregation of women, and supports the Taliban in Afghanistan. The group is linked to al-Qaeda and helped John Walker Lindh, the American who fought with the Taliban in Afghanistan, to get to Pakistan and enroll in a madrassa (religious school) to study Islam. They also helped al-Qaeda member Kamal Derwish recruit six Yemeni-American men in Lackawanna, New York, for the purpose of travelling to Pakistan to engage in al-Qaeda training camps in 2001.[49] Derwish was later killed in Yemen by an armed American Predator drone that fired a Hellfire missile into his vehicle.[50]

Nida'ul Islam

Nida'ul Islam, or "The Call of Islam," is an Islamist group based in Sydney, Australia. Nida'ul Islam's web site contains interviews with Osama bin Laden, Sheikh Omar Abdul Rahman (who orchestrated the 1993 World Trade Center bombing), and members of the Taliban. A feature article on the Nida'ul Islam web site is entitled "The Termination of Israel: A Qur'anic Fact," in which it is argued that Israel's destruction is mandated by the Koran. In another article entitled "How the West Came to Dominate the Whole Wide World," the writers condemn Christianity and Judaism and claim that slavery was the Christian response to the spread of Islam in Africa. The writers also argue that capitalism is an invention of Jews and Christians to ensure Western domination of the world. In the words of Nida'ul Islam,

> The globalization of trade in stolen goods was sanitized by the term, Capitalism. The trade was financed by the largest owners of capital, namely the (Christian) Church and Jews, underpinned by usury, sanitized by the term, "interest".... Little wonder that the capitalistic theories of Adam Smith — a Jew — are still popular under neo-colonialism.... In 1947 Palestine was handed over to the Zionists. The never forgotten objective of the Church, the recapture of Palestine, had finally been achieved.... The Jews returned under the New Secular Order, to dominate the socio-economic, political and foreign affairs of the Gentiles by indirectly ruling the Church.[51]

Other articles on the Nida'ul Islam web site include "The U.S. War on Islam" and "Australians, Shooting for Israel." Although Nida'ul is not necessarily a terrorist organization, its inflammatory language is clearly designed to encourage others to join in physical jihad against Israel and the West. Nida'ul Islam's strategy has been referred to by scholars as "the drip effect," which refers to a stream of constant negative criticism which gradually erodes belief among Muslims in the values of Western societies.[52] One may argue that the jihad (or the accompanying Western War on Terror) will never be won on the battlefield, but in the hearts and minds of Muslims everywhere. Nida'ul Islam is engaged in a serious effort to win the cultural struggle through the winning of hearts and minds, a strategy that thus far appears to be effective.

Union of Islamic Organizations of France

The Union of Islamic Organizations of France (UOIF) is a Salafist Muslim Brotherhood organization that preaches self-imposed separatism for European Muslims so as to avoid contamination of Islam through association with infidels. The UOIF declares that Europe is now dar al Islam (the area of the world under the rule of Islam) and therefore calls for the application of sharia in Europe. The UOIF works through Islamist charity networks and provides social services to the economically dispossessed in France, thus winning converts for Islam.[53] The UOIF was politically visible in France during the political fight over the hijab and gained sympathy from international human rights groups for being forced by the French state to abandon their cultural and religious traditions.[54] A spinoff organization of the UOIF is the Muslim Students of France (EMF) that provides social services to Muslim students on university campuses. Like the UOIF, the EMF typically targets the economic underclass in France and attempts to exploit their underprivileged status for political gain, much like the French communists did prior to the fall of the Berlin Wall. In the process, the EMF attempts to politicize and mobilize Muslim students into an Islamist political force.[55]

French Council of the Muslim Creed

At the end of 2002, the French Council of the Muslim Creed (CFCM) was established with an administration derived on a representative basis from each French Mosque. The CFCM quickly became dominated by the UOIF since the UOIF was the only organization that had effectively permeated the 1500 mosques throughout France. The vice president and most powerful member of the CFCM was Fouad Alaoui, who was also the secretary-general of the UOIF at the time.[56]

Milli Gorus

The Milli Gorus is a Turkish Islamist organization in Germany with connections to the Muslim Brotherhood. The German federal agency for the protection of the Constitution, the Bundesamt fur Verfassungsschutz, describes the Milli Gorus as Germany's largest Islamist organization and labels the group's activities among German youths as "disintegrative, antidemocratic, and anti–Western." The Bundesamt fur Verfassungsschutz has blacklisted the Milli Gorus, meaning that German governmental agencies are not allowed to maintain any form of contact with the Milli Gorus nor may German governmental agencies include the organization in discussions of German political problems.[57] The size of the actual membership of the Milli Gorus is unknown; however, one German politician perhaps put it best when he stated to Western scholar Jytte Klausen in 2004 that "we cannot meet with half of the Muslims in town because the Verfassungschutz says they are a danger to our values."[58]

Arab European League

The Arab European League (AEL) is an Islamist group based in Antwerp, Belgium, led by Dyab About Jahjah, a political refugee from Lebanon granted asylum in Belgium. The AEL is not known at present to be involved in terrorism, but its leader, Jahjah, has publicly expressed his admiration for the Madrid bombers and has boasted that his people "give as good as they get" when they meet "skinheads." Jahjah and the AEL reject homosexuality in particular, but also the legitimacy of Judaeo-Christian civilization in general.[59] Jahjah also claims on the AEL web site that the American invasion of Iraq was precipitated by Saddam Hussein's 1990 condemnation of imperialism. The AEL web site further claims that Saddam Hussein did not ever "gas" the Kurds, and terms Saddam as a "martyr" for the Arab people.[60]

American Muslim Associations

In general, American Muslims have taken advantage of the free speech and free assembly rights granted to all Americans under the First Amendment to form Islamic associational groups. Due to the First Amendment freedoms, the groups are virtually unregulated, so the opportunity for Islamists to form and infiltrate American Islamic groups is great. In the words of American Islamic scholar Salam al-Marayati, "It is our job to guide our community to an independent pathway. We can be more powerful than so many other Islamic groups because we live in a free society and we can organize politically and we can represent to help ourselves here and help others elsewhere."[61]

The first American Islamic association founded by Muslim immigrants to America was the Federation of Islamic Associations (FIA), founded in 1953.

The focus of the group was primarily on issues related to the Middle East and Palestine in particular.[62] A more successful group, known as the Muslim Student Association (MSA) was founded in 1963 by Muslim students with inspiration from the Muslim Brotherhood. The MSA later (1982) spawned another group accused of Islamist leanings known as the Islamic Society of North America (ISNA). The ISNA is a coalition of a number of different types of local groups including local Islamic centers and professional associations. The ISNA holds an annual conference, which is partly academic and partly commercial. The conference includes the usual workshops and discussions, but it is also a marketplace for Islamic books, CDs, clothing, and other goods.[63]

Clearly most of the individuals involved in the ISNA are not Islamists; however, it is also perhaps natural that Islamists would be drawn to such an organization. There are numerous Muslim associations and organizations in the United States that may have links to radicalism and terrorism. In particular, Steven Emerson argues that there are links between global terrorist organizations and nine American Muslim groups, which he names as the Muslim Arab Youth Association (MAYA), the American Islamic Group (AIG), the Islamic Cultural Workshop (ICW), the Council on American-Islamic Relations (CAIR), the American Muslim Council (AMC), the Islamic Circle of North America (ICNA), the Muslim Public Affairs Council (MPAC), the American Muslim Alliance (AMA), and the Islamic Society of North America (ISNA).[64] Similarly, Mohammed Hisham Kabbani, chairman of the Islamic Supreme Council of North America, claims that over 80 percent of the more than 3000 mosques in the United States are dominated by radical Islamist ideology and that the ideology is beginning to spread into the American universities.[65] Kabbani also argues that there are numerous Islamic charity organizations in the United States that fund Islamic extremism outside the United States. In the words of Kabbani,

> Our sources say that many, many millions of dollars have been collected and sent. They send it under humanitarian aid, but it doesn't go to humanitarian aid…. Some of it will go to homeless people and poor people but the majority, ninety percent of it, will go into the black markets in these countries and buying weapon arsenals.[66]

It should be noted, however, that Kabbani's contentions are disputed by the AMA, AMC, CAIR, MPAC, ICNA, and ISNA, who together with the American Muslim Political Coordination Council and the Muslim Students Association of USA and Canada issued a statement condemning Kabbani's arguments and demanding an apology, which Kabbani refused.[67]

American authorities have known about the problem of the diversion of funds from Islamic charities in the United States to radical and violent Islamist causes, at least since the first Persian Gulf War. During that conflict, the Saudi ambassador to Pakistan informed the American Consulate in Pakistan that Islamic charity organizations in California and Texas were funding violent jihad in Afghanistan. The CIA and FBI were made aware of the information, but apparently did not follow up with investigations.[68] In another incident, Osama bin Laden once apparently wired $210,000 to a contact in Texas to purchase a private cargo jet for use in transporting weapons to Afghanistan.[69]

The issue of aid to terrorists from American Muslims is just one more difficulty that American policymakers now face in their quest to stem the threat of global Islamist terrorism. One of the difficulties in stopping such "humanitarian" aid from going to terrorists is that many legitimate Islamic charities may be linked through multiple connections to terrorist groups, even sometimes without their knowledge. This is partially due to the fact that the lines between legitimate Islamic charities and terrorist groups become blurred, because many successful terrorist groups, such as Hamas in Palestine and Hizbollah in Lebanon, also perform social welfare functions, providing food and necessities to the impoverished. For American Muslim groups to therefore claim that the funding of Hamas is the funding of a legitimate charity organization is not completely false, but ignores the fact that the same organization that helps the poor also engages in horrific acts of terrorism.[70]

CHAPTER 4

The Culture-Clash Thesis

Some prominent scholars, such as Bernard Lewis[1] and Samuel Hunting-ton,[2] argue that Islam and Western societies are on a collision course based on culture clash and that the culture clash between Islam and the West has been endemic for centuries. In the words of Lewis, "for almost a thousand years, from the first Moorish landing in Spain to the second Turkish siege of Vienna, Europe was under constant threat from Islam."[3] To that, Huntington adds, "Islam is the only civilization which has put the survival of the West in doubt, and it has done that at least twice."[4] Huntington further argues that of the wars involving pairs of states of different religions between 1820 and 1929, 50 percent were between Muslims and Christians.[5]

Now that millions of Muslims have migrated to dwell within the West, some scholars and many Western statesmen contend that the presence of such a large population of Muslims in Western societies is likely to lead not only to terrorism, but also to culture clash between the diverse cultures of Muslims and those existent in their Western host countries. For example, Gilles Kepel, a noted scholar of Islam, states that Europe has become a cultural "bat-tlefield."[6] Similarly, American international relations scholar Samuel Hunt-ington has written an academic best-seller about relations between Islam and the West entitled *The Clash of Civilizations*. Huntington's thesis is that culture clash between Islam and the West has emerged as the new, dominant global conflict since the end of the Cold War.[7] This conflict and culture clash is per-ceived not only by Westerners, but by Muslims worldwide who, especially since 9/11, tend to believe that the U.S. has replaced its Cold War communist nemesis with Islam.[8]

Huntington essentially argues that religion is the primary source of iden-tity and value orientation for Muslims and that Western liberal values and Muslim values are irreconcilable. In the words of Huntington,

> In this new world the most pervasive, important, and dangerous conflicts will not be between social classes, rich and poor, or other economically defined groups, but between peoples belonging to different cultural entities. Tribal wars and

ethnic conflicts will occur within civilizations. Violence between states and groups from different civilizations, however, carries with it the potential for escalation as other states and groups from these civilizations rally to the support of their kin countries.[9]

Huntington further adds, "For forty-five years the Iron Curtain was the central dividing line in Europe. That line has moved several hundred miles east. It is now the line separating the peoples of Western Christianity on the one hand, from Muslim and Orthodox peoples on the other."[10] For good measure, Huntington includes Vaclav Havel's observation that cultural conflicts "are increasing and are more dangerous today than at any time in history" and Jacques Delors' statement that "future conflicts will be sparked by cultural factors rather than economics or ideology."[11]

In Huntington's conception, history for the last four centuries is the history of subjugation of the world by the West and "intercivilizational relations consisted of the subordination of other societies to Western civilization."[12] Huntington argues that the West expanded for four centuries until World War II, after which a revolt against the West began that has not ceased. Culture clash between Western culture and Islam has been unavoidable since World War II since the separation of religion and politics in Western culture clashes with the religion culture of Islam.[13]

Similarly, noted scholar Bernard Lewis argues that conflict between Muslims and Western culture is unavoidable because Muslims are unable to separate religion and politics as it is in the West and that Islam is essentially an entire system that encompasses religion, politics, economics, and private life. Furthermore, Lewis argues that "in any encounter between Islam and unbelief, Islam must dominate."[14] To that, Huntington essentially adds that both Western Christian culture and Islam are exclusive and unaccommodating. In the words of Huntington,

> Both are monotheistic religions, which, unlike polytheistic ones, cannot easily assimilate additional deities, and which see the world in dualistic us-and-them terms. Both are universalistic, claiming to be the one true faith to which all humans can adhere. Both are missionary religions believing that their adherents have an obligation to convert nonbelievers to that one true faith. From its origins Islam expanded by conquest and when the opportunity existed, Christianity did also. The parallel concepts of "jihad" and "crusade" not only resemble each other but distinguish these two faiths from other major world religions.[15]

Debates over "culture clash" are not limited to the halls of academia, however. American president George W. Bush, for instance, famously and repeatedly referred to Islamists as "evil" and "enemies of freedom." In a somewhat similar vein, former German chancellor Helmut Schmidt once argued that peaceful coexistence between Islam and Christianity is possible only in authoritarian states.[16] Meanwhile, Hirsi Ali, a Dutch legislator of Somali origin and self-described ex–Muslim referred to Mohammed as a "pervert" and argues that Islam is the cause of oppression for women in Muslim countries.[17]

While there is merit to the complaints of critics who contend that Bush, Schmidt, Ali, etc., are overbroad in their statements if not wholly incorrect, it is also clear that recent decades have witnessed continual conflict between Islamists and the West not only in the form of major terrorist attacks, but also within the conventional political arena of Western societies in the more mundane subjects of burying the dead, gay rights, polygamy, equal rights for women, forced marriages, laws of inheritance, divorce laws, religious holiday schedules, accommodations for prayers, the provision of building permits for mosques, the public ownership of all available cemeteries, concerns over animal rights that disallow ritual slaughter, issues of pastoral care for Muslims in prisons, and the propriety of translating the Koran into Western languages.[18]

Islamism and the Culture-Clash Thesis

Radical Muslims concur with the culture-clash thesis and reject Western infidelity to Islam. They also reject Western individualism as unIslamic, self-centered, anti-family, and anti-community. To the Islamists, this individualism is at the root of Western selfishness that has produced not only the Western consumer culture, but moral depravity, the destruction of the environment, the rape of resources from lesser developed countries, the economic imperialism of international corporations and the exploitive political colonialism of the past.[19]

While most Western Muslims are not Islamists and do not argue for the implementation of sharia in Western societies, the more radical Muslims in the West typically favor a system whereby Islamic religious law would be codified and applied in secular courts. It is this separatist model that is generally favored by Islamists, the basic idea being that Western liberalism is anti–Islamic in that secular law in Western countries legally takes precedent over sharia. Islamists believe that no law can take precedent over sharia due to a passage in the Koran (The Unbelievers 109: 1–6) that states:

> Say: Oh unbelievers! I do not serve that which you serve, nor do you serve Him Whom I serve: Nor am I going to serve that which you serve, Nor are you going to serve Him Whom I serve: You shall have your religion and I shall have my religion.

Based on this passage, Islamists argue that Muslims in the West should follow sharia regardless of Western law and Western law should not apply to Muslims. If there is one uniting principle of Islamists, it is this demand for sharia applied to all Muslims living in the West.[20] Conversely, because of the last line in the above passage, most Islamists accept that sharia does not apply to the unbelievers. Thus, conflict between Islamists and the state is endemic in the Western system of government because laws and rights theoretically apply to everyone equally and Muslims cannot legally ignore Western laws whether they conflict with sharia or not. For the Islamists, there is no need to update sharia, no matter how archaic it may appear to Western minds, because it is viewed as perfect since it was revealed by God. Thus, cultural conflicts between Muslims and the West are now playing themselves out in Western courts. For example, Western tradition dictates that the dead are buried in caskets, and the limitations of space have led to the development of cremation as a common practice in Western societies. Islamists, however, reject both the use of caskets (a legal requirement in some Western countries) and cremation in general. Furthermore, Islamists demand that the bodies of the dead must face Mecca, thus placing the graves themselves at odd angles in comparison with those of others in any particular cemetery. Islamists also argue that the grave is an eternal resting spot that cannot be disturbed, but in space-starved Europe, it is customary in some countries to reuse burial plots after 25 years.[21]

Over issues of marriage and divorce, Islamists conflict with Western societies in numerous ways, including the joint property laws, but also most conspicuously because Islam allows polygamy and Western societies do not. Islamists essentially skirt the Western ban on polygamy by marrying one woman in a civil ceremony recognized by the state, but marrying additional wives in religious ceremonies without state knowledge or sanction. According to the British Shariah Council, as many as 4,000 men are involved in such plural marriages in the UK alone.[22] Western courts do not recognize the legal standing of Muslim marriages if they occur outside of the auspices of the state; consequently, women married in religious ceremonies, polygamous or otherwise, without the knowledge of the state cannot initiate claims against their husbands in secular courts.

While no Western society is likely to allow polygamy any time soon and the dispute is therefore moot in a legal sense, culture clash over the issue can be expected to continue as Islamists informally skirt the Western laws. By the same token, secular courts will not yield to sharia in cases of divorce from a state-sanctioned marriage and will not award two-thirds of the jointly held property to the men as dictated by the Koran.

Xenophobic Western Backlash

The Roman philosopher Lactantius, once wrote, "Where fear is present, wisdom cannot be."[23] Lactantius could just as easily have been writing about Western xenophobic attitudes toward Islam in 2010 as ancient Rome since wisdom and reason do not always dominate Western democratic politics, especially when fear is present. Instead, the political right in the West is generally replete with nativist elements opposed to immigration, multiculturalism, and, in the case of American Protestant fundamentalists, any religion except evangelical Christianity. Unsurprisingly, polls of Muslims in Western countries therefore reveal Muslim discontent over what they view as bias against Muslims in Western countries. Muslims tend to perceive this bias regardless of whether they are Islamists or more secular in their approaches to politics and religion. In general, Muslims argue that Westerners exhibit "Islamophobia" due to ignorance and irrational fear of something that they do not understand. Muslims also denounce what they view as biased Western media and right-wing politicians in Western countries for fanning the flames of anti–Islamic xenophobia and dragging the general populations into anti–Islamic rhetoric as well.[24]

There is some statistical evidence to support the claims of the Islamists. In 1990, polling data suggested that three-fourths of the French public believed that there were "too many Arabs in France."[25] In 1994, a poll of Germans revealed that 47 percent would prefer not to have Arabs living in their neighborhoods.[26] In 1985, 47 percent of Danes believed that Muslims were "too culturally different" and 46 percent of Dutch polled in 2002 favored a zero-immigration policy.[27] In a 2004 poll conducted by the *Wall Street Journal*, 52 percent of Western Europeans and 49 percent of American respondents said that there was a "lot of disapproval of Muslims" in their countries.[28]

Politicians and other public figures both in America and in Europe have joined with the masses in expressing their disapproval of Islam. In the United States, Attorney General John Ashcroft asserted in 2002 that "Islam is a religion in which God requires you to send your son to die for him. Christianity is a faith in which God sends his son to die for you."[29] Similarly, U.S. Army General William Boykin in October 2003 framed the war on terror as a "religious war" and claimed that the Muslims worshipped an "idol."[30] In Germany, the president of the Christian Democrat Union/Christian Social Union coalition, Friedrich Merz, argued that a precise definition of German culture was needed so that immigrants would know what they were being integrated into. The Christian Democrat Union then adopted a new immigration platform that referred to "Western values, characterized by Christianity, the tradition

of Roman law, and the Enlightenment."[31] In Austria, popular politician Heribert Berrera argued in March 2001 that "too many immigrants constituted a
threat to traditional Austrian society."[32] Meanwhile, in Spain, the Spanish
minister of immigration issues, Enrique Fernandez-Miranda, argued that successful integration of immigrants in Spain required conversion to Catholicism.[33] In Italy, Cardinal Biffi called for limits to be placed on Muslim
immigration in order to defend Christian Europe. In the words of Biffi,

> Muslims come here with the resolve to remain strangers to our brand of individual
> or social humanity in everything that is most essential, most precious: strangers
> to what it is most impossible for us to give up as "secularists." More or less openly,
> they come here with their minds made up to remain fundamentally "different,"
> waiting to make us all become fundamentally like them.... I believe that Europe
> must either become Christian again, or else it will become Muslim.[34]

American Evangelical preachers have played leading roles in fanning the
flames of Islamophobia in the U.S., frequently condemning Islam as an evil
and violent religion and even denouncing the prophet Mohammed at a paedophile. According to a 2003 survey, 77 percent of evangelical Christian leaders reported that they had a negative image of Islam and perceived it as
inherently characterized by violence.[35] A 2002 book by M. Ergun and Emir
Caner entitled *Unveiling Islam*, where the authors argue that the God of the
Muslims and the God of the Christians are fundamentally different, became
a best-seller. In the 2008 presidential election, allegations that Democratic
Party candidate Barack Obama was a Muslim, attended a madrassa, had the
middle name Hussein and had a last name that rhymed with "Osama" were
all spread by his detractors in an attempt to discredit his candidacy.

Unfortunately, anti–Muslim sentiments in Western societies have sometimes translated into violence. The German Office for the Protection of the
Constitution reported 2283 acts of anti-foreigner violence, much of it directed
against Muslims, for the year 1992 alone.[36] On November 23, 1992, two young
Turkish girls and a Turkish grandmother were killed in a firebombing in
Molln.[37] In Britain, in spite of the fact that the Muslim Council of Britain
condemned the 9/11 attacks three hours after the incident, British Muslim
organizations and mosques suffered a rash of hate mail, offensive phone calls,
and arson attacks on the weeks following 9/11.[38] One British Islamic organization, the Islamic Human Rights Commission, published a report suggesting
that there were 674 attacks on Muslim targets in Britain that were directly
motivated by 9/11. In perhaps the most violent incident, a Muslim woman
was beaten by men wielding baseball bats, apparently only because she was
identified by her assailants as being a Muslim.[39] Media coverage of radical
Islam may have contributed to the anti–Muslim backlash by increasing focus

on the extreme elements among Britain's Muslims and presenting them as the stereotypical "enemy within." This combined with scapegoating by right-wing politicians to exacerbate the already volatile situation.[40]

Western Responses to 9/11

Western governments have adopted numerous approaches in efforts to stem the tide of radical Islam in their midst, but all have proven thus far to be insufficient, as evidenced by continued terrorist attacks and violence. This failure has contributed to the growth of xenophobic parties of the far right. Nearly all European countries have significant xenophobic parties and those that do not, such as the United States, have significant xenophobic groups such as the KKK, Neo-Nazis, and the "Minutemen," a citizens' group whose members sit in lawn chairs on the Mexican border with field glasses, scanning the horizon for illegal immigrants to report to the American border patrol.

In some respects, 9/11 only forced to a head anti–Muslim sentiments that had been percolating under the surface of Western politics for some time. Surveys in the United States in the years after 9/11 reveal a tendency for Americans to associate Islam with fanaticism.[41] Unsurprisingly, Congress passed the USA PATRIOT Act that eroded civil liberties in the interest of ensuring protection against Muslim terrorists. America, however, was not alone in taking action against the Islamist "threat."

In 1997, in a precursor of things to come, the Runnymede Trust in Britain published a report entitled *Islamophobia: A Challenge for Us All,* warning of the security threat posed by Radical Islam. Four years later, the events of 9/11, coupled with race riots in the British cities of Oldham and Burnley in May 2001, led to the passage of a new law on terrorism, crime, and security in December 2001. The new law increased the power of the police in information gathering and the monitoring of citizens.[42] The French government subsequently passed new restrictions on immigration that made it more difficult for the children of foreigners to become citizens, for families of foreigners to immigrate, and for foreigners to seek political asylum in France.[43] The xenophobic French attitude is perhaps best summed up by Pierre Lellouch, who stated in 1991, "History, proximity and poverty insure that France and Europe are destined to be overwhelmed by people from the failed societies of the south. Europe's past was white and Judeo-Christian. The future is not."[44]

In Germany, which has thus far avoided an Islamist terrorist attack on the scale of those in the United States, London, and Madrid, German officials have recognized that Germany is by no means immune to such attacks. Instead, Germany responded to 9/11 with the passage of two new anti-terrorist laws in December 2001 that increased funding for security forces and provided greater latitude for police in conducting investigations. The new laws also allowed armed German security agents on planes.[45]

Nativist Parties

In addition to the added security laws, the terrorist attacks of 9/11 also resulted in a rise in support for the nativist political parties throughout the Western world. In the UK, the nativist British National Party (BNP) launched campaigns with titles such as "Islam out for Britain" and "No to Fundamentalists" in an attempt to gain seats in the British Parliament.[46] Though the BNP did not win any seats in the 2001 Parliamentary elections, the Party did win 16.4 percent of the vote in Oldham and eight BNP councillors were elected to office in Burnley in 2003. The BNP's leader, Nick Griffin, made Muslims the center of BNP ire when he stated that Britain "does not have an Asian problem but a Muslim one."[47]

Similarly, in 1999, the Freedom Party won 27 percent of the vote in the Austrian elections on a nativist, anti-immigrant platform. The same year, the Belgian Vlaams Blok received 10 percent of the vote, but was declared illegal by the Belgian Supreme Court in 2004 due to its racist nature. In 2001, the nativist Progress Party won 15 percent of the vote in Norway. The next year, a Norwegian atheist organization petitioned the municipality of Oslo to be permitted to proclaim for a few minutes each day that God does not exist as a counterbalance to the Muezzin of Oslo.[48] Meanwhile, in the Netherlands, a Moroccan imam created a stir when he proclaimed on Dutch television that homosexuality was a disease and a danger to Dutch society.[49] The next year, the Dutch Lijst Pim Fortuyn won 17 percent of the vote in the Netherlands on a platform that claimed that Muslims were bigots that diluted Dutch liberal values.[50] Fortuyn, a sociology professor and open homosexual, was the first politician in the history of Dutch politics to have publicly expressed anti–Islamic sentiments. Fortuyn was subsequently murdered, but his political positions opened the floodgates.[51] In 2002, the Dutch Parliament adopted a law requiring training in Dutch language and culture for all foreign-born imams entering the country.[52] In the absence of Fortuyn, the Dutch Party of Freedom, headed by Geert Wilders, now vows to ban the Koran and boot Romania and Bulgaria from the European Parliament.[53]

Perhaps the largest and most powerful xenophobic party, however, is the National Front of Jean Marie Le Pen in France, which has garnered as much as 18 percent of the vote nationally, finishing second in the 2002 French presidential elections, with a platform against immigration and multiculturalism.

Le Pen surprised most political observers in France when he outpolled socialist prime minister Lionel Jospin.[54] In spite of his racism and neo–Nazi rhetoric, Le Pen's party has grown to the point that several cities in southern France, including Marignane, have National Front mayors. In a 1995 pamphlet distributed to French electors in the presidential election, Le Pen proposed the expulsion of 3 million non–Europeans from France.[55]

Such extremist rhetoric was nothing new for Le Pen, however. In 1987, Le Pen once referred to the Nazi gas chambers as "a point of detail of the Second World War," a comment for which he was fined 1.2 million francs. More recently, Le Pen declared in the far-right German publication *Rivarol* that Germany's occupation of France during World War II was "not particularly inhumane."[56]

Political correctness often forces a softening of the rhetoric, such as that of the Danish People's Party, which states that "foreigners should be absorbed into Danish society, but only under the condition that they do not pose a threat to social security and democracy." Consequently, the Danish People's Party supports revoking citizenship and expulsion for naturalized citizens convicted of crimes. The Danish People's Party is currently the third largest party in Denmark.[57]

The true influence of xenophobic parties, however, is not necessarily reflected in their vote percentages, since major parties and major party politicians often adopt nativist rhetoric in order to avoid losing votes to extremist parties. For example, In France, future president Jacques Chirac in 1990 declared publicly that "immigration must be totally stopped" and socialist interior minister Charles Pasqua argued in 1993 for "zero immigration."[58] German governmental officials have often issued warnings reminiscent of those issued by the Bush administration in the United States. For instance, interior minister Wolfgang Schäuble has argued that nuclear attacks in Germany are "only a matter of time."[59] Schäuble also questioned whether the German legal system could allow the authorities to do what is necessary to prevent terrorism. Schäuble proposed that Germany may need to take more coercive measures such as detaining terrorists without charge, deploying the German army in domestic operations, searching the computers of suspected terrorists without their knowledge, and conducting targeted assassinations of terrorists.[60] Similarly, German Defense Minister Franz Josef Jung publicly stated that if terrorists attempted to use airlines as missiles, he would shoot them down.[61]

Though the views of Schäuble and Jung are very controversial in Germany and Schäuble quickly found himself compared to George W. Bush and the American policies at Guantanamo Bay, which are intensely unpopular in

Germany, in 2006, Germany passed a "Flight Security Law" that would have allowed the German state to deploy the armed forces at home to protect against terrorist attacks and shoot down hijacked airliners. The German courts overturned the parts of the law that would have allowed the German state to kill some citizens to save others and deploy soldiers at home except to repel foreign invasions or deal with catastrophes. In short, the German courts ruled that the duty of the state to respect human dignity is absolute.[62] In spite of these limitations, Germany has passed thirteen other measures designed to limit terrorist threats including authorizing police and the German secret services to share data on terrorist suspects and more aggressive laws may be expected if Germany suffers from a major terrorist attack.

The German government also amended Article XVI of the German constitution guaranteeing political asylum and cut benefits to asylum-seekers. As a result, the number of persons granted political asylum in Germany dropped 71 percent between 1992 and 1994.[63] At the end of the 1990s, the Christian Democratic Party (CDU) worked against the 1999 German naturalization law that eased the process for Muslims seeking German citizenship by reducing residency requirements to eight years. CDU leaders argued that it was dangerous to naturalize such a large population of aliens and recommended a quota for the admission of immigrants and the requirement that all foreigners adhere to the values of the German Leitkulture (guiding culture). The Bavarian wing of the CDU even released a position paper arguing that foreigners living in Germany should embrace "values rooted in Christianity, the Enlightenment, and humanism."[64] The anti-immigrant sentiments of the CDU gathered steam in 2002 when CDU leader Edmund Stoiber in the 2002 electoral campaign warned against "uncontrolled immigration." Similarly, in 2004 Stoiber adopted nativist rhetoric in condemning a proposal to make Ramadan a German holiday. In the words of Stoiber, "That is not toleration, not integration, but the surrender of our cultural heritage. It must be stopped."[65]

In recent years, the Republican Party in the United States has assimilated anti-immigrant rhetoric and galvanized support under the banner of "securing America's borders." For example, in his State of the Union Address in January 2006, President George W. Bush catered to the nativists by stating,

> Keeping America competitive requires an immigration system that upholds our laws, reflects our values and serves the interests of our economy. Our nation needs orderly and secure borders. To meet this goal, we must have stronger immigration enforcement and border protection.[66]

In the UK, the government reduced its immigration to only approximately 50,000 a year in 1980 and the number of asylum-seekers permitted to remain in the UK was slashed over 50 percent between 1992 and 1994.[67]

By 1995, the Islamophobia had even spread to international organizations such as NATO, whose Secretary General that year declared Islamic fundamentalism to be "at least as dangerous as communism."[68]

Due to the prevalent xenophobia, Islamists in the West are more effortlessly able to sell the position that Muslims are stigmatized and thus co-opt more moderate Muslims to help them formulate a collective defense. Islamists use Western scholarly arguments such as those of Samuel Huntington, who described Muslims as an "indigestible minority" as proof that Westerners are biased against Muslims.[69] Their argument is bolstered by Huntington's call for cultural warfare against Muslim immigrants. Radical Islamism and anti–Westernism among Muslims living in the West therefore at least partially may be explained as a backlash against Western Islamophobia. Conversely, it is also true that Islamophobia would most certainly be lessened in the West if the media airwaves were not permeated with the frequent illiberal statements from radical Muslims in the news, and if history books over the last four decades were not filled with instances of horrific violence both in the West and elsewhere in the name of Islam. Finally, as if the continuing violence and hyperbolic political rhetoric is not sufficient in itself, Islamophobia is surely further exacerbated by high unemployment rates among Muslims in Europe. Unemployment among European Muslims in 2007 was estimated to be as high as 24 percent among Turks in Germany and 39 percent among North Africans in France.[70]

American Anti-Muslim Backlash

Muslims have, however, experienced some forms of anti–Muslim backlash since their arrival in the U.S. in significant numbers in the post–World War II era. After the Six Day War in 1967 and the rise in Middle Eastern political unrest and Islamic terror that followed that conflict, the Nixon administration in 1972 formed a special committee to restrict Arab immigration to the U.S., collect data on Arab immigrants already in the U.S., and compile dossiers on Arab American organizations and their leaders. The Nixon administration even considered preparing two military compounds in the Southern United States for the possible internment of Arbas and Iranians living in the U.S.[71] While these were the actions of a particularly extreme American president who shortly thereafter resigned under threat of impeachment for abuse of power, American Muslims discovered that a paranoid and nativist streak exists in the American polity.

In addition to these anti–Muslim domestic policies of the Nixon administration, American Muslims also tended to view American foreign policy then and now as pro–Israel and hypocritical, since the U.S. purports to support the concepts of freedom, democracy, and human rights, yet supports tyrannical despots in the Islamic world, supports the position of the Russian government against Muslim rebels in Chechnya, backs the undemocratic Egyptian government against the Muslim Brotherhood, and shares nuclear technology with Hindu India while supposedly allied with Islamic Pakistan.[72]

During the Clinton years of the 1990s, Muslims found American domestic policies to be more Muslim-friendly. Though many Muslims distrusted President Clinton because he was elected with the support of the pro–Israel lobby, and Clinton consulted with Israeli activists on his Middle Eastern policies, Clinton made efforts to reach out to Muslim Americans on numerous fronts. In 1993, the Department of Defense commissioned the first Muslim chaplain in the American armed forces. Subsequently, Muslim chaplains were appointed in all branches of the American armed services and an Islamic prayer hall was constructed on an American military base in Norfolk, Virginia. Clinton also hosted the first official Ramadan iftar (breaking the fast) dinner, and the event had essentially become an annual tradition by the end of the Clinton presidency.[73]

Immediately after the Oklahoma City bombing in 1995, however, major American media outlets jumped to conclusions and blamed Muslim terrorists before the evidence led authorities to a young Anglo Protestant fundamentalist and conservative ex-military gun-rights advocate named Timothy McVeigh. Nevertheless, Congress passed the Anti-Terrorism and Affective Death Penalty Act of 1995 that gave the federal government the power to try and incarcerate Arab-Americans suspected of terrorism without evidence. The Act also sanctioned airport profiling of Muslims as potential terrorists. Several months earlier, President Clinton banned contributions to Palestinian charitable organizations by American citizens in the interest of stopping the flow of American money to terrorists masquerading as humanitarian aid organizations.[74]

American Culture Wars and Crusade

An important factor that may contribute to the Islamist threat in the United States is the fact that the United States is much more religious than its European counterparts and therefore perhaps more likely than European countries to be viewed by Islamists as waging a "crusade" against Islam. In the words of Ahmed Hashim, the United States is a

> self-professed moralistic country that sees the world in black and white rather than shades of grey, and it conducts crusades. Its victory in the Cold War rein-

forced that, as did the terrorist tragedy of 9/11. It is in effect, as currently constructed, congenitally incapable of waging effective counter-insurgency (against radical Islam).[75]

The election of Protestant fundamentalist President George W. Bush in 2000 appears to have led to a bit of a change in direction for American policies concerning Muslims away from Clinton's assimilationist approach and toward the moralistic crusade described by Hashim. For instance, Muslims quickly noticed that there was no Muslim participation in any of President Bush's inauguration ceremonies while other religious groups, especially Protestant fundamentalists, were well represented. A few months later, the president cancelled a celebration of Eid-ul Adha to which Muslim leaders were invited. The message to Muslims was essentially that they were welcome as voters and donors to the Bush political machine, but they would remain spectators in things of political importance.[76]

In May 2001, the American-Arab Anti-Discrimination Committee published an advisory that reported an increased frequency of passenger profiling of Arab and Muslim Americans at airports.[77] This anti–Muslim atmosphere that Muslims perceived in the early days of the Bush presidency only intensified after the terrorist attacks of 9/11. When Congress passed the USA PATRIOT Act in October 2001 that sanctioned the monitoring of bank transactions, telephone conversations, email messages, book purchases and credit card transactions, American Muslims perceived it as disproportionately directed at them. Muslims were particularly outraged at what they viewed as government interference into Islamic charities, which are considered to be among the "five pillars of Islam."[78] Bush also angered American Muslims by appointing Daniel Pipes, whom many American Muslims view as a pro-Israel Muslim demonizer, to the U.S. Institute of Peace.[79] American Muslim leaders scheduled a meeting with the president in 2002 to discuss the issues, but the meeting fell apart when one of the participants, Abdullah al-Arian, was escorted out by a federal security agent who identified him as a security risk even though he had been vetted by security agents prior to the meeting. Other Muslim leaders were offended and subsequently walked out of their meeting with the president.[80]

Since 9/11, the repeated vilification by American politicians and the American press of any call to Islam as "fundamentalism" and the repeated portrayal of radical Islam as America's greatest enemy by the Bush administration has convinced many American Muslims that the American government opposes Islam and will not allow American Muslims to live as Muslims.[81] The Bush administration exacerbated these attitudes in 2003 with the arrest and deportation of almost 14,000 Muslim men who had been living in the United

States.[82] The problem of American Muslim alienation is well described by Mohommed A. Muqtedar Khan, who states,

> This attitude that Islam is a major threat to the West in the post-communist era alienates many American Muslims, putting them on the defensive and creating barriers that discourage their assimilation. Many American experts and scholars often fail to distinguish between accepting Muslims and accepting Islam. America will continue to alienate its Muslim population as long as it continues to demonize Islam each time it faces resistance to foreign objectives in Muslim states or from Muslim movements.[83]

Khan made this statement prior to 9/11, but the situation has been greatly exacerbated in the years since. It is also worsened in the eyes of American Muslims by what they view as a completely different approach by American politicians and the American media toward Jewish violence against Muslims. For instance, neither American politicians nor the American press vilified Judaism when Baruch Goldstein gunned down 29 Muslims at prayer in the Tomb of the Patriarchs in Jerusalem in 1994. The American press also turned a deaf ear to Jewish radicalism when Rabbi Dov Lior argued that Israel should use captured Arab terrorists as guinea pigs for medial experiments.[84] Nor was extremist Judaism denounced by the American press when Jewish radical Yigal Amir assassinated Israeli Prime Minister Yitzhak Rabin because of his conciliatory approach toward the Palestinians.[85]

American Muslims also point out that the American press and American politicians tend to ignore the extremism and anti–Muslim rantings of American evangelical Christians. For example, instead of condemning the assassination of Yitzhak Rabin, American evangelist John Hagee essentially supported the assassination of Rabin because he viewed the Israeli-Palestinian peace process as the work of the Antichrist. Instead of seeking peace in Palestine, Hagee looks forward to what he termed as the "most devastating war Israel has ever known" after which Hagee expects the long-awaited return of Jesus.[86] Similarly, Dallas pastor Mike Evans in his 1997 book, *Jerusalem Betrayed*, describes the Mideast peace process pursued by every American president since Jimmy Carter as "an international plot to steal Jerusalem from the Jews." Evans added that behind an international cast of collaborators was a "master conspirator who is directing the play" that Evans identified as the anti–Christ.[87]

The fact that American politicians and the American media are so careful not to upset the sensitivities of American Christians and Jews by condemning their radical statements and acts of terrorism (such as the abortion-related violence in the U.S. perpetrated by the Christian right) and so quick to denounce Islamist terrorism leads American Muslims to believe that the American government and American society is antagonistic toward Islam. As a result, American Muslims are more compelled to indulge in identity politics and defend their faith, which they view as under assault. An upsurge in identity politics among American Muslims could be expected to increase political conflict between Muslims and America at large as more Muslims come to view America as hostile to Islam.[88]

President Bush was perhaps the most important contributor to the Islamist perception of the United States as crusaders due to his invasions of two Islamic countries and several statements he made, where he essentially framed the War on Terror as a "crusade." Three days after the 9/11 terrorist attacks at what Bush declared as a "National Day of Prayer and Remembrance," Bush proclaimed in dichotomous language similar to that of the Islamists that "our responsibility to history is already clear: to answer these attacks and rid the world of evil."[89] Similarly, in an address to a joint session of Congress in January 2002, Bush proclaimed, "We will pursue nations that provide aid or safe haven to terrorism. Every nation in every region now has a decision to make. Either you are with us or you are with the terrorists."[90] Again, the "with us or against us," black or white, dichotomous thinking mirrored that of Bush's Islamist adversaries. Finally, in January in his State of the Union Address, Bush provided Islamists with perhaps their "smoking gun" proving that the United States is bent on destroying Islam, when he referred to the American invasion of Afghanistan as a "crusade" and declared, "Liberty is God's gift to every human being in the world."[91]

Bush, however, is not alone in his view that the War on Terror is a "crusade," and it is most likely that he used the term because many Americans view it as positive, rather than the extreme negative connotation that the word denotes in the Islamic realm. Currently, approximately 60 percent of Americans say that religion "plays an important role in their lives" and 80 percent claim to have experienced "God's presence or a spiritual force." Furthermore, over one-fifth of Americans identify as attending church more than once a week, whereas three-fourths of Americans report that they attend at least once a month.[92] For these Americans, accustomed to fervently singing "Onward Christian Soldiers, marching as to war, with the cross of Jesus..." without any real consideration of possible interpretations, Bush's call for a crusade was simply a call to the restoration of goodness and justice. For Islamists, the call to Islamic jihad has literally the same meaning.

Much like the jihadists, America has a long history of couching its military struggles in terms of religious moral crusades. In World War I, President Woodrow Wilson famously proclaimed that the United States was going to war to "make the world safe for democracy." In the Civil War, both sides essentially claimed that God was on their side, and the Union even began putting "In God we trust" on their coins in 1864 to suggest that the faith of the Union was superior to that of the "godless" South.[93] The Union's "Battle Hymn of the Republic" could hardly be more religious and the words speak of the civil war as a religious war, eerily similar to the way that Muslims speak of jihad in the twenty-first century. For example, the opening and closing lines to the first verse and the chorus read,

> Mine eyes have seen the glory of the coming of the Lord, / He has trampled down the vineyard where the grapes of wrath are stored... / His truth is marching on... / Glory, glory hallelujah.[94]

As if the message were not clear enough in the first verse, the final verse of the hymn is not only religious, but proclaims the war itself to be an act of religious martyrdom that very well parallels the views toward jihadist martyrdom held by most radical Islamists in the twenty-first century.

> In the beauty of the lilies Christ was born across the sea; / With a glory in his bosom that transfigures you and me; / As he died to make men holy, let us die to make men free, / While God is marching on.[95]

During the cold war of the 1950s, Congress endeavored to show that God was on the side of America when it directed the president to create a national day of prayer, designated "In God We Trust" to be the national motto, placed "In God We Trust" on American paper currency, and inserted the words "under God" into the American flag salute. In casting the War on Terror as a religious crusade, Bush was merely falling in line with a long American tradition.

Bush, however, was not intending to speak to the Islamists, but to the religious right in America, which is largely credited with his election in both 2000 and 2004. Support of this core group would be necessary if the president were to carry out a military campaign against radical Islam. There are multiple reasons for the marriage between the religious right and the George W. Bush administration, but the faith of the president himself appears to be an important factor and the president has made clear that he shares their values. For example, Anthony Evans of Dallas, a fundamentalist minister and confidant of George W. Bush, explained to a British journalist in 2003 that one of the impetuses for Bush's consideration of running for president in 2000 was Biblical teaching and direction from God. In the words of Evans, Bush "feels God is talking to him."[96] Similarly, journalist Bob Woodward wrote (based on his interviews with Bush) that "the president was casting his vision and that of the country in the grand vision of God's master plan."[97] Likewise, presidential advisor David Gergen told the *New York Times* that Bush "has made it clear he feels that Providence intervened to save his life, and now he is somehow an instrument of Providence."[98] Finally, Bush as much as admitted that he viewed his presidential role as part of a divine plan at the national prayer breakfast on February 6, 2003, when Bush stated, "We can be confident in the ways of Providence.... Behind all of life and all of history, there's a dedication and purpose set by the hand of a just and faithful God."[99] In Bush's case, however, the incentive is perhaps even greater since Bush owed his ascendancy to the White House perhaps as much to the religious right as to any other group. In each religious category in the 2000 election, whether evangelical, mainline Protestant, Catholic, or even Muslim, the higher the religiosity of the person, the more likely it was that they supported George W. Bush. For example, 84 percent of high-commitment evangelicals supported Bush. Similarly, Catholics, formerly a strongly Democratic demographic, supported Bush by approximately 60 percent.[100] With these kinds of Christian religious connections, it should not be surprising that Islamists view the president as the head of a Christian crusade against Islam.

As president, Bush acted accordingly and remembered those who put him in the White House by placing religious right conservatives in numerous key positions throughout the federal government. Bush appointed Kay Coles James, formerly dean of the Robertson School of Government at Pat Robertson's Regent University, as head of the Office of Personnel Management. David Caprara, a former director of the American Family Coalition, an affiliate of Sun Myung Moon's Unification Church, was appointed the head of AmeriCorps VISTA. Moon himself, a Bush supporter who controls the conservative pro–Bush newspaper the *Washington Times*, sponsored an inaugural prayer luncheon for Bush on January 19, 2001, where propaganda on the Unification Church was distributed. This partiality to the Reverend Moon is in spite of the fact that Moon is often condemned by other evangelical Protestants for asserting that he wants to take over the world, abolish all religions except the Unification Church (certainly including Islam), abolish all languages except Korean, and abolish all governments except his own, one-world theocracy.[101] Although Moon merely sponsored a prayer luncheon and was not appointed by Bush to a position in government, Bush did nominate J. Robert Brame III, a former board member of American Vision, a group that favored putting the United States under biblical law and opposed women's rights, to the National Labor Relations Board. Additionally, to chair the Food and Drug Administration's Reproductive Health Drugs Advisory Committee, Bush appointed W. David Hager, a person who recommended specific scriptural readings and prayers for headaches and premenstrual syndrome. Finally and most famously, Bush appointed John Ashcroft, a devout Pentecostal Christian who had his own head anointed with Crisco cooking oil before being sworn in as attorney general.[102]

Bush was not alone among Republicans at the time, however, in catering to the religious right. Other leading Republicans during the Bush years have tended to make statements favorable to the Christian right and support the policies they champion. Former Republican House majority leader Tom DeLay, for instance, exhibited his own consistency with religious right thinking when he assured a Texas Baptist audience that God had elevated Bush to the presidency in order to "promote a Biblical world-view." According to Benjamin and Simon,[103] DeLay's importance in Middle East policy is such that the White House asked for his clearance on President Bush's June 2002 speech on American policy in the Middle East, where Bush declared support for a Palestinian state. DeLay also refers to the Israeli-occupied territories in Palestine by their biblical names of Samaria and Judea and argues that they rightly belong to Israel.[104] On a visit to Israel, DeLay said of the West Bank, "I don't see occupied territory; I see Israel."[105]

Similarly, Dick Armey, DeLay's predecessor as Republican House majority leader, endorsed the transportation of Palestinians from Palestine to any other countries that would take them. Not to be outdone, Republican Senator James Inhofe of Oklahoma proclaimed to his fellow senators that Israel was entitled to the occupied territories "because God said so."[106] Again, with such leadership in Congress and the executive branches of the federal government, it is perhaps little wonder that Muslims in America and worldwide tend to view recent American policies as an anti–Muslim crusade.

Aiding the Islamists in their contention that the American invasion of Iraq and the accompanying War on Terror are anti–Muslim crusades was General William G. "Jerry" Boykin, an American general in charge of the hunt for Osama bin Laden and other top terrorist targets. Boykin is an evangelical Christian who has cast the U.S. War on Terror as that of a Christian nation locked in battle with Satan, and declared that his Christian God was bigger than that of the Muslims (obviously not understanding that Muslims and Christians worship the same God). Furthermore, Boykin told one group that "George Bush was not elected by a majority of the voters in the United States. He was appointed by God" and that the jihadists "will only be defeated if we come to them in the name of Jesus."[107]

Meanwhile, the leaders of the Christian right itself would spend the years of Bush's first term flailing from one anti–Muslim issue to another and inflaming culture war against Muslims in the process. As explained by Olivier Roy,

> In the United States the Christian Right is either openly hostile to Islam as a religion, in the name of the Bible (and will try to convert Muslims to Christianity,

something that would seem very odd in Europe), or sides with Muslims in the defence of religion in the public sphere (for example, prayers at school) and conservative values (against feminists or homosexuals, for instance). Europeans want secular Muslims, Americans want Protestant Muslims.[108]

Roy explains that for both Protestant fundamentalists and Islamists, intellectual and theological debates are secondary to a personal expression of faith and both movements acknowledge and condemn the depravity of society. Both movements also disparage intellectualism and the discipline of acquiring knowledge normatively. To both Protestant fundamentalists and Islamists, a personal relationship with the deity leads directly to truth, and rationality is rejected for emotion and "feeling." Both, however, believe that they are the minority of believers in the world fallen away from God and are intolerant of other religious perspectives.[109]

For instance, noted evangelist Franklin Graham in 2002 offended Muslims by referring to Islam as "wicked" and "evil." In his best-selling book, *The Name*, Graham characterizes Christianity and Islam as "eternal enemies," and joined in a "classic struggle that will end with the second coming of Christ."[110] Furthermore, in spite of the fact that Christians and Muslims both worship the God of Abraham, Graham argues that Christians and Muslims do not worship the same God, the two being as different as "lightness and darkness." Moreover, Graham characterizes the War on Terror as a religious war between "evil and The Name" rather than a conflict between Islamists and the West.[111] Meanwhile, the Reverend Jerry Falwell referred to the prophet Mohammed as a terrorist, and Dr. Jerry Vines, pastor of the First Baptist Church in Jacksonville, Florida, declared that Mohammed was a "demon-possessed paedophile."[112] Not to be outdone, the Reverend Pat Robertson referenced Mohammed as a "wild-eyed fanatic, a robber, and a brigand."[113]

A central focus of American Christian fundamentalists in terms of foreign policy is American support for the territorial integrity of Israel to the exclusion of a Palestinian presence, a position opposed by the vast majority of the world's Muslims. To some Christian fundamentalists, it is a threat to God's ultimate plan for Israel if the United States is to mediate the Arab-Israeli conflict. Thus, the American Christian right has become a major support group for the Israeli Likud Party that takes a much less accommodationist approach toward the Palestinians. For an example of such a position, one need look no further than the words of the Reverend Jerry Falwell who once claimed that "America's Bible Belt is Israel's safety belt."[114] The Reverend Malcolm Hedding, whose group, the International Christian Embassy, is the headquarters for Christian Zionists in Jerusalem, elaborated this position further when he stated, "We stand for the right that all the land God gave under the Abrahamic covenant 4,000 years ago is Israel's.... And He [God] will regulate the affairs of how Israel comes into its allotment which is hers forever.... Palestinian statehood is also irrelevant, since there is no such thing as a Palestinian."[115] Another American Christian fundamentalist group, known as the "Cattlemen of the Apocalypse," have spent their time since 9/11 shipping cattle to the Holy Land in an attempt to breed the Revelation-prophesied red heifer that would signal Israelis to rebuild their Holy Temple and thus usher in the "end times."[116]

Exhibiting a different Israel-centered view, John Hagee, a well-known Protestant fundamentalist minister and televangelist in San Antonio, announced that his congregation would give over $1 million to Israel for the resettlement of Jews from the former Soviet Union to the West Bank and Jerusalem in the Israeli-occupied territories of Palestine.[117] Simultaneously, still another religious right group raised money to hire lawyers to defend Israelis who were arrested for planning to blow up Jerusalem's Al-Aqsa Mosque.[118] Another fundamentalist Christian group, known as the International Fellowship of Christians and Jews, claims to have raised as much as $100 million for Israel, $20 million of it in 2003 and 2004 alone. Furthermore, it has sponsored the resettlement to Israel of 100,000 Jews from Russia and Ethiopia, in anticipation of the apocalypse.[119] Given these prevalent pro-Israel sentiments of American evangelical Christians and given the fact that President Bush won 78 percent of the Evangelical Christian vote in 2004, Bush's Middle East policies have been predictably pro–Israel, reflecting his support base, a fact not missed by Muslims, whether in the United States or abroad.

Finally, the Muslims' perception of the Iraq war as a crusade has been bolstered by the American Christian missionary efforts that have accompanied the American invasion and occupation of Iraq. In the words of Kyle Fisk, executive administrator of the National Association of Evangelicals,

> Iraq will become the center for spreading the gospel of Jesus Christ to Iran, Libya, throughout the Middle East.... President Bush said democracy will be spread from Iraq to nearby countries. A free Iraq allows us to spread Jesus Christ's teachings even in nations where laws keep us out.[120]

Similarly, Christian missionary Tom Craig stated that he and other evangelicals were in Iraq because "God and the President have given us the opportunity to bring Jesus Christ to the Middle East."[121] Nine evangelical churches opened in 2003 in Baghdad alone.

For support for the contention of the Islamists that the American invasion of Iraq is a crusade against Islam, they need little else, since American Christian evangelicals openly admit that a modern-day "crusade for Christ" is indeed their purpose. With such attitudes, a significant reactionary Islamist movement among American Muslims (not to mention those worldwide) should perhaps be the most logical expectation. A successful strategy against global Islamism undoubtedly requires that Americans understand the Islamist mindset as much as possible and rid themselves of black and white ideological predilections. The prevalence of the crusade by the religious right in America suggests that a very large segment of Americans, perhaps a majority and including the presidential administration of George W. Bush, are incapable of doing so. While the presidential administration of Barack Obama appears to be moving in a more conciliatory direction, no one should expect cultural change to occur overnight.

Islamists in Western Democratic Politics

Thus far, no Islamist party in the West has gained enough political support to even come close to winning in a major election in a Western country although the Islamist Refah Partisi polled over 20 percent of the vote in Turkey in 1994. Thus far, there appears to be a lack of cohesion among Muslims in Western countries as there is no significant Islamic party in France or the UK and the majority of American Muslims actually voted for George W. Bush in 2000 before the 9/11 tragedy allowed Bush to launch two wars in Islamic countries. Nevertheless, the presence of Islamist parties and Islamist interest groups on the Western political landscape actually contributes to the Westernization of Islamism as much as it contributes to the "Islamization" of the West. In other words, as long as Islamists form overt political pressure groups and political parties in Western countries, they are essentially playing the Western political game and the Islamist conception of Islamic jihad is compromised.[122] It should also be mentioned that Islamists in the West have a vested interest in the separation of church and state since their religion remains a minority religion in the West and any church-state blend would surely award preference to the majority Christian religion rather than Islam. That being the case, one may expect Islamists to fight within Western political systems to retain their religious autonomy and freedom from the state for all religions. Political battles over the hijab, halal foods, etc., fought by Muslims through conventional Western political means exemplify the Westernization of the Islamists' approach.

Muslims and the Western Political Left

Muslims at times find allies among the political left in Western countries who tend to be less xenophobic and more multicultural in approach. The political left in Western countries, however, contains numerous elements that are equally reprehensible to Islamists. In Europe and the United States, the political left is predominantly secular and anticlerical, positions that conflict with Muslims who desire to wear the hijab in the workplace, demand time off work for daily prayers, etc. The political left also tends to champion women's rights, gay rights and abortion rights, thus placing them at odds with Islamists. To compound matters in the United States, the American Democratic Party has typically been the party associated with the American Jewish vote, the Jewish lobby, and pro–Israel policies. That being the case, Islamists in American politics find themselves with a choice of voting with the hated Jews in the Democratic Party or the hated "crusaders" of evangelical Protestantism in the Republican Party. With such unattractive choices, it is perhaps reasonable to expect the Islamists to resort to less conventional means of influencing the Western political systems.

Recent Muslim Assimilation Problems

Generally, Muslims in the West appear to be overwhelmingly secular in outlook and supportive of core liberal values as a group. For example, a 1989 survey of ethnic Algerians in France revealed that 30 percent of those under age 26 neither observed Ramadan nor daily prayers. Overall, French authorities estimate that only about a third of Muslims living in France regularly attend the mosques on Fridays and the number would be even lower if the practice were not still nearly universal for Muslims in the over-fifty age bracket.[123] In other words, there is evidence that Muslims living in the West are generally becoming secularized along with the rest of the Western population, though their religiosity still remains higher than that of European Christians. The measure of weekly church attendance in France, for instance, now languishes in single digits.[124]

Nevertheless, there are ominous signs that some Muslims in the West are becoming poorly integrated into society and are retaining a separate Muslim identity based on religion rather than nationality. In the words of Benjamin and Simon,

> Most of the Continent's (Europe's) Muslims arrived in the 1950s and 1960s as workers to fill postwar Europe's labor shortage, and they stayed on in countries that, for the most part, neither expected nor wanted to integrate them into their societies. It soon became apparent, however, that there was no easy way to send these workers back or to stanch the flow of family members seeking reunification with loved ones — let alone to stop them from having children. As a result, Europe

has sleepwalked into an awkward multiculturalism. Its Muslim residents, many of them now citizens, live for the most part in ghetto-like segregation, receive second-rate schooling, and suffer much higher unemployment than the general population. Those who do work are more likely than their non–Muslim counterparts to have low-wage, dead-end jobs. Indeed, it is this marginality that helps to explain the appeal of radicalism.[125]

Benjamin and Simon's conclusions are supported by numerous measures. In France, the crime rates among Muslims have risen dramatically since 1990 and random violence by Muslim youths wielding knives or guns has become common as have full blown riots that last for days. In one of the most celebrated of such riots, police involvement in the death of a Muslim motorcyclist in October 1990 sparked four nights of stone-throwing and firebombing by Muslim youths in the Lyon suburb of Vaulx-en-Velin. Damage was estimated by French authorities at 25 million francs. In 2002, Paris mayor Bertrand Delanoe was stabbed in the chest by a radical Muslim who was targeting politicians and gays. Not surprisingly, opinion polls in France now suggest that the French electorate ranks crime as its most important concern.[126]

Part of the increase in crime and radical Islamic activities may be linked to increased marginalization among the European Muslim population. In Britain, for instance, unemployment among the Muslim population is three times that of the general population and four times the average for Muslim women. With such disparity between ethnic groups in employment and socioeconomic well-being, one might expect political unrest even if religion were not part of the mix. Once religion is added to the equation, however, the potential for long-term unrest appears to increase significantly.[127]

Other polling data suggests that a significant number of Western Muslims are not only failing to integrate, but may also be experiencing an identity crisis and becoming more Islamist. In one British poll, 80 percent of British Muslims indicated that they view themselves as Muslims first and foremost, rather than as citizens of the United Kingdom.[128] If there is a point on which European Muslims and the rest of the European population tend to agree, it may be on the subject of Muslims thinking of themselves first as Muslims, and as French, British, German, etc., second. In fact, many Westerners essentially view Muslims as inassimilable. For example, former French Algeria leader Jacques Soustelle spoke for many Westerners and Muslims alike in 1990 when he stated, "Islam is not only a religion, metaphysics and ethics, but a determining and constrictive framework of all aspects of life. Consequently, to speak of integration, that is to say assimilation, is dangerously utopian. You can only assimilate what can be assimilated."[129]

Furthermore, it appears that there may be a movement toward greater religiosity among Europe's Muslims. In one poll in France, for example, the percentage of Muslims who identified themselves as "believing and practicing" increased by a full 25 percent between 1994 and 2001.[130] Greater religiosity itself clearly may open the door for increased radicalism, but this is especially true in Europe, where its Muslim population remains marginalized and not well integrated. Europe's ghettoized and marginalized Muslims, not surprisingly, tend to feel that they are persecuted by the larger non–Muslim majority across Europe. Survey data reveal that one-third of Britain's Muslims report that they or someone they know has been persecuted because of their religion. Similarly, two-thirds of British Muslims agree that antiterrorism laws are applied unfairly against Muslims and the same percentage agree that Britain's Muslims are politically underrepresented in the British political arena.[131]

The propensity to radicalism is further enhanced, however, by the fact that there is a shortage of home-grown clerics in Europe, necessitating the import of Muslim clerics from the Middle East, North Africa, and South Asia, many of whom may have more radical views than those typically held by Western Muslims.[132]

Furthermore, the tension between Muslims living in the West and the general populations should perhaps be expected to worsen in the near future, as more than one million Muslims immigrate to the West annually. Additionally, the birth rate of Muslim population is triple that of the native European populations; consequently, Europe is expected to be 20 percent Muslim by the middle of the twenty-first century.[133]

Globalization and advanced communications technology in the West have the potential to exacerbate the probability of further cultural conflict, since it allows the West's Muslims to reach across state borders both to other Western Muslims and to those Muslims living in the Islamic realm, thus forging a global Muslim identity that supersedes national identities. Whereas much of this interaction is most certainly positive for Western Muslims and Western societies in general, the globalization of communications technology has also thus far proven to be a boon to radical Islamism in Western countries.

CHAPTER 5

Western Approaches to the Challenge of Islam

Muslim Immigration and Western Policy to 1980

Europe has a fairly lengthy history of religious toleration that emerged after the calamity of the Thirty Years' War in the seventeenth century. Although up to one-third of the population of Europe died in religious wars prior to the Treaty of Westphalia in 1648, England passed religious toleration in 1689, Holy Roman emperor and king of Hungary Joseph II issued the Edict of Toleration in 1781 that allowed dissenters to worship privately in the Hapsburg Empire, and France eliminated the monopoly of the Catholic Church with the French Revolution in 1789. In the United States, the free exercise of religion was guaranteed in the American Constitution of 1787 and state-supported religion was banned by the same Constitution. Muslims coming to Western countries after World War II therefore enjoyed the fruits of centuries-long traditions of religious toleration that allowed them to practice their religion freely in their new host countries.[1]

Because of French and Spanish geographic proximity to North Africa and because of the British colonial empire that extended to the Islamic realm, Europeans have had contact with Islam for centuries and a small number of Muslims were living and working in Europe prior to World War II. In Britain, the first mosque was constructed in Woking in 1889.[2]

French contact with the Islamic realm dates as early as 716 C.E. when a group of North African Muslim soldiers entered what is currently French territory and established a Muslim protectorate and mosque in Narbonne. Numerous Muslim invasions and French expulsions of the Muslim invaders occurred in southern France throughout the Middle Ages, resulting in the establishment of mosques and a small number of settlers. The French turned the tables and became invaders themselves in the nineteenth century with the conquest of Algeria in 1830, which became the first of several French colonies with large Muslim populations. Algeria remained a French possession until separating from France through revolt in 1958, but the French expanded their colonial empire in North Africa to include more of North Africa between 1830 and World War II. The first significant immigration from Muslims in French colonies to France, however, came during World War I as several hundred thousand Muslims were recruited by the French both to work in the factories and to serve in the French army. The flow of immigrants from Muslim lands to France became a flood after World War II, however, due to the acute labor shortage that existed in France after the war. By 1975, the Muslim population in France was estimated to be in excess of one million persons.[3]

Prior to the 1970s, European governments generally did not have any policies toward Muslim Western citizens since those that had immigrated to Europe during the 1950s and 1960s had immigrated as guest workers and were not expected to remain in Europe permanently.[4] Conversely, as guest workers, Muslims typically made few demands on Western governments. The first generation of Muslim immigrants to France after World War II, for example, were predominantly male and generally viewed themselves as temporary residents of France with plans to eventually return to their countries of origin. Under these circumstances, Muslims living in France typically remained apolitical and practiced Islam without creating any major political disturbances.[5]

The vast majority of Muslims living in the West prior to 1970 viewed conflict with Western sovereigns as inconsistent with Islam and believed that they had no authority in Islam to demand that their Western infidel sovereigns implement sharia. The South Asian Muslims of the United Kingdom, for instance, tended to keep their own creed and apply the sharia to themselves in their own separate community within the United Kingdom without provoking the intervention of the state. In Germany, where citizenship was by blood rather than residence, the Muslim population was even more inclined to live in closed groups and apply their religious beliefs informally to their separate society within the society at large.[6]

The situation began to change in the 1970s, however, as a global recession and unemployment brought on by the twin oil shocks of the 1970s reduced the need for guest workers in Western Europe. Consequently, European countries tightened their immigration laws, essentially closing their borders to low-skilled Muslim workers, but allowing the possibility of immigration for the purpose of family reunion or political asylum. In 1977, France went so far as to offer North African immigrants 10,000 francs to return to their countries of origin. The French government's efforts, however, had the opposite effect of that intended since few accepted the 10,000 francs and instead, many

Muslims living in France sought to change their status to that of permanent residents and to bring their families living elsewhere to France permanently.[7]

The restrictions on immigration then triggered a second wave of immigration as family members of the guest workers immigrated to Western Europe to reunite their families. The impact of the new immigration laws was to transform the European Muslim population from one of single male "guest" workers to one of families who desired to stay in the West permanently. As the number of permanent residents grew and their population demographics changed, Muslims living in the West began to view their situation differently and began to make demands on European governments. In Britain, for example, Muslims demanded halal (ritually slaughtered) meat in school lunchrooms and the creation of all-girls' schools.[8] In France, there were major strikes among Muslim immigrant workers between 1975 and 1978, and the Iranian-backed Shiite Muslim group Hizbollah carried out bombings in Paris in the 1980s. Consequently, the problems surrounding the integration of the new Muslim immigrants into Western society became an ever more pressing concern on the Western political agenda by the 1980s.[9]

Assimilation or Multiculturalism?

A major debate is currently raging in Western societies over whether any minority group, Islamic or otherwise, should remain distinct or whether they should put away unique features of their cultures and fully assimilate into society as indistinguishably as possible from other segments of society. Similarly, a debate rages among Muslims themselves living in the West over how much Muslims can compromise in the interest of assimilation or whether Muslims must isolate themselves from Western society so as to be true to Islam.

French Assimilationist Approach

France promotes a "melting pot" assimilationist (or integrationist) model where all immigrants, Islamic or otherwise, are encouraged to put away ethnic or religious separatism and assimilate themselves into French culture. In furtherance of this goal, France favors policies that reduce or eliminate cultural uniqueness. Consequently, the French government has taken a harder line against Islamists in particular and Muslims in general in areas where Islamic culture has clashed with the French culture at large.

In terms of actual policy, the assimilationist approach manifests itself in numerous ways, a few of which are worthy of note. First, the French have taken measures to prevent the further radicalization of French Muslims by refusing to grant political asylum to Islamist leaders so as to prevent them from infecting the general Muslim population in France with Islamic radicalism. In the early 1980s, the French state even initiated a policy of subsidizing the return of immigrants to their country of origin in the effort to keep France "French."[10]

Furthermore, the citizenship provision that guaranteed French citizenship to anyone born in France was eliminated in 1993. To be a French citizen, one must do more than simply be born in France; instead, one must become culturally French. Those that are unable to do so will be unable to attain full French citizenship and enjoy all the benefits of French citizenship. For example, the French government has interpreted Muslim adherence to the Islamic daily prayer schedule as an indicator of insufficient assimilation into French culture and grounds for disqualification of an application for French citizenship. Similarly, such individuals are disqualified from receiving any sort of public assistance.[11] This is in spite of the fact that the Grand Mosque in Paris was actually built by the French government in 1926 to recognize the contribution of French Muslim soldiers in World War I. At present, however, the Grand Mosque is supported by the Algerian government and the Mosque's rector is an Algerian Government employee. Finally, French law also generally disallows any sort of dual citizenship.[12]

The French also implement the assimilationist model in their approach to education. French students essentially receive no education about Islam in school except for cursory attention given to the realm of Islam in world history and geography classes.[13] As a consequence of the assimilationist approach to education, headscarves are banned in schools and the workplace in an effort to promote cultural unity and help Muslims integrate seamlessly into society.[14] As a result of this approach, literally hundreds of young Muslim women have been expelled from public schools over the years for refusing to remove their headscarves. Some of these women abandon their education altogether and some study by correspondence, but some adopt volunteer Muslim tutors; thus, the possibility for a radical Islamic indoctrination in their education is increased.[15]

In order to combat the problem of violence among Muslim youths in French cities and suburbs, the French have increased funding for education and social services in impoverished areas with large Muslim populations. Schools with immigrant populations that are 30 percent larger than the national average receive extra money for teachers and better facilities. Additional resources are directed by the education ministry toward violence-prone schools. A separate program targets poor minority residents for additional vocational training and assistance in integration-oriented ethnic associations.[16]

French Separation of Church and State

The French version of separation of church and state has its origin in the French Revolution during which revolutionaries disestablished the Catholic Church, seized most Church property, and outlawed most Catholic religious orders. Strict separation ended in 1801 when Napoleon Bonaparte signed an agreement with Pope Pius VII designating Catholicism to be the "religion of the great majority of French people," but not the established religion. In 1882, France passed the "Ferry Law," after Minister of Public Instruction Jules Ferry, that separated religion from the public schools, though schools were to designate one day a week where students could attend religious classes elsewhere if they so desired.[17]

In 1905, France eliminated special privileges for the Catholic Church and guaranteed freedom of religions with the Law of Separation. Article II of the law also prohibited public funding for any religion and declared that all expenses for religion should be eliminated from budgets of the state, departments, and townships. Additionally, religious symbols were stricken from public monuments.[18] Since 1959, however, the French state has paid the salaries of teachers in religious schools and 80 percent of the budgets for religious schools now come from government sources.[19]

Article 10 of the Revolutionary *Déclaration des droits de l'homme et du citoyen* of 1789 states that "no one may be troubled on account of his or her opinions, even religious ones, provided their manifestation does not disturb the public order established by law."[20] Unfortunately, thousands of French Muslims have expressed that they have been very much "troubled" in France on account of their religious opinions over the last several decades. This is largely because of the second clause, "provided their manifestation does not disturb the public order," which has led to a situation where in the public sphere, French citizens face numerous restrictions on their free exercise of religion. For instance, state employees are forbidden from engaging in any "exterior manifestation" of their religion while performing official duties. This includes praying in public, refusing to eat certain foods at a public facility, or wearing religiously distinctive clothing.[21] Such strict separation has been criticized by French Muslims with arguments that are eerily similar to the arguments of members of the Christian right in the United States, who decry the "religion of the secular humanism" that they claim the U.S. government forces on American children in the public schools. The French Muslim version of the same argument is echoed by Kamel Kabtane, the director of the Grande Mosque of Lyon, who has denounced what he termed as "extreme secularists who want to impose laicité [Church/State separation] as a new religion ... as in (Soviet) Russia."[22]

Concerning the religion of Islam itself, the French state grants it the same rights and duties as other religions in that its free exercise is guaranteed as long as it respects the public order. Islam is not, however, an "established" religion in that it is not recognized by the state and it does not receive any public funding. For example, the French government has not yet funded any Muslim schools, even though Islam is the second largest religion in France.[23] Essentially, the French argue that the government is not supposed to favor or support any religion; therefore, funding of private religious schools, Islamic or otherwise, violates the obligation of the French state to maintain religious neutrality.

Concerning official representation of Islam in France, in December 2002, then Minister of the Interior Nicolas Sarkozy worked with the Union of Islamic Organizations in France, the National Federation of French Muslims, and the Great Mosque of Paris to create the French Council on Islam (Conseil Francais du Culte Musulman), whose original board of directors were drawn from the Great Mosque and the other leading French Islamic organizations.[24] The presidency of the new French Council on Islam was granted to the rector of the Great Mosque of Paris. The principle of "vote by mosque" was decided on for all future elections of the Council, which also includes elections for a 4,032-member representative assembly and an administrative council along with the board of directors.[25]

The purpose of the Council is to allow dialogue between all of the different segments of Islam in France and the government and the model for the French Council on Islam had already been established by similar organizations for the Catholic, Protestant, and Jewish faiths in France.[26] Part of the motivation for the creation of the French Council on Islam is to bring Islam out into the open based on the premise that an underground or "secret" religion is prone to radicalism. In the words of Sarkozy, "we should all fear a secrecy which leads to radicalization." The French government is not neutral, however, when it concerns religions that are determined by the French state to be "dangerous." In 2001, France banned "dangerous religious sects," an act aimed specifically at scientology, but the law will also allow the government to expel radical imams from France whenever they deem it necessary.[27]

Assimilationist Approaches Elsewhere

Adopting a similar approach, a new German citizenship reform in 2000 requires German citizens to prove commitment to the values of the German Basic Law, a requirement that essentially disallows citizenship to members of a number of German Muslim associations. Additionally, persons that have ever been members of Islamist groups are denied public sector employment by the German government.[28]

Even Britain began to move toward the integrationist model in 2004 with new Home Office rules for "overseas ministers of religion" that require that immigrant clergy must show knowledge of, and engagement with, British civic life, including an understanding of other faiths in Britain. The Dutch impose similar requirements, but also require that imams attend a compulsory introduction course and take a language exam. Both Germany and Denmark prohibit visas to imams who do not speak the host language.[29]

British Multiculturalism

Due to a history of colonialism in South Asia, the British have experienced centuries of contact with Islam; concurrently, Muslims began settling in Britain in the eighteenth century as British companies sought a cheap labor force in the British industrial seaports. The first Muslim migrants to Britain were therefore mainly sailors and most of the small Muslim enclaves that developed in Britain formed in the major port cities of Liverpool, Newcastle, and London.[30] The Muslim influx in the nineteenth century was small, but significant enough that the first mosque was constructed in Woking in 1889. A much larger wave of Muslims arrived in Britain after World War II as a labor force to help rebuild Britain after the war. Although most Muslims arriving after the war intended to make a handsome sum of money and return to South Asia, for a variety of reasons many instead chose to stay in the UK permanently.[31]

The Muslims in Britain after World War II enjoyed a different legal status than Muslims in other European countries in that under the 1948 British Nationality Act, Commonwealth immigrants had access to all the rights and privileges of British citizenship. Persons born in Commonwealth countries were not subject to immigration controls, nor were they considered aliens. The intent of the policy was to allow white colonial subjects to gain automatic citizenship when they returned to the UK. The unintended consequence, however, was that non-white subjects in the British Commonwealth had the same right of entry and settlement in Britain.[32]

Perhaps predictably, the influx of immigrants led to a number of race riots in the 1950s and 1960s, resulting in a conservative, anti-immigrant backlash. In 1968, British nativist Enoch Powell famously delivered his "rivers of blood" speech in which he called for an end to all non-white immigration and the repatriation of non-whites to their countries of origin.[33] Though the Tories never adopted Powell's approach, his vitriolic hyperbole led to the development of the nativist National Front Party in the 1970s and the British National Party in the 1980s. Parliament also passed the 1962 Commonwealth Immigrants Act and other subsequent acts that placed limits on immigration. Thus, Britain became the first country in Western Europe to place tight controls on immigration.[34]

In spite of the restrictions, however, there was still a significant population of Muslims in Britain that had become citizens under the 1948 Act, and the population grew even larger in the 1960s as Muslims in Britain took advantage of British laws that allowed immigration for the purpose of reuniting families. As resident Muslims moved to quickly bring their families to the UK, fearing more immigration restrictions that could keep them shut out forever, Britain perhaps had little choice but to adopt a multicultural approach toward those that were already citizens of the UK.[35]

The British approach, in contrast to the French approach, promotes a "salad bowl" multiculturalism model and generally allows immigrant groups to retain much of their cultures of origin while living in Britain as long as they stay within British laws. The general idea is that the state should encourage cultural minorities to create their own organizational structures with the freedom to retain their own cultural and religious practices as they choose. For example, British schoolgirls are allowed to wear the Islamic headscarf (hijab) as long as it conforms to the color requirements of the school's uniforms.[36] Similarly, British Courts have ruled that schools cannot ban the wearing of a turban because it violates Britain's Race Relations Act that prevents racial discrimination.[37] British schools have also been flexible in other areas such as the provision of halal meat, time off for religious holidays, and accommodation of daily prayers.[38]

The British also stress multiculturalism in education, including requiring religious education classes that include information about religions other than Christianity.[39] In 1976, Parliament passed the Race Relations Act that prohibited discrimination on racial or ethnic grounds and created the Commission for Racial Equality to oversee race relations. The Act does not, however, specifically protect against religious discrimination, and many Muslims feel that they suffer from anti–Muslim prejudice and Islamophobia.[40] Similarly, the Human Rights Act of 1998 provides for the idea that religious freedom in Britain is a fundamental right that is protected against state intrusion, but the act does not specifically protect against religious discrimination by private entities.[41]

Even though Britain officially has a state-established church in the Church of England and requires religious education classes, the curriculum includes coverage not only of Christianity, but also Islam, along with Judaism and Sikhism. Essentially, Muslims benefit from centuries of political conflict between Catholics and Protestants in England that led to the passage of the Roman Catholic Relief Act in 1829 and the Jews' Relief Act in 1858 that recognized these religious groups and granted them the rights of political participation.[42] Britain also allows public funding of Islamic schools as long as they adhere to the national curriculum and, by 2004, 85 Islamic schools received public funding.[43] Although this is certainly representative of religious freedom, the approach aids in the development of Islamic institutions that many non–Muslims in Britain do not want and the chance for radicalization of children at Islamic schools with state funding is present.

Numerous other European countries are even more multiculturalist than Britain when it comes to state recognition of religion. In Austria, Belgium, Italy, and Spain, all religions are legally recognized. In Belgium, over 800 teachers of Islam have been hired with public funding. Belgium also provided for the development of a Belgian General Islamic Assembly, but the Belgian government reserves the right to reject Islamist candidates in advance. Similarly, Islam was officially recognized by the state in Austria in 1979 and there are now over 230 state-supported teachers of Islam in Austria. Islam was granted recognition by the state in Spain in 1992, providing for the institution of Islamic education in public schools. Furthermore, religious marriages have the same legal status as civil marriages.[44]

In furthering the multicultural approach, one potentially dangerous consequence is that the British have granted political asylum to radical Islamists from all over the world, with the result that London has become known as a hotbed of radical Islamist activity that includes radical preaching in the mosques, Islamist publishing, Islamist internet sites, recruitment for jihad elsewhere, and more recently, even terror attacks in the UK itself.[45] An estimated 3,000 British Muslims have passed through al-Qaeda training camps worldwide.[46] British Muslims have also been among those detained by American authorities at Guantanamo Bay.[47]

The German Hybrid Approach

The German approach to Islam should be considered as a "hybrid" approach that falls somewhere between the polar opposites of the British multiculturalist and French integrationist approaches to Muslim immigration. In Germany, due to very strict nationalization laws prior to reforms in 1999, very few Muslim immigrants are German citizens because very few actually had the right to become German citizens. Like France, Germany has also used a number of approaches to attempt to induce Muslim immigrants to return to their countries of origin, though the efforts have been largely ineffectual.

In regard to religion and schools, the German approach is much like Britain's in that the Basic Law stipulates that state schools provide formal religious instruction as part of the core curriculum. The German school authorities essentially view their role as one of helping the churches to teach their own doctrines and schools do not take a particular position on religious matters. Parents may choose whether their children receive Catholic or Protestant instruction or none at all.[48] What this means, of course, is the current situation is such that Muslims in most locations cannot receive state-supported Islamic instruction in schools, thus providing grounds for complaints of discrimination. In most of the German Länder (states), the closest that Muslims can get to state-sponsored courses in Islamic instruction are comparative religious courses.[49] Germany has, however, funded some Islamic schools and Islamic social welfare and cultural organizations, and mandated the teaching of Islam as a required course in public schools in some areas. The intent of the German state in adopting these multiculturalist policies is to ensure that the version of Islam taught in the schools is one less radical and more compatible with Western liberal democratic ideals.[50] In Berlin, the Federal Administrative Court ruled in 2000 that Berlin had to recognize the Islamische Foderation Berlin (IFB) as a religious society entitled to administer Islamic instruction in public schools. This was in spite of protests from Turkish journalists and the German Association of Turkish Parents, who denounced the IFB as an extremist organization. Their strongest evidence was that the IFB had distributed a form on the Internet requesting that Muslim families have their daughters exempt from co-ed classrooms.[51] In spite of this, and in spite of the fact that the IFB was under surveillance by the German Secret Service, the Federation now provides Islamic instruction to over 1,000 students in 28 schools throughout Berlin. In several Länder, Islamic education is provided as part of a Turkish language program for children of Turkish immigrants. In some cases, the Turkish government provides both personnel and logistical support for these education efforts.[52]

In regard to private schools, the German Basic Law establishes the right to operate private religious schools as long as they are approved by the Land government. Thus far, Land governments have approved two Muslim elementary schools in Munich and Berlin and the schools are eligible for public funding under regulations of the Länder governments. The school in Berlin is almost completely supported through public funding.[53]

Muslims in Germany enjoy the same free-exercise religious rights as those of other faiths in Germany. Furthermore, the Basic Law guarantees the "undisturbed practice of religion" and forbids the state from restricting civil liberties based on the "exercise of religious freedom." The Basic Law even protects the right not to work on Sundays and publicly recognized religious holidays. The Basic Law also grants conscientious objector status to individuals in regard to military service if that service is precluded for religious reasons.[54]

In regards to the relationship between religion and the state, the German Basic Law establishes formal separation of church and state, but provides for cooperation between religion and the state in the areas of education and social welfare. While the Basic Law stipulates that Germany is to have no state church, the Basic Law recognizes religious public corporations and the government is authorized to collect money from church members on the behalf of the church. The money collected by the state (in effect, a church tax) is then used for the religious, social welfare, and educational work of the churches. According to the Basic Law, however, the public corporation status for religious entities is not limited to Christian churches, but other religious communities are granted the same rights "upon application where their constitution and the number of their members offer an assurance of their permanency."[55] Each German Land government determines the eligibility of religious groups to achieve public corporation status and in order to qualify, a group must have existed for at least thirty years, its members must comprise at least 0.1 percent of the total Land population, and that group must respect German law. Thus far, no Muslim group has achieved public corporation status as Land governments have deemed them unrepresentative or undemocratic. Muslims, unsurprisingly, have criticized the decisions of the Land governments in this respect as biased against Muslims.[56]

Concerning the building of mosques, as in Britain and France, the building of religious facilities in Germany is regulated by local governments and zoning restrictions vary greatly. Though regulated, mosque-building has not been greatly hindered as evidenced by the existence of over 2400 mosques across Germany. Requests for permits to build mosques are sometimes met with resistance from local groups who oppose increased traffic and noise or violations of local architectural consistencies. In some cases, locals simply argue that the building of a mosque may attract more unwanted Muslims.[57]

Like Britain, Germany has a long history of Muslim immigration. In 1732 (over a century before the unification of Germany), King Friedrich Wilhelm I of Prussia set up an Islamic prayer room in Potsdam for twenty Turkish mercenaries. Berlin's first mosque was constructed in 1925 after an influx of Turkish laborers followed World War I. During World War II, the Nazi regime trained imams to lead prayers for tens of thousands of Muslims who fought for Germany. Like Britain and France, Germany faced a labor shortage after World War II and welcomed foreign guest workers (in this case, Turkish Muslims) with the assumption that they would return to their countries of origin when reconstruction was completed.[58] As a consequence, Germany did little in the first two decades after World War II to meet the educational, cultural, or religious needs of what was viewed as a temporary, largely male Muslim population.[59]

The oil shocks of the 1970s brought economic decline in Germany and Germany suspended its active recruitment of foreign workers, assuming that the guest workers in Germany already would return to their countries of origin. Instead, the new restrictions on immigration brought an immigration reaction among guest workers as those already in Germany summoned family members from their countries of origin, the immigration of family members being a kind of immigration that remained protected under Germany's Basic Law.[60]

The cessation of the recruitment of guest workers in 1973 led to a change in the political views of Germany's Muslims. Instead of viewing themselves as guest workers, the German Muslim population came to view themselves as permanent residents with housing, educational, welfare, and religious needs. The Muslim population also became a family population instead of a population of single males.[61] Muslims began forming their own organizations, such as the Verband Islamischer Kulturzentren and the Milli Gorus-affiliated Islamische Union Deutschlands. By 1980, such groups had over 20,000 members in Germany. The Turkish government also did its part to help Turkish Muslims living in Germany by establishing in 1972 a division of the office of religious affairs (Diyanet Isleri Turk-Islam Birligi) to help Turkish Muslims living abroad with their religious needs.[62]

In one sense, the German approach has been successful in that Germany has been thus far spared the type of massive terrorist attacks that has befallen New York, London, and Madrid. This could be due to German policies, but it may also be because more German immigrants are of Turkish origin as opposed to Pakistan, Saudi Arabia, North Africa, or the Middle East, and Turkey has a much quieter recent history in terms of terrorism than any of the aforementioned. In contrast, a major segment of Britain's Muslim population is of Islamist-infested Pakistani origin and the majority of the Muslims in France and Spain are of North African origin, another area with a violent twentieth-century history of Islamic violence and colonialism.

Islam and Islamism in the United States

Islam is the fastest growing religion in the United States and should soon supplant Judaism as the second largest religion in North America.[63] In general, the American Muslim community has thus far been less hospitable to jihadists and less radical than their counterparts in Europe. This is due at least in part to the fact that there are far greater numbers of Muslims in Europe, although exactly how many Muslims live in America is a matter of debate since the U.S. Bureau of the Census does not collect data on religious affiliation. In order to get an approximate count, researchers are forced to rely on self-identification, surname characteristics, and national origins, none of which are perfect measures. The best estimates appear to be that the United States is home to approximately 3 million Muslim people, or a little more than 1 percent of the American population.[64]

Muslim Assimilation in America

American Muslims appear to be much more integrated into American society than they are in Europe, where there is a tendency for Muslims to occupy low-wage jobs and reside in Muslim ghettoes. In contrast, American Muslims are better educated, more likely to be professionals, and more economically advanced. The average household income of American Muslims is higher than the median U.S. household income and a fourth of American Muslim households earn over $100,000 annually. Similarly, more than a third of American Muslims have graduate degrees, compared with 8.6 percent of the American population as a whole.[65]

Certainly, part of the reason that American Muslims appear to be better assimilated than those in Europe may be that American Muslims are much more diverse. While the majority of Muslims in France and Spain are of North African origin, those in the UK are in the majority of South Asian origin, and those in Germany are predominantly of Turkish origin, American Muslims are a mosaic of numerous ethnic, racial and national groups, the majority of whom are foreign-born and educated outside the United States.[66] American Muslims include people from over sixty countries and the countries of origin themselves often contain numerous ethnic, racial, linguistic, tribal, and national identities. The American Muslim population also includes a large number of American converts, especially African Americans, with a very different cultural identity from that of the Muslim immigrants.[67] In fact, as late as 1994, an estimated 46 percent of American Muslims were converts, and the majority of those converts were African Americans. Furthermore, approximately 30 percent of the African American converts to Islam in the United States converted to Islam in prison.[68]

Because of this diversity, unity among American Muslims has thus far remained elusive, and American Muslims have failed to articulate a cohesive domestic political agenda, instead concentrating on the politics of their countries of origin.[69] Even in the case of the Israeli/Palestinian conflict, all American Muslims cannot be united because African American Muslims tend to support American policies and the policies of the diverse countries in the Islamic realm are not identical toward Israel. For example, Egypt signed the 1978 Camp David Accords in which Egypt recognized the Israeli government and subsequently found itself expelled from the Arab League.[70]

Currently, the largest percentage of the American Muslim population is either foreign-born or descended from a wave of Muslim immigration that followed World War II. The vast majority of American Muslims came to the U.S. after the repeal of the Asia Exclusion Act in 1965.[71] Although the United States was not involved in the same type of domestic rebuilding project as experienced by Europe after World War II, the U.S. encouraged the immigration of Muslims to the United States to be educated in American universities as a way of combating radicalism and Marxism during the Cold War. American policymakers believed that Muslims educated in American universities would adopt the American worldview and subsequently go forth and spread the "American way" throughout the world.[72] The experiences of Islamists such as Sayyid Qutb, who famously came to America in the 1940s as a moderate and returned to Egypt as a committed Islamist, suggest that the American policies did not always achieve the intended results.

As for the Muslims who came to America and stayed, there was social pressure in American society to conform as Americans tend to favor assimilation to cultural uniqueness and prefer that foreign cultural elements be abandoned. The small number of Muslim immigrants who arrived prior to 1960 generally conformed to the American expectations while those who have arrived since are more likely to claim the right to retain their own cultural uniqueness, thus perhaps increasing the possibility of cultural conflict. Predictably, some conflict between American Muslims and the larger culture has developed. Specifically, American Muslims tend to favor the American version of separation of church and state, which they view as protecting their religion, but Muslims tend to believe that Protestant Christianity receives preferred treatment in the American system over Islam. This also creates conflict within the American Islamic community itself between accommodationists and the more strict Islamists who argue that the Koran dictates that there should be no separation between church and state.[73]

Muslim Separatism in America

This is not to say, however, that all American Muslims have chosen assimilation. A minority of American Muslims have viewed American society as Dar ul-Harb (the land of non-believers) and chosen to separate themselves into enclaves so as to either preserve their culture or practice a purer form of Islam. In the words of Maher Hathout,

> Most of our centers are institutions to deal with homesickness, not headquarters for driving and guiding the Islamic movement in America. Egyptians miss Egypt, so they form a part of Egypt here in Los Angeles, where they can come together. So it is with Pakistanis, and Palestinians, and so forth. Indeed, you can walk into a center and say that this is an Indian center, a Pakistani center, or an Egyptian center. From people to food to virtually everything — you can see, you can feel it in the air — these were not built here for America after all. They are built so that I do not feel lonely. I am scared out there and I need my buddies to come together the way we used to huddle back home.[74]

Obviously, a minority of Muslims argue for the building of Islamic institutions and organizations within American society so as to preserve their cultural identity and religious purity.[75] The ability of Muslims to successfully separate themselves into cultural and religious enclaves in North America, however, is questionable. As Maher Hathout explained,

> While we huddle together as Pakistanis or Egyptians or Iranians or whatever else, our children are, whether we believe it or like it or hate it or not, American kids. The question should be whether they will be Muslim-American kids or just American kids. Anyone who believes that he will raise an Egyptian boy in America is wrong; the maximum we can do is to have a distorted Egyptian kid. The grandchildren will be without doubt American.[76]

If Hathout is correct in his analysis, then it appears that the "America, the great melting pot" model is still in existence and American Muslims will be able to assimilate into American society much like other immigrant groups that have preceded them. In fact, it may be that there is no choice in the long run and the attempt to construct Muslim enclaves is a futile and temporary exercise.

The greater diversity and assimilation of American Muslims may explain why identity politics and liberation ideology are not greater among American Muslims. The greater diversity and lack of cohesion among American Muslims may also explain why the 9/11 terrorists do not appear to have been part of a vast network of Islamists within the United States. Given the religious, ethnic, and language diversity among America's Muslims, creating an Islamist terror network is made much more difficult.

The Moderate Character of American Muslims

Though there clearly are those in North America who believe it is their responsibility to invest their time and energy in developing an Islamist vision and agenda in North America, in fact, the majority of American Muslims tend to disassociate themselves from the very issue of Islam's presence in the United States and instead prefer an assimilationist approach.[77] While Islamists have as a goal the conversion of all the world to Islam, the North American Association of Muslim Professionals and Scholars (NAAMPS) rejected this view at its 1993 conference and instead argued that Muslims should strive to "illuminate it [America] with the light of Islam" and focus on changing the lives of Muslims for the better instead of on conversion.[78] With this as the prevailing view among American Muslims, Islamists find themselves isolated from the rest of the American Muslim community. The *9/11 Commission Report*, for example, documents a fairly solitary path of the 9/11 terrorists while they were in the United States. The terrorists evidently did not make contacts with other American-based groups of Islamists, and the terrorists apparently had more contact with individuals from foreign embassies than with other American Muslims.[79] The 9/11 terrorists did not belong to neighborhood Islamic communities, nor had they been schooled in radical madrassas. The behavior of the 9/11 terrorists suggests that if there were a radical Islamist network in the United States, the 9/11 terrorists were not associated with it, may not have known about it at all, and if they had, may not have trusted it.[80]

Subsequent federal government efforts to thwart radical Islamism within the United States also have not revealed a vast Islamic terror network in the United States. For example, in spite of the recent American focus on terrorism, according to Eggen and Tate, in the first almost four years after 9/11, only thirty-nine people were convicted of crimes tied to national security or terrorism in the United States, and of those, only fourteen had any links to al-Qaeda.[81] Among those fourteen were the celebrated cases of John Walker Lindh, the American who fought with the Taliban; Zacarias Moussaoui, the so-called twentieth hijacker; and Richard Reid, the notorious shoe-bomber.

Again, the diversity of American Muslims appears to be a factor inhibiting the spread of Islamism in the U.S. as the diverse group of Muslims who live in the U.S. do not always associate with each other and do not always agree with each other. Still, American Muslims are faced with many of the same challenges as those faced by their Islamic counterparts in Europe. In other words, how should American Muslims deal with the problems of interest in banking, mortgages, insurance, and car loans as well as the problems of halal meat, Friday prayers, and Islamic clothing. Can Muslims invest in the stock market or in individual retirement accounts? How should American Muslims approach marriage, which in the U.S. must be recognized through secular courts in order to be recognized by the state as valid? Women who wear the hijab or the veil in the United States are likely to be discriminated against and a significant women's movement in America opposes both as demeaning to women. Does Islam require that American Muslim women subject themselves to such discrimination? Perhaps most importantly in the age of the War on Terror, can Muslims fight in the U.S. Armed Forces and kill other Muslims on behalf of a non–Muslim state?[82]

A Fiqh Council of North America exists to provide answers to such questions, but there is still little agreement. Some religious leaders argue for a bold reinterpretation of Islamic law (ijtihad) so as to allow Muslims to accommodate the challenges of modern Western societies, while others even argue that Muslims should emigrate back to Muslim lands where they can practice a purer form of Islam within Muslim societies.[83]

African American Muslims

Most scholars view African American Muslims as unique and separate from the larger Muslim community in the United States and the movement itself is generally viewed as interwoven with black liberation ideology and the African American response to racism in American society.[84] The first African American Islamic group, the Moorish Science Temple of America (MSTA) was founded in Newark, New Jersey, in 1913 and declared Islam to be the true religion of blacks and other persons of color in North America. MSTA leader Noble Drew Ali argued that blacks had fallen into a state of material and existential deprivation because they had turned away from God.[85] Ali, however, admitted that his version of Islam varied from that of the prophet Mohammed and argued that "to Americanize the Oriental idea of Islam involves many changes that are more or less negative to the main purpose of the Islamic religion."[86] In short, Ali connected Islam to black liberation ideology.

In 1930, a more well-known group known as the Nation of Islam was founded in Detroit, Michigan, subscribing not only to Islam, but also to the idea that the primary source of black suffering was abuse at the hands of whites.[87] The Nation of Islam preached the myth of black superiority and the myth of the black race's original devotion to Islam. The Nation of Islam also preaches a separatist millenarianism, according to which the black race will be recognized as the superior chosen people of God at the end of time and the white race will be eliminated.[88] For example, Nation of Islam leader Elijah Muhammad in 1965 argued,

> The original man, Allah has declared, is none other than the black man. The black man is the first and last, maker and owner of the universe. From him came brown, yellow, red and white people. By using a special method of birth control law the black man was able to produce the white race.... The white race is not, and never will be, the chosen people of Allah. They are the chosen people of their father Yakub, the Devil.[89]

Elijah Muhammed also, however, stressed purity through the prohibition of alcohol, drugs, tobacco, and gambling, along with a celebration of family and marital fidelity. In this, Muhammed was consistent not only with the teachings of Islam, but with the teachings of conservative, white, Protestant fundamentalist preachers in America.[90]

In the 1940s, Muhammad earned for himself the status as an enemy of the state by denouncing the American effort in World War II and imploring blacks not to join. Muhammad spent time in federal prison during the war for his actions.[91] By the 1960s, the Nation of Islam became intertwined with the American Civil Rights movement, which essentially was pushing for inclusion into American society rather than separatism. By the mid–1970s, the nature of the African American Muslim movement began to change again as Imam Warith Din Muhammad transformed the Nation of Islam into Sunni orthodox Muslims, but resisted the absorption of the Nation of Islam into a subservient position among Sunni Muslim immigrants. Muhammad stressed the "Americanness" of the Nation of Islam and at one point called his organization the American Muslim Mission and placed American flags in his mosques and encouraged the enlistment of his followers in the American armed services. Muhammad expressed the separateness of African American Muslims again in 1991 by supporting American intervention in the Gulf War while most other American Muslims did not.[92] Similarly, though, Louis Farrakhan, the current leader of the Nation of Islam, has amicable relations with several leaders of foreign Muslim nations designated by the U.S. government as "harbouring terrorists," most immigrant Muslims disassociate themselves from his teachings and regard him as a heretic. Farrakhan broke with Warith

Din Muhammed in 1977 and redirected the Nation of Islam, but currently their membership is estimated at only 20,000 of the 3 million black Muslims in the United States. Though the majority of American conversions to Islam are products of the African American Islamic movement, and most identify with the teachings of Sunni Islam, most do not refer to themselves as members of the Nation of Islam, or Sunni Muslims, or even "black Muslims," but simply Muslims.[93] Nevertheless, Muslims of foreign origin still tend to view themselves as the true torchbearers of Islam in America and the only ones with the expertise to direct Islam in the United States.[94]

CHAPTER 6

Bones of Contention

In the decades since World War II, a number of contentious issues have arisen between Muslims living in the West and their non–Muslim Western hosts. Though many of the issues were present but under the surface before the Salman Rushdie affair that exploded in 1989, Muslims living in Western countries have been more vocal about contentious issues ever since. It should be stressed that though the Islamists are the most vocal and uncompromising on all of these issues, moderate Muslims have expressed their concerns and become involved in the politics surrounding these issues as well. The explosive Rushdie affair and other contentious issues that have arisen in the years since its emergence will be discussed below.

The Salman Rushdie Affair

The Salman Rushdie affair exploded suddenly onto the world political scene in 1989 when Ayatollah Khomeini of Iran, viewed by many at the time as the world's supreme Shiite leader, put out a call for the world's Muslims to execute Salman Rushdie, a British author (with no connections to Iran) who had written a critical book about Islam provocatively entitled *The Satanic Verses*. Khomeini's proclamation led to violent demonstrations and vitriolic diatribes throughout the Islamic realm, complete with ceremonial book burnings that invited comparisons with Nazi book burnings of the 1930s.

Though Khomeini's bold proclamation clearly gave the issue a violent shove, and it might not have become a global phenomenon without his participation, it is noteworthy that the Rushdie affair did not originate in Iran with the Ayatollah, but was instead initiated in the United Kingdom by Muslim groups that led a petition drive to prevent the book's publication in the UK. The issue then heated up after the book's publication when the Bradford Council of Mosques organized a series of marches to publicize their opposition to the book, and organized a book burning of Rushdie's work in Bradford in

January 1989.[1] Further demonstrations then spread throughout the UK, including more book burnings in the British city of Oldham.[2]

Khomeini's unconventional escalation of the Rushdie issue then became transformed into the conventional British political arena where Western Muslims demonstrated that they had become adept at playing the Western democratic political game. Working within the existing political system rather than raging against it, British Muslims assembled an ad hoc Muslim Action Committee in London that called for the expansion of some archaic British blasphemy laws, originally passed to protect the Church of England, but rarely referenced in the late twentieth century, to be extended to other religions such as Islam. The ensuing debate brought much negative publicity to British Muslims, but also galvanized moderate and radical Muslims alike who argued for equal treatment for their religion. In the end, the British government was unwilling to extend the blasphemy laws to include Islam, but Muslims had made their voices heard and proven that they could be a political force to be reckoned with in Western democratic societies.[3]

In response to the rebuff by Parliament, one Muslim activist, Kalim Siddiqui, created an informal Muslim Parliament, whose members claimed to "legislate in the name of all Muslim believers in the United Kingdom," thus suggesting that British Muslims should subscribe to a different set of laws than those that applied to other British citizens. The British Attorney General, however, did not recognize a separate set of laws for Muslims and ruled that British law offered no grounds for any civil suit to withdraw Rushdie's book from circulation. Britain's Muslims responded by taking to the streets in demonstrations. Fearing for his life, Rushdie first went into hiding and then announced that he himself had converted to Islam. Time and the eventual death of Ayatollah Khomeini eventually caused the fervor over Rushdie to subside, but British Muslims suddenly had become politically mobilized.[4]

Two decades have passed since Khomeini's proclamation against Rushdie and the Rushdie affair has faded from memory for many Europeans, both Muslim and non–Muslim (though at the time it received more press than most other cultural clashes in the West between Muslims and Westerners). Still, the affair was extraordinary at the time in that the leader of an Islamic country outside the West was able to mobilize Muslims living in the West to political action. In this regard, the Rushdie affair has proven to be far less unique in the years since, but was instead a foreshadowing of things to come. As contact between Muslims and the West has increased, and the number of Muslims living in Western countries has increased, the number of Muslims living in the West who remain connected to the politics of Muslims outside the West has also increased, thus leading to more opportunities for externally instigated conflict within the West itself.

Headscarf Controversy

Dale F. Eckelman and James Piscatori argue that symbols are the source of all political mobilization, including the political mobilization of Muslims.[5] That being the case, Eckelman and Piscatori argue that contention over symbols is the basis of Muslim political activism in the West. Given that there has been a series of major flaps over Islamic symbols (of which the headscarf is merely one) in Western countries, Eckelman and Piscatori appear to be on target.

Koranic Origins

The Koranic requirement that women wear headscarves is found in Light 24:60, where it is stated, "Such women as are past child-bearing and have no hope of marriage — there is no fault in them that they put off their clothes, so be it that they flaunt no ornament," and in the Confederates 33: 32–33 where it is stated, "Wives of the Prophet, you are not as other women. If you are godfearing, be not abject in your speech, so that he in whose heart is sickness may be lustful; but speak honourable words. Remain in your houses; and display not your finery, as did the pagans of old."

Obviously, the words in the Koran concerning the headscarf and other articles of women's clothing are a bit non-specific, but Muslims throughout history have used the commands to "flaunt no ornament" and to "display not your finery" to justify covering not only the entire female body, but the face as well, in drab material. Although seculars may question why any of it would matter if women are forbidden from leaving their houses anyway, Islamists interpret the verses as to command that women keep their hair covered with a hijab (headscarf). Others go even farther and insist that women must be veiled or covered entirely from head to foot with long, drab, and loose material. Secular Western citizens and Western Christians generally find such restrictions revolting, thus leading to conflict, but one might argue that these same Westerners would do well to look closer at their own wedding veils, traditional clothing for Catholic nuns, the wardrobes of Amish women in Pennsylvania, and the dress codes of seventeenth-century Puritans in Massachusetts Bay. Furthermore, Apostle Paul's biblical restrictions on appearance (avoidance of jewelry, women should have their heads covered, etc.) appear on the surface to be little different from Mohammed's Koranic restrictions. For example, the word "hijab" comes from the Arabic word "hajaba" meaning "to hide from view or conceal." The word is used in the West more specifically to refer to the headscarf, but in Arabic it properly refers only to the general obligation of women to dress modestly, a command with which most devout Western Christians would have little quarrel.[6] In practice, however, Muslims living both in and outside of the West have interpreted the Koranic command to "dress modestly" as a command that requires the wearing of the headscarf by Muslim women and, as a specific command from God, it cannot be discarded. Although it is surely true that there are some Muslim women that oppose the wearing of the hijab, many devout Muslim women prefer to wear the scarf voluntarily as a symbol of their Islamic faith. Muslim women also criticize Westerners for passing laws making it permissible to be nude in public under the guise of freedom of choice, while simultaneously denying the choice of wearing a headscarf to Muslim women.[7]

In contrast to the Muslim view, many Westerners (typically ignoring any parallels in Christianity) view the headscarf as a symbol of both the Muslim failure to fully assimilate into Western societies and the Muslim oppression of women. This is in spite of the fact that in most instances in Western political democracies, Western Muslims generally have not argued not for the compulsory wearing of the hijab, but instead have argued for the right to do so under the Western conceptions of religious freedom.[8] In this sense, the Muslim struggle for the freedom to wear the hijab finds Western Muslims playing the Western democratic political game and working within the political system rather than raging against it.

Multiculturalism, Assimilationism and the Hijab

The approach of most Western Muslims toward the headscarf is essentially multiculturalist in character and is guided by the idea that diverse cultures can live under the same political roof while simultaneously retaining their unique cultural identities. Those favoring the multiculturalist model (both Muslim and non–Muslim) consider legislation against headscarves to be discriminatory against Muslims, an infringement on freedom of religion, and an infringement on Muslims' right to choose. In the multiculturalist UK, policewomen, doctors, and nurses freely wear the headscarf as do many other women in the workplace and at school. The same is largely true for the Netherlands, and the headscarf has caused little controversy in the United States.[9]

Those that favor the assimilationist model, such as the French, therefore oppose the wearing of the headscarf on the premise that it discourages assimilation and integration and displays state support or preference for a particular religion over others. In Germany in 2002, for instance, the federal administrative court ruled that the only way a teacher could fulfill her duty to be religiously neutral was to remove her hijab during class. This is in spite of the fact that crucifixes and other Christian symbols are prevalent on the walls of many public schools in Germany.[10]

In France, where French law restricts religion in public life and therefore the wearing of veils and headscarves in school, Muslims began to clamor for the right to wear their religious clothing in schools at the end of the 1980s.[11] The French government claims that the wearing of Islamic headscarves in French schools is prohibited because of the European Convention on Human Rights that bans the degradation of women. Many of France's Muslim schoolgirls, however, protested that the scarf was not degrading, but a cultural preference. Simultaneously, however, a British court cited the same European Convention on Human Rights document to uphold an Islamic schoolgirl's right to wear an even bulkier covering known as a jilbab in British schools.

The Hijab in France

The hijab (headscarf) heated up on the Western scene as a political issue in France in 1989 when a French secondary school in Creil expelled three girls for wearing the scarf. The expulsions were generally consistent with the existing French assimilationist approach toward minorities that encouraged immigrants to adopt French cultural mores. The Muslim parents of the expelled schoolgirls, however, pushed back against the schoolmaster's policies, leading to negotiations with the schoolmaster over the issue. The schoolmaster and the students' families eventually reached a compromise whereby the students would be able to wear the hijab everywhere in the school except for the classroom, where they would have to slide it off of their heads and place it around their shoulders. The compromise, however, lasted only ten days after human rights groups and the Cardinal of Paris announced their support for the right to wear the hijab.[12]

French Education Minister Lionel Jospin responded by instructing public school principals not to expel Muslim girls who wore the hijab. Jospin's instructions were immediately denounced by French teachers' unions and Jospin's Gaullist political opponents. Jospin then called on the Conseil d'Etat, the highest French administrative court, to settle the matter.[13]

The Conseil quickly issued a ruling that the wearing of headscarves for religious purposes did not violate French law. The issue did not simply go away, however, with this ruling. Instead, those against the hijab fought back with significant energy. As a result, the next month, Jospin issued a series of government rules that awarded to school principals the authority to either ban or permit headscarves. Shortly thereafter, in January 1990, French teachers went on strike in support of a principal who had expelled students for wearing the headscarf, and the issue refused to go away. Ten years later, seventy teachers in Normandy went on strike during Ramadan in protest against girls wearing the headscarf.[14]

In 2004 the French National Assembly voted 494–36 in favor of legislation banning the wearing of ostentatious religious symbols in the schools. The French law does not single out Islam specifically since it also bans the Jewish yarmulke as well as the wearing of "oversized" crosses in schools.[15] The French ban is in spite of the fact that the European Convention on Human Rights grants everyone the right to freedom of thought, conscience, and religion. The Convention allows limitations on public expressions of faith, however, if they constitute threats to public order or may be construed as attacks on the freedom of conscience of others.[16] To be consistent with the Convention, the French Parliament is essentially arguing that the wearing of headscarves constitutes either threats to public order or attacks on the freedom of conscience. Neither argument may be sustainable.

The Hijab in Germany

In Germany, bans against the hijab are in effect at the Land (five Länder) level and were put into effect for civil servants and teachers in public schools and some other public employees, but not for students. Similar to the French laws, the German bans generally included not only the headscarf, but also large crucifixes and yarmulkes, though Bavaria also passed a law that requires the placing of crucifixes in public schools.[17] Evidently then, in Bavaria headscarves are viewed as threats to public order or attacks on freedom of conscience that are banned by the European Human Rights Convention, while crucifixes are not. One does not have to be a Muslim to see the duplicity in this legislation. The German bans were also put into place in spite of the fact that the German Constitution states, "No person shall be favored or disfavored because of faith or religious opinions" and "freedom of faith and of conscience, and freedom to profess a religious or philosophical creed shall be inviolable."[18] The German bans affect only governmental employees under the premise that the wearing of the hijab by governmental employees violates state neutrality toward all religions and gives the impression that the state supports Islam. Obviously, the Bavarian law placing crucifixes in school gives the impression that the state supports Christianity, but German lawmakers are evidently comfortable with this contradiction. The German law does allow some teachers in certain Länder, such as Hamburg and Brandenburg, to wear the hijab, but in any case, the "inviolable" right to profess a religious or philosophical creed in Germany is not consistent from Land to Land. In all cases in Germany, the bans apply only to governmental employees in contrast to France, where the recent bans apply only to students. Under German law, forbidding a student to wear the hijab violates the student's inviolable right to profess a religious or philosophical creed.[19]

The Hijab in Britain

The British have been fairly tolerant of the headscarf under a multiculturalist approach, but they have proven to be less tolerant on the issues of the veil, jilbab, or burqa. For example, in one particular case of a sixteen-year-old girl who was expelled from school for wearing the jilbab (a long, drab, baggy article of clothing that covers the entire female body), the British lower courts sided with a Muslim principal who expelled the girl. The girl, Shabina Begum, appealed and was supported in her appeal by the Muslim Council of Britain. Her brother, Sherwas Rahman, a supporter of the Islamist group Hizb-ut-Tahrir, accompanied Begum to the courtroom where she won her case on appeal. Radical Islamist young men also took to the streets to picket the school where Begum had attended. In a final odd twist, the British Court of Appeals that decided that the school could not prevent Begum from wearing her jilbab based their decision on Article 9 of the European Convention on Human Rights, the same Article under which the French government justifies banning the headscarf.[20]

The Hijab in the United States

Though generally tolerant of the headscarf due to its multiculturalist approach, the United States has not been completely immune to the headscarf controversy. In general, American courts allow dress codes in the workplace and Muslims (and Sikhs) have found that they may lose their livelihoods and unemployment compensation when their religiously prescribed clothing conflicts with the workplace regulations of the employer.[21] These rulings appear consistent with the approach in Denmark where an Islamic cashier was fired by a supermarket for wearing a headscarf on the grounds that it was a safety hazard that might get stuck in the till.[22]

Although the hijab per se has not been ruled as a safety hazard in the U.S., the Equal Employment Opportunity Commission (EEOC) in the 1960s ruled that employers may ban clothing that is distracting or attracts attention in the workplace. Although the original rule was passed to allow employers to ban attention-getting or distracting mini-skirts, the regulation has been enforced more recently to prevent the wearing of headscarves and other religious coverings. In 1992, however, the EEOC allowed a Presbyterian retirement home to forbid a receptionist from wearing the hijab because it represented a non–Christian religious belief inconsistent with the Christian mission of her employer.[23]

In 1984, the subject of the hijab in American public schools arose when a Muslim woman was fired in the Philadelphia public schools under an 1895 Pennsylvania law that banned the wearing of "religious garb" by public school teachers. The U.S. court of appeals ruled that accommodating the hijab would require the state of Pennsylvania to sacrifice a compelling state interest in preserving the secular appearance of its public school system.[24] In other words, in the case of the hijab in the workplace, the separation of Church and state constructed from the establishment clause trumps the free exercise of religion.

Free exercise of religion for public school students, however, is a different matter. In Protestant-fundamentalist-dominated Muskogee, Oklahoma, in 2004, a Muslim schoolgirl was sent home because her headscarf violated the school district dress code. The U.S. Justice Department intervened in the trial on the side of the student, arguing that the school district dress code violated the girl's Constitutional rights under Title IX of the Civil Rights Act of 1964. As a result, the Muskogee Public School District has revised its dress code and allowed the girl to wear the scarf.[25]

Regardless of the outcome of the court rulings on the hijab, it is noteworthy that Muslims in the United States worked within the legal system to claim their rights to freely practice their religion. Options not taken include judicial assassinations, demonstrations, riots, suicide bombings, or burning 9,000 cars in Philadelphia. Instead, the Muslim Americans' legal struggles demonstrate that they are willing to work within the system and accept the outcome, even if it does not go in their favor, without staging extralegal activity. In doing so, they are implicitly investing themselves in the larger community, even through the acts of seeking to change it.

Simultaneously with the litigation approach taken by American Muslims to secure the right to wear the hijab, the hijab has been under attack on the political front by liberal American seculars and feminists who tend to oppose the forcing of anyone to wear the headscarf as a violation of religious choice and degrading to women. In this perspective, the headscarf is viewed as demeaning to women and it is assumed that women would not choose the headscarf if the option of abandoning it were available.[26] In some cases, it may be true that women are forced to wear the hijab by male authority figures in the family and it is this that seculars and feminists so vehemently oppose. The Pennsylvania and Oklahoma legal cases, however, suggest that many American Muslim women prefer to wear the hijab as a symbol of Muslim identity and are willing to fight for their rights to do so. As one American Muslim woman put it, she was

> empowered wearing hijab and loose clothing. I feel like no man has the right to undress me anymore with his eyes. Sure they can use their imagination, but my body is protected. I am not a sex object, and to be the "American Dream Girl" is a nice skin to shed. I feel empowered by prayer and the security of Allah's promise directly to me.[27]

Anyone familiar with the feminist perspective in the United States will recognize the similarity between the Muslim woman's statement above and the arguments of American feminists railing against male sexism. Even in arguing for the right to wear the hijab, Muslim women can evidently sound eerily like Western feminists with whom they disagree.

The Hijab in Canada

To many Canadians, the headscarf is a symbol of a group that remains unabsorbed and threatening to the social relations of Canadian society. According to Esamail Shakeri, in Canada, "the majority norm is considered right, and any behavior that deviates from it is regarded as inferior, and by some even deviant."[28] Nowhere in Canada is this more correct than in Quebec where natives tend to view the hijab as a symbol of Islamism and a betrayal of French identity. In fact, Quebec's policy on immigration and integration emphasizes the "French identity" of Quebec.[29]

The controversy came home to roost in 1994 in Montreal when two Muslim students enrolled in two different school districts were sent home by school officials for wearing the hijab. Muslim groups in Montreal immediately staged protests, charging the school boards with racism.[30] The largest teachers' union in Quebec, the Central de l'Enseignment du Quebec (CEQ) voted to ban the hijab the following May.[31] Those opposed to the hijab argued that the headscarf is more than just religious clothing, but is a symbol of radical Islam, which is associated with religious zealotry, violence, terrorism, sexism, and intolerance. In the words of one hijab-wearing Canadian Muslim woman, Rahat Kurd, "As long as the Muslim identity is portrayed as alien, linked to turbulence in Muslim countries, Islamic dress will seem shocking, foreign, and rootless in Canadian soil."[32] The hijab controversy thus far, however, appears to be limited mostly to Quebec as Canadian schoolboards elsewhere have thus far allowed the hijab.[33]

Feminists and the Hijab

French feminists contributed to the headscarf controversy in December 2003 when a group of French feminists and intellectuals placed an advertisement for a petition in the fashion magazine, *Elle,* where they argued that Muslim women are oppressed by the headscarf and in need of the legal protection of a law that would forbid them to wear it. In a rare case of the French political left and right working together, French president Jacques Chirac expressed his support for a headscarf ban and prime minister Jean-Pierre Raffarin also favored the ban on the headscarf ostensibly to protect French culture and help further Muslim integration into French society.[34]

It should be noted, however, that French feminists are not the only Western feminists that tend to oppose the wearing of the hijab. Western feminists in general, who are generally known for supporting multiculturalist views, tend to view the hijab and the veil as overt symbols of male oppression. Western feminists also generally argue that the veils and headscarves are the equivalent of the tacit admission that women are the source of evil in society and that women must hide themselves in public to protect society from their evil. Canadian feminist Michele Lemon well explains the feelings of many Western feminists when they see women wearing the hijab. In the words of Lemon,

> I feel I've been punched in the stomach. Her oppression, for oppression it is, becomes a symbol of the difficulty all women once faced and a startling reminder that the struggle for equality has not ended. How could anyone defend the outfit as preserving anything but the low regard and true unimportance of women, all protestations of respect to the contrary?[35]

Similarly, Catherine Mocks argues that though she does not violently object to the hijab in Islamic societies, they have no place in the Western world. In the words of Mocks, after seeing Muslim women wearing the hijab in her own Canadian neighborhood,

> I found the sight of these women with their hidden faces disturbing. It's one thing to see covered faces as the exotic and mysterious product of another culture you can leave behind when you return home. But finding them on my home turf, I have to confront my fears about what this kind of dress represents for me, and for all women: backwardness, submissiveness, degradation.[36]

The reactions of Lemon and Mocks essentially call into question whether or not Western societies can be sufficiently flexible and open to allow Muslims the freedom to determine their own forms of self-definition.

There is some hope for the multiculturalist model, however, even in assimilationist France. In 1997, the Conseil d'Etat ruled that the headscarf itself is not "ostentatious," and overturned 41 of 49 expulsion cases between 1992 and 1999. Unfortunately, however, many Muslims lack the resources to mount legal challenges and still suffer expulsions. Some school districts have followed the lead of the courts and allowed the hijab, while others have not. The result is that, currently, a mosaic has appeared on the French political scene where the most important determinant of whether Muslim students are able to wear the hijab is often the political leanings of the school principal along with the demographics of the area where the school is located. Principals in districts with large Muslim populations generally allow students to wear the hijab while those in districts with few Muslims appear less likely to do so.[37]

Halal Slaughter

Another contentious issue between Islamists and their Western hosts is the issue of halal (permissible) slaughter of animals. Western animal rights laws generally require that animals be stunned or anaesthetized prior to butchering. The Islamic requirement is that animals must be alive and healthy at the time of slaughter, and the slaughter of the animal must be accomplished by severing the jugular vein, carotid artery, and windpipe with a single swipe of a sharp knife. The animal must be alive at the time of slaughter, because ingesting blood is haram (forbidden) and therefore the heart must be kept beating as long as possible so as to drain all the blood from the animal's carcass. Additional requirements include that the animal for slaughter must be fed as normal and given water prior to slaughter. The knife must be four times the size of the animal's neck and razor sharp, the slaughterer and the animal should face Qibla or Mecca during slaughtering, and the animal must not be suffering with any illnesses or lacerations. Finally, a recitation by a Muslim (who need not be an imam) must be made dedicating the meat for consumption. To make the issue even more difficult for Muslims, all pork is haram as are all pork products; consequently, gelatine and candies that contain gelatine are forbidden as is the collagen used in cosmetics.[38]

Without control of the slaughterhouse and meatpacking industries in Western countries, Islamists who stick to the letter of the law on halal food have been unable to secure government enforcement of halal rules among companies that advertise and sell halal food. For example, in New Jersey, a Muslim coalition pushed the New Jersey state government to regulate the halal food industry, but the New Jersey Attorney General's Division of Consumer Affairs declined to issue any halal guidelines or regulations under the auspices of separation of church and state.[39]

Lacking confidence in perhaps slipshod halal food industries that have emerged in Western societies, Islamists in the West have run afoul of authorities for taking the job of animal slaughtering upon themselves. This is especially the case during the Islamic festival of Eid al-Adha (Feast of Sacrifice) when traditional Muslim families slaughter a sheep. Instances of Muslim immigrants keeping animals to be slaughtered in their urban apartments have been common, as have been instances of Muslims butchering animals in their bathtubs.[40] For instance, during Eid al-Adha, it is estimated that 20,000 sheep are slaughtered in private homes in Brussels alone. This is in spite of the fact that Belgian law forbids the slaughtering of animals at home and forbids the slaughter of animals without anaesthesia, including chickens.[41]

As long as there are no reliable supplies of halal meat, then it appears that the practice of home slaughter is likely to continue regardless of Western restrictions. Due to obvious public health concerns, Western societies are unlikely to relax their laws in this area; consequently, conflict over home slaughtering can be expected to continue until Muslims live in sufficient numbers everywhere in the West to support reliable halal meat industries and supplies.

Funding of Mosques and Madrassas

In some Western countries, such as the United States, there is no government funding of Islamic schools or madrassas due to either strict assimilationist policies or separation of church and state. Most schools, however, even in assimilationist France, where there is also a strict view of separation of church and state, make multicultural concessions such as the provision of non-pork meals for Muslims and Jews. Muslims could, however, receive public funding for Islamic schools even in France if their schools were open to non–Muslim students, but so far no Muslims in France have taken that approach to constructing an Islamic school.[42]

In spite of this exclusive nature of Muslim schools, there is some support throughout Europe for the British multiculturalist model that allows state funding of Islamic schools and even mosques. In the Netherlands, for instance, a mosque was built with public funding prior to a 1983 law that banned government construction of houses of worship (Christian or otherwise). In Belgium, Islam was recognized by the state in 1974 and now receives over 3 percent of the Belgian government funding of religion. Approximately 100

Belgian imams receive their salaries from the state. Similarly, in Sweden, four mosques have been constructed with public funding.[43]

Leading the theoretical argument in favor of such government support for Islam is Farah Karimi, an Iranian political refugee and member of the Dutch Parliament, who argues that mosques and Islamic schools should be publicly funded so as to prevent control of the schools and mosques by more radical foreign elements (namely Saudi Arabia and Iran). Currently, there are over 6,000 mosques in Western Europe, with at least one imam associated with each mosque.[44] Insufficient funding has led to a shortage of Islamic theological institutions in the West, thus leading to a shortage of Western-educated imams. As a result, many mosques and madrassas in the West are forced to import imams from abroad in order to satisfy local demands in Western countries.[45] While Turkey is the largest source of imams in Western Europe and Algeria is the largest foreign supplier of imams to France, the final result is the radicalization of some Western mosques due to the leadership of radical imams imported from Saudi Arabia and Pakistan.[46] In the words of Muslim Labour Party peer Nazir Ahmed,

> Young British Muslims go to the mosque and hear an imam delivering a sermon in a foreign language about the past. It has no relevance to ... the problems affecting Muslims in Britain. At the same time, it fills them with absurd notions about the British. They leave the mosque feeling angry and confused and walk straight into the arms of extremist groups such as al-Muhajiroun which talk to them in a language they understand.[47]

Ahmed argues that the best way to remedy the problem is through state-funding of the training of imams. The basic idea is that if the madrassas and mosques are publicly funded, the imams and teachers will be home-grown and therefore less radical. Furthermore, European governments may be able to influence the directions of Islam at least partially through the power of the purse. Common sense suggests that the threat of the denial of government funding to radical mosques and madrassas would provide incentive for them to avoid adopting radical Islamist positions. Governments could also perhaps influence Muslim associations and madrassas by requiring them to conduct their business with the government and their school instruction in the national language.[48] A further benefit of public funding of madrassas and mosques is that it seems to be congruent with what Muslims themselves often advocate. In the words of K.S. Butt, the chair of the Islamic Resource Center in Birmingham, UK, "when we ask for equal rights, for our own schools like other faiths have their own schools, the government tells us that they will be divisive, and that they will create a ghetto mentality. It is Islam that has been ghettoized by the Establishment."[49] What Butt seems to be saying here (and many other

Muslims agree), is that Muslims living in Western countries want the state to recognize their religion and accommodate them fairly and justly in conformity with other religious groups. Some European governments appear to be listening. After the Madrid bombings of March 11, 2004, the Spanish government essentially adopted the British approach by ending special funding privileges for the Catholic Church and providing public funding for all religions, including Islam.[50]

A possible mitigating factor, however, may be that religious knowledge among Western Muslims may be becoming increasingly divorced from formal religious institutions. Many young educated Western Muslims view themselves as experts in religion and do not necessarily defer to religious authorities. Religious debate, once the exclusive jurisdiction of the ulama, now has become a sphere for everyone.[51] Prominent Western Islamists such as Abu Hamza even urge young Muslims to reject the direction from Islamic scholars. In the words of Hamza, "The people who have been bestowed ijaza give us nothing but headache…. What's the use of all this Islamic knowledge if it's not bringing anything positive to Muslim people and Islam?"[52]

Furthermore, many of the prominent Islamists in the West are not graduates of religious universities or madrassas. Abu Hamza of London, for instance, is an engineer, and Jamal Badawi, a prominent Islamist in Canada, is a professor of management. Hassan Iquioussen, a famous video preacher in France, has a degree in history. Similarly, Sheikh Hamza Boubakeur, the dean of the Grand Mosque of Paris, is a cardiologist.[53]

Western Discrimination against Muslims

In the fall of 2005, France exploded into a series of nightly Muslim-dominated riots that resulted in the destruction of over 9,000 automobiles, most of them by fire, before it had run its course. According to the BBC, the riots were best explained as a reaction by Muslims against the negative perception of Islam in French society at large, and widespread French social discrimination against Muslim immigrants. The BBC further stated that there was a "huge well of fury and resentment among the children of North African immigrants in the suburbs of French cities" and proclaimed that "Islam is seen as the biggest challenge to the country's secular model in the past 100 years."[54] Although no one died in the violence except for the two boys who provided the spark for the riots at the outset, and the riots may have been linked to poverty, unemployment, and discrimination as much as religion, the unrest in France served as another reminder that the potential exists for violence between large populations of marginalized Muslims and non–Muslim majorities in Western countries.

France is also certainly not the only country where discrimination against Muslims has become a major issue. For example, the Islamic Human Rights Commission claims that British refusal to extend British laws against racial discrimination in employment, housing, and education to include religious discrimination is in practice a form of discrimination against Muslims. Furthermore, the Islamic Human Rights Commission has argued that riots involving Muslims, such as that in Oldham in 1989 surrounding the Rushdie affair, are linked to discrimination against Muslims.[55] Similarly, college students interviewed by the *Chicago Tribune* in the United States suggested that discrimination and harassment of Muslims from the American government has become common under the Bush administration's War on Terror and that the discrimination is causing America's young Muslims to become politically active.[56]

It also appears that discrimination and marginalization of Muslims in the West serves as a recruiting tool for jihadists. A report released by Dutch intelligence in March 2004 concluded that many Muslims in Europe are drawn into the jihadist network because they are outraged by the perceived discrimination and poor treatment that they receive in their adopted countries. Put more succinctly, the Dutch concluded that "the group of young people who feel treated disrespectfully is a major potential target for radicalization and possibly recruitment processes (for jihad)."[57] That being the case, it appears that it may be prudent for Western societies to dedicate themselves to addressing the problem of discrimination against Muslims in the West as quickly and as thoroughly as possible if they are to stem the tide of growing Islamism in Western countries.

CHAPTER 7

Islamist Terror in the West

Samuel Huntington argues that "the civilizational 'us' and the extracivilizational 'them' is a constant in human history, but in the world of the twenty-first century, advancements in transportation and communications (not to mention weaponry) have produced more frequent and more intense conflict."[1] Huntington also points out that while differences in material interests can be compromised, differences in values are much more difficult to negotiate.[2] For instance, could the French perhaps compromise and allow Muslim women to wear headscarves in the workplace every other day? Huntington suggests that we cannot. Instead, Huntington argues that it is "human to hate" and that for self-definition and motivation people need enemies, and naturally distrust and view as threats those who are different than themselves.

While we are not in this case presenting Huntington's argument as fact, let us suppose for a moment that Huntington is correct. If conflicts over headscarves and halal meat were the most important issues, then perhaps the Muslim diaspora in the West would not be so worthy of concern. Unfortunately, however, the cultural conflict between Muslims and Westerners has thus far proven to be dangerous, violent, and escalating throughout Europe and the United States.

Islamist violence within Western countries had its beginning when the Muslim-Israeli conflict spilled over into Europe and onto the world stage at the 1972 Olympic Games in Munich. In an event that shocked the world, the Palestinian terrorist group Black September (a group that few Europeans had ever heard of and understood even less) slaughtered eleven Israeli athletes during the Olympic Games. The next year, Black September caught the world's attention again when a plot to kill Israeli PM Golda Meir at the Rome airport was foiled by Israeli and Italian intelligence.[3]

Papal Assassination Attempt

In the next decade, however, terrorist targets in the West were not so lucky as Golda Meir. In 1981, Islamic terrorists had proven that no one is immune to terrorism when a young Turk named Mehmet Ali Agca, a member of a Turkish terrorist group known as the Gray Wolves, attempted to assassinate Pope John Paul II in St. Peter's Square in Rome. Agca's attempt was extremely close to being a success. Agca's first 9mm bullet penetrated the pontiff's stomach, small intestine, and colon. A second bullet struck the pope on the right hand, while a third hit him higher on the same arm.[4] Two years earlier, Agca had murdered the editor of a pro–Western Istanbul newspaper and was convicted, but he escaped from prison with the help of the Gray Wolves.[5]

Agca trained for his mission in a terrorist camp in Iran, where he began each day by reciting a long list of hatreds which included imperialists, NATO, apostate Muslim governments that had refused to cut off oil from the West, and most of all, the United States, whom Agca called upon Allah to destroy in a manner eerily similar to the rantings of Osama bin Laden two decades later.[6] After he had recovered from the terrible attack, Pope John Paul II visited Agca in prison. Agca informed the pope that the plot to kill him had been forged and nurtured in Tehran. After leaving the prison, John Paul repeatedly informed his staff that the coming conflict in the world was no longer going to be between the U.S. and the Soviet Union or between capitalism and communism, but between Islamic fundamentalism and Christianity.[7]

Western Jihad in the 1980s

The assassination attempt on the pope turned out to be a precursor of events to come as Islamist violence in the West increased in the 1980s. In 1982, Palestinian gunmen shot and wounded Israel's ambassador in London, with the result that three days later, Israel invaded Lebanon in retaliation.[8] In April 1984, Hizbollah bombers killed eighteen American servicemen in a restaurant in Torrejon, Spain.[9] In October 1985, Palestinian terrorists took over the Italian cruise ship *Achille Lauro* and held twelve American passengers hostage. The Islamic terrorists made an example of elderly Jewish-American tourist Leon Klinghoffer by shooting him in the back and casting his body overboard.[10] In December 1985, terrorists under the command of Palestinian terrorist Abu Nidal gunned down 19 tourists, including five Americans, at El Al (Israeli airline) ticket counters in Rome and Vienna.[11] In March 1987, amidst a clash in the Gulf of Sidra between Libyan leader Moammar Qaddafi and the Reagan administration, two American servicemen were killed and fifty were wounded by an explosion in a Berlin nightclub. President Reagan retaliated by bombing Qaddafi's house, and Qaddafi retaliated with the bombing of Pan Am flight 103 over Lockerbie, Scotland, which killed 259 passengers, including 37 American college students and 11 people on the ground.[12]

Obviously, President Reagan's policy of "tit for tat" with Islamic terrorists had proven to be a very deadly policy, but the terrorists' shocking violence was such that it could not be simply ignored either, and conversation with people who indiscriminately killed hundreds of innocent people hardly seemed like it could be productive. Thus, the conflict between radical Islam and the West continued unabated into the next decade.

French Jihad

France in particular was victimized by a wave of Islamist terror attacks in the 1980s carried out by Lebanese Shiites linked to the revolutionary government of Ayatollah Khomeini in Iran. No sooner had this wave of violence abated when another wave of Islamist terror swept through France in the 1990s as the Algerian civil war spilled over into Europe.[13] In 1995 and 1996 alone, France experienced a series of eight Islamist attacks that left 10 dead and 175 injured. Included in the French attacks was a gruesome beheading of the Trappist monks of Tibehirine in May 1996.[14]

Leading players in the unrest were the Groupe Islamique Armee (GIA), an Algerian Islamist organization that favors the establishment of an Islamist government in Algeria. In 1994, the GIA proved that it is much more than an irritating propaganda agency in the West when four Algerian GIA terrorists hijacked an Air France jet with plans to fly it into the Eiffel Tower. French authorities fooled them into thinking they lacked enough fuel to make it to Paris and diverted them to Marseilles, where they were all shot to death by French commandos.[15] The next year in Belgium, Belgian authorities seized a GIA training manual with a preface dedicated to Osama bin Laden that explained how to make bombs using a wristwatch as a timer.[16] In July 1995, GIA terrorists led by Khaled Kelkal, a Muslim immigrant to France living in the Lyon ghetto, blew up a Paris train, killing twelve people and wounding over eighty. Several weeks later, French security forces found Kelkal and shot him to death. As for his accomplices, twenty-four were tried, convicted, and incarcerated on the charges of possessing weapons, preparing terrorist actions, and threatening public order by intimidation or terror.[17]

The turn of the millennium brought only more conflict between Islamism and the West in France, beginning with the spectacular terrorist attacks of 9/11, since Zacarias Moussaoui, the so-called twentieth hijacker, is a French citizen.[18] Four years later in October and November 2005, France erupted in an explosion of Muslim (and other immigrant) violence when two young Muslims, Bouna Traore, 15, of Malian background, and Zyed Benna, 17, a Muslim of Tunisian origin, were accidentally executed at an electricity sub-station near Paris. Witnesses stated that the boys were in the process of fleeing from police (an allegation that the French police authorities denied) and French Muslims blamed what they viewed as overzealous and discriminatory French police for the boys' tragic deaths.[19] Riots and demonstrations erupted and quickly spread from Paris to dozens of other locations throughout France, including all fifteen of France's largest cities. The riots began on October 27 and escalated daily for twenty nights until almost 9000 vehicles had been burned in the violence and approximately $200 million worth of property had been destroyed. French president Jacques Chirac was forced to declare a state of emergency on November 8, which the French Parliament extended to three months, ending on the January 4, 2006, election in France. The French emergency law allowed local authorities to impose curfews, ban public gatherings, and conduct house-to-house searches in attempts to curb the violence. Following the trend established previously in the United States, the cherished Western freedoms were quickly sacrificed in the interest of safety and order.[20]

Although the head of French intelligence denied that Islam was a factor for the unrest, instead citing high unemployment rates among immigrants in France from North Africa, the *New York Times* reported on November 5, 2005, what most citizens in the Western world had already assumed, that the majority of those involved in the riots were young Muslim males of North African origin, thus suggesting that, to most Westerners, Islam was indeed a factor.[21]

Though France now has been a hotbed of Islamic violence for the better part of three decades, it is difficult to conclude that it is the French assimila-tionist model that spawns the violence since France has not had a monopoly on Islamic violence and terror threats. Instead, virtually every Western country has experienced some form of Islamic terror since the Munich Olympics in 1972 and several were directly connected with the 9/11 attacks on the U.S., including Germany and the United Kingdom.

German Jihad: The Hamburg Cell

In 2001, Hamburg, Germany, served as the logistics and planning base for the 9/11 terrorist attacks on the United States, and the Hamburg al-Qaeda cell was composed of what has been described as a group of very "Westernized" young Muslim men.[22] The Islamists took advantage of Western freedoms that allowed foreign students to stay in Germany as long as they wanted, travel anywhere in the European Union, and even have their university tuition paid for them by the German government. Germany in particular enshrined tolerance in its Constitution after the experience of World War II and the Holocaust and, because of their commitment to tolerance and avoiding any redevelopment of the forces that led to the rise of Nazism, allowed acknowledged terrorist groups to legally recruit and raise money in Germany as long as their plans did not include terrorism against Germany itself.[23]

The Hamburg cell was further aided by the fact that German security forces at the time focused primarily on Turkish and Kurdish organizations; consequently, Atta (of Egyptian origin) and his cohorts went about their terrorist planning undetected. The German legal system, which requires a strict burden of proof on the state in order to protect those accused of crimes against arbitrary government power (a reaction to Nazism after World War II), clearly provided an advantageous environment for terrorists.[24]

Blame for the blind eye to terrorists cannot be placed solely on Germany, however. The members of the Hamburg cell applied for visas to the U.S. and only Atta's roommate, Ramzi bin al-Shibh, was denied a U.S. visa on the grounds that Yemenis were known to outstay their welcome in the U.S. Bin al-Shibh remained an active member of the plot, however, as the liaison between the group and Khalid Sheikh Mohammed, who is generally credited as being the mastermind behind the "flying planes into buildings" plan.[25] Bin al-Shibh was arrested in Pakistan the next year, tortured, and interrogated at a CIA black site. Though his interrogation would yield little of value, his captured computer contained a wealth of al-Qaeda contact information, including the passport numbers of al-Qaeda members.[26]

Atta and al-Shibh finalized the details of the 9/11 plot in the Spanish resort town of Salou and fellow 9/11 terrorists Khaled al-Mihdhar and Nawaf al-Hazmi arrived in Los Angeles in January 2000 and resided in the United States for the better part of two years prior to the 9/11 attacks.[27] Atta, al-Mhidhar, and al-Hazmi enrolled at two different flight schools near Venice, Florida, while bin al-Shibh wired funds to the other three cell members.[28] The rest of the hijackers were unemployed Saudi fanatics personally selected by bin Laden, all of whom secured easy entry into the U.S. due to the friendly relations between the U.S. government and the government of Saudi Arabia. By July 2001, all 19 hijackers were in the U.S., residing in Florida and New Jersey. The Saudi Arabian muscle men visited American fitness centers while the pilots made surveillance flights on the aircraft they planned to hijack. The only detection of the plan by American authorities was the result of Zacarias

Moussaoui's odd behavior at flight school where he indicated an interest in flying, but not landing.[29]

Atta and fellow 9/11 pilot Marwan al Shehhi also demonstrated a significant degree of Westernization in another way between July and December 2000, when they regularly drank beer in a Venice, Florida, bar while attending flight school. Of al Shehhi, bartender Lizsa Lehman stated that he was "friendly and jovial and ... always eager to interact with bartenders and patrons.... I, to this day, have trouble seeing [Al Shehhi] doing it."[30] Similarly, Atta was evidently a regular patron at another bar known as the 44th Aero Squadron Bar. According to bar owner Ken Schortzmann, Atta never caused any problems and did not drink heavily or flirt with the waitresses. Meanwhile, the owner of the apartment unit where Atta lived stated that Atta and his friends smoked "a strange tobacco, which smelled like marijuana." During this time period in America when Atta was drinking beer and certainly chainsmoking tobacco, if not smoking marijuana, he never visited a mosque in southwest Florida and avoided any contact with the other Muslim residents.[31] It would have been difficult for those who knew him casually under these circumstances to conclude that he was an Islamist determined to kill thousands of innocent people in an attack on the United States.

Two of Atta's comrades also exhibited Western influences, but in a different way, on the night prior to the 9/11 attacks when they watched a pay-per-view porn film in their motel room.[32] The Hamburg cell that planned the 9/11 attacks therefore represents a new breed of Islamist terrorists in that they had been "Westernized" to a significant degree and had successfully assimilated into Western culture. Unfortunately, subsequent attacks in the West since 9/11 have followed a similar pattern.

Londonistan

In the United Kingdom, a section of London in the 1980s became known as "Londonistan" due to its large Muslim population and reputation as a sanctuary for Islamist radicals. The Finsbury Park mosque in Londonistan became known as a place of radical activities, radical ideas, and fiery Islamist preaching from the radical cleric Abu Hamza, who openly advocated terrorist training in Pakistan.[33] Predictably, it was only a matter of time before the radical words produced violent actions.

In 2003, the British intelligence agency MI5 drew up a list of 100 terror suspects in the UK. Among those were 45 British Pakistanis who had been involved in the jihad in Kashmir, including Mohamed Bilal, a British Pakistani from Birmingham, who blew himself up with a car bomb outside an Indian army barracks in Kashmir.[34] Londonistan was the place of residence for two Tunisian jihadists who journeyed to Afghanistan and assassinated Afghan Northern Alliance commander Ahmed Shah Massoud two days prior to 9/11.[35] Richard Reid, the notorious shoe-bomber who was arrested for attempting to blow up a flight between France and the United States in December 2001, is a British citizen associated with the Finsbury Park mosque, as was the so-called twentieth 9/11 hijacker, Zacarias Moussaoui.[36]

With British Islamists becoming involved in violence outside the country, it was perhaps predictable that British Islamists would become involved in violence inside the UK. In London on March 30, 2004, eight British citizens of Pakistani origin, including Omar Khyam, who had trained for the action in Pakistan, were arrested after being caught with large stocks of ammonium nitrate fertilizer.[37] This, unfortunately, was merely a precursor of things to come. The next year on July 7, 2005, 56 people were killed and 700 injured in Islamist bombings on the London transportation system. The bombings were carried out by British Muslims led by Mohammed Siddique Khan.

Two weeks after the 7/7 bombing, four more British Muslims, all first-generation immigrants from the Horn of Africa and followers of Abu Hamza at the Finsbury Park mosque, Mukhtar Said Ibrahim, Yassin Omar, Omar Ramzi Mohamed, and Hussein Osman, took homemade bombs on to London's transport system on July 21, 2005, in an attempt to repeat the carnage of 7/7. The plot was thwarted by British authorities and all four men were convicted of conspiracy to commit murder.[38] A fifth bomber in the plot, Manfo Kwaku Asiedu, abandoned his bomb at the last moment and fled the scene, but pleaded guilty to conspiracy to cause explosions. Asiedu claimed that he was forced into taking part in the attack by Ibrahim and that he was too frightened to tell the other men that he did not want to kill himself and that is why he abandoned his bomb. A sixth suspect, Adel Yahya, was an Ethiopian immigrant who had studied for a degree in computer networking at London Metropolitan University. Yahya also frequented Abu Hamza's Finsbury Park mosque. Yahya was charged with conspiracy to murder, but convicted of a lesser charge of collecting information that was useful to a person preparing an act of terrorism.[39]

Yahya's case is similar to many others that have been brought to British courtrooms. Between the terror attacks of 9/11 and March 2007, 1228 arrests were made in the UK in relation to terrorist offenses. Of those, only 241 ended up being actually charged with terrorist offences, 318 with other criminal offenses, and 669 were eventually released without charges of any kind.[40]

The Netherlands and the Death of Theo van Gogh

In the Netherlands in November 2004, the country was shocked when Theo van Gogh, a well-known Dutch filmmaker, television producer, and writer, not to mention relative of Vincent Van Gogh, was murdered in Amsterdam by an Islamic fanatic. Van Gogh was an anticlerical filmmaker who had publicly disparaged trends in Christianity and Judaism as well as Islam. Specifically, van Gogh had worked with Somali-born Dutch liberal MP Ayaan Hirsi Ali to make a film exposing Muslim maltreatment of women.[41] Van Gogh's Islamist assailant shot him twenty times, stabbed him repeatedly in the chest, and slit his throat so badly that he was almost decapitated. The murderer, Mohammed Bouyeri, a Dutch-born Muslim of Moroccan ancestry, pinned a five-page letter to van Gogh's chest with a knife that warned van Gogh's film collaborator, Ayaan Hirsi Ali, and several Dutch leaders of a similar fate.[42] Bouyeri then fled the scene of the crime and shot both a Dutch policeman and an innocent bystander, both of whom were injured critically, while attempting to make his getaway on foot. Bouyeri was eventually shot in the leg by Dutch police and apprehended, partially because his traditional Islamic clothing impeded his ability to run.[43]

Bouyeri was a student dropout from Dutch institutions of higher learning who had joined a terrorist group known as the Hofstad Network, which had plans to blow up Schiphol airport and kill conservative Dutch MP Geert Wilders. Nevertheless, Bouyeri was essentially acting on his own as no Islamic cleric had issued a fatwa against van Gogh.[44]

The violence in the Netherlands did not stop, however, after Bouyeri was taken into custody by Dutch authorities. Instead, the murder inspired an anti–Muslim backlash. One day after the murder, 20,000 people demonstrated to denounce the van Gogh killing and 30 people were arrested by Dutch authorities for inciting hatred against Muslims. In the weeks that followed, over twenty Muslim schools and mosques were burned down in the Netherlands by angry Dutch citizens in retaliation. Islamic radicals then responded in kind with the burning of Christian churches.[45]

The aftershocks of the van Gogh murder also led to backlash from Dutch immigration authorities who produced a video to convey to immigrants the nature of Dutch culture. The video includes bits of Dutch history and landscape, including tulips and windmills, but also footage of naked sunbathers and a gay wedding. Furthermore, the Netherlands' security minister, Rita Verdonk, is leading a fight to outlaw the wearing of the burqa. Meanwhile, Germany responded to the van Gogh murder by introducing more rigorous citizenship tests designed to keep radical Muslims out of Germany.[46]

Spanish Jihad

On March 11, 2004, Islamist terror bombings on the Spanish transit system killed 191 people and wounded over 1800 when ten bombs planted by Islamists were detonated in four different blast zones. The bombs detonated as four trains were en route toward Atocha station. If the trains had been running on time that day, they would have converged at the station just as the bombs exploded, most likely collapsing the railway station and killing thousands. It is possible that a collapse of the Atocha station would have been the most deadly terrorist attack in European history. Clearly the date (3/11), the selection of public transit, and the selection of four trains were intended to mimic the 9/11 attacks, suggesting an al-Qaeda connection. Two days later, a videotape was discovered in a trash bin near one of Madrid's main mosques. On the tape, a man named Abu Dujan Al-Afghani, who claimed to be al-Qaeda's military spokesman in Europe, announced that the Madrid attacks had been carried out because of Spain's cooperation with "the criminal Bush and his allies."[47] Additionally, the London-based *Al-Quds* newspaper reported an email from a group calling itself the Abu Hafs Al-Masri brigades that claimed credit for the attacks on the behalf of al-Qaeda. Whether either the video tape or the email were authentically al-Qaeda or not, the Spanish public needed little convincing and subsequently punished their political leaders. Less than a month later, a second attack was foiled when a bomb aboard a train from Madrid to Seville was discovered and defused before detonation.[48]

The bombings led to a change in the Spanish government in the next election as the ruling party of Prime Minister Jose Maria Aznar was defeated. The tragedy also had global political implications outside the Spanish borders since the newly elected Spanish government subsequently withdrew 1300 troops that they had committed to the American-led war in Iraq championed by American president George W. Bush. In response, al-Qaeda announced that there would be a truce called in Spain.[49]

The Madrid bombings drew attention to the fact that Spain had become a crossroads for terrorists due to its Western freedoms and its proximity to Islamic Morocco. This is in spite of the fact that Morocco traditionally had not been known as a hotbed of Islamism.[50] Spain has a large Muslim population, both legal and illegal, due to its geographic location across the Strait of Gibraltar from North Africa. Spain is therefore a major port of entry for Muslim immigration from North Africa as immigrants cross the straits at night in a flotilla of small boats. While most of the immigrants are merely seeking economic opportunity in Europe, some of them are Islamists engaged in jihad. For example, during the Algerian Civil War of the 1990s, Islamists fleeing North Africa frequently used Spain as a stopover on the way to safe havens in Britain and Canada.[51] Furthermore, the principal meeting to plan and finance the 9/11 attacks was held in Tarragon, Spain, in July 2001 and was attended by Mohamed Atta as well as Ramzi bin al-Shibh (mentioned previously as part of the Hamburg cell), who was connected to both Khalid Sheikh Mohammed and Osama bin Laden.[52]

Importantly, the Madrid bombings were not designed, funded, or executed by al-Qaeda or any other international Islamist organization, but were carried out by local Muslims in Spain, who, though perhaps inspired by bin Laden and al-Qaeda, were at that time unconnected to any other international terrorist organizations. Only one Madrid bomber, Hassan Al-Heski, had any military training or experience fighting in jihads abroad, and his exact role in the bombings remains unclear.[53]

The discovery of a bag containing a cell phone that was connected to an explosive device led Spanish authorities to the arrest of a North African immigrant named Jamal Zougam. Zougam had been arrested but released by Spanish police in 2001 for his connection to a number of known militants, including French convert jihadist David Courtailler, Syrian jihadist Imad Eddin Barakat Yarkas (alias Abu Dahdah), and the radical Moroccan preacher Fiazi.[54] The Madrid bombings thus demonstrate the global impact of Islamist ideology separate from al-Qaeda and the international terrorist network, some of which had developed indigenously in the West.[55] In the words of Benjamin and Simon, "Madrid shows all too plainly that people who hold these ideas and want to act on them live in the heart of the West. Their number is growing, and so too is the danger they pose."[56] The van Gogh killing later that year, the London bombings in July 2005, and the burning of more than 9000 cars in France by disgruntled French Muslim youths in the fall of 2005 were grim reminders of the same lesson.

One of Zougam's contacts, Abu Dahdah, was one of the most important Spanish jihadists and became the leader of a Syrian jihadist group in Madrid that became known as al-Qaeda in Spain. Abu Dahdah's group is alleged to have contact with senior al-Qaeda figures and sent volunteers to train in Afghanistan and Indonesia. Abu Dahdah, however, was arrested in Spain in 2001 and sentenced to 27 years in prison in 2005 for his role in leading a terrorist group and conspiring in the 9/11 attacks. After his arrest, al-Qaeda in Spain was taken over by a Tunisian Islamist named Abdelmajid Fakhet.[57] Fakhet died along with six other Madrid bombers in April 2004 in the Madrid suburb of Leganes when they detonated their explosives in their apartment as it was being stormed by police. One Spanish police officer was also mortally wounded in the bombing and one of the Islamist martyrs was blown across the apartment courtyard and hurled into a swimming pool.[58]

With eight of the Madrid bombers dead (seven at Leganes and another died fighting in Iraq), twenty-eight other defendants were rounded up by police and tried in Spanish courts. Of those tried, fourteen were Moroccans, nine Spanish, two Syrian, one Egyptian, one Algerian, one Lebanese. Three of the defendants were convicted of the attacks and given multiple sentences for the murders. Jamal Zougam in particular was found guilty of 191 murders and 1856 attempted murders and sentenced to 30 years in prison for each of the murders and 20 years each for the attempted murders. Fellow Moroccan Otman Al-Ghanoui received similar sentences. Abdelmajid Bouchar was sentenced to 18 years for warning the others at Leganes that they were surrounded by police. Evidence suggests that Bouchar had joined the terrorist cell because his father had kicked him out of the house for his laziness and he had nowhere else to go. Others were given sentences from 3 to 23 years for their complicity in the attacks or belonging to a terrorist group.[59] Egyptian Rabei Osman was found innocent in spite of a taped phone conversation where he boasted, "The operation in Madrid was prepared by me. Do you understand?... It was my project, the group, do you understand?... I was the thread behind the operation."[60]

The Madrid bombings also perhaps represent a watershed in Islamism in Europe. Prior to 9/11, Europe had clearly provided a sanctuary where Islamism could grow and plan. With the Madrid bombings, however, it appears that Europe has emerged as a battlefield for Islamist jihad. Consequently, the security paradigm on which European immigration policies concerning Muslims were predicated has been invalidated and European governments may seek new models for dealing with Islam in their midst.[61] At the very least, the Madrid bombings proved that the answer cannot be in merely prohibiting the immigration of radical Islamists since the Madrid bombers had all been in the country for years.[62]

Danish Cartoon Wars

In September 2004, an obscure Danish newspaper, *Jyllands-Posten*, published a dozen cartoons depicting the prophet Mohammed. Given that numerous Islamist sects ban all images, photographs, drawings, etc., of the human form, thousands (if not millions) of Muslims worldwide viewed the cartoons as a blasphemous abomination. To make matters worse in the eyes of Islamists, one of the cartoons portrayed Mohammed with a bomb in his turban, thus suggesting that the holy prophet of Allah was a terrorist. Given the obscurity of *Jyllands-Posten*, the cartoons would not have created much of a stir if it were not for the efforts of Danish imams to bring the cartoons to the attention of the larger Muslim world.[63]

Ahmed Abu Laban, the Palestinian-born leader of Denmark's largest Islamic Association, and Ahmed Akkari, a Lebanese imam that settled in Denmark in 1994, began spreading the news of the cartoons. They contacted Muslim embassies in Copenhagen and collected 17,000 signatures in a petition asking the Danish government to denounce the cartoons. When the actions did not achieve the desired results, the imams took their fight global on the Islamist website IslamOnline.net. Akkari and a number of other imams then embarked a tour of the Middle East to stir up opposition to the cartoons. To ensure that they could get a response, they added three more inflammatory images to their set of cartoons that were not published in *Jyllands-Posten*. One depicted Mohammed as a paedophile, another showed a praying Muslim being raped by a dog, and another showed a bearded man with a pig's snout and ears that carried the caption, "This is the true picture of Mohammed." The imams also claimed that *Jyllands-Posten* was owned by the Danish ruling party, thus causing those in the Muslim world to believe that the cartoons represented official Danish policy.[64]

The Muslim world both within and outside the West erupted in violence and demonstrations that Denmark's prime minister Anders Fogh Rasmussen summed up as a "global crisis that has the potential to escalate beyond the control over governments."[65] At least ten people worldwide died in protests following the publication of the cartoons, several in two incidents in Afghanistan when protesters attacked a Norwegian peacekeepers' base and an American military base. Western embassies in Syria, Lebanon, Indonesia, and Iran were also attacked. In Khartoum, Sudan, a crowd of an estimated 50,000 people took to the streets to demonstrate against the cartoons and shouted, "Strike, strike, bin Laden."[66] The Organization of the Islamic Conference (OIC) called on all Muslims to restrain themselves to peaceful protests, but called on the Danish government to condemn the drawings. Similarly, the Arab League condemned the Danish government for its inaction against the authors of the cartoons.[67] At the very least, the cartoon affair proved that not only could politics in Islamic countries spill over into the West, but politics in Western countries could unintentionally spill over into the Islamic realm and create political unrest in the process.

Governments in Islamic countries joined the protesting fray, with Saudi Arabia, Syria, Libya, and Iran all withdrawing ambassadors from Denmark, and Iran placing an embargo on Danish imports. In Saudi Arabia, 700,000 signatures were collected condemning the Danish government.[68] In both Yemen and Jordan, newspaper editors who republished the cartoons were arrested and their newspapers were shut down. In Syria, where protesters burned the Danish and Norwegian embassies, mass protests were evidently orchestrated by the government where witnesses reported government officials with walkie-talkies directing the crowds, and camera crews followed arsonists into buildings to film the torching of Western-associated buildings.[69] In Libya, Moammar Qaddafi declared that those who published the cartoons were "infidels" and that European school children were being taught that Mohammed was a liar. Libya also sponsored demonstrations against comments made by Italian MP Roberto Calderoli, who had announced that he intended to have the cartoons printed on T-shirts.[70]

While most European Muslims exhibited calm amid the global storm of protests over the cartoons, the fact that the initial rabble-rouser in the cartoon affair was a European Muslim is symbolic of the challenges facing the West in attempting to accommodate its Muslim populations. While free speech and free press remain linchpins of democratic values, radical Muslims living in the West appear ready to compromise those values when they view them as conflicting with Islam. The chilling impact of radical Muslims living in the West on Western free speech and free press was exemplified in the Danish cartoon affair when British and American newspapers were reluctant to reprint the cartoons due to fears of Muslim violence. Similarly, President Bush called on world governments to "be respectful" and Britain's foreign secretary denounced the cartoons as "insensitive" and "unnecessary," instead of defending the rights of the cartoonist's free speech.[71]

Simultaneously, Islamist organizations in Europe condemned the cartoons as part of an overall Western "war on Islam." For example, the Muslim Association of Britain staged a protest in London against the cartoons and issued a press statement condemning the cartoons as representative of Islamophobia. Similarly, the Alk-Ghurraba group in the UK compared the cartoons to the Crusades and held demonstrations in London. One Islamist at the Alk-Ghurraba-organized protest, Umran Jjaved, was arrested and later convicted of soliciting murder after he urged a London crowd to bomb Denmark and the United States.[72]

In September 2007, the cartoon issue arose again when Swedish artist Lars Vilks made a drawing depicting Mohammed's head on a dog's body. Shortly thereafter, Abu Omar al-Baghdadi, the leader of al-Qaeda in Iraq, placed a $100,000 bounty on Vilks' head and called for his assassination. The bounty would be increased to $150,000 if Vilks was "slaughtered like a lamb." In addition, al-Baghdadi offered a $50,000 bounty for the assassination of the chief editor of the Swedish newspaper, *Nerikes Allehanda*, which reprinted Vilks' cartoon.[73]

In order to protect Vilks, Swedish police took him from his home and placed him in a guarded, secret location. The Swedish prime minister, Fredrik Reinfeldt, much like President George W. Bush in the Danish cartoon controversy, called for "mutual respect between Muslims, Christians, and nonreligious groups," but was mum on the issue of the protections of free speech in Western societies.[74] Obviously, the effect on free speech of the Islamist death threats against cartoonists was so chilling that Western heads of state dared not be its champions lest they risk being accused of encouraging terrorist attacks. In Berlin, a performance of Mozart's opera *Idomeneo* was cancelled in 2006 because it depicts a beheading of Mohammed. In the Netherlands, the government responded with a bureaucratic agency called the Interdepartmental Working Group on Cartoons.[75] That being the case, it appears that the Islamists already have been somewhat successful at eroding one of the pillars of Western society through the erosion of free speech that has accompanied their threats of terrorism. Perhaps one Iranian living in Denmark stated it best when he complained, "It is an irony that I am today living in a European democratic state and have to fight the same religious fanatics that I fled from in Iran many years ago."[76]

Islamism in the United States

Like other minority groups in America, many American Muslims argue that they suffer from specific and deliberate discrimination and an American fear and distrust of Islam. As has been demonstrated over and over in other settings, these attitudes are often very much connected to Islamism. While it is clear that the majority of American Muslims are not radical Islamists, and the radical Islamists in the United States thus far appear to be few in number, it is also true that some have indeed arrived, including a select few that are native citizens of the United States, such as John Walker Lindh. As early as 1996, for instance, FBI agents using wiretaps on bin Laden's businesses were able to draw a map of the global al-Qaeda network and concluded that many of bin Laden's al-Qaeda associates had ties to the United States.[77]

American Jihadists

Other celebrated cases of radical Islam in America include that of Sami Omar al-Hussayen, a Saudi graduate student, who was charged in 2002 with raising funds for terrorist organizations, including Hamas, and managing web sites that supported terrorism. Al-Hussayen was acquitted, but was quickly deported for immigration violations.[78] In another case, Iyman Faris, a Columbus, Ohio, truck driver with links to al-Qaeda, was arrested in 2003 for a ridiculous plot to bring down the Brooklyn Bridge by cutting its suspension cables with blowtorches. One could assume that a solitary Islamist on the Brooklyn Bridge applying blowtorches to the cables would have been quickly reported and arrested unless he was also a reincarnation of the eponymous protagonist in H.G. Wells' *Invisible Man*. Finally, in Virginia, a local imam, Ali el-Timmimi (the same imam who rejoiced at the crash of the space shuttle *Columbia*), was convicted in April 2005 and sentenced to life in prison for "soliciting others to levy war against the United States and contributing services to the Taliban" after he had called on young American Muslims to join the jihad in Afghanistan five days after the 9/11 attacks. Nine others were convicted along with el-Timmimi and given sentences ranging from four years to life in prison.[79]

The conviction of the el-Timmimi ring was the first time since the conviction of Sheik Omar Abdel Rahman in 1995 (in the case of the first World Trade Center bombing) that someone had been convicted in American courts for his words rather than for actually carrying out terrorist activities. Most disturbing in the case to many, however, was the fact that el-Timmimi and five of the nine convicted were Muslim American citizens born in the United States.[80] The el-Timmimi case is one of several indicators that suggest that the Islamist movement in the United States, though small, like the American Muslim population in general, may be growing. Further evidence of Islamism in the United States developed in 2002 in the unlikely location of Lackawanna, New York.

The Lackawanna Six

In Lackawanna, New York (as mentioned previously), six Yemeni-Americans (the Lackawanna Six) associated with Jamaat al-Tabligh were arrested in September 2002 on charges of providing material support for terrorists after they had travelled to Afghanistan and attended an al-Qaeda training camp.[81] A major break in the case of the Lackawanna Six came from a captive at Guantanamo Bay, Juma al-Dosari, who revealed under interrogation that he had been an al-Qaeda recruiter in the U.S. and had met with men in the Yemeni community of Lackawanna, New York, with the intention of recruiting them for jihad. The interrogation of al-Dosari also revealed an alias for Kamal Derwish, another American member of al-Qaeda. Derwish was born in Buffalo, but returned to Yemen and Saudi Arabia with his family as a youth. Derwish returned to Western New York in 1998 at age 25 where he eventually became the spiritual leader of the Lackawanna group and led a group to a terrorist training camp in Afghanistan in 2001. Derwish had communications with Osama's son, Saad bin Laden, and Tawfiq bin Attash, one of the planners of the bombing of the USS *Cole*.[82] Derwish was eventually killed by a Hellfire missile fired from an American Predator drone aircraft in Yemen.[83]

A second break in the Lackawanna case came when Bahrain police arrested Mukhtar al-Bakri on his wedding day in Bahrain at the urging of President Bush. Al-Bakri had departed from Buffalo, New York, and travelled back to the Middle East from where he authored emails to the men in Lackawanna in which he discussed a wedding. CIA analysts sounded alarms because they believed the word "wedding" and the phrase "big meal" to be codes for an attack. In this case, however, al-Bakri was merely planning his wedding, a fact known by the FBI, but not shared with the CIA at the time.[84] Al-Bakri explained to interrogators that he had trained in an al-Qaeda camp in Pakistan along with six men from Lackawanna. Al-Bakri named the six men as Jaber Elbaney, Sahim Alwan, Yahya Goba, Faysal Galab, Shafal Mosed, and Yasen Taheir. All six had been well-assimilated men in Lackawanna's Yemeni community. Galab was part owner of a local gas station and Taheir was the captain of his high school soccer team and voted "friendliest" in his high school class. All six men played soccer in local soccer leagues. Although Elbaney was out of the country when al-Bakri was interrogated, the other five men were arrested immediately after al-Bakri provided their names.[85]

American Islamism, Islamophobia, and the War on Terror

President Dwight D. Eisenhower in 1957 spoke at the opening of the Islamic Center in Washington and proclaimed, "We shall fight with all our might to defend your right to worship according to your conscience."[86] This right to "worship according to your conscience" has been present in American society since the colonial period and is embedded in the First Amendment of the Constitution.

Since World War II, however, there has clearly been a growth in anti–Muslim sentiments in the United States that has accompanied the rise in Islamism and terrorism across the globe and now threatens the basic First Amendment rights of Muslims in the United States. The reasons for the American cultural shift against Muslims are many, but among the American

Christian right, anti–Muslim sentiments are due to religious conviction and little other motivation is necessary; however, Samuel Huntington argues that a "quasi-war" has raged between Islam and the West since the 1970s.[87] The slaying of the Israeli athletes at the 1972 Olympics by Islamic extremists, the Iranian hostage crisis in 1979, the truck bombing of the American marine compound in Lebanon in 1983, the first Gulf War in 1991, the World Trade Center bombing in 1993, the Africa bombings in 1998, the *Cole* bombing in 2000 and finally 9/11 and the accompanying War on Terror have all combined with dozens of other incidents to produce a recent history that does appear to conform to Huntington's "quasi-war." The natural result has been a rise in American Islamophobia. While American Muslims complain that the media coverage and government analysis of the events in question tend to be biased, the fact remains that the volume of Islamic terror against and related to the U.S. has been significant since World War II and an anti–Muslim backlash should be the expected result under such circumstances. The facts are that no other ethnic or religious group has had a hand in so many American deaths since the end of the Vietnam War.[88]

The first Gulf War (1991) in particular had a profound impact on American Muslims. Congress passed new immigration laws restricting the immigration of people from Muslim countries, although the new restrictions did not apply to America's Gulf War ally, Saudi Arabia. Simultaneously, Saudi Arabia cut off aid to a number of American Muslim organizations in North America that had opposed the Saudi position in the Gulf War.[89] Similarly, the first World Trade Center bombing in 1993 had an impact on American Muslims as the American government essentially recognized that the Muslim terrorists that carried out the attack were "soldiers" in a struggle "involving a war against the United States." Consequently, the U.S. government charged the terrorists with intending "to levy a war of urban terrorism against the United States."[90] Huntington concludes that "if Muslims allege that the West wars on Islam and if Westerners allege that Islamic groups war on the West, it seems reasonable to conclude that something very much like a war is underway."[91]

Thus far, direct violence perpetrated against Muslims in the U.S. has been minimal, though there have been a few uncelebrated attacks. In 1985, the offices of the Arab-American Anti-Discrimination Committee were bombed, resulting in the death of one person, Alex Odeh, by persons thought by the FBI to be associated with the Jewish Defense League. Mosques have also been bombed or burned in Texas, Indiana, and California.[92]

American editorialists typically argue that Americans should distinguish between "good Muslims and bad Muslims," and the American ethos has been decidedly against religious or ethnic bigotry since the civil rights movement of the 1960s. More recently, however, Muslims have become targeted again by nativists who argue that America must "secure its borders." No event, however, has had more impact on Muslims in America than the terrorist attacks of 9/11.

9/11 and American Muslims

Almost immediately after the terrorist attacks of 9/11, President Bush launched a comprehensive "War on Terror" that included everything from an invasion of Afghanistan to the increased screening of passengers at airports, to restrictions on financial institutions and greater surveillance of American residents. The impact of the president's War on Terror is in dispute, with the president claiming success and his political opponents claiming otherwise, and it is possible that it remains too early to provide comprehensive conclusions concerning the impact of the War on Terror and Islamism in the United States. It is worth noting, however, that in one substantial academic study, New York University's Center on Law and Security concluded that President Bush's legal war on domestic terrorism thus far has been largely unsuccessful in curbing the spread of Islamism. In the words of the New York University's Center on Law and Security, Bush's efforts in the War on Terror have

> yielded few visible results. There have been relatively few indictments, fewer trials, and almost no convictions on charges reflecting dangerous crimes. Either the government is focused primarily on using arrests to obtain information rather than conviction, or the legal war on terror, as fought in the courts, is inconsequential.[93]

The post–9/11 era, however, does appear to be developing a mild backlash in the American Islamic community against what some American Muslims view as discrimination and injustice against Muslims perpetrated by the Bush administration during the War on Terror. In the words of one Chicago college student,

> Our new awareness is also a reaction to the treatment of Muslims in this country. After 9/11, the older generation who ran the show thought it best to lie low.... As that happened, the younger generation was uncomfortable with this, especially at colleges and universities. We decided we must become active.[94]

This particular student's new radicalism is perhaps an inevitable reaction to the fact that more than 750 immigrants in the United States, many of them Muslims, were arrested and detained by the Bush administration in the four years following the 9/11 terror attacks. Dozens were jailed for weeks or months without charges and without rights to counsel.[95] In some cases, the Justice

Department of Attorney General John Ashcroft was clearly overzealous. In November 2001, Ashcroft announced that the government would conduct investigations of almost 5,000 Muslims living in the United States. Of these, only approximately twenty people were arrested and charged and none of those were charged with terrorist activities. Nevertheless, by the end of 2002, the Justice Department announced more than 3,000 additional investigations.[96] In Detroit in 2002, for instance, Ashcroft announced the arrest of a supposed "sleeper cell" of terrorists in Detroit that were suspected of being connected to the 9/11 attacks. The only conviction, however, was for a minor immigration offense, and even that was later overturned. The charges, it later was discovered, were based on misinterpretation of some pieces of evidence and the exclusion of some exonerating evidence.[97] Similarly, FBI agents arrested a Muslim American lawyer in Portland, Oregon, in 2004 on suspicion of collaboration in the Madrid bombing earlier that year. The condemning evidence that led to the man's arrest embarrassingly later turned out to be nothing more than his son's Spanish homework.[98] In December 2002 more than two hundred Iranians were held for several days without charges before being turned over to the INS for registration. In what to some was a mostly humorous incident, one of President Bush's own secret agents was expelled from an American Airlines plane on Christmas Day 2001.[99]

Individuals, however, were not the only targets of increased federal scrutiny. Because charitable giving, or zakat, is one of the five pillars of Islam, there are numerous Muslim organizations that exist in the United States for this purpose. Some of the money given to these organizations is designated for foreign relief work, and the line between what types of organizations overseas are strictly involved in benevolence and which ones sponsor terrorism is often unclear. For example, is Hamas a benevolent organization, a political organization, or an organization that sponsors terrorism, or all three? Because the U.S. has listed Hamas as a terrorist organization and many Muslims in the U.S. view it differently, many Muslim organizations that funnel money to Hamas have been the target of federal investigations under a program known as the Green Task Initiative. Consequently, the federal government seized more than $10 million in assets in 2002 from the Holy Foundation for Relief and Development, the Global Relief Foundation, and the Benevolence International Foundation. Muslim academic think tanks such as the Institute of Islamic Thought and the University of Islamic and Social Sciences were also targeted.[100]

Immigration policy in the United States concerning Muslims also became more restrictive after 9/11. In November 2001, a 20-day waiting period was imposed for all men between ages 18 and 45 coming from predominantly

Muslim countries. In June 2002, the federal government began requiring photographs and fingerprints of all new arrivals and regular surveillance of foreigners in the country for less than 30 days.[101]

Islamists in Bosnia

In 1990, as communism was collapsing across Eastern Europe, an Islamist named Alija Izetbegovic began an Islamist political party in Bosnia known as the Stranka Demokratske Akcije (SDA). In the November 1990 elections, the SDA swept the Muslim vote in the democratic elections for the presidency of the Yugoslav Republic of Bosnia-Herzegovina. Itzetbegovic was to become the first democratically elected Muslim president of a secularized country in Europe. Itzetbegovic is an Islamist who had been imprisoned by communist authorities for his 1970 book, *The Islamic Declaration*, in which he argues that Islam and non–Islamic systems are incompatible. In the words of Itzetbegovic, "There can be neither peace nor coexistence between the Islamic religion and non–Islamic social and political institutions." Itzetbegovic contends that Islam must eventually take power and create an Islamic republic. Furthermore, Itzetbegovic argues that in the Islamic state, education and the media "should be in the hands of people whose Islamic moral and intellectual authority is indisputable."[102]

The collapse of the Soviet Union in 1991 unleashed hostility that existed between Muslims and Christian Serbs in Bosnia and the hostility quickly divulged into full-scale civil war. In 1992, as the ethnic and religious conflict raged, some 4000 jihadists from Afghanistan and other Muslim countries around the world arrived in Bosnia to wage jihad, with financial backing from Iran. Additionally, the Sunni International Muslim Brotherhood joined the fray by calling for jihad against the Serbs. Beginning in 1992, $150 million in aid began flowing into Bosnia from Wahhabist Saudi Arabia. Atrocities were committed on both sides, but Islamists both within Bosnia and internationally noticed only those committed by the Serbs and pointed to the ethnic cleansing in Bosnia carried out by Serbs as proof that Muslim assimilation in Western countries is futile.[103]

The first jihadist fighting group to arrive from abroad in Bosnia was headed by Abu Abdul Aziz, a Saudi who had also fought in Afghanistan and Kashmir. In 1993, the El Mujahid brigade, made up completely of foreign volunteers and radical Bosnian Muslims, became part of the Bosnian army. Western Muslims from Turkey, France, and Germany also fought in Bosnia.[104]

The tactics of the jihadists that arrived in Bosnia, however, shocked

Western sensibilities with their brutality. Photographs of Arab jihadists holding the severed heads of Christian Serbs or crushing them under their boot heels caused international outcry against the Muslim warriors. Foreign jihadists also used the war as an opportunity to attempt to impose sharia in Bosnia, including destroying businesses they deemed un–Islamic and forcing women to wear veils and men to wear beards. The attempts to impose sharia were generally disparaged in the European press. Bosnian president Izetbegovic, once considered Islamist himself, but exhibiting pragmatism after becoming president, reacted by inviting all foreign volunteers to leave Bosnia in 1995 and allow themselves to be replaced by American peacekeepers. For his efforts, Izetbegovic was denounced by other Islamists as a "traitor" to Islam, but his transformation from Islamism to pragmatism suggests that the best option for diffusing Islamic radicalism in the West is the integration of the Islamists themselves into Western politics.[105]

Although the foreign jihadists were humiliated by the suggestion that they should give way to the infidel Americans, most quickly departed from Bosnia, with the result that Bosnia's Muslims largely returned to the practices of liberalism and secularism that typify most Muslim communities in Europe.[106] Although the Bosnian case clearly represents the dangers of religious strife, by 2006 Bosnia also appears to represent the possibility that religious differences between Muslims and others in Europe can be overcome. Unfortunately, part of the way they have been overcome is through ethnic cleansing as Muslim refugees have fled "Christian" areas and non–Muslim Serbs and Croats moved away from areas controlled by the Islamic government of Bosnia. The Islamic Bosnian government discriminated against non–Muslims in hirings and promotions and the Bosnian army became "Islamized" with 90 percent of its personnel Muslim by 1995.[107] In the words of Samuel Huntington, "overall, the Balkans have once again been Balkanized along religious lines," although the lines have been redrawn between the realm of Eastern Orthodox Christianity and the realm of Islam. Huntington further concludes that Bosnia has been transformed from being the "Switzerland of the Balkans" into the "Iran of the Balkans."[108]

Islamism in Chechnya

Beginning in the early 1990s, a jihadist civil war has raged in the Russian enclave of Chechnya between Islamists, who desire an independent Islamic state, and the Russian authorities, who desire continued sovereignty in the area. Both sides in the conflict demonized the other, with the Islamists in

Chechnya denouncing the Russians as infidels who could be legitimately killed according to Islam, and Russian leader Boris Yeltsin referring to the Chechen rebels as "mad dogs" who "must be shot."[109]

In 1994, Chechen leader Dzhokhar Dudayev proposed that Chechnya become an Islamic state governed by sharia. Chechen troops wore scarves with the word "gavazat," meaning "jihad" in Chechen, and shouted, "Allahu Akbar," as they launched a holy war against Russia.[110] Radical Western Muslims from France and Germany have since become involved in Chechnya in what radical Islamists view as a jihad.[111]

In 1999, Chechen rebels launched incursions and bombings into neighboring Dagestan and carried out a series of bombings in residential apartment buildings in Moscow that killed more than 300 people. In 2002, Chechen rebels seized a theater in Moscow and took 800 people hostage. In December 2002, Chechen rebels blew up the headquarters of the Russian-backed Chechen government and killed 80 people.[112] In September 2004, the conflict experienced its most horrific event when Islamists took more than 1000 people hostages in a school in Beslan. By the time the siege was over, 300 civilians were dead, more than half of them children.[113] The Chechen rebels are linked to al-Qaeda and share bin Laden's goal of creating an Islamic state and waging jihad against the West.[114]

CHAPTER 8

The Boys Next Door:
Western Islamists

As Western countries (some more than others) have become hotbeds of Islamist activism, some Western and "Westernized" Islamists have gained more notoriety than others. Below, some of the more notorious individual Western and Westernized Islamists are discussed under the premise that a pattern emerges from a brief look at the persons themselves. Perhaps what is most striking about these Islamists as a group is a relatively high degree of Westernization and the fact that their experiences with the West have produced radical rejection of the West along with a tendency to adopt, whether knowingly or unknowingly, some aspects of Western technology and culture. For example, one study of Islamists in the UK revealed that they were disproportionately likely to own mobile phones.[1]

In many cases, the Islamists were not known to be radical Muslims upon their arrival in the West, but became radicalized after moving to the West and living within the Western countries themselves. In other cases, the Islamists were religious men in their countries of origin before they came to the West and merely continued their religious beliefs and practices in a new location. In either case, the "boys" typically wore Western clothing, used Western transportation and communications, attended Western universities and experienced Western entertainment. Unfortunately for the West, as Michael Vlahos has argued, "Entertainment does not equate to cultural conversion."[2] In other words, driving a Japanese car does not make one Japanese any more than using a Nokia phone makes one sympathetic to the culture of Finland.

A review of the Westernized Islamists below reveals that they well fit the Islamist profile outlined by Samuel Huntington.[3] As Huntington would have predicted, the Westernized Islamists profiled below are mobile, modern-oriented young men that typically have higher education in technical fields, engineering, and sciences. Perhaps most frightening, they often belonged to the more "modern" sectors of the European Muslim middle class. They also tended to be recent migrants to cities.

Although these similarities exist among the jihadists themselves, most persons that fit the jihadist profile (young male Muslims, significant contact with the urban West, technical or science education, etc.) do not become Islamists and pose no more threat to society as a whole than any other group.[4] Exactly why some persons choose radicalism and others do not remains largely a mystery. The decision to choose Islamist activism cannot be well explained by merely stating that the Islamists have been somehow deprived or injured by the West, because multitudes of Muslims living in the West who do not adopt radical Islamist views could easily stake the same claims. As Leon Trotsky once explained, "The mere existence of privations is not enough to cause an insurrection; if it were, the masses would be always in revolt."[5] Similarly, Steven Levitt and Stephen Dubner find that martyrs for Hizbollah are less likely to come from a poor family (28 percent versus 33 percent), and more likely to have at least a high school education (47 percent to 38 percent). Levitt and Dubner also found that in analysis of Palestinian suicide bombers, only 16 percent were from poor families and more than 60 percent had continued their education beyond high school.[6]

The decision to become a member of an Islamist organization in Western countries in the post–9/11 world is clearly not an easy one since public sentiment in the West is overwhelmingly against Islamist terrorism in all Western countries. Islamist activists therefore risk public condemnation and alienation from friends, family, and the mainstream Muslim community along with surveillance, arrest, and detention by Western governments. Additionally, Islamist activism may take significant commitments of time and energy for religious training, evangelism, public demonstrations, and, in the most extreme cases, terrorism, martyrdom, and other violent jihadist activities. In short, Islamist activists clearly must face the prospect of giving their lives for what they believe in, a decision that cannot be taken lightly. Given that Western political systems allow numerous less demanding and less risky alternatives to political violence and radicalism, it is quite impressive that so many choose such a difficult path. Clearly, the power of "belief" in these cases triumphs over reason.

The Boys of al-Qaeda and 9/11

Ayman al-Zawahiri: Bin Laden's Mentor

Egyptian physician Ayman al-Zawahiri is the man generally thought of as Osama bin Laden's mentor, #2 man in al-Qaeda, and the most important al-Qaeda ideologue. While Osama bin Laden may be the most important face of al-Qaeda and the most important person in terms of securing funding for al-Qaeda, Zawahiri may be the most important person in terms of political ideology. In December 2001, Zawahiri released a manifesto entitled "Knights under the Prophet's Banner" which explains that al-Qaeda had attacked the United States on 9/11 in hopes of creating a cataclysmic event that would mobilize the masses and reverse the decline in jihadist recruiting that had occurred since the Soviets pulled out of Afghanistan in 1989. In addition, Zawahiri explains that 9/11 was only a stepping stone on the path toward the eventual goal of a global Islamic state.[7]

Zawahiri fits the profile of the educated radical Islamist who was well acquainted with the West, but rejected Western culture as decadent. Zawahiri was trained as a physician in Egypt and eventually served as Osama bin Laden's personal doctor, but also travelled extensively in the United States in the 1980s. On one trip to California, Dr. Ali Zaki, a gynecologist in San Jose who accompanied Zawahiri to mosques in Sacramento and Stockton, described Zawahiri as a "well-balanced, highly-educated physician."[8]

Zawahiri was raised in a very Westernized suburb of Cairo in a Westernized household where his more progressive mother did not wear a veil. Zawahiri's close relatives include thirty-one persons who are doctors, chemists, or pharmacists, all closely associated with the latest in Western medical technology, scattered about the Arab world and the United States.[9] As late as the 1980s, Zawahiri's mother-in-law brought Western toys from Fisher-Price to Zawahiri's children as gifts.[10]

In spite of these Western influences, by age 15, Zawahiri had already joined an Islamist group, and by 1981, when he was involved in the jihad in Afghanistan, Zawahiri was already planning to wage holy war on the United States. Shortly thereafter, Zawahiri was charged with aiding or planning the assassination of Egyptian President Anwar Sadat.[11]

In spite of this charge, as late as 1993, Zawahiri was operating freely in the United States on a visa, and met with Muslim scientists in Silicon Valley to raise funds for jihad against America through a tour of California mosques. Zawahiri arrived in the United States from Bern, Switzerland, posing as Dr. Abdul Mu'iz and representing the Kuwaiti Red Crescent. Zawahiri told admiring crowds that he was raising money for Afghan children who had been injured by Soviet land mines. Evidently, American Muslims were not so mesmerized that they were willing to give much monetarily for the Afghan children, however, since Zawahiri was unable to raise more than $2000 on his American tour.[12] Zawahiri was accompanied on his tour of American mosques by an undercover FBI agent, but he was neither arrested, detained, nor deported, in spite of his links to the Sadat assassination, and his speeches urging jihad.[13]

Although the entire scope of Zawahiri's travels after 1996 are unknown, he evidently spent time in both Switzerland and Bosnia, and at one time sought political asylum in Bulgaria. Zawahiri also nominally edited the Islamist newspaper *Al-Mujahideen*, which had its office in Copenhagen, though it is unknown whether or not Zawahiri actually travelled to Copenhagen. Zawahiri was also rumored to have travelled to the Netherlands for the purpose of establishing an Islamist satellite television to counter the "secular" al-Jazeera.[14] A fake passport once carried by Zawahiri did show, however, that he travelled to Malaysia, Taiwan, Singapore, Hong Kong, and Chechnya. Zawahiri evidently believed that an Islamist regime could be created in Chechnya from which a jihad could be spread throughout central Asia, connecting radical Muslims in Chechnya through central Asia to Islamists in Pakistan.[15]

In 1996, Zawahiri and two associates were detained in Russia by the Russian Federal Security Service for travelling without visas and entering the country illegally. At the time, Zawahiri held in his possession four different passports from four different countries with four different names. Zawahiri stood trial and was sentenced to six months in jail, most of which he had already served while awaiting trial. At the end of his term, Zawahiri was taken to the Azerbaijani border and expelled from Russia without the Russians ever knowing his true identity.[16]

Osama bin Laden

Zawahiri's cohort in the Afghan jihad and al-Qaeda, Osama bin Laden, has never been to the United States, but fits the profile of the jihadists in the West as intelligent, educated, and Westernized, at least to a degree. As the son of wealthy construction magnate Mohammed bin Laden, Osama grew up with Western influences even though he remained in Saudi Arabia. As a child, Osama watched Western television (his favorite shows were *Fury* and *Bonanza*), wore Western clothes, including a jacket and tie to his school, and remained clean-shaven into his teens. Unfortunately, Osama experienced a religious awakening at age 14 and rejected Western culture and clothing. In spite of his religious epiphany, however, Osama did not object to driving Western automobiles (his first car was a Chrysler, followed by a Toyota jeep and a Mercedes). After getting married and having children, Osama was evidently known for enjoying taking his family to the beach.[17] At home, Osama listened to Western music, allowed pictures of horses on the walls of his house, and allowed his children to play the latest video games, though such activities were banned in Afghanistan by the Taliban.[18]

Even after joining the jihad in Afghanistan, bin Laden seemed to have little problem with Western technological advantages, including not only weapons, but the use of cell phones, construction machinery, and Toyota Land Cruisers, while supposedly rejecting everything "Western." Osama is also known for having relatively permissive attitudes toward his wives. One wife, Um Hamza, is a professor of child psychology, while another, Umm Khaled, taught Arabic grammar. Both kept their university jobs and commuted to Saudi Arabia while Osama was exiled in the Sudan.[19] Another wife, Umm Abdullah, was known to use Western cosmetics and wear Western lingerie.[20]

Bin Laden also has proven that he does not object to being surrounded by other "Westernized" jihadists, including Ayman Zawahiri, but also his personal secretary, Wadih el-Hage, an American citizen who had an American wife, April Brightsky Ray, by whom he fathered six children. El-Hage was born in Lebanon and was raised a Catholic, but converted to Islam and gained his American citizenship after his marriage to Ray.[21] El-Hage studied city planning at Southwestern Louisiana State University in Lafayette, Louisiana, and later worked as a manager of a tire shop in Fort Worth, Texas, before becoming involved in al-Qaeda's East Africa bombings in 1998.[22]

Like Zawahiri, bin Laden also had relationships with Islamist publications based in the West, and along with Zawahiri signed a fatwa in 1998 urging Muslims everywhere to kill Americans and their allies anywhere. The fatwa was published on February 23, 1998, by the London-based newspaper *Al-Quds al-Arabi.*[23]

Khalid Sheikh Mohammed

Khalid Sheikh Mohammed, often referred to by American authorities simply as "KSM," regarded as one of the most senior operatives in al-Qaeda, is another in a growing list of "Westernized" jihadists and the uncle of Ramzi Yousef, the first World Trade Center bomber. KSM was born in Kuwait and became a radical Islamist by age 16, joining the Muslim Brotherhood in Kuwait and becoming involved in the global jihad. In 1983, however, KSM became immersed in Western culture when he left Kuwait to study in the United States at Chowan College, a small Baptist college in Murfreesboro, North Carolina. After only one semester at Chowan, Khalid transferred to North Carolina A&T University, a predominantly black school in Greensboro, NC, where he earned a degree in mechanical engineering in 1986. Shortly after graduation, Khalid travelled to Pakistan in 1987 where he trained in an al-Qaeda terrorist camp. Khalid remained associated with al-Qaeda and global Islamic terrorism until his capture after 9/11.[24]

KSM had a minimal involvement in the first World Trade Center bombing in 1993 in that he wired $660 from Qatar to an associate of Ramzi Yousef's in the U.S. Yousef's success in the first World Trade Center bombing evidently inspired KSM to become involved in the planning of further attacks on the U.S. According to KSM, his hatred for the U.S. did not stem from his experiences in the U.S. as a student (like Sayyid Qutb), but instead from his opposition to U.S. foreign policy that he viewed as favoring Israel.[25]

KSM has travelled extensively throughout the globe, including meetings with Osama bin Laden in Afghanistan and a stint as the secretary for bin Laden's spiritual mentor, Abdullah Azzam. Azzam's "spirituality," however, evidently did not completely take hold with KSM, since he is known to have enjoyed a sensuous lifestyle that included alcohol and loose women.[26] In 1994, Mohammed joined his nephew, Ramzi Yousef, in Manila to plan "Operation Bojinka," a terror plot through which they intended to simultaneously explode twelve 747 jumbo jets in the air after the planes departed from the Philippines, a plot for which KSM was indicted in the U.S. While in Manila with Yousef, Khalid and Yousef developed plans to assassinate President Clinton and to bomb U.S.-bound carriers by smuggling jackets containing nitrocellulose on board.[27]

KSM travelled widely in the 1990s, from Sudan, to Yemen, to Malaysia, Brazil, and Afghanistan, knowing that American authorities were searching for him. In 1996, Khalid met with bin Laden in Afghanistan and proposed the plan to fly planes into buildings in the U.S.[28]

KSM was eventually captured by Pakistani authorities working with the CIA in March 2003 and remains in U.S. custody. KSM is currently being held by the United States at Guantanamo Bay, but in March 2007, during a hearing to determine whether he should remain at Guantanamo Bay as an enemy combatant, KSM confessed to organizing and planning the 9/11 attacks, but also confessed to playing roles in thirty other terrorist plots, including the decapitation murder of American journalist Daniel Pearl (though British-born Omar Saeed Sheikh, who attended a private school in Essex, was actually sentenced in Pakistan for the kidnapping of Pearl), the 1993 World Trade Center attack, the shoe-bombing attempt by Richard Reid, and plots to assassinate Pope John Paul II and Bill Clinton. Although Mohammed was clearly an important al-Qaeda operative, and most certainly played a role in planning the 9/11 attacks, most view his confessions as unreliable and a demented form of self-aggrandizement.[29] In fact, evidence suggests that KSM's confession was obtained through waterboarding and other extreme tactics, including extraordinary rendition and torture in Egypt, and therefore is highly suspect.[30]

Ali Abdelsoud Mohammed

Zawahiri's guide in the United States was a man suspected of being a double-agent for the CIA and al-Qaeda known as Ali Abdelsoud Mohammed. Mohammed was an ex–Egyptian soldier who spoke fluent English, French, and Hebrew, in addition to Arabic, and had been in the same unit of the Egyptian Army as Anwar Sadat's assassin, Khaled Islambouli. In 1984, Mohammed offered his services to the CIA as an informant. The CIA then sent Mohammed to a Hamburg mosque with the intention of infiltrating Hizbollah, but Mohammed revealed to other American agents at the mosque that he was an American spy. Consequently, Mohammed was placed on State Department watch lists, but he was still able to make his way to California on a visa-waiver program sponsored by the CIA that was designed to shield individuals who had performed clandestine services for the United States. Mohammed married an American woman, Linda Sanchez, in California and then enlisted in the U.S. Army. Mohammed was then stationed as a supply sergeant by the Army at the John F. Kennedy Special Warfare Center and School at Fort Bragg, North Carolina. Mohammed received special commendations from his commanding officer for "exceptional performance" and won fitness awards in competition with other American soldiers.[31]

While in the U.S. Army, Mohammed pursued a Ph.D. in Islamic studies and cooked his meals according to Islamic dietary restrictions. The U.S. Army was so impressed with his dedication to Islam that they asked him to teach a class on Middle East politics and culture and to make videotapes explaining Islam to U.S. soldiers. In this capacity, Mohammed prepared and executed over 40 country-orientation sessions for U.S. military teams deploying to the Middle East.[32]

Unfortunately, Mohammed the decorated American soldier was also photocopying American training manuals for use as al-Qaeda training manuals and spending his leave time commuting to Brooklyn and Jersey City where he trained jihadists in military tactics. Among those trained by Mohammed was el-Sayyid Nosair, an Egyptian Islamist who was charged with killing radical Israel-supporter Rabbi Meir Kahane in 1990 after a pro–Israel speech in New York City. Nosair was originally acquitted of murder due to a lack of eye witnesses, but was convicted on gun possession charges. Nosair also later was convicted as a co-conspirator with Sheikh Omar Abdel Rahman in the 1993 World Trade Center bombing, for which he received a life sentence.[33]

In 1988, Ali Abdelsoud Mohammed, double-agent and trainer to jihadists in America, took leave from the U.S. Army and went to Afghanistan to fight in the jihad against the Soviet army. While there, Mohammed trained al-Qaeda volunteers in unconventional warfare, including kidnappings, assassinations, and airplane-hijacking techniques that he had learned from the U.S. Army Special Forces. Mohammed then left active military duty in 1989 for the U.S. Army Reserve and applied for positions as a translator both at the CIA and FBI. Although unsuccessful with those agencies, Mohammed obtained a job as a security guard for a defense contractor in San Jose, California, that made a triggering device for the Trident missile system.[34]

While working in San Jose, Mohammed caught the attention of the FBI for his involvement in making fake driver's licenses. The FBI contacted the Department of Defense, which dispatched a counterintelligence team to San Jose to question Mohammed. Mohammed informed DOD officials of his journeys to Afghanistan and his training of al-Qaeda jihadists, even mentioning Osama bin Laden, of whom DOD officials had never heard in 1993. In the words of Lawrence Wright, "Mohammed openly revealed himself as a trusted member of bin Laden's inner circle, but that meant nothing to investigators at the time."[35]

Mohamed Atta

As previously discussed, the leader of the famed "Hamburg Cell" of al-Qaeda and the captain of the 9/11 suicide bombers was Mohamed Atta. Atta is believed to be the pilot of the first plane that hit the World Trade Center on 9/11. In spite of his role in one of the world's most outrageous terrorist attacks and his rabid anti–Semitism, Atta fits the profile of the Westernized Islamist well since he appeared to be well assimilated into German society as a student of urban planning. Atta was born in Egypt in 1968 where he earned a degree in architectural engineering and then worked as an urban planner in Cairo. Atta's father was an attorney in Cairo and both of his sisters also attended the university in Cairo, suggesting that his family held more moderate views and his Islamist ideas were not necessarily learned at home in Egypt.[36] Alison Pargeter, however, presents evidence that Atta's family in Egypt was actually very religious, and his father viewed the United States as hypocritical and run by oil companies.[37] That being the case, it appears that Atta merely built in Germany upon the religious beginnings he developed in Egypt.

At any rate, Atta moved to Germany in 1992 to continue his studies in urban planning at the Technical University in Hamburg.[38] In fact, Atta wrote his master's thesis on how to preserve the pluralistic Islamic-Christian urban fabric in the traditional quarters of the Syrian city of Aleppo. In his thesis, Atta praised the harmonious coexistence of Muslims and Christians in Aleppo and received an excellent grade from his professor for his efforts.[39]

Atta was described by those who knew him as an elegant and delicate perfectionist with even an array of effeminate mannerisms; so much so, in fact, that those meeting Atta sometimes had a difficult time reading his sexual orientation.[40] In spite of his effeminism, Atta evidently had overtly negative attitudes toward women. For instance, Atta stated in his will that "no pregnant woman or disbelievers should walk in my funeral or ever visit my grave. No woman should ask forgiveness of me. Those who will wash my body should wear gloves so that they do not touch my genitals."[41] Exactly why Atta thought that there would be any genitals left to touch after flying planes into buildings is unclear; however, there is speculation that his animosity toward women stemmed not only from Islam, but from his own confused sexuality.[42]

Atta briefly returned to Cairo in 1995 only to again return to Germany. After his return to Germany, it appears that his religious opinions became more radical, and he grew a full beard and began to communicate only with an exclusive group of friends in Arabic, though he possessed full command of the German language. Atta and his cohorts worked to stop laughing in public so as to symbolize their Islamic piety.[43] Atta prayed regularly on the floor of his office and his religiosity was noticed by his employers. In the words of one of the partners at the firm where he worked, "he was very, very religious."[44]

Atta attended the radical al-Quds mosque in Hamburg where the imam known as Al-Fazizi made a tape, later confiscated by German police, where he argued that Christians and Jews should have their throats slit.[45] Atta himself often displayed rabid anti–Semitism and delusional conspiracy theories involving Jews. Atta reportedly often stated that Jews controlled the media, banks, newspapers, and politics, from what he viewed as their world headquarters in New York City. Atta also blamed the Jews for planning the wars in Bosnia, Kosovo, and Chechnya, where thousands of Muslims were killed in part of a Jewish plot to restrain Islam. Atta even believed that Monica Lewinsky was a Jewish agent sent to undermine American President Bill Clinton, who had displayed too much sympathy for the Palestinian cause.[46]

Atta formed the Hamburg cell with his roommate, Ramzi bin al-Shibh, a Yemeni he had met in a radical mosque, and together they recruited cell members from European mosques whose imams focused on the Afghan jihad. Seven men from the al-Quds mosque Atta attended were eventually arrested by German authorities on terrorist charges.[47] Atta, al-Shibh, and two other friends, fellow student Marwan al Shehhi from the United Arab Emirates and Ziad Jarrah, a radical Muslim from Lebanon, journeyed to Afghanistan for a preliminary terrorist training course in 1999. It was in Afghanistan that Atta and the members of the Hamburg cell met Osama bin Laden and others with plans for spectacular attacks on the United States. The Hamburg cell arrived back in Germany in early 2000 and shaved off their beards so as to better blend in with Western culture.[48] In July 2000, Atta enrolled at Huffman Aviation International in Venice, Florida, and five months later he moved to the Miami area to practice his piloting skills on a Boeing 727 flight simulator. Atta lived in the United States essentially assimilated into American society and raising no eyebrows of either neighbors or authorities for over a year.[49]

Ramzi Bin al-Shibh

Ramzi Bin al-Shibh was born in Yemen in 1972 and worked for the International Bank of Yemen as a clerk until 1995. In 1995, Bin al-Shibh applied for a U.S. visa, was denied, and went to Germany instead where he applied for asylum under a false name, claiming to be a Sudanese citizen. Bin al-Shibh was denied asylum by the German authorities and returned to Yemen, but subsequently returned to Germany under his own name and registered as a student in Hamburg. Bin al-Shibh flunked out of school, but met Mohamed Atta in a Hamburg mosque and began sharing an apartment with Atta in 1998. Bin al-Shibh was radically anti–Israel and perceived a global Jewish "conspiracy," but was generally known within the Hamburg Muslim community as "sociable, extroverted, polite, and adventuresome."[50] In other words, in spite of his radical anti–Semitism, other Muslims in the Hamburg Muslim community did not evidently view him as someone who would be plotting mass murder.

Bin al-Shibh and the members of the Hamburg cell travelled to Afghanistan and met with Osama bin Laden with their plans for what eventually became the 9/11 attacks on the United States. Of the members of the Hamburg cell, only bin al-Shibh was denied a U.S. visa. Bin al-Shibh would remain an active member of the plot, however, as the liaison between the group and 9/11 "mastermind" Khalid Sheikh Mohammed.[51] Bin al-Shibh would be arrested in Pakistan the next year and his captured computer contained a wealth of al-Qaeda contact information, including the passport numbers of numerous al-Qaeda members.[52]

Marwan al Shehhi

Marwan al Shehhi was born in the United Arab Emirates in 1978 and grew up in the Ras al-Khaimah Emirate in a middle-class family. His father is a muezzin in the UAE and one of his half-brothers is a policeman.

Al Shehhi departed for Germany in 1996 as part of a military scholarship program in conjunction with his work as a soldier in the army of the United Arab Emirates. Al Shehhi lived with a German family for several months before moving into his own apartment. Though he was known to be very religious, friends also described him as a "regular guy," wearing Western clothes and travelling about Europe in automobiles.[53]

Al Shehhi experienced academic difficulties in Bonn, however, and applied for permission to continue his studies in Hamburg, evidently a request motivated by his desire to join fellow radicals Atta and bin al-Shibh. Al Shehhi had more academic difficulties in Hamburg, and subsequently moved back to Bonn, and then again back to Hamburg in 1999 to study shipbuilding at the Technical University where he reunited with Atta and al Shibh.[54] After his return to Hamburg, however, acquaintances reported that al Shehhi became more radical, demanding halal food, wearing inexpensive clothing, and watching no television. When asked why he never laughed, al Shehhi is reported to have replied, "How can you laugh when people are dying in Palestine?" Al Shehhi leased an apartment in Coral Springs, Florida, with Mohamed Atta in April 2001 and visited both Georgia and Virginia prior to 9/11.[55] On 9/11, Al Shehhi was the pilot on United Airlines Flight 175, the second commercial jetliner in the U.S. headed for mass murder and suicide at the World Trade Center.[56]

Ziad Jarrah

Ziad Jarrah was born in Lebanon in 1975 to an affluent, Westernized family. Jarrah's father is a mid-level bureaucrat in the Lebanese government and his mother, from a well-off family, is a teacher. The family car for the Jarrahs while Ziad was growing up was a Mercedes, and Jarrah attended private Christian schools in Lebanon before going abroad to continue his studies at a college in Germany.[57] In April 1996, Jarrah enrolled at a junior college in Greifswald, Germany, with the intention of studying dentistry. Jarrah was not an Islamist when he arrived in Germany, but instead had a reputation for frequenting the discos and beaches in Beirut. After arriving in Germany, Jarrah attended student parties and drank beer in Greifswald as many other Western college students do.

After a trip to Lebanon in late 1996, however, Jarrah began putting away his old lifestyle and living more strictly according to sharia. In September 1997, Jarrah enrolled at the Technical University of Hamburg-Harburg with the intention of studying aircraft engineering. Jarrah grew a full beard, began praying regularly, and alienated his previous girlfriend in the dentistry program at Greifswald by criticizing her lack of religiosity.[58]

Jarrah evidently met Ramzi bin al-Shibh at the al-Quds mosque in Hamburg and travelled with Atta, Binalshibh, and Shehhi to Afghanistan for terrorist training in an al-Qaeda camp in November 1999. Jarrah eventually ended his life as the pilot of United Airlines Flight 93 that crashed in a field in Pennsylvania after passengers foiled the plot of the hijackers to hit their target in Washington.[59]

Said Bahaji

Said Bahaji is the only German citizen of the famed "Hamburg cell." Bahaji is the son of a Moroccan immigrant who was educated in Morocco, but returned to Germany to study electrical engineering at the Technical University of Hamburg-Harburg. Bahaji even spent five months in the German army before obtaining a medical discharge, an experience that obviously requires a tremendous amount of Western culturalization. Bahaji has been described by those who know him as an "insecure follower with no personality" and possessing a "limited knowledge of Islam," but Bahaji lived with Atta and bin al-Shibh for eight months and Atta and bin al-Shibh used Bahaji's computer for internet research.[60] Though warrants have been issued for Bahaji's arrest in both Spain and Germany, Bahaji is one of the few involved in the 9/11 plot that remain at large at this writing.[61]

Mounir el Motassadeq

Mounir el Motassadeq is a Moroccan who came to Muenster, Germany, in 1993 at age 19 and moved to Hamburg in 1995 to study electrical engineering at the Technical University of Hamburg-Harburg. The degree to which Motassadeq had been Westernized after a decade in Germany is attested to by university officials in Hamburg, who, after his 2002 arrest on terrorism charges, described Motassadeq as a "normal student" eager to take his exams.[62]

Motassadeq became acquainted with bin al-Shibh and Mohamed Atta and took part in radical discussions at Atta's home where he evidently organized film sessions that included speeches by bin Laden.[63] Motassadeq became extremely radical in his thinking and reportedly even stated that he would kill his entire family if his religious beliefs demanded it. Motassadeq was also evidently anti–Semitic, and another witness reported that he remembered Motassadeq referring to Adolf Hitler as a "good man."[64]

Motassadeq eventually became the treasurer for the Hamburg cell, handling funds for the living expenses of three of the 9/11 hijackers.[65] In 2005, Motassadeq received a seven-year prison term in Germany for membership in a terrorist group, and in 2006, he was convicted of being an accessory to more than 3000 counts of murder stemming from his role in the 9/11 attacks.[66]

Zakariya Essabar

Zakariya Essabar is another member of the Hamburg cell who was born in the Islamic world, but became radicalized after moving to the West. Essabar was a Moroccan citizen who moved to Germany in 1997 and to Hamburg in 1998 to study medical technology. In Hamburg, Essabar became acquainted with bin al-Shibh and other members of the Hamburg cell through his attendance at a radical mosque.

Evidently, Essabar adopted a radical form of Islam suddenly in 1999 against the will of his parents, who made repeated attempts to dissuade him from his radical Islamic thinking. Essabar is credited with being a messenger from the Hamburg cell who travelled to Afghanistan to communicate the date of the 9/11 attacks to the al-Qaeda leadership in Afghanistan. At this writing, Essabar remains at large.[67]

Abdelghani Mzoudi

Abdelghani Mzoudi was a member of the Hamburg cell that witnessed the execution of Mohammed Atta's will in 1986. Like Zakariya Essabar, Mzoudi was a Moroccan citizen who moved to Germany in the 1990s (1993 in his case) to study science (physics and chemistry). Also like Essabar, Mzoudi was not an Islamist upon his departure from Morocco, but adopted a more radical form of Islam at some point after arriving in Germany.

Mzoudi studied in Dortmund, Bochum, and Muenster before moving to Hamburg in 1995 where he evidently became acquainted with Mohamed Atta and Mounir el Motassadeq of the Hamburg al-Qaeda cell.[68] Mzoudi was charged with terrorist activities in Germany, but acquitted in 1994 for lack of evidence and deported by German authorities back to his native Morocco in 1995.[69]

Zacarias Moussaoui

Zacarias Moussaoui, the so-called twentieth hijacker, is a native French citizen of Moroccan descent and son of a Moroccan cleaning woman who moved to France after enduring domestic violence in Morocco. As a young man in France, Moussaoui reportedly became an avid handball player and outstanding academic.[70]

Prior to 2001, Moussaoui had been a resident of Britain, and held a master's degree in business (1995) from Southbank University in the United Kingdom. Moussaoui had travelled to Afghanistan on several occasions and trained in al-Qaeda training camps before coming to America for flight school. Moussaoui became associated with Islamism at the Brixton mosque in London where he also became associated with shoe-bomber Richard Reid and other Islamists. Moussaoui, however, was evidently too radical even for other Islamists at the mosque, as he was expelled for wearing combat fatigues and pressuring the imam to give him information on joining the global jihad.[71]

In February 2001, Moussaoui arrived in Norman, Oklahoma, where he attended flight school and joined a gymnasium, but he ended his attendance at flight school prior to finishing his training. In August 2001, Moussaoui attended another flight school in Minneapolis, Minnesota, for simulator training on the Boeing 747. It was here that Moussaoui alarmed flight-school trainers by showing interest only in how to steer a jumbo jet, while showing no interest in learning to take off or land. Moussaoui evidently also asked strange questions about the flight patterns around New York City and whether or not the doors of a cockpit could be opened during a flight. Prior to 9/11, the FBI was unable to arrest Moussaoui simply because they believed he might be a potential hijacker, but Moussaoui was turned over to the Immigration and Naturalization Service, who arrested him as a French citizen who had overstayed his visa. The FBI seized Moussaoui's laptop, but could not search it because they could not show probable cause to justify the search. After 9/11 when the rules of probable cause were significantly relaxed, Moussaoui's laptop was found to contain information connecting him to the 9/11 plot, and Moussaoui was charged with being an accomplice in the 9/11 attacks. Moussaoui was also discovered to be receiving money from Ramzi bin al-Shibh of Mohammed Atta's 9/11 Hamburg cell.[72]

Abdullah Azzam

Among those mujahadeen receiving American assistance for waging jihad against the Soviet Union in Afghanistan in the 1980s was Abdullah Azzam, once a spiritual leader and role model to Osama bin Laden. Azzam, however, did not limit his struggle to Afghanistan, but also distributed pamphlets in the 1980s calling for jihad on the Iberian Peninsula. To Azzam, Spain and Portugal constituted Muslim lands that had been usurped by infidels in the fifteenth century.[73] During the 1980s, Azzam visited the United States annually, including visits to the American heartland in Kansas City, St. Louis, and Dallas, along with a tour through the mosques of New York, Seattle, Sacramento, Los Angeles, and San Diego. During these visits, Azzam sought money and recruits for the Afghan jihad, all the while denouncing the decadent West that funded the Afghan jihad (in the interest of anti-communism) and allowed him the freedom to travel and recruit in the West. Altogether, Azzam and Osama bin Laden's organization, the Services Bureau, opened branches in thirty-three American cities.[74]

Azzam's recruiting stories of the Afghan jihad were replete with mythology and apocalyptic fantasy. In the words of Wright,

> He spoke of mujahideen who defeated entire columns of Soviet troops single-handed. He claimed that some of the brave warriors had been run over by tanks but survived; others were shot, but the bullets failed to penetrate. If death came, it was even more miraculous. When one beloved mujahid expired, the ambulance filled with the sound of humming bees and chirping birds, even though they were in the Afghan desert in the middle of the night. Bodies of martyrs uncovered after a year in the grave still smelled sweet and their blood continued to flow. Heaven and nature conspired to repel the godless invader. Angels rode into the battle on horseback, and falling bombs were intercepted by birds, which raced ahead of the jets to form a protective canopy over the warriors.[75]

Exactly how anyone living in the West, Muslim or non–Muslim, could believe such nonsense on the surface boggles the mind, but one must remember that approximately a third of Americans also believe the Bible to be literally true and thus accept as reality the stories of talking snakes, talking donkeys, angels, demons, global floods, the parting of the Red Sea, the sun standing still in the sky, and manna from heaven. With such a mindset, a belief in birds that intercept falling bombs does not take a huge leap of faith.

Mohammed Loay Baizid

One American Muslim who was persuaded by Azzam to join the jihad, Mohammed Loay Baizid, a Syrian immigrant to the U.S., explains that he was not even a believer before he met the charismatic Islamist Azzam. According to Baizid, he was a typical middle-class 24-year-old American man in 1985 who frequented shopping malls and ate American fast food. Baizid's story is corroborated by another Syrian immigrant at University of Missouri at Kansas City, who described Baizid as an easygoing and quick-witted young man who enjoyed playing cards and hanging out at the Country Club Plaza.[76]

Baizid was studying engineering at a community college in Kansas City when he came across a copy of a tract from Abdullah Azzam explaining all the miracles in Afghanistan. Baizid found Azzam's testimony sufficiently compelling that he decided he should fly to Afghanistan and see the miracles for himself. Baizid secured a flight to Islamabad, Pakistan, and called the number for Azzam that was on the mimeographed tract he had read. If the phone number on the tract had not been a working number, Baizid would have had no idea whatsoever how he could have reached Azzam or the mujahadeen. Fortunately for Baizid, Azzam answered, and Baizid soon found himself in the company of the mujahadeen. Though Baizid had planned only to stay three months, he was captivated by the camaraderie and dedication of the mujahadeen warriors who sought martyrdom for God. In the words of Baizid, "Everything was totally strange. It was like I was born just now, like I was an infant, and I have to learn everything new. It was not so easy after that to leave and go back to your regular life."[77]

Baizid journeyed with Azzam to Afghanistan and joined forces with Afghan mujahadeen commander Gulbuddin Hekmatyar. Baizid did not see major action with the mujahadeen and his unit of jolly jihadis fairly quickly disbanded because they were not needed, but the captivating ideology of Islamism had been powerful enough to take a 24-year-old college student from Kansas City to the killing fields of Afghanistan, where he was willing to become a martyr.[78] According to John Lumpkin, a senior fellow at GlobalSecurity.org, a defense-policy research firm, Baizid eventually became a major figure in the founding of al-Qaeda. In Afghanistan, Baizid evidently changed his name to Abu Rida al Suri, whom the Department of Homeland Security lists as an al-Qaeda financier who lived in Kansas City in the 1980s, in addition to Tucson, Arizona. Evidently, Abu Rida not only travelled to Afghanistan, but also to the Sudan in or around 1990 to search for a base for al-Qaeda. Abu Rida also may have been present and taken notes at the very first meeting in Pakistan where al-Qaeda was founded.[79] Abu Rida was also involved in supplying weapons to a radical Islamic Sudanese militia group and in attempting to purchase uranium in the Sudan in the early 1990s.[80] During this same time period when Rida was attempting to purchase uranium for al-Qaeda, he also obtained an Illinois driver's license and became the leader of a charity organization known as the Benevolence International Foundation, which was eventually shut down by the federal government for funnelling money to al-Qaeda.[81]

Imad Yarkas (Abu Dahdah)

Imad Yarkas, also known as Abu Dahdah, is a Spanish businessman of Syrian origin who is considered to have been part of the first wave of Islamists that helped bring radical Islam to Spain. After arriving in Spain in the 1980s, Yarkas became the head of a radical Syrian group in Madrid, and the name Abu Dahdah became almost synonymous with al-Qaeda in Spain.[82] Yarkas arranged a July 2001 meeting between 9/11 hijacker Mohammed Atta, and Ramzi Bin al-Shibh, Atta's roommate and fellow 9/11 plotter from the Hamburg cell. Yarkas is also accused of recruiting jihadists for terrorist training in Afghanistan. Yarkas was eventually convicted of conspiracy to commit murder in connection with the 9/11 terror attacks and was sentenced in October 2005 to 27 years in prison for his role in the 9/11 plot.[83]

Khalil Deek

Khalil Deek is an American citizen who is credited with creating an electronic version of the al-Qaeda terrorist manual, the *Encyclopaedia of Jihad*, on CD-ROM. The 9/11 terrorists evidently obtained a copy of the *Encyclopaedia* from Deek. Deek was also involved in making travel arrangements for al-Qaeda members to go to Afghanistan and receive terrorist training. Deek was arrested in Pakistan for his role in the millennium plot in Jordan.[84]

The First World Trade Center Bombers

Sheikh Omar Abdel Rahman

In the American zeal to combat Soviet communism in Afghanistan in the 1980s, recruitment centers for the Afghan jihad were set up in American universities and Islamic student associations welcomed radical preachers and jihadists from the Middle East. Islamists took advantage of American immigration laws that favored applicants from Muslim countries to immigrate to the U.S.[85] In one glaring case of American blindness during the Afghan jihad, in 1986, only two years after his release from prison in Egypt for his involvement in the assassination of Anwar Sadat, the blind Sheikh Omar

Abdel Rahman, known by the CIA as the founder of Gamaa Islamiya in Egypt, obtained a visa to the United States through the CIA. In 1991, just two years before he was involved in the first World Trade Center bombing, Rahman received a permanent resident's visa on the grounds that he was a minister at a mosque in Jersey City, where he operated freely until his arrest for connections to the first bombing of the World Trade Center.[86] Rahman gained asylum in the United States in spite of the fact that he was listed as a terrorist on a State Department watch list. Once in North America, he travelled widely in both the U.S. and Canada, giving sermons against the decadent West, and often denouncing Americans as "descendants of apes and pigs who have been feeding from the dining tables of the Zionists, Communists, and colonialists."[87] Rahman called for an Islamic jihad against the West and specifically argued that Muslims should "cut the transportation of their countries, tear it apart, destroy their economy, burn their companies, eliminate their interests, sink their ships, shoot down their planes, kill them on sea, air, or land."[88]

Rahman and his followers had plans to assassinate numerous American political figures and destroy the George Washington Bridge, the Lincoln and Holland tunnels, Federal Plaza, and the building of the United Nations, in simultaneous bombings in New York. The reasons for the attacks, ostensibly, were due to American support for Egyptian President Hosni Mubarak. Rahman's efforts were at least partially funded by Osama bin Laden and al-Qaeda.[89]

Ramzi Yousef

Rahman, however, was far from alone. The area where he resided in Jersey City by the end of the 1980s had become known as "little Egypt." Rahman's accomplice in the first World Trade Center bombing, Ramzi Yousef, received an electrical engineering degree in the United Kingdom prior to training for jihad in a camp in Afghanistan in 1990. Yousef then came to New York City in 1992 with a fake passport he had purchased in Pakistan, with the idea of launching a terror attack on the United States in retaliation for American aid to Israel.[90] Yousef was not a particularly devout Muslim and therefore may have been motivated more by his hatred of the Jews and the Palestinian cause than by radical Islam; nevertheless, Yousef became the first Islamist terrorist to attack the American homeland.[91]

Before Yousef arrived in New York, the Brooklyn terror cell had been experimenting with pipe bombs, but Yousef's ambition to bring down the World Trade Center expanded the ambition of the group. Yousef hoped that he would kill 250,000 people in the World Trade Center bombing through collapsing the building and lacing his bomb with deadly poisons.[92] Yousef's bombing of the World Trade Center killed six people and injured more than a thousand while causing $500 million in damage, including a 200-foot-wide crater under the building.[93] Yousef temporarily escaped to Pakistan, and then to Manila, where he planned to blow up a dozen 747s simultaneously, assassinate the pope and President Clinton, and crash a plane into CIA headquarters.[94]

Yousef was caught and brought to trial in the United States after one of his associates returned to the car rental company from where they had rented the vehicles used in the World Trade Center bombing, seeking his deposit. Yousef also hindered his ability to remain a fugitive with letters to New York newspapers claiming responsibility for the attacks. In his letters, Yousef demanded that the United States end aid to Israel, break relations with Israel, and pledge to end interference in Muslim countries.[95] The Yousef case demonstrates how Islamists in the West have been able to become interconnected with global terrorism. Not only did Yousef train in jihadist camps in Afghanistan after the World Trade Center bombing in 1993, he flew to Pakistan and stayed in a safe house funded by Osama bin Laden.[96]

Yousef explained to the FBI that he felt guilty about the deaths in the bombing, but his remorse over the deaths was overridden by his desire to do whatever he could do to stop the killing of Muslims by Israeli troops.[97]

Londonistan Islamists

Omar Bakri Mohammed and Hizb ut-Tahrir

Omar Bakri Mohammed was born in Syria in 1958 and schooled at an Islamic boarding school between the ages of five and fifteen. At age 15, he joined the Muslim Brotherhood, and then fled Syria, where the Muslim Brotherhood was persecuted under the regime of Hafez al-Assad. In Lebanon, Bakri Mohammed joined the Islamist group Hizb ut-Tahrir. In this, Bakri Mohammed differs from many other Western Islamists in that his Islamist beliefs were well entrenched before he ever arrived in the West.

In 1979, Bakri Mohammed attended al Azhar University in Cairo where he clashed with his professors due to his radical views. Consequently, six months later, Bakri Mohammed moved to Mecca to study at the Islamic School of Saltiyah. While in Mecca, Bakri Mohammed started a cell of Hizb ut-Tahrir. Given that the group was officially banned in Saudi Arabia, the Hizb ut-Tahrir cell in Kuwait officially expelled Bakri Mohammed out of fear of the Saudi government in 1983. Undaunted, Bakri Mohammed then started his own radical Islamist group, al-Muhajiroun (the emigrants).[98]

Bakri Mohammed slowly built his organization to approximately 70 members, but was arrested and expelled by the Saudi government in December 1985 for teaching from banned literature published by Hizb ut-Tahrir and for preaching against the Saudi government. Bakri Mohammed fled to London in January 1986 and quickly organized a branch of Hizb ut-Tahrir in London. In 1990, Bakri Mohammed was granted political asylum in England because his life would be in danger if he returned to either Syria or Saudi Arabia. In 1991, during the Persian Gulf War and just months after he had been granted political asylum in England, Bakri Mohammed gained notoriety for stating publicly that British prime minister John Major should be assassinated if he went to Saudi Arabia.[99]

In 1995, Bakri Mohammed again made the news when he publicly called for Queen Elizabeth to convert to Islam and stated that the ultimate goal was that the "black flag of Islam flies over Downing Street."[100] For this statement, Bakri Mohammed was expelled from the international Hizb ut-Tahrir organization. Bakri Mohammed responded by launching al Mujahiroun in the UK. Bakri Mohammed's new group (later renamed the Saviour Sect) differed from Hizb ut-Tahrir in that while both favor establishment of Islamist government and reestablishment of the caliphate, Hizb ut-Tahrir argues for focusing on countries where an Islamist government is a more realistic possibility while Bakri Mohammed calls on all Muslims everywhere to work toward the establishment of Islamist government in all countries. Al Muhajiroun also differed from Hizb ut-Tahrir in that Bakri Mohammed argued that British Muslims must actively support jihad while Hizb ut-Tahrir theoretically supports jihad, but does not view it as an obligation for Western Muslims. Under Bakri Mohammed's leadership, al Muhajiroun became the most visible Islamist movement in the UK, with branches in thirty cities and 700 followers taking weekly religious lessons from Bakri Mohammed. Branches of the Saviour Sect have also been opened in Lebanon, Ireland, Pakistan, and the United States.[101]

Mohammed Sidique Khan

Mohammed Sidique Khan was born in 1974 in Leeds, UK, to a foundry worker of Pakistani origin. Khan attended high school in Leeds where most of his friends were white Britons and Khan was described by friends as considering himself to be Western. High school friends also described Khan as enamored with all things American after he made a trip to the U.S. and Khan was generally known by the Westernized nickname "Sid." As a high school student, Khan's classmates also reported that he exhibited little interest in religion and therefore most certainly was not at that point an Islamist.[102]

After leaving school, Khan worked for the British government as a low-level bureaucrat in the Benefits Agency and later in the Department of Trade and Industry before returning to school to pursue a degree in business at Leeds Metropolitan University. Khan graduated with a degree in business studies in 1996.[103]

Khan married Hasina Patel, the daughter of award-winning British teacher Farida Patel, in 2004 and resided in Dewsbury, UK. Hasina worked as a community enrichment officer and Khan worked as a learning mentor at Hillside Primary School in Beeston, UK. While at Hillside, Khan developed a reputation for being good with children and became involved in running school clubs and activities. The former head of Hillside Primary School, Sarah Balfour, is married to Member of Parliament John Trickett, who gave Khan a tour of the Houses of Parliament as his personal guest in 2004. Khan's employment record, however, became tarnished by absences in 2004 with the result that Khan was eventually forced to resign his post in December 2004.[104]

Khan's extended family is also from all outward appearances quite Westernized, with significant stakes in British society. Khan's mother-in-law, Farida Patel, who moved to the UK in the 1970s, was the daughter of an anti-apartheid activist, and a co-opted member of the British government's council of religious leaders from 1996 to 2000. In 1998, Farida Patel was the first Asian woman to attend a garden party at Buckingham Palace due to her work as a teacher in bilingual studies. The next year, Farida was invited to Downing Street where she was given an award by Prime Minister Tony Blair for her work on the Inner City Religious Council. The ceremony was also attended by the queen, Prince Charles, and the Duke of Edinburgh. In July 2004, Farida was again a guest at a Buckingham Palace garden party along with her husband and her daughter, Hasina, the wife of Mohammed Sidique Khan. At the 2004 event, Farida Patel received an award for her work as a teacher.[105]

While Khan's family members were being rewarded by Western society for their accomplishments, Khan was apparently drifting off course in 2004 as evidenced by his spotty attendance record at the primary school where he worked and had previously flourished. Khan used a EU grant that he received through the Leeds City Council to establish gymnasiums for Muslims, which on the surface appears rather innocuous. Eventually, however, these gyms became known as centers of Islamic extremism where Khan is believed to have preached his extreme anti–Western ideas to young Islamic men.[106] Khan evidently began attending a radical mosque in Dewsbury and then journeyed to

Pakistan for jihadist training.[107] By the late 1990s, Khan had narrowed his focus to the mosques, the Pakistani youth clubs that he helped run, and a bookshop where he gave talks.[108] Khan then completed the transition from words to action with the London transportation bombings of 2005, of which Khan is generally considered to be the mastermind.

Khan originally came to the attention of Western officials through President Bush's surveillance program conducted outside of judicial surveillance by the National Security Agency (NSA). Through the NSA's secret surveillance program, they discovered emails between Khan and American citizens, one of whom was Ahmed Omar Abu Ali, a Virginia resident and valedictorian of the Islamic Saudi Academy in Alexandria, Virginia. In their correspondence, Khan and Ali discussed Khan's plans to come to the United States and the desire to blow up synagogues on the east coast. As a result, the CIA and FBI put Khan on a "no-fly list" and prevented his entry into the United States. Khan then returned to his job as a schoolteacher in Leeds and worked with other Muslim radicals on conducting the attacks on the London subways on July 7, 2005.[109] Khan's purpose evidently was global jihad as he explained on his suicide video where he stated, "as you kill us, you will be killed, as you bomb us, you will be bombed."[110]

Abu Doha

Abu Doha was the leader of an Algerian radical group known as the al-Qaeda Organization in the Islamic Maghreb. Doha was born in Algeria and trained with al-Qaeda in Afghanistan, but went to London in the late 1990s where he coordinated the activities of extremists from the notorious Finsbury Park mosque. Doha was arrested in 2001 for carrying a false passport and is currently fighting his extradition to the United States. Doha has also been linked to Ahmed Ressam and the plot to blow up the Los Angeles airport as well as the ricin plot in the UK.[111]

Kamel Bourgass

Kamel Bourgass was an associate of Abu Doha's in the Al-Qaeda Organization in the Islamic Maghreb. Like Doha, Bourgass is an Algerian who moved to London and became involved with the radical Islamist movement at the Finsbury Park Mosque. In 2003, Bourgass murdered a British detective who was tracking him in a suspected plot to spread the poison ricin throughout London. In addition to the murder, Bourgass was convicted in April 2005 for "conspiracy to cause public nuisance by use of poisons and/or explosives."[112]

Esa al-Hindi

Esa al-Hindi was once the head of al-Qaeda in the UK and the author of casing reports drawn up in 2000 and 2001 on New York's Citicorp headquarters the New York Stock Exchange, the Prudential Tower in Newark, and the World Bank headquarters and International Monetary Fund Building in Washington.[113] Al-Hindi, also known as Dhiren Barot, was arrested in the UK in August 2004 for planning what became known as "the Gas Limos Project" to explode three limousines packed with gas cylinders and explosives in underground parking garages in the UK.[114]

French Jihad

Khaled Kelkal

Khaled Kelkal was born in Algeria in 1971, but came to France with his mother as an infant to join his father in Vaulx-en-Velin, a suburb of Lyon. Like so many other radical Islamists in the West, Kelkal was known as a good student in school and even earned the nickname "Mr. Smiley" because of his pleasant countenance.[115] Unfortunately, in his late teens Kelkal apparently lost interest in school and subsequently became involved in criminal activity, being sentenced to four months' probation in 1990 for trafficking stolen automobiles. Several months later, Kelkal was arrested for violent thefts where he used cars as battering rams to enter private properties. Kelkal was sentenced to four years in prison, but while in prison, he adopted a radical form of Islam. His Islamic mentor is believed to have been an Algerian inmate who was involved with Islamists in Algeria. In an interview with a sociologist in 1992, Kelkal argued that there was no justice for Arabs in France and he referred to Algeria, rather than France, as his real home.[116] Several months after his release from prison in 1992, Kelkal travelled to Algeria ostensibly to visit family. While in Algeria, he was evidently recruited by the Algerian GIA.[117]

Kelkal returned to France and quickly became involved again in petty crime, but he also began frequenting the Bilal mosque in the Thibaude quarter of Vaulx-en-Velin. Kelkal reconnected with childhood friend and fellow Islamist Karim Koussa, and the two developed a small, radical GIA cell and watched GIA videos together. It was through other Islamists they met in the Bilal mosque that they became acquainted with the Algerian Ben Ali Boualem Bensaid, who was eventually arrested, tried, and sentenced to life in prison for his part in the French bombings. Under the guidance of Bensaid, Kelkal and Koussa were evidently ready to put their radical ideas into action.[118]

In 1995, Kelkal was involved in the assassination of Imam Sahrouri, a moderate imam in Paris who was opposed by the GIA. In July 1995, a bomb was detonated in the Saint-Michel rail station in Paris. In August of the same year, a similar bomb that had not detonated was found near the Paris-Lyon railway with Kelkal's fingerprints on the bomb. A month later in September of that year, Kelkal attempted to kill Jewish schoolchildren in a suburb of Lyons with a car bomb, but the bomb detonated before school let out and killed no one.[119] Kelkal was designated "Public Enemy #1" by French authorities and 170,000 photographs of Kelkal were distributed throughout France. On September 29, 1995, Kelkal was located in the forest of Malval near Lyon and shot dead by French authorities while resisting arrest. Camera footage of the gun battle showed a French policeman shouting "Finish him off" while another kicked him to make sure he was dead. Thus, Kelkal became a symbol for the anti-racism movement among French minorities and Kelkal's death sparked riots across France.[120] At the time of his death, however, Kelkal was carrying an address book that allowed police to arrest his accomplices, including Boualem Bensaid, his captain in the GIA terrorist cell. Further investigations revealed that the radical GIA cell was also planning a bombing in a market in Lille and had been responsible for the bomb that exploded in front of a Jewish school in September 1995.[121]

The Canadian Boys

Ahmed Ressam

Ahmed Ressam is best known as a then 32-year-old Algerian-born Muslim who was arrested in Port Angeles, Washington, in December 1999 with 130 lbs. of explosives in his Chrysler sedan and outlines of plans to blow up the Los Angeles International Airport. Ressam had essentially formed his own ad hoc al-Qaeda cell in Montreal after training in an Al-Qaeda camp in Afghanistan. His closest connection to Osama bin Laden was a phone call he made to Afghanistan prior to his failed attack on the Los Angeles airport, but Osama never called him back.[122] Though raised in Algeria, Ressam fits the profile of a Westernized jihadist in that neither his mother nor his sisters wore veils and inside his boyhood home, they wore pants, dresses, and other Western-style clothing and fashions. Ressam himself wore Western designer jeans and frequented Algerian nightclubs. In the words of his friend Yousfi Boualem, "Ahmed liked to dress himself well and go search for women. He had nothing to do with Islam.... He was a handsome young man. He was cool and had no problem finding the young girls. Not women of the street, but nice young girls."[123] Another friend, Morad Cherani, says that Ressam and his friends drank wine, smoked hashish, and frequented a seaside nightclub that had a swimming pool, all activities forbidden by the Koran and detested by Islamists.[124]

At age 16 (1983), Ressam was sent to Paris by his father for medical treatment for a stomach ulcer. Ressam returned to France fleeing political unrest almost a decade later when Algeria erupted in Islamist violence. Ressam only had a 30-day visa, however, so after his legal stay in Marseille expired, he went to Corsica illegally with a fake passport under the name Nasser Ressam. Ressam was arrested in Corsica in 1993 and repatriated to Algeria. Ressam had no intention of remaining in Algeria where the political situation had perhaps even worsened, however, and departed for Montreal under the name Tahar Medjadi in February 1994. Upon his arrival in Montreal, Ressam was arrested for travelling with a fake passport, but he applied for political asylum. Ressam's application for asylum was denied, but he was subsequently released by Canadian authorities on his own recognizance with the understanding that he was to be deported.[125]

While in Montreal, Ressam lived on welfare and lived in a small, run-down apartment in a low-income neighborhood in Montreal, but still frequented nightclubs and wore $1000 Armani suits that he stole from Montreal department stores. When not shoplifting, Ressam drank coffee with friends and enjoyed kicking a soccer ball in the yard of his Montreal apartment. In 1995, Ressam was arrested for stealing a suit at a Montreal department store, fined $100, placed on two years' probation, and ordered to leave Canada. Ressam, however, did not depart from Canada, and instead continued his life of petty theft. In October 1996, Ressam was arrested for pickpocketing, fined $500, sentenced to two years' probation, and again set free on Canadian society.[126]

Ressam journeyed to Afghanistan in 1998 to train for jihad, and departed Afghanistan with $12,000 in cash from al-Qaeda and instructions to rent a safe house in Canada, purchase passports and weapons, and build a bomb to be used in the United States.[127]

Ressam's route to Canada came through the Los Angeles airport where U.S. officials confiscated his passport and noted that he carried a shampoo bottle filled with glycol and a Tylenol bottle of hexamine tablets, both ingredients that could be used in making explosives. Ressam was travelling under the name Benni Noris, which was not on any sort of terrorist watch list; consequently, the American Immigration and Naturalization Service allowed Ressam to fly on to Vancouver. A month later, Ressam made his way to Montreal, rented an apartment, and began building his terrorism cell.[128]

Ressam decided on the Los Angeles airport as his target and planned to coordinate his terrorist attack with the passing of the millennium. In November 1999, Ressam and an associate, Abdelmajid Dahoumane, travelled to Victoria, rented a room, and built their terrorist bomb for the Los Angeles airport. Ressam then placed the bomb in the trunk of his Chrysler and took the ferry from Victoria to Port Angeles, Washington, where he was apprehended by American officials when his nervous activity tipped off U.S. Customs officials. In conjunction with Ressam, the FBI also arrested Abdelghani Meskini in Brooklyn based on communications the FBI had intercepted.[129]

Ressam was eventually convicted on nine counts, including conspiracy to commit an act of international terrorism, and faced up to 130 years in prison. Faced with this grim future, Ressam struck a deal with the FBI to turn over information about al-Qaeda and his associate in the Los Angeles airport plot, Mokhtar Haouari. In return, Ressam had his sentence reduced to 27 years.[130]

Fateh Kamel

Fateh Kamel was a French Algerian involved with the GIA who had fought in Afghanistan and had also fought and been wounded in the jihad in Bosnia. Kamel had moved to Montreal in 1988, married a Canadian woman who worked for a suburban school system, became a naturalized Canadian citizen, and opened his own arts and crafts business. This, however, was not Kamel's only business. In Canada, Kamel made money on the side by procuring documents (passports, credit cards, etc.) for al-Qaeda terrorists. Among those whom Kamel purchased identification from was Ahmed Ressam, who sold identification to Kamel that he had stolen from Canadian citizens. Kamel eventually made his way to Jordan, where he was arrested by Jordanian authorities on suspicion of terrorism and extradited to France for trial.[131]

Abderraouf Hannachi

Abderraouf Hannachi is a Canadian Muslim associated with the same Montreal mosque that was attended by Ahmed Ressam. Hannachi claims to have trained with Osama bin Laden in Afghanistan and learned about explosives and rocket-propelled grenades. Hannachi worked as a recruit for Osama bin Laden in Afghanistan and helped coordinate the entry of recruits into the Afghan jihad. In late 1996, Hannachi helped facilitate the travel of Ahmed Ressam to Afghanistan for training in an al-Qaeda terrorist camp.[132]

The Converts and Exports

Converts to Islam can be expected to be important players in the Western political landscape in the future because there is a tendency toward zealotry among converts in virtually any religion, and Islam should be no exception. In the words of Mickelthwait and Wooldridge, "The more that people choose their religion, rather than just inherit it, the more likely they are to make a noise about it."[133] That said, conversion to Islam among Western citizens is on the rise (in France, for example, 50,000 persons convert to Islam annually) and with the rise in conversions a disturbing trend has developed in the form of a rise of radical Islamism among converts to Islam in the West. "A second disturbing trend has developed concurrently in an increase in the export of jihad from Islamists in the West back to Islamic countries, including the participation of converts.[134] Converts also present another problem in that they know the culture and consequently can more easily maintain their cover. In August 2003 this problem was confirmed by al-Qaeda member Abu-Muham-mad al-Abaj in *Al Majalla* magazine, where he claimed that al-Qaeda had attracted "blue-eyed members" who conceal their Islamist leanings and are "all over U.S. institutions."[135] Similarly, an Islamist calling himself Rakan Bin Williams stated in the *Al-Sharq Al-Awsat* newspaper in 2005 that

> Al-Qaeda's new soldiers were born in Europe of European and Christian parents. They studied in your schools. They prayed in your churches and attended Sunday Mass…. They are currently roaming the streets of Europe and the United States planning and observing in preparation for upcoming attacks.[136]

Converts also present Western countries with a further problem in that they cannot merely be deported to their countries of origin as can resident aliens.[137]

Studies of converts reveal that they typically have a background that is unrelated to Middle East conflicts, colonialism, or radical madrassas. Instead, it appears that most have little Islamic education, and many are middle-class Westerners with science backgrounds, though a good number of Western converts to Islamism, including Richard Reid and Jose Padilla, were directionless working-class dropouts and thus fit the pattern of "rebels" who found a "cause."[138] Padilla (Latino) and Reid (Caribbean), along with Germaine Lindsay (Caribbean who participated in the London bombings), were also all members of ethnic minority groups.[139]

In 2005, a study by the French Security services of 610 French converts to Islam, 49 percent had no college education and only 20 percent were students or attending college. Furthermore, unemployment among the converts was more than five times the rate of the general population.[140]

Similar to the factors that spawned the black Muslim movement in the

United States in the 1960s, it appears that many minorities are attracted to Islam because Christianity is viewed by some as a "white man's religion." Perhaps as a consequence, an estimated 60 percent of the members of the radical Brixton mosque in the UK are black converts of Caribbean origin. One Islamist convert at the mosque, Sheikh Abdullah Faisal, distributed racially provocative cassettes and DVDs with titles such as *The Devil's Deception of the 21st Century House Niggers*.[141] The danger of such a message is obvious since London bomber Germaine Lindsay is believed to have been influenced by Faisal's rantings.[142]

In the cases of young, disaffected minorities, the causes of their radicalism may be linked to the same sociological factors that have been linked to other forms of radicalism, violence, and gang activities among young Western low-income ethnic minorities for decades. For some, conversion appears to be a cultural fashion statement, complete with Islamic rap songs that rail against Islamophobia. Conversion in some cases has become intertwined with gang culture and is sometimes used by the converts to justify their criminal activity.[143]

Others may convert to Islamism simply out of a need for group acceptance. In such cases, the mosque often becomes the new family to the new convert and the old family is shunned. German Islamist Thomas Fischer, for instance, who died in Chechnya in 2002, reportedly had no friends at age 14 when he was converted by a Turkish man from his local mosque. The mosque and his new religious brothers then became his primary social group.[144] Similarly, Richard Reid was described not only as a person from a low-income household, but also as a "loner" who was "never one of the crowd." It was while incarcerated for 24 robberies and 22 thefts at Feltham Young Offender Institution that Reid converted to Islam. After his release, his aunt explained, his brothers at the mosque became his "family."[145] Similarly, British Islamist Wayne Derby, who was brought to Islam by Al-Muhajiroun, stated, "I was drinking alcohol, lack of work, lack of family around me, didn't have no family. Now I've got one billion point ... so many brothers around me. I couldn't ask for a bigger family."[146]

The pattern of conversion tends to be often associated with one radical mosque and one particular radical imam. The Caribbean converts at the Brixton mosque clearly fit this pattern. In this, Islamist conversion appears to fit the same pattern that produces Islamization among other Muslims. In either case, the Islamists tend to uproot themselves from society and live separately from it as a close-knit group while living within the greater society.[147]

The Muslim conversion pattern also appears to mirror the conversion patterns of Western fundamentalist Protestants. Islamists typically stress not worldly victories but the otherworldly victories of salvation and a looming day of judgment. Rewards should not be expected on earth, but in heaven, and the return to God begins with individual self-discipline and submission to God. In the words of one Islamist sheikh (al-Albani), "establish Islam first in your heart, then society can become Islamic."[148]

Finally, since the collapse of the Soviet Union and the communist bloc, Islam arguably has been the only legitimate challenge to Western culture. In some cases, conversion has served as a means to protest and combat Western policies. One jihadist that fits this profile is French convert Lionel Dumont, who served in a French peace-keeping force in the Horn of Africa and returned to France embittered against Western policies in the region. Dumont then put his disaffection into action by joining the jihad in Bosnia. After his arrest, Dumont described the Bosnian conflict for him as a "humanitarian war."[149]

Exports

Unfortunately, a recent disturbing trend among converts and Western-born Muslims has been the export of Islamic radicalism from Western countries to local conflicts in the Islamic realm. For example, Scotland Yard estimates that as many as 3,000 British citizens have trained in al-Qaeda training camps. British Muslims have fought in Bosnia, Chechnya, and Afghanistan, and seven British Muslims were interned at Guantanamo Bay after being captured by the U.S. in Afghanistan during the U.S.-led campaign against the Taliban.[150] In 2003, a British Muslim was captured in Iraq while fighting for Ansar al-Islam, an Iraqi-based al-Qaeda group.[151] Hundreds of British Muslims, most of South Asian descent, have also journeyed to Kashmir to wage jihad against the Indian army. Specific examples are legion. Mohammed Bilal, a young Muslim from Birmingham, England, blew himself up in a car outside an Indian army barracks in Kashmir, killing several Indian soldiers and Muslim Kashmiri students. Ahmed Omar Saeed Sheikh, a British-born graduate of the London School of Economics, was arrested in Kashmir for his role in several kidnappings in 1994. In 2002, he was sentenced to death for his role in the kidnapping and slaying of American journalist Daniel Pearl.[152]

The Western export of jihad, however, is in no way limited to the UK. For instance, it is estimated that in the 1990s between 1,000 and 2,000 American Muslims fought in jihadi causes in Bosnia, Chechnya, and Afghanistan. French Muslims have been actively involved in jihadist causes in Algeria and Morocco. Two French converts, Joseph Jaime and David Vallat, were sentenced to prison in France in 1997 for providing support to the Algerian

GIA.[153] German Muslims of Turkish origin played significant roles in the Bosnian conflict in the 1990s.[154] In 2005, a Belgian woman, Muriel Degauque, journeyed to Iraq and blew herself to bits in a suicide bombing.[155] Profiles of some of the more significant converts and exports are presented below.

Christopher Caze

Among the most famous radical Islamist converts in the West is a young Frenchman named Christopher Caze, a former medical student, raised Catholic, who travelled to Bosnia to work as a hospital medic in the 1990s and returned to France as a radical Islamist. While in Bosnia, Caze apparently converted to a radical form of Islam and joined the Muslim jihad against the Serbs. The extreme nature of Caze's conversion is attested to by reports that while in Bosnia, Caze enjoyed playing soccer with the severed heads of Serbian fighters.[156] Upon his return to France, Caze became a leader of a GIA group based in Roubaix, France, that made their living by robbing banks, armored cars, and supermarkets, and using masks, machine guns, and grenade launchers. In March 1996, Caze's group attempted to assassinate the leaders of the free world with a car bomb at a G7 meeting in Lille, France. French police discovered the bomb and killed four of Caze's gang in a gun battle at a Lille apartment. Caze escaped, only to be gunned down be French police the next day as he attempted to run a police roadblock in his car.[157]

Asif Mohammed Hanif and Omar Khan Sharif

Asif Mohammed Hanif and Omar Khan Sharif were both British citizens who were raised and educated in the UK. Sharif enjoyed an upper-middle-class lifestyle in Britain and attended the prestigious Repton Preparatory School, an expensive public institution whose list of graduates includes children's writer Roald Dahl, playwright Christopher Isherwood, and Lord Ramsey, the archbishop of Canterbury. Hanif lived in Hounslow near the Heathrow Airport, was known to be an avid cricket fan, and attended business classes at Cranford Community College, where he was described by the headmaster as a "model pupil." In the late 1990s, Hanif and Sharif attended radical Islamist instructions hosted by the radical group al Muhajiroun. Some of the instructions were from the leader of al Muhajiroun, Omar Bakri Mohammed himself. Both Hanif and Sharif became active in al Muhajiroun activities and Sharif took part in distributing al Muhajiroun leaflets in the British city of Derby.[158]

In April 2003, Hanif and Sharif attempted to bomb a bar near the U.S.

embassy in Tel Aviv with explosives hidden in copies of the Koran. Sharif's bomb failed to go off, but Hanif's bomb detonated, killing three and injuring 35. Hanif died in the blast and Sharif's body was found floating in the water-front near the bar twelve days later.[159]

John Walker Lindh

John Walker Lindh, commonly known as the American Taliban, was the 20-year-old son of a California lawyer and former U.S. Justice Department employee. Lindh was known as a good student with an affinity for basketball and hip hop music when he converted to Islam at age 16 after reading a biography of Malcolm X. Soon after, Lindh unofficially changed his name to Sulayman, began wearing a long white robe and turban and quit listening to Western music. Lindh travelled to Yemen in 1998 to learn Arabic, and subsequently returned to California before he departed for Yemen again in February 2000. Lindh then journeyed to Pakistan to enroll at a madrassa, but once there, he also joined a paramilitary training camp run by Kashmiri militants. Evidently, Lindh came into contact with the Taliban at the camp and decided to join, thus becoming an American Taliban and jihadist export to a Muslim country. Lindh explained to a *Newsweek* reporter that he joined the Taliban to help the Islamic government because the Taliban was the only government that actually provided Islamic law. While in Afghanistan, Lindh trained in an al-Qaeda training camp called Al Farooq that was funded by Osama bin Laden, and Lindh may even have met bin Laden personally, though he claimed that he had not ever heard of al-Qaeda, and he found a speech given by bin Laden at the camp to be "boring," and he fell asleep.[160] At the Al Farooq camp, however, it is believed that Lindh was given only Taliban military training to fight the Northern Alliance rather than al-Qaeda terrorist training, though Lindh did admit that he was asked by an Egyptian member of al-Qaeda if he would like to perform a martyrdom operation in the U.S. or Israel, but Lindh declined. Lindh also stated that he never had the occasion to use his rifle at his sentry post.[161] When questioned by Western media about his experience (that most assumed he would view as a mistake), Lindh stated that his experience was "exactly what I thought it would be" and that he was "definitely" fighting on the right side of the struggle.[162]

It should be noted, however, that at the time that Lindh arrived in Afghanistan in the summer of 2001, the United States under the incoming Bush administration had just announced a grant of $43 million to the Taliban government for the purpose of fighting the opium trade and the Bush administration did not yet view the Taliban as a hostile government in spite of their relations with Osama bin Laden. Instead, the State Department issued a press release in the spring of 2001 after announcing the $43 million grant where Secretary of State Colin Powell stated, "We will continue to look for ways to provide more assistance to the Afghans."[163]

By October of that same year, however, American bombs were falling on Afghanistan and Lindh's Taliban unit was captured by Northern Alliance troops in November. Video tape of Lindh's capture shows a starving, filthy, and neglected Lindh with a bum leg from a gunshot wound being kicked by a Northern Alliance commander and threatened with death by CIA officers if he did not talk (both violations of the Geneva Conventions).[164] Lindh, however, had no real intelligence value and later eschewed terrorism at his trial where he was not convicted of terrorism and conspiring to kill Americans as charged, but of supplying services to the Taliban. For these lesser charges, Lindh was sentenced to 20 years in prison.[165] The Lindh case was particularly disturbing to the American public at large because given that Lindh was white and middle class, it suggested that any convert to Islam, regardless of class, ethnicity, or background, was susceptible to Islamic extremism.[166] It appears that Lindh, however, never intended to fight against the United States, but instead joined the Sunni Taliban to fight against the Shiite Northern Alliance, a fact that was very well missed by the American public.

Jose Padilla

Jose Padilla is a U.S. citizen of Puerto Rican origin, born in Brooklyn and raised in Chicago, who was designated by President Bush as an "enemy combatant" and held without habeas corpus for allegedly planning to detonate a "dirty bomb" in the United States. Padilla was raised Roman Catholic, but converted to Islam after becoming involved in Chicago street gang activities in the 1980s.[167] In the late 1990s, Padilla allegedly had trained in Pakistan with explosives where he met with senior al-Qaeda leaders and discussed the dirty bomb plot. Padilla was arrested at Chicago's O'Hare Airport in May 2002 and shortly thereafter turned over to the Department of Defense, who placed him in a military brig in Charleston. Padilla was considered an important enough prisoner by the Bush administration at one time that he merited a visit and interrogation from Bush's legal team that included the president's counsel, Alberto Gonzalez; the vice president's counsel, David Addington; and Secretary of Defense Donald Rumsfeld's chief counsel, William J. "Jim" Haynes II.[168] Padilla was held incommunicado and in solitary confinement from the time of his arrest in May 2002 until his case made it to the Second Circuit Court of Appeals in July 2003. During this time, Padilla was denied the right to see the evidence against him, denied the right to discuss it with counsel, and denied the right to challenge his detention in court.[169] In November 2005, Padilla was indicted for "aiding terrorists and conspiracy to murder U.S. nationals overseas," but the long-sought indictment made no mention of the "dirty bomb" plan.[170] In August 2007 a federal jury found him guilty of conspiracy to murder, kidnap and maim overseas, of conspiracy to provide material support for terrorists, and of providing material support to terrorists. He was sentenced to 17 years and four months in prison.

Richard Reid

Richard Reid is the British-born son of a Jamaican father and English mother from the generally low-crime, middle-class London suburb of Bromley. Reid's father spent most of Reid's childhood in prison and son Richard was imprisoned in the 1990s for a string of muggings. Fitting a pattern that has become familiar, it was in prison that Reid converted to Islam. After his release, Reid became associated with Islamists, perhaps including Zacarias Moussaoui, at the Brixton Mosque in south London. Reid changed from wearing Western-style clothes to traditional Islamic garb. In 1998, Reid departed from London and spent time in Pakistan, Egypt, Israel, Turkey, Belgium, the Netherlands, France, and possibly Afghanistan. During this time he evidently learned to construct the shoe bomb that he attempted to detonate in December 2001 on a flight from Paris to Miami. Reid was overpowered by passengers and crew after attempting to light a fuse connected to the explosives. A computer captured by American authorities in Afghanistan connected Reid's plot to al-Qaeda and he was quickly charged in the United States with international terrorism along with attempted murder.[171]

In 2003, Reid was convicted on terrorism charges in federal court. During the proceedings he stated that he was an Islamic fundamentalist and enemy of the United States in league with al-Qaeda and Osama bin Laden. Reid was sentenced to life imprisonment and fines in excess of $7 million.[172]

Raed Hijazi

Raed Hijazi is a former Boston taxi driver and U.S. citizen who was arrested (along with 16 others) and is facing execution in Jordan for his role in the millennium plot to blow up the 400-room Radisson Hotel in Amman, Jordan, on January 1, 2000. Hijazi had also planned to bomb the border crossings from Jordan into Israel along with two Christian holy sites at times when the locations were likely to be crowded with Western tourists. For the millennium plot, Hijazi accumulated 5200 pounds of nitric acid that he stored in a basement dug by his co-conspirators underneath a rented house.[173]

Hijazi was born in San Jose, California, to a wealthy family of Palestinian origin and grew up travelling frequently between the United States and the Middle East. In 1986, he enrolled at California State University in Sacramento to study business administration. Evidently, it was at this American university that Hijazi met a radical cleric that convinced him to travel to Afghanistan and join the jihad against the Soviet Union. In the late 1990s, Hijazi returned to the United States and used his job with a Boston cab company to raise money for his eventual jihad overseas. According to Jordanian prosecutors, Hjazi sent over $13,000 to a Jordanian terror cell.[174]

American Jihadist: Nidal Malik Hasan

On November 5, 2009, U.S. Army Major Nidal Malik Hasan, a Virginia-born Muslim of Jordanian descent, committed the worst mass murder on an American military base in U.S. history when he opened fire on his fellow soldiers at Fort Hood in Killeen, Texas, killing twelve people and wounding 31. At this writing, the military investigation into the incident has not been concluded, but early evidence suggests that Hasan's Islamist views may have provided his motivation for the shooting rampage. Hasan was reported to be upset about his pending deployment to Iraq where the U.S. Army had been killing Muslims for six years.[175] Two years earlier, Hasan had argued in a slide presentation at the Walter Reed Army Medical Center that Muslims in the army should be able to claim conscientious objector status when their deployment would require them to kill Muslims in a war. In the same presentation, Hasan stated, "It's getting harder and harder for Muslims in the service to morally justify being in a military that seems constantly engaged against fellow Muslims." Hasan further added, "Muslim soldiers should not serve in any capacity that renders them at risk to hurting/killing believers unjustly."[176] One of Hasan's classmates in medical school, Dr. Val Finnell, stated that Hasan "equated the war against terror with a war against Islam."[177] Six months prior to the incident, Hasan came under investigation by the Department of Defense's Criminal Investigative Services assigned to the Joint Terrorism Task Force for his communications online with Islamist cleric Anwar al-Awlaki. Ultimately, however, the investigation was halted.[178] Hasan had evidently posted items on the internet where he discussed the possibilities of committing suicide bombings and other horrific acts of violence.[179]

Major Hasan was an army psychiatrist who had practiced medicine for six years at the Walter Reed Army Medical Center in Washington where his training included a fellowship in disaster and preventive psychiatry. He had been promoted to the rank of major just six months earlier, but told his family that he wanted out of the military after being informed that he was to be deployed to a predominantly Muslim country in Iraq or Afghanistan.[180]

Although at this writing Hasan has not made a statement since the shooting rampage, currently the evidence is suggestive that Hasan's thought processes are very consistent with those of Osama bin Laden, who declared war on America in retaliation for the deaths of Muslims at the hands of American soldiers in the Middle East and the presence of American troops in what he viewed as the "Holy Land." Given that Hasan was born and raised in America, his case is one more reminder that the immersion of Muslims into Western culture is not a cure-all for the dangers posed by radical Islam. Unsurprisingly, internet bloggers followed the Fort Hood tragedy by lighting up the web with Islamophobic writings highlighting this fact.

The Rest of the Boys

Hassan al-Turabi

Hassan al-Turabi, the man who was the Islamist head of state in Sudan that harbored bin Laden and al-Qaeda in the 1980s, was another example of a prominent Islamist that was well acquainted with the West. As a Sudanese college student and Koranic scholar, al-Turabi travelled throughout the United States in 1960, staying with ordinary American families. Al-Turabi received a master's degree in law from the London School of Economics in 1961 and a doctorate in law from the Sorbonne in Paris in 1964. Like Sayyid Qutb, however, al-Turabi's experience in the West only led him to denounce Western culture and Western capitalism in favor of Islamist revolution in his country of origin.[181] Al-Turabi returned to the Sudan and became a leader in the Sudanese Muslim Brotherhood in the early 1960s that later became known as the National Islamic Front (NIF) in the 1980s. Al-Turabi envisioned the creation of an international Muslim community with himself as its spiritual guide. Al-Turabi's group participated in Western-style parliamentary elections in the Sudan in the 1980s, a tactic that appears to be inconsistent with Qutb's condemnation of everything that is un–Islamic. Similarly, Al-Turabi himself condemned party politics as "a form of factionalism that can be very oppressive of individual freedom and divisive of the community, and it is, therefore, antithetical to a Muslim's ultimate responsibility to God."[182]

Al-Turabi reconciled his participation in parliamentary elections with his condemnation of party politics by calling for one-party rule from the NIF, thus justifying Islamists' participation in democratic party politics under the premise that it can be used as a means to the eventual righteous end of Islamic rule. Al-Turabi's party came in third in the 1986 Sudanese elections, but he proved that his commitment to Islam was much greater than his commitment to the democratic process when his party effectively seized power in a military coup in 1989. From behind the scenes, the NIF then imposed an Islamic police state dedicated to imposing sharia in the Sudan, complete with amputations, summary executions, and wholesale slaughter of their political opposition.[183]

Once in power, al-Turabi opened the doors of the Sudan to any Muslim, regardless of nationality, with no questions asked, in an effort to unite all Muslims in the global ummah. Often, those who heeded al-Turabi's invitation were radical Islamists, such as Osama bin Laden, who were unwanted elsewhere.[184] In 1991, al-Turabi placed his regime at odds with the American government when he established the popular Arab Islamic conference for the purpose of opposing the American involvement in the 1991 Persian Gulf War.[185] Al-Turabi has also alienated other Islamists, however, by advocating the reconciliation of the ancient breach between Shiites and Sunnis and by advocating women's rights, including the idea that women could vote, counsel men and lead prayer.[186] At this writing, the political winds in the Sudan have changed and al-Turabi is imprisoned in Khartoum. From prison, however, al-Turabi has continued his reformist approach, arguing that "intelligent mujahideen must exercise restraint and refrain from initiating war and must limit operations to military, not civilian targets."[187] Apparently, the man who once notoriously harbored Osama bin Laden now objects to bin Laden's tactics. That being the case, al-Turabi's change of heart provides a ray of hope since it suggests that even the most hardened Islamists can change their political perspectives.

Musa Kousa: Lockerbie Bomber

Musa Kousa was the Libyan ambassador to the United Kingdom in the 1980s who is generally believed to have been involved in the planning of the bombing of the Pan Am flight over Lockerbie, Scotland, in 1988. Kousa was also involved in the bombing of a French airliner, UTA 772, over Niger in 1989, killing 170.[188] Prior to his career in the Libyan government of Moammar Qaddafi, however, Kousa had been a student at Michigan State University where he received a master's degree in sociology in the 1970s. By 1980, Kousa worked for the Libyan government in London as head of the Libyan Mission, essentially Qaddafi's ambassador to London. While working in that capacity,

Kousa informed a reporter for *The Times of London* that Libya financially supported the IRA, and that two Libyan opponents of Qaddafi living in London would be killed. Soon afterwards, two Libyans were found dead in London and Kousa was expelled from the U.K.[189]

After 9/11, Libyan leader Moammar Qaddafi and other prominent Libyans desired to get themselves off of the list of states that sponsor terrorism and enjoy all the benefits that accompany a return to the world community. Consequently, Qaddafi returned Kousa to the U.K. in 2001 with names and locations of Islamic terrorists in Europe, North Africa, and the Middle East that Kousa turned over to Western intelligence. Among the names turned over by Kousa was that of Ibn al-Sheikh al-Libi, who became the first major American capture in President Bush's War on Terror.[190] The U.S. then delivered al-Libi to Egypt, a country not known for being squeamish about torturing people, for "interrogation."[191]

Mir Amal Kasi

A month before the first World Trade Center bombing in 1993, Mir Amal Kasi, who received a master's degree in English literature from Baluchistan University (Pakistan) in 1989, shot and killed two CIA employees who were waiting in their cars to enter the gates at CIA headquarters. Kasi had been convinced that the CIA was responsible for the deaths of thousands of Muslims worldwide, and he viewed his act as justified due to Muslim deaths at the hands of the CIA.[192] Kasi was later apprehended in 1997 by Afghan agents working for the CIA in Afghanistan.[193]

Yazid Sufaat

An associate of Riduan Isamuddin, also known as Hambali, the leader of Jemaah Islamiyah, the affiliate of al-Qaeda in Southeast Asia. Sufaat was an al-Qaeda biological weapons man who had a degree in chemistry and laboratory science from California State University in Sacramento. Sufaat was picked up by Malaysian police in December 2001 and handed over to American authorities in late 2002 for questioning.[194]

Trends and Tendencies

From this review of the Western Islamists themselves, it is evident that a good number of patterns are emerging among Western Islamists. First, the

Islamists operate globally, travel widely, and are not limited to any particular country or territory. The 9/11 hijackers well exemplify this "deterritorialization" in that they were generally schooled in the West, yet trained in their terrorist arts in Afghanistan and connected to al-Qaeda in both South Asia and the Middle East. The bombers hatched the 9/11 plot in Germany, met in Spain, and conducted attacks on the United States with international funding from al-Qaeda. Second, many of the Western Islamists, such as the Madrid bombers, are Western citizens and some were even born and educated (often with education in technological fields) in Western countries. Many of the Western Islamists, such as Fateh Kamel, are married to Western women and therefore did not follow Islamic traditions of arranged marriages and marrying cousins. One European Islamist, Kamel Daoudi, even met his Hungarian wife through the Internet.[195] Third, the jihad by Western Muslims is now being waged not only in Western countries; some Western Islamists, such as Redouane Hammadi and Stephane Ait Idir, are exporting jihad from Western countries back to locations within the Islamic realm. Fourth, much of the Islamism in the West appears to be connected to the political situations in the larger Islamic world. Some of the unrest stemming from radical Islam in France is connected to Islamism in Algeria and the Algerian GIA. The Madrid bombers were apparently sympathetic to the Islamist movement in Morocco, and Islamism in the UK is often connected to the political unrest in Pakistan and Afghanistan. Finally, Western converts to Islam, such as John Walker Lindh, Richard Reid and Jose Padilla, are now playing roles in the global jihad.

CHAPTER 9

Western Freedoms and Jihad

Perhaps inevitably, the allegiance that Islamists display toward their religion and the horrific acts of terrorism that have occurred worldwide over the last several decades have caused many Westerners to consider rethinking Western liberalism and the Western conceptions of civil rights. Jihadists have clearly taken advantage of Western freedoms of speech, religion, and traditions of asylum not only to obtain transport and residency in the West, but also to protect themselves against detection and prosecution for terrorist conspiracies and other radical activities. For instance, the first words uttered by one Islamist captured after an attempted suicide bombing in London were, "I know my rights."[1] Similarly, numerous Islamists who find themselves at odds with the political authorities in their countries of origin attempt to solve their problems by seeking asylum in the infidel West. Even West-hating Osama bin Laden sought asylum in Britain following his expulsion from the Sudan in the 1990s.[2]

Meanwhile, radical Muslims publish their Islamist propaganda under the cover of the Western protections of free press. For example, the Egyptian Islamist group Gamaa Islamiya set up a headquarters in Copenhagen rather than in Egypt, whereas the Algerian Armed Islamic Group (GIA), a group that has killed thousands in Algeria in an extended campaign against the government since a cancelled election in 1991, published its propaganda newspaper, *Al-Ansar*, in Stockholm and London rather than Algeria. *Al-Ansar* has featured headlines such as, "Thank God, We Have Cut 200 Throats Today!" and "Our Brother Beheaded His Father for the Sake of Allah."[3] Such a publication could easily be shut down by the authoritarian states of Algeria and Egypt, but a more favorable climate for publication is found in the free and open societies of the West. The irony that these Islamist publications are only free to spew their venom in the societies that they denounce continually is evidently lost on the publications' sponsors and readers.

In the United Kingdom, asylum was granted to so many militants from all over the world that militants declared Britain a sanctuary where no acts of terrorism were to be committed. In particular, an Egyptian Islamist group known as Talai al-Fath (the Vanguard of Conquest) set up its operations in London.[4] The London bombings of July 2005, however, are proof that some militants no longer consider Britain to be off limits to terrorism, thus leading to changes in British policy.

The statement "I know my rights," echoed by an Islamist suicide bomber under arrest reveals that the would-be terrorist in this case had become to some degree Westernized or he would not have made such a claim, though he also seems to be oblivious to the fact that a basic premise of rights in the Western world is the "right to life," which would be very much precluded by successful detonation of his suicide bomb. As a result, some Western countries, and especially the United States under the Bush administration, have begun to erode traditional protections against search and seizure, torture, speedy and public trials, and a whole host of privacy and criminal rights normally present in Western societies.[5]

The British had promoted a multicultural model, but more recently has moved away from the multiculturalist model because it tends to promote separateness rather than integration.[6] Unfortunately, the integrationist model has not eliminated terrorism and disharmony in France, so one should perhaps not expect the changes in the British approach to immediately produce more harmonious results.

Jihad and Rights in the United States

After the terror attacks of 9/11, American president George W. Bush announced the beginning of a war on terror that eventually included invasions of both Afghanistan and Iraq, with the stated purpose of bringing "freedom and democracy" to both lands. Similar to numerous other American presidents before him who launched military campaigns for "noble causes" while simultaneously limiting the rights of Americans at home, President Bush's actions during the War on Terror have had a profound impact on American civil rights. Whether that impact is permanent or merely temporary (as has been the case with his predecessors) remains to be seen.

Winston Churchill once proclaimed,

> The power of the executive to cast a man into prison without formulating any charge known to the law, and particularly to deny him the judgment of his peers, is in the highest degree odious, and the foundation of all totalitarian government whether Nazi or Communist.[7]

Unfortunately, American history is replete with executives doing exactly that. In 1798, Congress under John Adams passed the Alien and Sedition Acts that led to the imprisonment of Adams' political opponents for criticism against his government during America's "quasi-war" with France. Similarly, during the Civil War, President Abraham Lincoln suspended habeas corpus and imprisoned critics of his government, including a former Congressman. In 1917, Woodrow Wilson asked Congress for a declaration of war against Germany to "make the world safe for democracy." Simultaneously, Wilson and the American Congress made dissent illegal and cast those that criticized Wilson's war effort into prison. Similarly, in 1941, Franklin Roosevelt called for war against the Axis for the purpose of creating a world of four fundamental freedoms: freedom of speech, freedom of religion, freedom from want, and freedom from fear. Unfortunately, Roosevelt then famously signed an Executive Order that interned Japanese Americans on the west coast into concentration camps for the duration of the war. During the first presidency of the new millennium, George W. Bush also launched war for the purpose of "making the world safe for democracy" and securing "freedom from fear." In the process, however, much like his predecessors before him, the actions of Bush's executive branch during the time of war were such that freedom of speech and religion, and freedom from want, as well as American criminal rights protections, were significantly compromised in a manner similar to the threats to liberties that occurred during World War II, World War I, the Civil War, and the "quasi-war" with France during the John Adams administration.

The narrowing of individual rights under the Bush administration is based largely on the perceived need for tightened security following the terrorist attacks of 9/11, but also consistent with the traditional conservative ideological preference for order over freedom. Unfortunately, however, the limitations on liberties have been largely inconsistent with most scholarly conceptions of the democracy and freedom that Bush's administration was theoretically fighting for.

Search and Seizures

Most notorious among Bush's civil rights innovations is a controversial piece of congressional legislation known as the USA 1. Under this Act, the federal government was granted the authority to develop a project to promote "total information awareness." Under this program, the federal government gained the authority to obtain all sorts of information on American citizens without probable cause. This includes the authority of the federal government to monitor religious and political institutions and organizations, certainly including mosques and other Islamic organizations (again, the government does not have to show probable cause), perhaps violating First Amendment free exercise and assembly rights as well as criminal due process protections. Evidently, the purpose behind the act is to allow the federal government the authority to eavesdrop on mosques and other Islamic organizations in order to snoop for terrorist activity. Federal authorities even have the authority to secretly enter homes without warning and wait for months before informing residents that they were there. Federal agents involved in such investigations can receive warrants for searches by merely stating that something in a house they have secretly searched without a warrant might have some connection to the investigation of some agent of a foreign power. Warrants are then granted from secret courts that are structured so that warrants are almost never denied.[8] Under the USA PATRIOT Act, the federal government has the authority to monitor every web site that anyone in the U.S. visits on the internet, keep lists of all emails, monitor phone calls, and read all mail, search all library records for books checked out by suspects, and attend all public meetings, all without warrants from courts.[9]

The result, however, obviously violates long-standing legal traditions protecting Americans against government infringement on their personal lives without probable cause. Numerous violations of the rights of ordinary Americans with no connections to terrorism, however, have already occurred. In one instance, 20 peace activists, including nuns and high school students, were detained as security risks for saying that they were traveling to a rally to protest against U.S. military aid to Colombia. Furthermore, the entire high school wrestling team from Juneau, Alaska, was held up at airports seven times because one member was the son of a retired Coast Guard officer on the FBI watch list.[10]

Detention and Secrecy

The PATRIOT Act also made life difficult for immigrants to the U.S. and political refugees. John Ashcroft's Justice Department quickly arrested and detained over 1200 persons of Arab descent and detained them for varying lengths of time, cleared them all, but never released the names of those detained, the reasons for their detention, or their actual locations.[11] According to James Reynolds, the chief of the Terrorism and Violent Crime Section in the Criminal Division of the Justice Department,

> releasing the names of the detainees who may be associated with terrorism and their place and date of arrest would reveal the direction and progress of the investigations by identifying where DOJ is focusing its efforts. In effect, it would allow terrorist organizations to map the progress of the investigation and thereby develop the means to impede them. Even disclosing the identities of those

detainees who have been released may reveal details about the focus and scope of the investigation and thereby allow terrorists to counteract it.... The rationale that underlies the withholding of the names of the detainees similarly supports the nondisclosure of their lawyers' identities.... Release of such a list may facilitate the identification of the detainees themselves and the harms described above could ensue.[12]

Such secrecy obviously opens the door to abuse. In one particular case, Anser Mehmood, a citizen of Pakistan who had overstayed his visa, claims he was arrested on October 3, 2001, shackled in handcuffs, leg irons, and a belly chain, thrown against a wall, and denied even a phone call for two weeks. Mehmood was then allegedly kept in solitary confinement for months, charged with using an invalid Social Security card, and deported eight months after his arrest.[13]

The number of political refugees coming to the United States declined 70 percent between 2001 and 2003 due to tighter immigration restrictions. To make matters worse, at this juncture, hundreds of persons are still being held in prison at the U.S. naval base at Guantanamo Bay, Cuba, without being formally charged of anything. Of those detained there at one time or another, three were children (the youngest age 13), several were over 70, and one claimed to be over 100. The detainees have been denied the rights of habeas corpus, the rights to speedy and public trials, the rights to counsel, and perhaps, protections against cruel and unusual punishment. The extent that these limitations deviate from the norm is perhaps underlined by the fact that in the case of *Rasul v. Bush*, Shafiq Rasul, a prisoner at Guantanamo Bay, is the first person in more than 150 years of American law that was not informed that litigation was underway on his behalf.[14] The Bush administration essentially suspended the right to counsel for detainees under the pretense that seeing a lawyer would somehow disrupt the government's interrogation of its prisoners and therefore endanger national security. Thus, detainees cannot consult attorneys until interrogation, which could last for years, is complete.[15]

Torture and Abuse

September 17, 2001, President Bush issued a fourteen-page directive to the CIA ordering the agency to hunt, capture, imprison, and interrogate terrorism suspects around the world. Bush's directive set no limits on what the CIA could do in the War on Terror. The direction laid the foundation for a system of secret prisons where CIA officers and private contractors working for the CIA could use harsh interrogation techniques, including torture. The torture itself ended up being severe, as evidenced by the conviction of one CIA contractor for beating an Afghan prisoner to death.[16]

President Bush's directive also gave the agency a new and extraordinary authority to turn kidnapped suspects over to foreign security services for interrogation and to rely on the confessions that were extracted under torture.[17] Under Bush's directive, the CIA began to function as a global anti-terrorism police force and hundreds of suspects were abducted and thrown into secret CIA prisons in Afghanistan, Thailand, Poland, and Guantanamo Bay, Cuba. Hundreds more were handed off to the intelligence services of Egypt, Pakistan, Jordan, and Syria for "enhanced interrogation."[18] According to former CIA director George Tenet, the CIA abducted and detained more than 3,000 people after 9/11, but as few as fourteen people among the 3,000 were high-ranking figures within al-Qaeda and its affiliates.[19]

In March 2008, Congress attempted to end the torture of terror suspects by the United States and passed a bill that would have eliminated coercive interrogations, including waterboarding. President Bush, however, vetoed the measure, claiming that such coercive interrogation techniques had been effective in helping prevent further terrorist attacks on the United States. Bush's presidential successor, Barack Obama, has promised to close Guantanamo Bay, but at this writing, the facility remains open.[20]

Islam, Guantanamo Bay, and Civil Liberties

Guantanamo Bay

Among the actions of the Bush administration that spurred the most resentment among American Muslims (as well as those around the world) was the detention of as many as 6,000 Muslims at Guantanamo Bay, Cuba (and other secret American prisons throughout the world), without charges and without rights under either the U.S. Constitution or international law. Camp Delta at Guantanamo Bay alone has housed over 800 prisoners from more than 40 countries.[21] Although the Bush administration claimed, and many Americans believed, that the detention facilities were packed with the world's most dangerous terrorists, Major General Michael Dunlavey arrived in Guantanamo Bay in February 2002 for the interrogation of high-level terrorists only to discover that as many as half of the prisoners at the base had little or no intelligence value.[22] Dunlavey then departed for Afghanistan where he complained to his superiors that there were too many "Mickey Mouse" prisoners being sent to the base. General Dunlavey also later stated that some of the prisoners at the base were "older than dirt."[23] Commanders in Afghanistan admitted to the problem, but explained that they had nowhere else to send suspects.[24]

In March 2002, Lieutenant Colonel Bill Cline, the deputy camp commander at Guantanamo Bay at the time, reported that a good number of the prisoners were innocent "victims of circumstance" who had simply been in the wrong place at the wrong time. Evidently, dozens of prisoners described in classified intelligence reports as farmers, cab drivers, etc., were shipped to the prison though there was no evidence they were involved in terrorism. One prisoner arrived at Guantanamo with a severe head wound and was nicknamed "half-head Bob" by the American soldiers at the base. Another prisoner, obviously insane, ate his own feces and drank his own urine. Americans at the base referred to him as "Wild Bill." Another prisoner, Faiz Muhammed, claimed to be 105 years old. The shrivelled, partially deaf old man was referred to by his interrogators as "Al-Qaeda Claus."[25] In August 2002, intelligence officials determined that there were "no big fish" among the six hundred prisoners then held in Guantanamo Bay.[26]

The "Mickey Mouse" nature of the prisoners at Guantanamo Bay appears to be a result of the way in which the prisoners were captured in the first place. Evidently, only about 5 percent of the prisoners at Guantanamo Bay were captured on the battlefield by the United States. The vast majority were instead captured by the Northern Alliance, Afghan tribal warlords, or Pakistani intelligence. The United States created an uncertain situation in the Afghan war by littering Afghanistan with leaflets offering to pay cash bounties of $5,000 for each member of the Taliban and $20,000 for each member of al-Qaeda.[27] The obvious conclusion is that many innocent people were essentially captured and turned over to the U.S. by their captors for the purpose of gaining the American-paid bounties. State Department intelligence official Pierre Richard Prosper summed up the situation thusly, "We thought the detainees were all masterminds.... It wasn't the case. Most of them were just dirt farmers from Afghanistan."[28] Lieutenant Colonel Thomas Berg, who was part of the original team set up by the Pentagon to work on military prosecutions at Guantanamo, echoed a similar sentiment by stating, "In many cases, we had simply gotten the slowest guys on the battlefield. We literally found guys who had been shot in the butt."[29]

American Muslims generally view Guantanamo Bay as evidence of how the United States has made the War on Terror into a war on Islam. The reports of torture and prisoner abuse, including as many as thirty-seven deaths, as well as the reports of flushing a Koran down the toilet, have become potent symbols to American Muslims (as well as for the global body of Muslim believers) of an anti–Muslim campaign by the government of the United States.[30]

Abrogation of the Geneva Conventions

According to President Bush, the detainees at Guantanamo Bay are "illegal enemy combatants" and the Geneva Conventions that prevent the abuse of prisoners of war do not apply. Bush's attorney general, Alberto Gonzalez, concurred with the president and wrote a memo on January 25, 2002, where he argued that the 9/11 attacks "renders obsolete Geneva's strict limitations on questioning of enemy prisoners and renders quaint some of its provisions."[31] The next month, President Bush issued an order that the prisoners captured during the War on Terror would not be protected by the Geneva Conventions.[32]

Members of President Bush's own administration disagreed with Bush's decision. Secretary of State Colin Powell informed the president that the United States had never denied the applicability of the 1949 Geneva Conventions. Powell argued that the junking the conventions would deprive the U.S. of the right to invoke the Conventions to protect American soldiers. Powell also warned the president that abandoning the Conventions would provoke widespread condemnation from America's allies and actually hinder the War on Terror by discouraging America's allies from cooperating with the U.S. Powell also argued that abandoning the Geneva Conventions would "undermine U.S. military culture" by introducing uncertainty, and that the U.S. abandonment of the Conventions would encourage other countries to do the same.[33]

William Howard Taft IV, the legal advisor to the State Department, also argued that abandoning the Conventions broke with established U.S. military practice and deprived American troops of claims to protections under the Conventions. The military lawyers with the Joint Chiefs of Staff also objected to the abandonment of the Conventions and argued that the president should treat all detainees as if the Conventions applied.[34]

The interpretation of the Geneva Conventions by Bush and Gonzalez is clearly incorrect from a legal standpoint. The Geneva IV (Civilian) Convention of 1949, signed by the U.S. after World War II with the maltreatment of civilians by belligerents during World War II freshly in mind, was intended to apply directly to civilians. The exact wording of the Convention is that it applies to all people "who, at a given moment and in any manner whatsoever, find themselves" in the custody of an enemy. The Convention protects people even if they have committed acts of violence and acted as "unlawful combatants." According to the commentary on the Convention prepared by the International Committee of the Red Cross,

> Every person in enemy hands must have some status under international law: he is either a prisoner of war and, as such, covered by the Third Convention, [or] a civilian covered by the Fourth Convention.... There is no intermediate status; nobody in enemy hands can fall outside the law.[35]

The United States signed this Convention in 1949, its provisions had been followed by the U.S. Army since that time until the War on Terror, and the U.S. had adhered without protest to the Geneva bans against violence to civilian life and person, cruel treatment and torture, outrages upon personal dignity, and humiliating and degrading treatment, all found in the Convention, until the directives from the Bush administration in conjunction with the War on Terror.[36]

Furthermore, the U.S. military has a long history of opposing the abuse of prisoners during wartime. For example, during the Filippino Rebellion in 1900, American military officer Major Edwin F. Glenn used what was known as a "water cure," forcing prisoners to ingest large amounts of water, as an interrogation technique. Glenn was court-martialed for his action, but in his defense he argued that his action had been a matter of urgent military necessity and that the insurgents did not comply with the laws of war. The judge advocate general at Glenn's court-martial rejected this argument, instead stating that the U.S. Army banned torture to extort confessions and he concluded that the "necessity" defense failed completely, "inasmuch as it is attempted to establish the principle that a belligerent who is at war with a savage or semicivilized enemy may conduct his operations in violation of the rules of civilized war. This no modern state will admit for an instant."[37]

Although there have been some aberrations, the U.S. has generally followed the rules of the Geneva Conventions ever since. For example, in World War II, the Conventions required that prisoners be provided the same living conditions as the soldiers who guarded them. When POWs arrived faster than the U.S. was able to construct barracks, the prisoners had to sleep in tents. Consequently, American POW camp commanders ordered their own troops to sleep in tents as well so as to be in compliance with the Conventions.[38] Similarly, General Douglas MacArthur directed the American forces under his command to abide by the "detailed provisions of the prisoner of war convention" during the Korean conflict.[39] The U.S. also followed the conventions during the Vietnam War where only one in six of those captured was actually a uniformed POW. In fact, in Vietnam every soldier was given a card that stated, "You must not mistreat your prisoner, humiliate or degrade him, take any of his personal effects which do not have significant military value, refuse him medical treatment if required and available."[40]

Torture as Policy

Nevertheless, U.S. attorney general Alberto Gonzalez in the summer of 2002 asked his colleagues John Yoo and Jay Bybee at the Office of Legal Counsel in the Justice Department whether U.S. agents (such as the CIA) were constrained by the 1994 torture statute passed by Congress and the UN Convention against Torture. In August 2002, Bybee and Yoo answered in their famous "torture memo" in which they defined torture as requiring excruciating or agonizing pain equivalent to the intensity of the pain accompanying serious injury, such as organ failure, impairment of bodily function, or death. To make matters worse, Yoo and Bybee argued that the defendant must show that the government had the "intent" to torture and that the torturers would be immune from prosecution if the torture itself were directed by the president. Yoo and Bybee further advised that the president is not answerable to Congress when acting in his role as commander-in-chief, and that the powers of the president as commander-in-chief override the Fourth Amendment protections against unreasonable search and seizure. In other words, when acting in his capacity as commander-in-chief, the president can ignore the Constitution. Yoo and Bybee's memo is so sweeping in its grant of power to the executive that it even allows the use of military force inside an American city to raid terrorist dwellings even when innocent third parties could be killed or injured by exchanges of fire.[41]

Evidently, the same types of tortures that were so graphically and publicly revealed to have been endured by Iraqi POWs in Abu Graib prison in Iraq were also applied to the detainees in Guantanamo Bay. This is in spite of the directions in the U.S. Army's own field manual (written in 1992 during the last year of the previous Bush administration) that not only prohibits torture, but states unequivocally that torture does not work. As stated in the manual,

> Experience indicates that the use of prohibited techniques is not necessary to gain the cooperation of interrogation sources. Use of torture and other illegal methods is a poor technique that yields unreliable results, may damage subsequent collection efforts, and can induce the source to say what he thinks the interrogator wants to here.... Revelations of the use of torture by U.S. personnel will bring discredit upon the U.S. and its armed forces while undermining domestic and international support for the war effort. It may also place U.S. and allied personnel in enemy hands at a greater risk of abuse by their captors.[42]

The field manual goes on to explain to American soldiers what is essentially the equivalent of the golden rule and instructs soldiers to ask the question,

"Would a reasonable person in the place of the person being interrogated believe that his rights, as guaranteed under both international and U.S. law, are being violated or withheld, or will be violated or withheld if he fails to cooperate?"[43] The same field manual goes on to explain that direct questioning is most effective and that statistics reveal that in World War II it was 90 percent effective. Furthermore, in Vietnam, Just Cause, and Desert Storm, direct questioning was 95 percent effective.[44] In contrast, the U.S. officially denounced confessions that the Japanese extracted from American aviators through torture during World War II.[45]

Nevertheless, when Brigadier General Rick Baccus, who was base commander at Guantanamo Bay, demanded that the prisoners be treated in a manner consistent with the Geneva Conventions, he found himself replaced by Major General Geoffrey Miller, a commander who had no prior experience running a detention facility, but who was committed to using his position to "produce actionable intelligence for the nation."[46] Under General Miller, prisoners could be subjected to solitary confinement for up to thirty days at a time, prisoners could be hooded during interrogations, which could last for up to twenty hours and include light deprivation and auditory stimuli. Prisoners could be stripped of all clothing and all items necessary for grooming, dogs could be used to induce stress, and prisoners could be put in stress positions for extended periods. To top it all off, prisoners could be subjected to what amounted to mock executions.[47] Defense Secretary Donald Rumsfeld approved of such tactics and even wrote in one memo, "I stand for 8–10 hours a day. Why is standing limited to 4 hours?"[48]

If, however, interrogators at Guantanamo Bay are unable to achieve the desired results, prisoners are evidently sent to other countries, such as Jordan or Egypt, that are less timid with their interrogation techniques.[49]

Reports of abuse at Guantanamo Bay have been legion. In December 2002, for instance, the chief psychologist for the Navy Criminal Investigative Service, Dr. Michael Gelles, reported "abusive techniques and coercive psychological procedures at Guantanamo Bay." Similarly, Alberto Mora, the Navy's general counsel, denounced the interrogation techniques as "unlawful and unworthy of military service."[50]

On July 14, 2004, T.J. Harrington, the deputy assistant director of the FBI Counterterrorism Division, wrote a letter to Major General Donald Ryder of the Army's Criminal Investigation Command, in which he advised Ryder of several incidents observed by FBI agents involving "highly aggressive interrogation techniques being used against detainees at Guantanamo." According to Harrington, an FBI agent observed an interrogation where the detainee was shackled and his hands were cuffed to his waist. The FBI agent,

Special Agent Clemente, observed a female soldier identified as Sergeant Lacey apparently

> whispering in the detainee's ear, and caressing and applying lotion to his arms (this was during Ramadan when physical contact with a woman would have been particularly offensive to a Muslim male). On more than one occasion the detainee appeared to be grimacing in pain, and Sergeant Lacey's hands appeared to be making some contact with the detainee. Although Special Agent Clemente could not see her hands at all times, he saw them moving towards the detainee's lap. He also observed the detainee pulling away and against the restraints. Subsequently, the marine who had previously taped the curtain (in the observation room) and had been in the interrogation room with sergeant Lacey during the interrogation re-entered the observation room. SA Clemente asked what had happened to cause the detainee to grimace in pain. The marine said Sergeant Lacey had grabbed the detainee's thumbs and bent them backwards and indicated that she also grabbed his genitals. The marine also implied that her treatment of that detainee was less harsh than her treatment of others by indicating that he had seen her treatment of other detainees result in detainees curling into a fetal position on the floor and crying in pain.[51]

Unfortunately, the above case was not the only incident of abuse observed by the FBI at Guantanamo Bay. In his letter to General Ryder, Harrington also discusses an incident in 2002 where FBI agents observed that

> a canine was used in an aggressive manner to intimidate detainee #63 and, in November 2002, FBI agents observed detainee #63 after he had been subjected to intense isolation for over three months. During that time period, #63 was totally isolated (with the exception of occasional interrogations) in a cell that was always flooded with light. By late November, the detainee was evidencing behavior consistent with extreme psychological trauma (talking to non-existent people, reporting hearing voices, crouching in a corner of the cell covered with a sheet for hours on end).[52]

According to *Time* magazine, detainee #63 was also forced to bark like a dog and growl at pictures of terrorists. During another interrogation, he had a leash tied to his neck and was forced to perform a series of dog tricks. Interrogators hung pictures of scantily clad women around his neck and taped a picture of a 9/11 victim on his pants. Another time, he was forced to wear a woman's bra and had a thong placed on his head. He was also told that his mother and sister were whores and he himself was a homosexual and that other prisoners detained at Guantanamo Bay knew of his homosexuality.[53] Unfortunately, these cases appear to be far from the worst. As of February 2006, at least ninety-eight prisoners had died in U.S. custody, and these may be merely the ones that the Bush administration admits have perished.[54] In such an atmosphere, if accurate news of what has really been going on in American detention centers becomes widespread, the potential perhaps exists for the ignition of Muslim hostility and violence within the United States similar to that experienced in recent years throughout Europe. To make matters worse, many American Muslims believe that they themselves have suffered some form of discrimination, abuse, or erosion of their rights since 9/11. Survey data suggest that almost 75 percent of American Muslims "either know someone or have themselves experienced an act of anti–Muslim discrimination, harassment, verbal abuse, or physical attack since September 11."[55]

In January 2003, Defense Secretary Donald Rumsfeld ordered a study of the Guantanamo Bay interrogation procedures as a response to domestic and international criticism. Rumsfeld's working group concluded that an interrogator had not committed a crime unless the pain or suffering was of such "high intensity that the pain is difficult for the subject to endure," but in any case, the Defense Department argued that the president's power as commander in chief renders the entire anti-torture statute irrelevant.[56] The conclusions of Rumsfeld's working group were in spite of the fact that Thomas Romig, the judge advocate general for the U.S. Army, concluded that the techniques used at Guantanamo Bay were unlikely to produce reliable intelligence, would endanger U.S. military personnel, and would destroy the POW safeguards the U.S. had worked hard to establish and protect since World War II.[57]

The international response to the American treatment of prisoners at Guantanamo Bay has been one of almost unanimous condemnation. The International Committee of the Red Cross termed the treatment of prisoners at Guantanamo Bay as "tantamount to torture."[58] Congress responded to public concerns concerning Guantanamo Bay in 2006 with the McCain Amendment, which specifically prohibits the "cruel, inhuman and degrading treatment" of prisoners in American custody. The McCain Amendment passed both houses of Congress with veto-proof majorities, but President Bush issued a signed statement essentially claiming that he could ignore the law at his discretion, and all evidence suggests that he continued to do so for the rest of his presidency.[59] Ironically, while the Bush administration was doing everything it could do to ignore international law, congressional statutes, and the Constitution; it demanded that the Taliban adhere to international law when they seized American missionaries in Afghanistan.[60] Bush's own State Department in its 2004 report on Turkey condemned the Turks for using "torture methods that did not leave physical traces, including ... exposure to cold, stripping and blindfolding, food and sleep deprivation, threats to detainees of family members ... and mock executions."[61] Similarly, the State Department condemned China for using "prolonged solitary confinement, long confinement in contorted positions, and sleep deprivation" along with "secret prisons and detention centers outside the national prison system."[62]

No Recourse in Law

The Bush administration declared that the detainees are not POWs, and therefore do not receive the protections of the Geneva Convention under international law, but the Bush administration also claimed that the detainees are also outside of the jurisdiction of any American civil or criminal court, being in Guantanamo Bay, Cuba. Essentially, the Bush administration has created a new designation outside of the protections of any law, and those designated as "detainees" are at the complete mercy of the Bush administration. The vast majority of the detainees are foreign nationals, but a number of U.S. citizens have also been detained for months without charges, including Yaser Hamdi, seized in Afghanistan and transported to Guantanamo Bay, and Jose Padilla. At least five American citizens have also been detained by the U.S. military in Iraq.[63] As a consequence, legal scholars, such as Yale international law professor Harold Hongju Koh, have condemned the Bush administration for creating an international law double standard where there is one set of rules for the U.S. and another separate set of rules for the rest of the world. In the words of Koh, "The emerging doctrine has placed startling pressure upon the structure of human rights and international law that the U.S. itself designed and supported since 1948. In a remarkably short time, the United States moved from being the principal supporter of that system to its most visible outlier."[64]

This is perhaps most important to note since the Bush administration cited Iraq's violations of international law as reason enough for invasion, yet the same administration has tossed international law aside when international legal principles were deemed to be inconsistent with American interests. Koh further argues that shift in American policy toward international law and human rights is not due to a shift in American national culture, but instead is a result of "short-sided decisions made by a particularly extreme American administration." In other words, Bush's assault on liberties reflects the traditional conservative ideological preference for order over freedom.[65]

International Impact of American Policies

Bush's compromise of American civil rights has, predictably, encouraged similar behavior by foreign governments abroad. In Indonesia, for example, the army cited America's Guantanamo detention center as a model for a proposal to build an offshore prison camp on Nasi Island where detainees can be held without charges indefinitely. In China, the founder of a pro-democracy magazine was imprisoned for life on the charge of terrorism. In Egypt, the government extended for three years its emergency law that allows it to detain suspected terrorists indefinitely.[66] Obviously, the message that others have received from Bush's action is that if international law is irrelevant to the U.S., it is irrelevant to others as well.

International Law has not proven to be irrelevant to everyone, however, and it turns out that not all other countries view President Bush's War on Terror as preempting their own laws. For instance, in February 2007, a judge in Italy ordered the indictment of the CIA's Rome station chief, the Milan base chief, and two dozen more CIA officers for their role in the abduction of a radical cleric in Italy who subsequently spent several years in Egypt suffering brutal interrogations. Similarly, a court in Germany charged thirteen CIA officers with the wrongful kidnapping in Germany and imprisonment of a Lebanese-born German citizen. Taking a different approach, the government of Canada formally apologized and paid $10 million to one of its citizens who had been seized by the CIA while changing planes in New York after a family vacation. The man was then transported by the CIA to Syria where he suffered brutal interrogations for ten months.[67]

USA PATRIOT Act

Bush's compromise of civil liberties does not stop with international law, however. The USA PATRIOT Act also erodes American Fourth Amendment protections against unreasonable searches and seizures by giving the federal government the authority to seize citizens' papers and effects without probable cause if it is in conjunction with a terror investigation. The federal government even has the authority to review which books one checks out at the library and librarians are prohibited from informing individuals of federal inquiries under threat of incarceration.[68] The CIA was given new powers to spy on the American people, including the power to read secret grand jury testimony without a judge's prior approval, and to obtain private records of corporations and other organizations. The CIA can also review banking and credit data on American citizens and American corporations.[69] In April 2003, the Terrorism Section of the Justice Department, in an arrangement with the U.S. district court in Alexandria, VA, began the practice of the "instantaneous subpoena" whereby Western Union was allowed to notify FBI and CIA about which location money was being wired to and who was picking it up.[70] Although the CIA has spied on American citizens before in American history, it had never been granted the authority to do so and those previous actions were not only illegal, but almost universally condemned when they became public. Now the CIA had broad powers to spy on the American people with the support of Congress and the president, but without judicial oversight.[71]

The USA PATRIOT Act also infringes on the right to counsel by granting the federal government the authority to monitor federal prison conversations between attorneys and clients and deny the right to counsel completely to those accused of terrorism activities. Finally, the PATRIOT Act denies the right to habeas corpus, the right to confront witnesses, and the right to a speedy and public trial, and allows the federal government to incarcerate suspected terrorists indefinitely without a trial.[72]

The right to habeas corpus was once described by the Supreme Court as "the precious safeguard of personal liberty."[73] Sometimes referred to as the Great Writ, habeas corpus has been part of been part of American legal tradition since its founding and is enshrined in the Sixth Amendment of the U.S. Constitution. Under the federal habeas statute, the government must establish that a prisoner's custody does not violate the Constitution or laws or treaties of the United States, and the government must establish the factual and legal basis for a prisoner's detention.[74]

While it is true that the United States detained and tried for war crimes twenty-seven Germans captured in China after the surrender of Germany during World War II, those prisoners had right to counsel and could examine the evidence against them prior to trial, call witnesses for their defense, cross-examine witnesses, and challenge the admissibility of the government's evidence. The detainees in Guantanamo Bay and other American secret prisons around the world have often been denied all of these rights.[75]

Among the more controversial actions of the Bush administration in the War on Terror has been President Bush's October 4, 2001, orders to the National Security Agency to conduct wiretaps and eavesdrop on the communications of suspected terrorists within the United States without judicial warrants.[76] This action appears to violate the Foreign Intelligence Surveillance Act of 1978, passed in the post–Watergate era of the Carter administration, which prohibits warrantless surveillance of domestic electronic communications. Under a classified presidential order signed in 2002, the National Security Agency has monitored messages of perhaps thousands of American citizens without warrants.[77] The Bush administration argued that these invasions of liberty are necessary in order to ensure safety from terrorism. Tyrants throughout history have frequently so argued. The dangers of such thinking should be obvious to all, but are perhaps best summed up by Benjamin Franklin in 1759, who argued, "They that can give up essential liberty to obtain a little temporary safety deserve neither."[78]

At this writing, it is early in the first year of the Obama administration and though the candidate Obama denounced the detention center at Guantanamo Bay and announced his intention to close the facility, at this writing, the facility remains open and the USA PATRIOT Act and other Bush administration adjustments to American civil liberties largely remain intact. Evidently, restoring civil liberties is somehow more difficult than taking them away.

The Iraq War and Islamism in the West

Bernard Lewis in making his case that the West and Islam were involved in a "clash of civilizations" argued that "Muslim rage" was rooted in "that perhaps irrational but surely historic reaction of an ancient rival against our Judeo-Christian heritage, or secular present, and the worldwide expansion of both."[79] "Irrational" or not, Lewis warned that the West should guard against any equally irrational reaction against Islam. In the words of Lewis, "It is crucially important that we on our side should not be provoked into an equally historic but also equally irrational reaction against the rival."[80] Unfortunately, it appears that the events of 9/11 may have provoked American president George W. Bush to do just that with his invasion of Iraq.

Whether Bush's invasion of Iraq should be termed as an "irrational reaction" or not depends somewhat on what information was at his disposal in 2002 when he made the decision to invade Iraq. It is at least certain, however, that regardless of the quality of the information at his disposal, Bush violated the age-old military adage of "know thine enemy." This precept was enunciated by President Dwight Eisenhower in 1959 at Langley, Virginia, where he went to lay the cornerstone for what would be the new headquarters for the CIA. In his dedication speech, Eisenhower argued that,

> In war nothing is more important to a commander than the facts concerning the strength, dispositions, and intentions of his opponent, and the proper interpretation of those facts. In peacetime the necessary facts ... and their correct interpretation are essential to the development of policy to further our long-term national security and best interests.[81]

In March 2003 the United States under President George W. Bush invaded Iraq ostensibly to rid the world of weapons of mass destruction amassed by Iraqi leader Saddam Hussein and rid the world of an imminent threat the United States and the world faced due to those weapons. According to the president and other members of his administration, the American conclusions concerning Iraqi weapons of mass destruction were based on "sound intelligence." Much went wrong with the American invasion of Iraq, but the fact that the American leaders did not understand the "facts concerning the strength, dispositions, and intentions of their opponents and the proper interpretation of the facts at their disposal" may be paramount.

Beginning with the fact that the Americans were unable to find the weapons of mass destruction that supposedly prompted the invasion, the fact that the American soldiers were not greeted warmly as the Bush administration evidently believed, and the fact that at this writing, the war continues to rage with no end in sight after seven years (when the Bush administration clearly anticipated a far shorter war), it is glaringly obvious that numerous Bush administration assumptions about America's "enemy" in this case proved to be off base. Among the things that clearly went wrong was the fact that the Iraq war has also given a boost to Islamism both in Iraq and around the world, including within Western democracies. That this result was unanticipated by the Bush administration merely demonstrates how little care Bush and his top advisors took to "know their enemies."

Given the wealth of literature on Islamism that was available at the time, it is difficult to understand why the Bush administration could not foresee what was coming. The expansion of Islamism on a global scale as a result of the Iraq war was even predicted by the Islamists themselves. On the al-Qaeda web site al-Nida, internet jihadist Yusef al-Ayeri argued prior to the American invasion of Iraq that the invasion would bring the best possible outcome for al-Qaeda, soaking extremism throughout the Persian Gulf and South Asia, and achieving the same kind of radicalizing quagmire that bin Laden had hoped would occur in Afghanistan.[82] Although al-Ayeri's prediction could have been easily dismissed as propaganda, the Bush administration's own CIA later vindicated al-Ayeri's predictions in 2006 when they concluded that the American invasion and occupation of Iraq had become "the cause celebre for jihadists, breeding a deep resentment of U.S. involvement in the Muslim world and cultivating supporters for the global jihadist movement."[83] Similarly, the same year, the National Counterterrorism Center released its annual *State Department Country Reports on Terrorism* that showed that acts of terrorism had increased nearly fourfold in 2005.[84] Similarly, the Bush administration's own 2006 *National Intelligence Estimate* stated that "the Iraqi jihad is shaping a new generation of terrorist leaders and operatives" and that "if this trend continues, threats to U.S. interests at home and abroad will become more diverse, leading to increasing attacks worldwide."[85] Rash action without knowledge and understanding, it turns out, is a dangerous and risky business.

The Iraq War and Islamist Propaganda and Recruiting

Islamists proudly display evidence of their attacks on Americans in Iraq and Afghanistan on the Internet so as to demonstrate their resolve and virtue, as well as to provide evidence that they are winning. They also post pictures of Iraqis killed at the hands of Americans so as to play on people's emotions and thus boost their recruiting. Short propaganda and recruitment videos have been produced and posted on the Internet by Islamists showing images of oppressive American military operations and grieving Muslim families, including narrations that explained the American war on Islam and the struggle between good and evil.[86] That the American invasion of Iraq has provided a boon to Islamist recruiters should be obvious to all. For specific evidence, Israeli scholar Reuven Paz analyzed the biographies of 154 foreigners who died in Iraq. Paz concluded that the fallen insurgents were not seasoned veterans from the jihad of Afghanistan or elsewhere, but new, young recruits who had never taken part in any terrorist activity before the American invasion of Iraq. In other words, the American invasion is spawning Islamic terrorists and the terrorists in Iraq have emerged in response to recent political developments, rather than as a response to a lifelong commitment to jihad.[87] In a similar study of some three hundred Saudis captured in Iraq, Saudi scholar Nawaf Obaid concluded that

> the largest group is young kids who saw the images on TV and are reading the stuff on the internet. Or they see the name of a cousin on the list or a guy who belongs to their tribe and they feel a responsibility to go.[88]

An imam from a British mosque in Beeston, United Kingdom, from where the mastermind of London's transportation bombers, Mohammad Sidique Khan, resided, concurred that the American invasion of Iraq created jihadist sentiments among his congregation. In the words of the imam, "A big thing is Iraq and Afghanistan. Lots of youngsters, whether they have Islamic knowledge or not, get automatically affected. It triggers something."[89]

Captured jihadists themselves have confirmed the observations of Obaid and Khan. One insurgent captured in Iraq, Walid Muhammad Hadi al-Masmudi, cited television as the primary influence on his decision to leave his native Tunisia and go to Iraq. In the words of al-Masmudi,

> We also watched clerics on television and on Al-Jazirah declaring jihad I Iraq.... There was a statement, fatwa, by a list of 40 scholars from the Arab and Islamic world on Al-Jazirah.... They used to show events in Abu Ghraib, the oppression, abuse of women, and fornication, so I acted in the heat of the moment and decided ... to seek martyrdom in Iraq.[90]

Another Tunisian jihadist captured in Iraq, Muhammad bin Hassan Rabih, also cited the images on Al-Jazirah and the abuses at Abu Ghraib in particular as the reasons he left his homeland to go to Iraq to wage jihad.[91] It is only reasonable to conclude that a certain percentage of these new jihadist recruits like Hassan Rabih will eventually take up residence in the United States and Western countries themselves. As a final note, it should be reiterated that the 3/11 Madrid bombers and the 7/7 London bombers clearly referenced the Iraq War as a motivating factor.[92]

Abu Ghraib

At a press conference in the Rose Garden in May 2004, President George W. Bush boasted that one of the major achievements of the United States in Iraq was that "there are no longer torture chambers or rape rooms."[93] A week later, a scandal erupted involving American abuse of Iraqi prisoners at Saddam Hussein's Abu Ghraib prison. Iraqi prisoners had been sodomized with broomsticks, one had been beaten to death, and photographs were circulated throughout the media of naked Iraqi prisoners in humiliating and compromising positions. One photograph showed an American soldier with a smirk on her face and a dog leash around the neck of an Iraqi man. Another showed a hooded Iraqi man wearing something resembling a blanket standing on a box with electrical wires attached to his testicles. Regardless of American explanations and contentions by the Bush administration that the abuses were isolated incidents, the revelation destroyed American credibility in the minds of most Iraqis (not to mention other Muslims and non–Muslims alike all over the world), and memos on torture and the Geneva Conventions written by the president's counsel (later attorney general) Alberto Gonzalez that essentially condoned torture only added fuel to the fire. No high-ranking American official was held accountable for the abuse and only low-level enlisted personnel faced charges stemming from the scandal.[94]

For Muslims, Abu Ghraib symbolized the hypocrisy of American policies, since the United States was supposedly occupying Iraq in order to bring freedom to the Iraqi people, but had shoved aside the Geneva Conventions, that had governed the treatment of prisoners of war for decades, and evidently condoned maltreatment of Muslim prisoners. Radical Islamists throughout the Muslim world quickly utilized Abu Ghraib as a rallying cry and recruiting tool for jihad. For example, one radical Imam in Paris, Farid Benyettou, was arrested in Paris on charges of recruiting young boys for terrorism (some as young as thirteen) and sending them to Iraq. Benyettou's lawyer described his client's approach to recruitment thusly:

> He would talk to his disciples about Abu Ghraib, the abuse of Muslims and say, "What are you going to do about it?" He was like a ... guru who claimed to know the sacred texts ... and he convinced them that the texts said it was their duty to go to Iraq to fight for the cause.[95]

Three of Benyettou's recruits were known to have died in Iraq, and another, a thirteen-year-old boy named Salah, was working with jihadists in Syria preparing fighters for the conflict in Iraq.

While the Bush administration claimed that "we are fighting them over there, so that we don't have to fight them over here," evidence suggests that the Iraq War created a situation where America was "fighting them over there" when many of them otherwise wouldn't be fighting against America at all. Furthermore, America was continuing to fight radical Islam at home with the Department of Homeland Security, the USA PATRIOT Act, new restrictions in airports, etc. If defeating the threat posed by radical Islam to America was the goal, it is difficult to demonstrate how the goal was advanced through the invasion of Iraq.

CHAPTER 10

Islamism and the Internet

Joseph Goebbels, Adolph Hitler's minister of propaganda, once said,

> It would not have been possible for us to take power or to use it in the ways we have without the radio.... The radio is the most influential and important intermediary between a spiritual movement and the nation, between the idea and the people.[1]

Radio, of course, was the most important and most high-tech medium of the 1930s and it was used by the Nazis as a propaganda tool almost to perfection. Unfortunately, perhaps the same can be said of Islamists and their use of the Internet some seventy years later. In recent years, the global expansion of the Internet has meant that the Internet itself has become a major tool for Islamists in propagating Islamist ideology and winning converts to Islamism throughout the globe. At the time of the 9/11 attacks, one source had identified only twelve jihadist web sites. By 2008, the figure was 9,000.[2] Given that the War on Terror is as much a war of ideas as it is an actual battlefield and in reality is a war for the hearts and minds of Muslims, the Internet has assumed major importance.

The Islamists themselves appear to understand, perhaps better than their adversaries thus far, that the war of ideas is the most important element of the struggle. For example, it is estimated that over 60 percent of the material on Islamist web sites deals not with current events, military instruction, or footage of war, but with ideological and cultural questions within Islam.[3] According to the American *National Intelligence Estimate* in April 2006, "The radicalization process is occurring more quickly, more widely and more anonymously in the Internet age, raising the likelihood of surprise attacks by unknown groups whose members and supporters may be difficult to pinpoint."[4] The jihadists themselves appear to agree with this assessment. From its very beginning, al-Qaeda has sought and made use of the latest technologies, whether in the form of cell phones and Toyota Land Cruisers or shoulder-fired missiles, but the internet in particular is of tremendous use to them due to both the ability of the internet to reach a global audience at a low cost and the ability to encrypt their messages so as to avoid detection. Some jihadist websites place their most dangerous information in password-protected areas where they are able to do some screening and grooming of potential recruits. The Internet allows the jihadists to push their perspectives on a global scale, free of government censors or mainstream media filters, while simultaneously preserving their anonymity.[5]

The Internet also allows the Islamists to tailor their messages in such a way to suggest that the world is more hostile to Islam than it actually is, and thus create stress among those who visit Islamist web sites. For example, while there may be much that is negative associated with the American invasion of Iraq, there must be something positive that has occurred as a result of the invasion as well. Through the use of the Internet, Islamists can ignore those positives and show only negative images that reinforce the Islamists' already-paranoid view of the West in general and the United States in particular.

Al-Qaeda's Ayman al-Zawahiri himself argues that Islamists should use the media as a means of convincing the Muslim masses that the global jihad, in which he views himself as engaged, involves every Muslim in the world.[6] The Internet allows Islamists to essentially erase the geographical boundaries of Dar al-Islam (the realm of Islam) and Dar al-Harb (the realm of war) and transform the entire cyberspace world into Dar al-Islam.[7] Much as online dating services can match like-minded individuals living continents apart who otherwise would have no way of meeting, so can online Islamist websites link Islamist radicals. Islamists across the globe can go online and give themselves a sense of taking part in jihad at a very low risk and even contribute monetarily to the cause online with their credit cards.

The center of Islamist internet publishing is not the Middle East or South Asia, but London, where Islamists using the internet are able to use Western media to link various Islamist battles being waged in different spots throughout the world in order to create the image of a coordinated global jihad in cyberspace. Through cyberconnections, jihadists can link attacks in Iraq with those in Palestine, Egypt, Algeria, Afghanistan, and anywhere else to provide the impression of coordination of jihad even where none exists.[8]

The Internet has essentially given rise to what the *Economist* refers to as the "terrorist-journalist." In fact, al-Qaeda regularly uses the internet to send out what it refers to as "news bulletins," complete with masked reporters, footage of destroyed American Humvees, and ticker tapes that tell of how many Americans have been killed. Insurgent groups use the Internet to extol their successes and denounce their enemies, often in grandiose hyperbole. For example, on some web sites, battle scenes in Iraq and Afghanistan are compiled into short films with accompanying musical soundtracks.[9]

Islamists take advantage of the freedom of speech and press that exist in Western societies, freedoms that are not present in the Islamic realm to the same degree, in order to publicize their propaganda criticisms of the West as morally decadent and engaging in a crusade against Islam. In fact, the European Islamist preacher Tariq Ramadan acknowledges that a revival of Islam can take place in the West because Muslims living in the West are free to develop an Islam that is a "pure faith," freed from ethnicized doctrines and rituals that characterize countries of origin and free from the limitations imposed on Muslims from the despotic governments in the Islamic world.[10] Consequently, Islamists are able to use the new media to forge new directions for a "purer" Islam.

Islamists also use the Internet to extol the greatness of martyrs and champion the glorious afterlife that is purported to follow martyrdom. For example, online jihadist Hamid al-Ali declares in a video recording online that martyrs go to paradise where they "enjoy delicious food, drink and a wife who will astonish your mind and much else besides; her vagina never complains about how much sex she had, and afterwards she reverts back to being a virgin."[11]

Islamists use tactics similar to Western right-wing extremists in promoting their propaganda. In other words, the use of quotations with little reasoning or analysis is common. The use of true, outrageous cases that are actually statistical outliers, but presented by the Islamists as the norm, are also common. Broad statements are made with no supporting evidence, and bold assertions are made on the basis of purely erroneous or at least insufficient evidence. When scholars are consulted or scholarly sources are used, the presentation avoids anything in depth. In some cases, blatant untruths are presented as fact. For instance, Islamist Internet postings after the American assault on Fallujah in November 2004 claimed that the United States had resorted to the use of chemical weapons because conventional weapons were insufficient to dislodge the insurgents.[12] Similarly, al-Qaeda estimates of American deaths in Iraq posted on jihadist web sites far exceed the estimates published by the Pentagon.[13]

In other words, the propaganda tactics once used by Nazi Germany and Stalin's Soviet Union are employed to the fullest, but with more advanced technology. For instance, there is even now a jihadist video game entitled "Night of Bush Capturing" where participants have the first person video experience of shooting American soldiers and President George W. Bush.[14] A jihadist website was even established modeled after the popular YouTube where jihadists could post their battlefield videos. The website was aptly named Youbombit.com.[15] The importance of such propaganda should not be understated since the propaganda efforts in Nazi Germany compelled millions of otherwise seemingly rational-thinking German people to support the Nazi Party, the 1939 invasion of Poland, and the attempted genocide against the Jews. In the words of Zawahiri to Zarqawi in an intercepted letter, "more than half of this battle is taking place in the battlefield of the media."[16]

There are literally thousands of Islamist organizations with web sites, which if not based in the West, are certainly accessible to radical Muslims living in the West. Many are in Arabic, but many others are in English, French, and other languages of Western countries. According to Gabriel Weimann of Haifa University in Israel, the number of web sites related to terrorist groups number over 4400.[17] This certainly includes both the Muslim Brotherhood and al-Qaeda, which after the U.S. invasion of Afghanistan became much less of a military base of terror operations and much more of a database that connected jihadists all over the world via the Internet.[18]

As of 2005, the most common subjects of the Islamist web sites are jihadist attacks on Americans in Iraq. Other web sites, as explained by Benjamin and Simon,

> present cartoons, interactive games, fables, adventure stories — as well as images of children with real weapons playacting as terrorists. For adolescents, there are rap videos, like Sheikh Terra's Dirty Kuffar [infidel], which flashes images of Marines cheering as one of them shoots an Iraqi on the floor; a rolling list of the fifty-six countries that are said to have been the victims of American aggression since World War II; a Russian soldier being blasted by a Chechen guerrilla with an AK-47; and pictures of Colin Powell and Condoleezza Rice with the words "still slaves" superimposed on them. As the heavy beat goes on, the rappers guffaw in the background while on the screen the destruction of the Twin Towers is replayed.[19]

The Internet essentially allows the jihadists to counter Western media dominance in a way that they otherwise could not. The usefulness of such web sites to the Islamists for their recruitment is obvious. Web sites allow Islamists to recruit those with skills needed for their cause by placing advertisements for chemists, computer experts, electronics experts, etc., online. Other web sites provide prospective recruits with directions on how they may best make their way to the jihad in Iraq via Syria or other bordering countries.[20]

Still other web sites provide films, manuals, PowerPoint slides, etc., that include directions for bomb-making, the home manufacture of poisons, the best assassination techniques, or the best ways to attack urban targets.[21] For example, the Islamist web site Alm2sda.net provided detailed instructions on the types and characteristics of explosives that work best on improvised explosive devices (IEDs) as well as instructions on types of detonators and timers and the best way to build a car bomb.[22] Another web site advertises itself as the "Encyclopaedia of preparation." Still others provide instructions on how to disable American armored vehicles and tanks.[23] Other Islamist web sites direct jihadists concerning what targets should be hit. For example, in February 2002, an online article appeared explaining the advantage of bombing oil tankers. Perhaps not coincidentally, the French tanker *Limburg* was bombed eight months later.[24]

Other web sites issue fatwas or Islamic legal rulings and answer questions presented to Muslims by everyday life in the West. For example, should a Muslim man living in the West refuse to shake the hand of a woman? Does purchasing a house and assuming a home mortgage violate Islamic prohibitions against interest? The web sites, of course, have no way of enforcing their fatwas, but they may be able to influence Western Muslims into actions that Westerners would typically view as sexist, bigoted, or just backward and stupid.

It should also be noted, however, that the Internet can also backfire on Islamists as it gives Western authorities an opportunity to monitor their activities and communication. Jihadists regularly instruct readers not to "divulge secrets," warn of surveillance by authorities, and advocate communicating through mosques rather than the internet due to the obvious danger and lack of secrecy that is the nature of the internet.[25]

Irhabi 007

A prime example of why jihadists caution radical internet users of the risks involved occurred in October 2005 in Bosnia where police, due to monitoring of jihadist web sites, arrested Mirsad Bektasevic, a Swedish teenage cyber-jihadist who referred to himself as "Maximus," for plotting terror attacks in Bosnia and across Europe. In Bektasevic's apartment, police found 19 kg of explosives, weapons, and a video with instructions for how to make a suicide vest. On his computer, there was also information connecting him to a notorious cyber-terrorist known as Irhabi 007. Two days later, British police raided a house in West London and arrested Younis Tsouli, a 22-year-old man of Moroccan origin and a student of information technology. Tsouli turned out to be the infamous Irhabi 007.[26]

Like so many other young Islamists, Tsouli was a student of a technical field (information technology). His co-defendants, Waseem Mughal and Tariq al-Daour, also fit the Western-educated jihadist profile. Mughal is a British-born graduate in biochemistry while al-Daour was an immigrant law student in Britain from the United Arab Emirates.[27]

Tsouli's arrest demonstrates how difficult it is for authorities to combat online jihadist activities and prevent others from picking up where Tsouli left off (which they have). In raiding Tsouli's residence, British authorities found stolen credit card information and discovered that the pilfered cards were used to pay American Internet providers on whose servers Tsouli posted jihadist propaganda. Only after finding these connections did the British law enforcement authorities understand that they had apprehended Irhabi 007.[28]

Irhabi 007, like many of the other persons and groups that construct Islamist web sites, is of non–Western origin, but like many other cyberjihadists, was a radical Islamist living and conducting his jihadist activities in the Western countries themselves. The number of organizations and web sites based in Western countries that are radical Islamist in character are simply too many to mention in this space, but a few prominent ones will be noted here.

The name "Irhabi 007" is essentially a play on words that combines "Irhabi," the Arabic word for "terrorist," with the code number for Ian Flemming's famous fictional spy, James Bond. Irhabi 007 has been credited with being a central figure in enabling al-Qaeda to reconstitute itself after the American invasion of Afghanistan disrupted al-Qaeda's safe haven. Irhabi 007 essentially worked as a "webmaster" for numerous jihadist web sites including that of the late Abu Musab al-Zarqawi, who was the notorious leader of al-Qaeda in Iraq prior to being killed by Western troops. Zarqawi was also famous for launching perhaps the most successful online terrorist public relations campaign in history through the placement online of a video of Nicholas Berg's beheading, which was downloaded over half a million times in the first twenty-four hours.[29]

Irhabi 007 was not only a webmaster, however, but a significant computer hacker, translator, and advisor on all things associated with jihad. Via the internet, Irhabi 007 distributed CIA manuals on making explosives, Navy SEAL guides on sniper training, video slides of how to make car bombs, and cyber-tips on how jihadists using the internet could avoid online detection.[30] At one point, Irhabi even hacked into the computers of the Arkansas Highway and Transportation Department and distributed their video files to jihadists via the Internet.[31]

In his short internet-jihad career, young Tsouli was able to cast his Internet jihadist net far and wide. Not only did he help Zarqawi and al-Qaeda in Iraq spread their propaganda via the internet, he was at the forefront of jihadist efforts to defeat online security in the West while at the same time enhancing online security for the jihadists themselves.[32]

Tsouli's downfall, however, has allowed Western authorities to also bring down some of his fellow cyber-jihadists. In Denmark, a 17-year-old man of

Palestinian origin was convicted in February 2006 for involvement in Mirsad Bektasevic's ("Maximus") terrorist plots. Similarly, two men in Atlanta, Georgia (Syed Ahmed, 21, and Ehsanul Sadequee, 19), were charged with planning attacks on targets in Washington, D.C., and the World Bank. Ahmed and Sadequee had sent Tsouli photographs of proposed targets and travelled to Canada to meet with fellow jihadists concerning attacks. Tsouli may also have been linked to the failed July 2007 attempts by a group of London Muslim physicians and other medical personnel to set off car bombs in London and Glasgow. One of the messages on Tsouli's computer, in a folder labelled "jihad," stated, "We are 45 doctors and we are determined to undertake jihad for Allah's sake and to take the battle inside damaged America."[33] The "doctors' message" also outlined a plot to attack a naval base in Florida and destroy the aircraft carrier *John F. Kennedy* along with other ships and topless nightclubs. The author of the posting estimated "pig casualties" at 200–300. Tsouli, Mughal, and al-Daour all pled guilty to the charges of incitement to murder and conspiracy to murder. Tsouli received a sentence of ten years in prison for his activities while Mughal and Daour received shorter sentences.[34]

Abu Musab al-Suri

Abu Musab al-Suri (a.k.a. Mustafa Setmariam Nasar, Omar Abdel Hakim) was a member of the Syrian Muslim brotherhood who was exiled from Syria in the 1980s and eventually fought with bin Laden and the mujahadeen in Afghanistan. In 1987, al-Suri settled in Spain and became a Spanish citizen through marriage to a Spanish woman. In 1995, al-Suri moved to the UK where he became a European intermediary for al-Qaeda and affiliated with North African Islamist groups. In particular, al-Suri became editor of the publication for the Algerian Armed Islamic Group (GIA) known as *Usraat Al-Ansar*. Al-Suri moved to Afghanistan in 1998 after the takeover by the Taliban and spent his time there training jihadists for the Taliban. Colin Powell announced a $5 million reward for information leading to the capture of al-Suri in November 2004. Al-Suri promptly posted an official response on his own Internet home page.[35]

Al-Suri also posted a 1600-page opus on the internet called *The Global Islamic Call to Resistance* where he advocated self-starting, independent terrorist cells, not directly affiliated with existing groups, which could stage spectacular attacks. The 3/11 Madrid bombers, to whom al-Suri had no direct connection, very well fit the profile as outlined by al-Suri. Unfortunately, other autonomous groups similar to the Madrid bombers can be expected to surface in Western countries in the future, at least in part due to the writings online of al-Suri and other cyberjihadists like him. Al-Suri was captured by Pakistani authorities in Pakistan and turned over to American authorities in 2006. At this writing, his actual whereabouts is unknown, but it is suggested that he was returned to Syria for his interrogation and detention there.[36]

The Cyberwar of Ideas

Arrests of individuals such as Tsouli and al-Suri may be counted as victories for the West in the War on Terror, but they are only representative of individual battles won and do not reflect Western success in winning the war. Instead, since the War on Terror is really a war for the hearts and minds of young Muslim men throughout the globe, the proliferation of jihadists websites suggests that it is a war that the West may not be winning. Instead of invasions of rogue states such as Iraq and Afghanistan, which seem to promote cyber-jihad, a better approach may be a system of counter-propaganda in support of a more Western-friendly version of Islam. For every cyber-jihadist that Western authorities are able to catch up to and take off the net, another is there to quickly take his or her place. For instance, though Irhabi 007 may be off the net, another cyber-jihadist has taken his place who refers to himself as Irhabi 11 and posts the same sort of Islamist rhetoric.[37]

CHAPTER 11

Hope: The Evolution of Islam

At present, Islamism continues its expansion in the West along with the political unrest and terrorism that has too often accompanied its dissemination. The expansion of Islamism in the West is most certainly due to the pull factors of economic opportunities in the West that have drawn Muslims from around the world to Western societies, but it is also due to the push factors associated with authoritarian regimes in the Islamic realm that tend to purge their Islamist opposition and thus create thousands of asylum-seekers that flee to the West for refuge. The expansion of Islamism in the West is therefore made possible in part by the freedoms in the West that allow persons the privacy rights and privileges to practice their religion as they please, and the fact that the West is viewed by many Islamists as a place of political refuge for those persecuted in their countries of origin. European Muslim spokesman Tariq Ramadan, for instance, argues that Muslims can practice Islam better in the West than in Muslim countries because so many Islamic countries are led by apostates that interfere with the practice of purer Islam.[1] Similarly, the radical Islamist British imam Abu Hamza argues for Muslim immigration to the West because apostate leaders in host countries prevent Muslims from practicing a purer form of Islam.[2] In some ways, the freedoms of the West therefore provide greater potential for Muslims living in the West to live up to the strict tenets of radical Islam. Western freedoms, however, do not include the freedom to make bombs and plot mass murders, and the West is therefore void of terrorist training camps in the al-Qaeda mode, but Islamist ideas actually disseminate much better with the cover of free speech and the aid of the Internet.

Separate from the issues of Western freedom and immigration, however, a contributing factor to the expansion of Islamism in the West has been Western foreign policies that have a history of placing foreign armies in Islamic lands, leading to the deaths of thousands of Muslims across the globe, and inflaming ordinary Muslims to a more radical form of Islam both in the occupied Muslim lands themselves and among Muslims living in Western democracies. That being the case, tremendous potential exists for Westerners to reduce the number of Islamists living among them simply by refraining from invading Muslim countries without provocation, refraining from detaining people indefinitely with charges, refraining from torturing people, and refraining from indiscriminately killing civilians in Muslim lands. In other words, at least a portion of the problem of radical Islam in the West can be solved if Western countries will simply live up to their own human rights ideals.

Playing the Western Political Game

If Islamic fundamentalism is to follow the pattern of other religions, such as Christian fundamentalism, then it should be expected to soften over time as the religion fights the struggle between purity and respect in Western societies. Just as Christian fundamentalists no longer burn witches, execute heretics, or flog people for fornication, Islamists perhaps may be expected over the long haul to abandon beheadings, amputations, terrorism, and stonings, since to a large degree they are already playing the Western political game without even realizing that this is what they are doing. It is noteworthy, for instance, that Western Islamists tend to defend Islamism in Western language and on terms consistent with a Westernized approach. For example, sharia is exalted by Islamists theoretically for doing a better job of ensuring women's rights than Western laws.[3]

Another indication of the ability of fundamentalist Muslims to adapt to Western society is the situation where Muslim associational groups use existing public laws to defend the rights of Islam. For instance, in the United States, the Council for American Islamic Relations (CAIR) lobbies for the protection of Islam in the name of the religious freedoms guaranteed by the U.S. Constitution. CAIR has initiated numerous lawsuits on the grounds of First Amendment religious freedoms as well as under American equal opportunity laws and won numerous lawsuits against American governmental and corporate entities for discriminatory practices against Muslims.[4] Similarly, Muslim women in the West have staged political demonstrations in public and sued in court for the right to wear the hijab in the workplace, thus exemplifying the fact that conservative Muslims are quietly adopting Western political ways even while rejecting much that is Western in their rhetoric. Just the fact that women are in the workplace at all is a violation of Taliban-style Islamism. The fact that they are in the workplace wearing the hijab may display their Muslim faith, but the fact that the hijab is also often worn in the West with jeans, T-shirts, and athletic shoes displays the fact that these same Muslims are becoming immersed in Western cultural ways. For instance, the web site of the Islamic Information Society of Calgary, Canada, advertises karate for both men and women as well as women's soccer, though it also advertises a class in "The Reality of Jinn, Exorcism, and Magic." Similarly, the Islamic Food and Nutrition Council of America recently declared food at McDonald's to be halal.[5]

The fact that these hijab-wearing Muslims then sue in Western courts for protection of their individual rights places them squarely within the Western political game along with other non–Muslim minorities who sue for their own individual rights protections. In the long run, it is possible that the Islamists' denunciation of everything Western will fail simply because living in the West and becoming surrounded with Western culture, they will have become Western themselves in most respects. If one is a member of the second largest Western religion, lives in a Western country, uses the Western political system to one's advantage, is employed in the Western workplace, uses Western technology, lives in a Western home, etc., then at a certain point, that person is Western whether they don a hijab or not.

Muslim associational groups in the West also lobby to defend the interests of Muslims in foreign policy and tend to support pro-Palestinian positions regarding the Arab-Israeli conflict. Muslims have also proven that they will punish politicians at the polls that ignore their foreign policy interests. For example, American Muslims supported George W. Bush in 2000, but not in 2004 after he took a pro–Israel stance in Palestine and invaded two Muslim countries.[6]

Furthermore, the very idea that there is a distinct "Islamic culture" or "Islamic identity" is itself a Western construct, as is the very idea that Muslims in Europe should be recognized as a minority group with its own values and mores. In other words, the multiculturalist and minority rights claims made by Islamists in the West are essentially tacit admittance of their acceptance of Western pluralism. The claim of Western Islamists that Muslims in the West constitute an "identity group" is no different than the identity-group claims in the United States of fundamentalist Christians or American Jews. Also similar to Christian fundamentalists, Western Islamists tend to exhibit an "us against them" mentality and view themselves as a select group of true believers struggling in the sea of iniquity to follow the straight path commanded by God.[7] If fundamentalist Christians can reside in harmony in Western societies with this mindset, then it stands to reason that Islamists should be able to do the same.

Shared Values

Clearly, in spite of their differences, Islamists and Westerners actually share many of the same values. Britain's Prince Charles, for instance, stated, "This crucial sense of oneness and trusteeship of the vital sacramental and spiritual character of the world is something important we can learn from Islam."[8] Even the most radical Islamists espouse some values that are consistent with Western ideals ("Thou shalt not steal," for instance), and especially those of American evangelical Christians. This is extremely important in the search for common ground between Westerners and Islamists, because as Samuel Huntington points out, "cooperation depends on trust, and trust most easily springs from common values and culture."[9] In spite of Huntington's concern over "culture clash," it is clear that Islamists actually share the same basic values as all human societies, including reverence for the family, a moral sense of right and wrong, and even the conviction that murder is one of those wrongs.[10] Although this might not be evident to most Westerners who witnessed the video clips of Islamists flying planes full of innocent people into buildings, Islamists, like Westerners, also delineate a moral difference between murder, which they view as immoral, and the taking of human lives in war, which is not. Avoiding bloodshed at the hands of Islamists in the future may therefore hinge on convincing as many Muslims as possible that there is no war between Islam and the West, a feat made much more difficult by the still unresolved Western invasions of two Islamic countries spearheaded by President George W. Bush.

Partially due to Western religious freedom and diversity, and much like Western fundamentalist Christians, Islamists in the West view their faith as under attack and decry the erosion of societal moral values. Their view that the religious sky is falling is at least partially due to the fact that the majority of Muslims in the West reject the rigid religious interpretations of the Islamists. In the view of the Islamists, pure Islam is therefore being corrupted. For instance, 48 percent of male Algerian immigrants polled recently in France responded that they were not Islamic believers and 64 percent responded that believer or not, they did not practice. For those that did observe some religious traditions, such as fasting during Ramadan or other pillars of the Islamic faith, many viewed it as observance of communal customs rather than acts of faith.[11]

Islamic fundamentalists, like their Christian counterparts, stress family, traditional gender roles, dedication to God, charity, commitment to their religious community, religious education, personal discipline, and religious freedom. Muslim and Christian fundamentalists in Western societies in the future can perhaps be expected to join hands in fighting for government funding of religious schools, the rights of free exercise of religion, the rights to wear religious articles in the workplace and schools, and in opposition to what they view as the decadence and immorality of Western culture. Fundamentalist Christians and Muslims both abhor what they view as decadence in television, movies, magazines and popular music. In the words of one Muslim mother,

> I don't like them (the children) to watch commercials or dancing, rap music, dating situations, looseness on TV — anything which you can see by turning it on for two minutes or less. Also I don't want them to get used to musical instruments or music which has adult rock and roll rhythm even if it has children's lyrics.[12]

While these comments are from an American Muslim mother, they might as easily be spoken by a fundamentalist Christian anywhere in the West, but especially in the southern United States. The idea of "being in the world but not of the world" is as Muslim as it is Christian. If Western society can accommodate fundamentalist Christians who believe the earth is only 6,000 years old, that God created the universe in six days, that there is no such thing as evolution, and that a talking snake induced the first humans into immorality, then surely it can also accommodate fundamentalist Muslims who believe the same.

Islamists have also Westernized Islam through their attempt to make everything religious. As so well stated by Olivier Roy, "When everything has to be Islamic, nothing is."[13] The irony of this statement is that as the Islamists attempt to make everything religious, they actually end up secularizing Islam. For instance, the leaders of religion in Iran (and in Afghanistan under the Taliban) are also governmental policy leaders, thus playing large secular roles in their societies. In such an arrangement, the propensity of politics to dominate religion in the long run is the dominant trend, whether one is discussing the decision of American Mormons to abandon polygamy or the Catholic Church decision to abandon the prohibitions against usury.

New Interpretations of Islam

Thomas Jefferson once wrote, "Man, once surrendering his reason, has no remaining guard against absurdities the most monstrous, and like a ship without rudder, is the sport of every wind."[14] Islamism obviously surrenders Jefferson's reason to faith and emotion and therefore lends itself to absurdities; however, if Jefferson is correct, then it is also the "sport of every wind" and is subject to change.

Supporting Jefferson's "sport of every wind" argument is nineteenth-century Iranian Islamist Sayyid Jamaluddin al-Afghani, who denounced the view of Islam that holds it to be incompatible with science. Afghani, who believed in pan–Islamism and was among the most influential Islamists of his time, criticized Islamic civilization for attempting to stifle science. Afghani explained that because of the Muslim belief that Islam has all the answers, true believers had no incentive to seek scientific proof, thus the realm of Islam fell behind the West in technological advancement.[15] If Afghani could advocate an approach to Islam that was more compatible with science in the 1880s, then so could Islamists in the twenty-first century. One of Afghani's disciples and co-workers, Muhammad Abduh, was an advocate of ijtihad, which is essentially the use of independent reasoning to reach Islamic juridical conclusions. Abduh issued fatwas based on his own ijtihad in areas that were previously not considered open to discussion. For example, Abduh issued a fatwa in 1903 authorizing the establishment of interest-based banking, a precedent that legitimized Western-style financial institutions that aided in economic development in Egypt in the early twentieth century.[16] Similarly, Egyptian scholar Taha Hussein argued that after World War I Islamic civilization was based on the willingness of Muslims to borrow freely from other cultures and that Egypt should borrow as needed from the developed West.[17] More recently, Mahathir bin Muhammad, then Prime Minister of Malaysia, speaking at the International Conference on Islamic Thought in Kuala Lumpur in 1984 stated,

> If Muslims really want an Islamic social order, then they must examine every aspect of modern life from the perspective of Islam and make necessary corrections.... Then they should integrate the new knowledge into the corpus of the Islamic legacy by eliminating, amending, reinterpreting and adapting its components according to the world view of Islam.[18]

Reflecting the fact that Mahathir bin Muhammad is not alone in his sentiments, since the time of Afghani, Abduh, and Taha Hussein, Islamist jurists have frequently employed ijtihad and reinterpreted Islam in ways that alter Islam to be consistent with social realities in twenty-first-century Western societies. As a consequence, a new mosaic of Islamic rulings has emerged as Islamic jurists have often disagreed over major points, such as whether Muslims can live in the infidel West or must immigrate back to Muslim lands. For example, in 1909 when Bosnia-Herzegovina was ceded to Austro-Hungarian control, an Ottoman jurist announced that all Muslims in Bosnia-Herzegovina must immediately immigrate to an Islamic country. Rashid Rida, the most prominent jurist of the time in Egypt, responded by pointing out that the prophet Mohammed himself had allowed Muslim converts to live outside the realm of Islam. Rida further argued that there is no distinction between prayer performed in Islamic lands or those performed elsewhere and that Muslims may live a proper Islamic life in non–Muslim countries. The real issue, according to Rida, was not whether the leaders of a country were Muslims, but whether Muslims could practice their religion in the land in which they were living. Rida cited the opinion of an eleventh-century Muslim jurist, al Mawardi, as his legal authority in the matter. Rida did not necessarily bind all Muslims to his way of thinking, however, because in his fatwa, he stated that ultimately it was the Bosnian Muslims who were the best judges of their own affairs.[19] Although other jurists may not agree, Rida had provided a way for Islam to adapt to social and political changes, and placed the responsibility for the adaptation and evolution of Islam in non–Muslim lands squarely upon the Muslims living in those lands.

Rida further releases Muslims living in non–Muslim lands from Islamic civil and criminal laws, arguing that in non–Muslim territories, Muslims are bound only to follow the laws pertaining to acts of worship. Instead, Rida argues that Muslims are bound by the laws of the host state. That being the case, Rida argues that Muslims may borrow and lend money with interest and may build and lease out a hotel even to people who will sell or serve alcohol. In short, Rida argues that civil and criminal laws in Islam are all based on ijtihad (juridical reasoning) and that ijtihad is context-specific; consequently, Islamic civil and criminal law has no applicability in non–Muslim lands. Similarly, twelfth-century jurist Abu Bakr Al-Kindi argues that Muslims residing in non–Muslim lands may work, own land, and farm, even if it means paying unjust taxes to a non–Muslim state.[20] Collectively, these rulings are eerily similar to Apostle Paul's admonition to Christians in Romans 13:1–6 to be good citizens and honor the king. Practically, it demonstrates how even some of the most conservative Islamic jurists allow Islam to adapt.

While many other Islamist jurists clearly disagree with Rida and Al-Kindi, the disagreement itself suggests that Islam, like other religions, is able to evolve with its surroundings and a single conservative Islamists path is not preordained. While most Muslims living in the West may be comfortable with the idea that maxims of seventh-century Islam are still applicable today, the reality is that Western Muslims continually review and reinterpret Islam to fit their current situations and the Islam of the twenty-first century in Western societies is quite different than that of the time of Mohammed.[21]

This approach is reflected by the Fiqh Council of North America that was organized in the 1970s to provide sharia-based advice and counsel to American Muslims. The North American Fiqh counselors are charged to respect the opinions of the classical jurists, but they are not bound by them unless the existing sharia rulings, such as the ban on eating pork, are clear and unambiguous. In other cases, the Fiqh council views its role as one of providing satisfactory answers when classic ones are outdated. In other words, the North American Fiqh council helps facilitate the adaptation of Islam to Western society and therefore the long-term evolution of Islam. To make matters even more flexible, Fiqh counselors often offer dissenting opinions that Muslims may choose to follow instead, thus allowing even greater flexibility.[22] Similarly, scholars of Islam at the University of Ankara in Turkey are working on a new version of the Hadith where Mohammed's sayings are placed in context. Mehmet Gormez, a theology professor at the university, argues that the Hadith forbidding women from travelling alone, for instance, was "clearly not a religious injunction, but was related to security in a specific time and place."[23] This is quite a departure from the Saudi Arabian interpretation of the same verse that they use to prevent women from driving.

Even some of the more ridiculous Islamist interpretations provide some hope that they can in the future change their interpretations of Islam away from the interpretation that impels them to violence and toward one that embraces non-violence. For example, the Koran is very explicit in condemning suicide, yet the Islamists interpret the Koran so as to make suicide bombers into martyrs that receive the gifts of 72 virgins in heaven. The contradiction in this is glaring. While the Islamists argue for strict interpretations of the Koran, they have simultaneously reinterpreted the Koran's ban on suicide to allow blowing one's self to pieces. Any clear-headed person who subscribes to reason, whether Muslim or not, might beg to differ with the Islamists' interpretation. If Islamists are essentially arguing for interpretations of the Koran that appear on the surface quite unreasonable, then the possibility exists that reason may be used by more moderate Muslims to convert the radicals away from their extremism.

Similarly, Islamists have also re-interpreted the Koran to sanction the martyrdom of female suicide bombers, though it is exceedingly unclear how the 72 virgins awaiting the martyr in heaven might benefit the martyred females when they get there. The point, other than that the Islamists' logic is clearly suspect, is that if Islamists are currently reinterpreting the Koran (though they deny it), then they may also reinterpret it in the future in a way that will render even the more conservative forms of Islam much more consistent with Western culture and (hopefully) much less violent. After all, their Christian fundamentalist counterparts were able to do the same thing with the command of Exodus 22:18 (Thou shalt not allow a witch to live) since even the late reverend Jerry Falwell, who blamed Hurricane Katrina on the fact that New Orleans native Ellen Degeneres is gay, did not still advocate hunting down those suspected of witchcraft and applying capital punishment.

In a similar vein, there is hope in the future that Islamists in the West can again reinterpret the Koran to discard violent jihad through terrorism, and instead focus on spreading Islam through peaceful means based on Mohammed's clear command to "Aggress not, God hates the Aggressor."

Given the fact that it took Christians literally thousands of years after the writing of Exodus to cease witch hunts, however, it may be merely wishful thinking to expect Islamists to abandon violent jihad in the near future, even if there is hope eventually provided by clear evidence of the Westernization of Islam that is already under way.

Religious Freedom and Islamic Diversity

Another subtle process of Westernization among Islamists is occurring among Western Muslims due to the Western concept of separation of church and state. Given that even in Western countries, where there are official state churches that receive state support, there is also religious freedom, including the freedom to think differently and even think secularly, Western Muslims are beginning to resemble these patterns among Western Christians in that great diversity is developing among them. Islamist thought is only one of those directions and it is clearly a small minority in comparison to the numerous other directions of Islam in the West. Given the choice between the radical Wahhabi Sunni ideology exported from Saudi Arabia and a more permissive and secularized Islam, most Western Muslims do not choose Islamist sects. Furthermore, even more conservative Muslim groups that support the ideas of the halal meat, traditional marriages, and traditional roles for women often oppose violence. For instance, the Union of Islamic Organizations in France supports the obligation of women to wear the hijab, yet publicly opposes al-Qaeda.[24]

Western Protestant-style individualism also appears to be influencing Islam in the West as Western Islamists regularly introduce innovations to Islam. For example, the contention of some Islamists that jihad, or holy war, is a "sixth pillar" of Islam is a clear alteration of the orthodox "five pillars" of Islam outlined by the prophet. Western Islamists with little or no religious training and no status as clerics or Islamic jurists often take it upon themselves to issue fatwas and decide for themselves the meaning of sharia in any particular situation. Osama bin Laden himself conforms to this individualism through his issuing of fatwas when he himself has no religious authority in Islam to do so.[25]

Western Islamists are becoming further Westernized in that their preference for emotion, faith and charismatic preachers over law and orthodoxy resembles the approach of Western Protestant fundamentalists. As such, radical Muslims typically eschew ethnicity-based mosques in favor of those that are faith-based, often led by radical preachers imported from Saudi Arabia or Pakistan.[26] Western Islamist preachers often appeal to their flocks through emotion and wail and cry in front of crowds in displays that resemble those of Western television evangelists. Additionally, the new Western Islamist preachers are typically less interested in the strictures of religious rituals, such as fasting and praying five times daily, preferring instead the moral and emotional messages akin to those of Western Protestant evangelists.[27] One European Turkish group, the Tablighi, even have adopted Western-style door-to-door evangelism tactics that include campaign tours by missionary teams by ordinary Muslims rather than by the ulama.[28]

Muslim student organizations in the West tend to resemble this faith-based "universalist" model where Muslims of all ethnicities and languages are drawn together under a common faith. The very nature of these student organizations is to a degree Westernizing in that the groups are largely student-led, thus subverting the more traditional approach that places a premium on deference to elders. Radical Muslim student groups also become to a degree Westernized as they join hands with Protestant fundamentalists in Western mass politics to oppose abortions, gay rights, and other activities they view as immoral in society.[29] The "Westernized" nature of American student organizations is well-exemplified by the Muslim student web site at the University of Houston where students ask questions concerning the permissibility of body piercing and sex change operations in Islam.[30]

An additional Westernizing factor among Western Muslims is the fact that Muslims in the West are ethnically and linguistically diverse. For instance, since Arabs constitute only 20 percent of all Muslims, efforts to ferment global jihad and a single interpretation of Islam through web sites constructed exclusively in Arabic are doomed to failure. Some level of deculturation is therefore necessary for Islamists in the West in order for them to be able to communicate with each other. In American mosques, for instance, 97 percent of attendees speak English as their primary language.[31] That being the case, the radical Wahhabis of Saudi Arabia are at a disadvantage since they speak only Arabic, thus hindering their own ability to project their radical message.

Religious Revival

Samuel Huntington observes that the non–Western world has been experiencing "unsecularization" or a religious revival over the last century as a response to modernization.[32] Huntington points out that religion provides a sense of identity and direction amid societal change, fills a vacuum in chasms of political chaos, and provides order amid the disorder. For immigrants to the West, Huntington argues that religion provides emotional, social, and material support. The fact that religion, including Islam, does provide these things for people suggests that Islamism is not going away any time soon. It should be remembered, however, that the current wave of "unsecularization" is not the first of such waves experienced by Western society, nor should it be expected to be the last. The Protestant Reformation in Europe obviously was not without its social upheaval, but the unrest did eventually pass. The Great Awakening in the eighteenth century United States and the second Great Awakening in the nineteenth century United States were clearly waves of "unsecularization," but much less violent. This suggests that "unsecular-ization" does not necessarily have to follow a violent path. Hope certainly exists that this is as true of Islam as it is of any other religion.

It is possible, however, that for Islam to shed its radical streak in Western society, Muslims must find more ways to separate religious issues from politics. Salman Rushdie recently made this argument, stating, "The restoration of religion to the sphere of the personal, its depoliticization, is the nettle that all Muslim societies must grasp in order to become modern.... If terrorism is to be defeated, the world of Islam must take on board the secularist-humanist principles on which the modern is based."[33]

Hope also exists in the fact that in many areas the Koran even as interpreted by Islamists do not necessarily clash with Western society. In the words of Daniel Pipes,

> Pious Muslims can cultivate the sciences, work efficiently in factories, or utilize advanced weapons.... The sharia has nothing to say about the changes that accompany modernization, such as the shift from agriculture to industry, from countryside to city, or from social stability to social flux; nor does it impinge on such matters as mass education, rapid communications, new forms of transportation, or health care.[34]

As a consequence, even the most conservative Muslims are free under Islam to work in Western urban centers, attend Western universities, use Western communications and transportation technology, and take advantage of superior Western health care. Though these advantages did not prevent Osama bin Laden, Mohammed Atta, and a host of others mentioned and not mentioned in this book from becoming terrorists, for every "terrorist" example, there are perhaps thousands of other non-violent Muslims living in the West and simultaneously retaining their Muslim faith while flourishing in Western society. If Catholicism, Protestantism, Judaism, Hinduism, and Buddhism, each with its own segments of intolerance, can flourish within Western society without resorting to mass terror, then logic suggests that Islam may evolve to do the same.

Hope in Education

Western education clearly offers promising prospects for converting Islamists from their right-wing authoritarian mindsets to something more compatible with Western society. As long as new learning can occur, the possibility remains that individuals, Islamist or otherwise, can learn to view the world differently as they assimilate new information. Islamists and other right-wing authoritarians do not tend to be critical thinkers, a condition that Western higher education is generally designed to correct. In the words of Robert Altemeyer,

> Compared with others, authoritarians have not spent much time examining evidence, thinking critically, reaching independent conclusions, and seeing whether their conclusions mesh with the other things they believe. Instead, they have largely accepted what they were told by the authorities in their lives, which leaves them with time for other things, but which also leaves them underpracticed in thinking for themselves.[35]

Altemeyer provides empirical evidence that the attitudes of right-wing authoritarians in the United States are often significantly altered and softened by the university experience.[36] If this is true of American right-wing authoritarians, then one should expect Western universities to have a similar impact on Islamists. Unfortunately, as the Mohamed Atta example illustrates, the university education will not provide the solution in every case, but it appears that Western university education helps reduce right-wing authoritarian (and therefore Islamist) attitudes in the aggregate. Some of this is due to the nature of college curriculum, but some of it is also because it is more difficult in the Western university setting for right-wing authoritarians of any stripe, Islamist or otherwise, to keep themselves constantly surrounded with like-minded people that reinforce their flawed reasoning as is their preference.

Moral Criteria of Religious Truth and Religious Recruitment

There is also hope that Islamism will eventually soften its approach in an attempt to gain new members, just as fundamentalist Protestantism had done. In spite of the often inflammatory rhetoric of Falwell, Pat Robertson, James Dobson, etc., none advocate killing the enemies of Christianity as commanded by Jesus himself in Luke 19:27 where Jesus clearly states, "but bring here those enemies of mine, who did not want me to reign over them, and slay them before me." While many Christian fundamentalists in the West may be comfortable with denunciation of gays, lesbians, abortionists, feminists, liberals, and the ACLU as sinners and abominations before God, very few could be found that would go out and slay the enemies of Jesus as he commanded (though I here recognize that most fundamentalist Christians can be expected to argue that I have misinterpreted Jesus' statement in the "parable" in Luke 19:27 and Jesus did not command his followers to kill his enemies). Given that fact, Christian fundamentalist leaders refrain from such a call because it would most certainly alienate most, and thus hinder rather than help recruitment.

This is largely because an interpretation of Luke 19:27 as a command to kill the enemies of Jesus is theologically questionable to most Christians because their consciences tell them that it is morally wrong. As John Shepherd argues, there are "moral criteria of religious truth, and religions need to be held accountable in these terms."[37] In other words, most Christians can be expected to reject any command in the Bible to slay the enemies of God because they view such actions as morally wrong. Similarly, most Muslims can be expected to ignore the commands in the Koran to slay infidels. Instead, moderate Muslims, such as Khaled Abou El Fadl, who holds a chair in Islamic Law at UCLA, call for a new interpretation of Islam that is consistent with universal humanist ideals of goodness and beauty that will resonate with both Muslims and Western non–Muslims.[38] In a similar vein, five days after the 9/11 attacks, Hamza Yusuf, a white American convert to Islam, denounced the 9/11 terrorists as

> enemies of Islam ... mass murderers, pure and simple.... I think that Muslims, and I really feel this strongly, have to reject the discourse of anger.... We have to move to a higher moral ground, recognizing that the desire to blame others leads to anger and eventually to wrath, neither of which are rungs on a spiritual ladder to God. It's times like these that we really need to become introspective.[39]

Western Muslims are morally little different from Christians and they exemplify this human morality in that the vast majority do not engage in a violent jihad against the West, and for every suicide bomber, there is a far greater number uncomfortable with anti–Western rhetoric. Islamists can never win the majority of Western Muslims to jihad and martyrdom any more than could Western Christian fundamentalists coerce the majority of Christians to rise up and slay the enemies of Jesus. In order to gain a broader audience in the West, both Christian fundamentalists and Western Islamists will have to adopt a degree of moderation. In other words, in order to achieve real mass appeal and win over the majority of Muslims, the radical Islamists will be forced to become less radical and even at times less Islamic. In the words of Fathi Osman, the former editor of the London-based magazine *Arabia*, "Unless Muslims can convince the technologically advanced, materially rich and militarily superior world that Muslims and Islam have something to offer and to contribute, no one will listen to us."[40] Muslim recruitment is obviously greatly hindered if it calls for violence and martyrdom or is so oversimplified that it considers every modern institution as superficial and every Western effort at human improvement as hypocritical.

It should be noted that though Islamists brought the entire world to their attention on 9/11, this did not result in bringing a single society closer to sharia nor did it move Islamic society closer to the return of the caliphate, two major goals of Islamists. Furthermore, Islamists were unable to follow 9/11 with further attacks that toppled the far enemy and subsequent attacks in Madrid and London were less spectacular in comparison. Public opinion among Muslims, both in and outside the West, since 9/11 has been greatly divided over the tactics of the Islamists. In Saudi Arabia, the indiscriminate killing of Muslims by Islamists has apparently shifted the dominant view against the Islamists. In Iraq, al-Qaeda in Iraq under Zarqawi succeeded in alienating the majority of the population with attacks on the Shiite majority.[41]

Thus, while American Protestant fundamentalist Pat Robertson may call for the assassination of Venezuelan leader Hugo Chavez, he does not organize a group for that purpose and popular European Muslim leader Tariq Ramadan similarly does not organize a group for the purpose of committing terrorist attacks in Europe. While this does not mean that there will not be more extremists and more terrorism, both Christian and Muslim, in the West, it does mean that the extremists, both Christian and Muslim, have already lost the battle for the hearts and minds of the majority, even if they are unaware of that fact. It is, however, this fact that the extremists will not be able to win the hearts and minds of the majority without moderating their approach that perhaps provides the greatest hope.

In Western societies, the prevailing view is that religion must be held accountable to the society at large and it cannot violate the freedom, health, safety, well-being, or public morals of the larger society. One of the acid tests in this respect is religious conversion or the freedom of religious people to leave their religion. Islamists typically oppose the freedom to leave the faith even to the point of calling for the death penalty for apostates. In Saudi Arabia, for instance, even attempting to convert Muslims from the faith carries the death penalty.[42] Islamists, as well as other religious extremists, reject the suggestion that the morals of their religion can be trumped by the larger society. Nevertheless, human history is replete with examples of just that. American Mormons abandoned polygamy under pressure from the U.S. government, Western Jews no longer stone women caught in adultery, and Hindus living in Western societies are not allowed to burn their wives to death if their dowries are insufficient. Hence, there is little reason to believe that Islamists are so radical that they cannot eventually conform their behavior to that of the larger society. In order to do so, Western society clearly will need some help from more moderate Muslims. Egypt's grand mufti, Ali Gomaa, provided some of that help in 2007 when he caused a stir in the Islamic world by publishing an article where he argued for religious freedom. Similarly, the religious AK Party that currently rules in Turkey under PM Recep Tayyip Erdogan has banned the death penalty and retained laws keeping abortions legal. Turkey also bans headscarves at the universities.[43] Thus far, Erdogan's government has produced virtually no legislation that would change the fundamental nature of the secular Turkish state. This may be related to the fact that a pro-secular rally two weeks after Erdogan's election, the largest political rally in Turkey's history, occurred under the slogan, "Turkey is secular and it will remain secular." Furthermore, military leaders issued a statement indicating that they were pledged to be the "absolute defender of secularism."[44]

Moderation of Islamism from within Islam

The final solution is not in the elimination of Islam, but in the moderation and Westernization of the religion itself. Although outside pressure from secular society (such as the U.S. Supreme Court rulings against Muslim polygamy) may play a role, the largest impetus for change may have to come from within the Western Muslim community. For example, in 2002, Michael Wolfe, an American Muslim, edited a collection of essays by American Muslims who argued for "taking back" their faith from the Islamists who had hijacked it.[45] Similarly, 2002 Harvard valedictorian Zayed Yasin, in his commencement speech entitled "My American Jihad," claimed that there is a unity between Islamic and American values and that the word "jihad" has been misused and abused by Islamists. Instead, Yasin argued that his jihad, a struggling to do right in the name of God, is consistent with American values.[46] Similarly, M.A. Muqtedar Khan, a political scientist of Indian-origin from Georgetown, wrote an essay entitled "A Memo to American Muslims" and posted it on his web site. Khan spoke for many Western Muslims when he stated,

As an Indian Muslim I know for sure that nowhere on earth, including India, will I get the same sense of dignity and respect that I have received in the U.S.... In the U.S., bigotry and xenophobia has been kept in check by media and leaders.... It is time that we acknowledge that the freedoms we enjoy in the U.S. are more desirable to us than superficial solidarity with the Muslim world. If you disagree then prove it by packing your bags and going to whichever Muslim country you identify with.... It is our responsibility to prevent people from abusing Islam. It is our job to ensure that Islam is not misrepresented.[47]

The "America, love it or leave it" portion of Khan's essay could have just as easily been written by conservative American politician Pat Buchanan. Similarly, in 2002 American moderate Muslim leader Shayk Kabbani denounced Wahhabism and equated it with the communist threat during the Cold War, stating, "And in that ideology [Wahhabism], of course, people are going to be violent. Until today no one tried to stop that kind of ideology. It's equal to communist ideology, which America always came out against and fought."[48]

If radical Islam truly is similar to "communist ideology" as Khan proposes, then it also makes sense that it can be combated the same way that communism was combated, and that means not by attacking it directly, but the institution of a policy of containment would be in order. Communism and Islamism (as well as fascism and Nazism) are clearly flawed and extreme ideologies that contain the seeds of their own destruction. Islamism, like other extreme ideologies, disallows diversity of thought, thus not only depriving itself of recruits, but also constricting development and therefore jeopardizing their own competitiveness and long-term survival. The authoritarian Islamists can tolerate no criticism, much like the communists of the former Soviet Union, but history has proven that the preservation of a hospitable environment for inquiry and debate, with a diversity of voices and free press, is a requirement for the long-term competitiveness of a society. In the words of Walter Lippman, "There can be no liberty for a community which lacks the information by which to detect lies."[49] Islamism, like other authoritarian ideologies, lacks such information.

Communism famously collapsed from within near the close of the twentieth century, partially due to the reforming efforts of the communist leader of the Soviet Union, Mikhail Gorbachev. As of yet, no Muslim Gorbachev has emerged (unless one desires to reach all the way back to Kemal Ataturk), but progressive voices have emerged. Afshin Ellian, for instance, an Iranian-born intellectual, argues that Islam needs its own versions of Nietzsche, Voltaire, and Marquis de Sade. Dutch Parliamentarian Ayaan Hirsi Ali has denounced Mohammed as a "perverted tyrant" and called for "liberal jihad."[50]

As previously discussed, Islamists have also used Western freedoms to their advantage. In no Western society, however, does liberty rightly conceived include a right to harm others. A liberal state, like any other, must operate on the basis of substantive values based on moral conceptions of human well-being, and the radical Islamic threat poses challenges not only to security, but to the values and institutions that are the foundation of freedom and democracy in the West; consequently, Western societies cannot be legitimately neutral between issues of danger and safety, deceit and integrity, or cowardice and courage. Thus, if Western societies regulate other negative externalities that are contrary to the good of society as a whole, such as environmental pollution, then they may also regulate extreme ideologies that threaten the very existence of Western freedoms. Although George W. Bush may be guilty of over-reaction, it may also be true that an effective response to the Islamic threat may require altering long-standing policies in numerous areas, including, but not limited to, immigration and civil rights. In other words, Mr. Bush may be correct in that some liberties may have to be eroded in Western societies in efforts to curb the dangers posed by radical Islam in the future. This is unfortunate, but recent deadly events have proven that things could not continue as they were. Advanced security measures at airports, for instance, can be expected to be continued, while permanent detention without charges and torture can be expected to be abandoned.

Unfortunately, the attacks of 9/11 (and other subsequent terrorist attacks in London, Madrid, the Netherlands, etc.) have aroused Western fears and the aroused fears have distorted Western judgment. Western leaders have proven too eager to use public anxiety for political gains and shed the long-standing restraints on governmental power that free and open societies require. The overreacting Western governments have threatened freedoms in their own societies at home while overreaching abroad and thus elicited a self-defeating Islamist backlash against themselves. American attempts at imposing hegemony have thus far mostly only stirred resentment and the prospect of a war on terror with no end has unravelled both Western liberties and the Western regimes that launched the ill-fated wars in Iraq and Afghanistan.

In a world with deep moral disagreements, it would appear that the wisest course would not to be to stipulate Western values that all the people in the world must adopt as a premise, but to facilitate means of social cooperation in hopes that the divides between Islamists and the West can be bridged. America in particular has proven for most of its existence that a society can be both religious and modern with individual rights and democratic values. Liberty, however, is trampled when a religious group condemns apostates to death for heresy or leaving the faith. Thus far, few Muslims living in the West have spoken out unequivocally for the right to leave the faith or even to hold dissonant views in safety. The challenge then is to construct free and democratic political regimes that also protect individual rights, but allow individuals to practice their religions freely within the rights-protecting set of liberal democratic rules. Muslims must therefore produce their own Voltaires that argue that "I do not agree with what you have to say, but I'll defend your right to say it." Given that most religions have actually had their beginning as heresies, one of the hallmarks of a democratic society is that arguments within freely constituted groups, religious or otherwise, may unfold peacefully. Furthermore, if those disputes lead to new political and religious divides, that too must be a peaceful process free of violence and coercion.

After 9/11, there was a flurry of interfaith events all across the United States as local churches hosted classes, seminars, and social gatherings with local Muslims in an attempt to bridge the religious and cultural divide. During this period, Muslims proved that they could reach across the aisle to their Christian brothers without calling for their execution and condemning them to everlasting hell. Although much of this handshaking was very short-lived, it is certainly suggestive that many Western Muslims, as well as Christians, are dedicated to coexistence, and much like the tiny sound remaining after Pandora opened her box, hope therefore remains.

Chapter Notes

Preface

1. Joselyne Cesari, *When Islam and Democracy Meet* (New York: Palgrave/Macmillan, 2004), 3.

2. Ibid., 4.

3. Ibid.

4. S. Sayyid. *A Fundamental Fear: Eurocentrism and the Emergence of Islamism* (London and New York: Zed Books, 2003), 17.

5. Ibid.

6. Bernard Lewis, *The Political Language of Islam* (Chicago: University of Chicago Press, 1988), 72–73.

7. Oivier Roy, *The Failure of Political Islam* (Cambridge, MA: Harvard University Press, 1994), 157.

8. Ibid., 153.

9. Lewis, *The Political Language of Islam*, 72–73.

10. Ali A. Allawi, *The Crisis of Islamic Civilization* (New Haven and London: Yale University Press), 2009.

Chapter 1

1. Samuel Huntington, *The Clash of Civilizations and the Remaking of the World Order* (New York: Simon & Schuster, 1996), 66.

2. Ron Geaves and Theodore Gabriel, "Introduction," in *Islam and the West: Post 9/11*, edited by Ron Geaves, Theodore Gabriel, Yvonne Haddad, and Jane Idleman Smith (Burlington, VT: Ashgate Publishing, 2004), 3.

3. John Mickelthwait and Adrian Wooldridge, *God Is Back: How the Global Revival of Faith Is Changing the World* (New York: Penguin Press, 2009), 5.

4. Jytte Kausen, *The Islamic Challenge: Politics and Religion in Western Europe* (Oxford and New York: Oxford University Press, 2005), 6. See also Olivier Roy, *The Failure of Political Islam* (Cambridge, MA: Harvard University Press, 1994), 16.

5. Klausen, *The Islamic Challenge*, 6.

6. Joselyne Cesari, *When Islam and Democracy Meet* (New York: Palgrave/Macmillan, 2004), 15.

7. Klausen, *The Islamic Challenge*, 6.

8. Huntington, *The Clash of Civilizations*, 200.

9. Mickelthwait and Wooldridge, *God Is Back*, 279.

10. Syed Z. Abedin and Saleha M. Abedin, "Muslim Minorities in Non–Muslim Societies," in *Oxford Encyclopaedia of the Modern Islamic World* (Oxford, UK: Oxford University Press, 1994), 112.

11. Cesari, *When Islam and Democracy Meet*, 17.

12. Mickelthwait and Woodridge, *God Is Back*, 279

13. Klausen, *The Islamic Challenge*, 1, 189.

14. Cesari, *When Islam and Democracy Meet*, 61–62.

15. Klausen, *The Islamic Challenge*, 192.

16. Olivier Roy, *Globalized Islam: The Search for a New Ummah* (New York: Columbia University Press, 2004), 22.

17. Geaves and Gabriel, "Introduction," 5.

18. Mickelthwait and Wooldridge, *God Is Back*, 340–341.

19. Brian Moynihan, "Hardline Holland," *The Sunday Times* (February 27, 2005), 34.

20. Efraim Karsh, *Islamic Imperialism: A History* (New Haven, CT: Yale University Press, 2006), 228.

21. Lawrence Wright, *The Looming Tower: Al-Qaeda and the Road to 9/11* (New York: Alfred A. Knopf, 2006), 171.

22. Huntington, *The Clash of Civilizations*, 247.

23. Gilles Kepel, *The War for Muslim Minds: Islam and the West* (Cambridge, MA: Belknap Press of Harvard University, 2004), 102.

24. Ibid., 94–95.

25. Ibid., 94–95.

26. Ibid., 97–98.

27. Ibid., 98.

28. Michael Burleigh, *Earthly Powers: The*

Clash of Religion and Politics in Europe, from the French Revolution to the Great War (New York: HarperCollins, 2005), 39.

29. Ibid., 39, 46.

30. Owen Chadwick, *The Victorian Church: Part II* (Oxford, UK: Oxford University Press, 1970), 430.

31. Roy, *Globalized Islam*, 19.

32. David Hume, *Dialogues and Natural History of Religion*, ed. J.C.A. Gaskin (Oxford, UK: Oxford University Press, 1998), 134–196.

33. Roy, *Globalized Islam*, 10.

34. Shireen T. Hunter, *The Future of Islam and the West: Clash of Civilizations or Peaceful Coexistence?* (Westport, CT: Praeger, 1998), 110.

35. Roy, *Globalized Islam*, 29

36. Wright, *The Looming Tower*, 12–14.

37. Ibid., 15.

38. Ibid., 15–16.

39. Ibid., 18.

40. Ibid., 20.

41. Ibid.

42. Ibid., 22.

43. Ibid.

44. Ibid., 23.

45. Bernard Lewis, "The Roots of Muslim Rage," *Atlantic Monthly* 266, no. 3 (September 1990): 55–59.

46. Hunter, *The Future of Islam and the West*, 111.

47. Ibid.

48. Ibid., 113.

49. Roy, *Globalized Islam*, 2.

50. Ibid., 2.

51. Ibid., 4–5.

52. Ibid., 138.

53. Ibid., 141.

54. Klausen, *The Islamic Challenge*, 141.

55. http://www.meforum.org/448/we-will-domdinate-you.

56. Klausen, *The Islamic Challenge*, 140–141.

57. Ibid., 151–152.

Chapter 2

1. Mark Juergensmeyer, *Terror in the Mind of God: The Global Rise of Religious Violence* (Berkeley: University of California Press, 2003), 7.

2. John Shepherd, "Self-critical Children of Abraham? Roots of Violence and Extremism in Judaism, Christianity and Islam," in *Islam and the West: Post 9/11*, edited by Ron Geaves, Theodore Gabriel, Yvonne Haddad, and Jane Idleman Smith (Burlington, VT: Ashgate, 2004), 43.

3. Mark Juergensmeyer, *Global Rebellion: Religious Challenges to the Secular State, from Christian Militias to Al Qaeda* (Berkeley: University of California Press, 2008), 217, 255.

4. Reinhold Niebuhr, *Moral Man and Immoral Society* (New York: Scribner's, 1932), 277.

5. Ibid.

6. Bernard Lewis, *The Political Language of Islam* (Chicago: University of Chicago Press, 1988), 3.

7. Juergensmeyer, *Global Rebellion*, 183.

8. Chip Berlet and John Salvi, *Abortion Clinic Violence and Catholic Right Conspiracism* (Somerville, MA: Political Research Associates, 1996), 8.

9. Gary North, *Backward Christian Soldiers? An Action Manual for Christian Reconstruction* (Tyler, TX: Institute for Christian Economics, 1984), 267.

10. Ibid., 267.

11. Juergensmeyer, *Global Rebellion*, 184.

12. Ibid., 2.

13. Ibid., 185.

14. John Kifner, "Suspect in Kahane Case Is Muslim Born in Egypt," *New York Times* (November 7, 1990), B13.

15. Juergensmeyer, *Global Rebellion*, 186.

16. Ibid.

17. Ibid., 191.

18. Ibid.

19. Gerald Baumgarten, *Paranoia as Patriotism: Far-Right Influences on the Militia Movement* (New York: Anti-Defamation League, 1995), 17.

20. Bruce Hoffman, "Holy Terror: The Implications of Terrorism Motivated by a Religious Imperative," *Studies in Conflict and Terrorism* 18 (1995): 271–284.

21. Morris Dees, *Gathering Storm: America's Militia Threat* (New York: HarperCollins, 1996), 154.

22. Juergensmeyer, *Global Rebellion*, 187–188.

23. Theodore Adorno, Daniel Jay Levinson, R. Nevitt Sanford, and Else Frenkel Brunswick, *The Authoritarian Personality* (New York: W.W. Norton, 1950, 1993), v–ix.

24. Stanley Feldman, "Enforcing Social Conformity: A Theory of Authoritarianism," *Political Psychology* 24, no. 1 (2003): 41–44.

25. John T. Jost, Jack Glaser, Arie W. Kruglanski, and Frank J. Sulloway, "Political Conservatism as Motivated Social Cognition," *Psychological Bulletin* 129, no. 3 (2003): 339–375.

26. Juergensmeyer, *Global Rebellion*, 224.

27. Robert Altemeyer, *The Authoritarian Specter* (Cambridge, MA: Harvard University Press, 1996, 78–79).

28. Albert Bandura, *Aggression: A Social Learning Analysis* (Upper Saddle River, NJ: Prentice Hall, 1973), 124–128.

29. Lawrence Freedman, *A Choice of Enemies: America Confronts the Middle East* (New York: Public Affairs, 2008), 494.

30. Stanley Milgram, *Obedience to Authority: An Experimental View* (New York: Harper Perennial, 1969), 1.

31. Ibid., 205.

32. Al Gore, *The Assault on Reason* (New York: Penguin Press, 2007), 155.

33. Milgram, *Obedience to Authority*, 127–134.

34. Wendell Steavenson, *The Weight of a Mustard Seed: The Intimate Story of an Iraqi General and His Family during Thirty Years of Tyranny* (New York: HarperCollins, 2009), 117.

35. Ibid., 118.

36. Ibid., 119.

37. Joseph LeDoux, *The Emotional Brain* (New York: Simon & Schuster, 1996), 19.

38. Altemeyer, *The Authoritarian Specter*, 9.

39. Ibid.

40. Ibid., 10.

41. Ibid., 84.

42. Robert Baer, *See No Evil* (New York: Three Rivers Press, 2002), 74–75, 234.

43. Altemeyer, *The Authoritarian Specter*, 84.

44. Ibid.

45. Ibid., 10.

46. Robert Altemeyer, *Enemies of Freedom* (San Francisco: Jossey-Bass, 1988), 47–151.

47. Altemeyer, *The Authoritarian Specter*, 11.

48. Ibid., 30–31.

49. Ibid., 20–21.

50. Ibid., 144–145.

Chapter 3

1. John Mickelthwait and Adrian Wooldridge, *God Is Back: How the Global Revival of Faith Is Changing the World* (New York: Penguin Press, 2009), 5.

2. Ibid., 280.

3. Paul Belien, "Meet the Mayor of Brussels: She's a Muslim," *The Brussels Journal* (16 January 2006), www.brusselsjournal.com/node/671.

4. Marcia Hermansen, "The Evolution of American Muslim Responses," in *Islam and the West: Post 9/11*, edited by Ron Geaves, Theodore Gabriel, Yvonne Haddad, and Jane Idleman Smith (Burlington, VT: Ashgate, 2004), 85.

5. Lawrence Freedman, *A Choice of Enemies: America Confronts the Middle East* (New York: Public Affairs, 2008), 98.

6. Fouad Ajami, "The Moor's Last Laugh: Radical Islam Finds a Haven in Europe," *Wall Street Journal* (March 22, 2004), A18.

7. Gilles Kepel, *The War for Muslim Minds: Islam and the West* (Cambridge, MA: Belknap Press of Harvard University, 2004), 253.

8. Ibid., 286.

9. Jytte Klausen, *The Islamic Challenge: Politics and Religion in Western Europe* (Oxford and New York: Oxford University Press, 2005), 210.

10. Joan Trevor, "Anti-Bans, Anti-Hijab," *Worker's Liberty*, 12 August 2004, www.workersliberty.org/node/2320.

11. Klausen, *The Islamic Challenge*, 33–35.

12. Sacha Ismail, "What Is the Muslim Association of Britain," *Worker's Liberty*, March 15, 2007, www.workersliberty.org/node/3026.

13. Martin Bright, "Radical Links of UK's 'Moderate' Muslim Group," *The Observer* August 14, 2005, http://observer.guardian.co.uk/uk_news/story/0,6903,1548786,00.html.

14. Klausen, *The Islamic Challenge*, 34.

15. Ibid., 35.

16. Ibid., 32.

17. Union Des Organisations Islamiques Des France, *Actualite*, January 16, 2007, www.uoif-online.com/&prev=/se.

18. Klausen, *The Islamic Challenge*, 38.

19. Quintan Wictorowicz, *Radical Islam Rising* (Lanham, MD: Rowman and Littlefield, 2005), 1–2.

20. Klausen, *The Islamic Challenge*, 20.

21. Ibid., 45.

22. Abul Taher, "Banned Extremists Regroup," *The Sunday Times* (October 29, 2006), www.timesonline.co.uk/tol/news/uk/article616692.ece.

23. Wictorowicz, *Radical Islam Rising*, 6–7.

24. Ibid., 7.

25. The Jamestown Foundation, *Al-Muhajiroun in the UK: An Interview with Sheikh Omar Bakri Mohammed*, www.jamestown.org/terrorism/news/article.php?search=1&articleid=23622.

26. Adrian Morgan, "UK Islamist Guilty of Soliciting Murder," *Spero News* (January 8, 2007), www.speroforum.com/site/article.asp?id=7364.

27. The Insight Team, "Focus: Undercover in the Academy of Hatred," *Times Online* (August 7, 2005), www.timesonline.co.uk/tol/news/uk/article552687.ece.

28. Richard A. Clarke, Glen P. Aga, Roger W. Cressey, Stephen E. Flyn, Blake W. Mobley, Eric Rosenbach, Steven Simon, William F. Wechsler, and Lee S. Wolosky, *Defeating the Jihadists: A Blueprint for Action* (New York: Century Foundation Press, 2004), 61.

29. Olivier Roy, *Globalized Islam: The Search for a New Ummah* (New York: Columbia University Press, 2004), 111.

30. Klausen, *The Islamic Challenge*, 45.

31. Ibid.

32. Suha Taji-Farouki, *Muslim Identity and the Balkan State* (New York: New York University Press, 1996), 3.

33. Michael Whine, "Al-Muhajiroun: The Portal for Britain's Suicide Terrorists," *International Policy Institute for Counter Terrorism* (May 21, 2003), www.ict.org.il/articles/articledet.cfm?articleid=484, pp.1–8.

34. Klausen, *The Islamic Challenge*, 45.

35. Whine, "Al-Muhajiroun," 5.

36. Al-Bab, "Abu Hamza and the Supporters

of Sharia," March 7, 1999, http://www.al-bab.com/yemen/hamza/hamza1.htm.

37. Ibid.

38. Ibid.

39. Ibid.

40. "Cartoon Wars," *The Economist* (February 11, 2006): 9.

41. "Special Report: Islam and Free Speech," *The Economist* (February 11, 2006): 24–26.

42. Ibid., 26.

43. Human Rights Watch, "Human Rights in Saudi Arabia: A Deafening Silence," December 2001, www.hrw.org/backgrounder/mena/saudi.

44. International Policy Institute for Counter Terrorism, "SpotLight: Hilafet Devleti," January 28, 2004, www.ict.org.il/spotlight/det.cfm?id=245.

45. Joan Bakewell, "The Believers Who Despise Our Ways," *New Statesman* (May 29, 2000), www.newstatesman.com/200005290011.

46. "Profile, the Caliph of Cologne," *BBC News* (May 27, 2004), http://news.bbc.co.uk/2/hi/europe/1705886.stm.

47. International Policy Institute for Counter Terrorism, "SpotLight: Hilafet Devleti."

48. "Profile, the Caliph of Cologne," *BBC News*, May 27, 2004.

49. Clarke et al., *Defeating the Jihadists*, 57–58.

50. Ron Suskind, *The One Percent Doctrine: Deep Inside America's Pursuit of its Enemies Since 9/11* (New York: Simon & Schuster, 2006), 181.

51. Caroline Cox and John Marks, *The West, Islam, and Islamism* (London: Civitas, 2003), 64.

52. Ibid.

53. Kepel, *The War for Muslim Minds*, 254, 263.

54. Ibid., 264.

55. Ibid., 263–265.

56. Ibid., 265.

57. Klausen, *The Islamic Challenge*, 43.

58. Ibid.

59. Rosemary Belcher, "Europe's Malcolm X," *New Humanist* (July/August, 2004): 8–12.

60. Ibid., 12.

61. Salam Al-Marayati, "Formulating an Agenda of Political Actions for North American Muslims," in *Islam: A Contemporary Perspective*, edited by Mohammad Ahmadullah Siddiqi (Chicago: NAAMPS, 1994), 94.

62. Joselyne Cesari, *When Islam and Democracy Meet* (New York: Palgrave/Macmillan, 2005), 81.

63. Ibid., 81–82.

64. Steven Emerson, *American Jihad: The Terrorists Living Among Us* (New York: Simon & Schuster, 2003), 178–221.

65. Cox and Marks, *The West, Islam, and Islamism*, 67.

66. Ibid.

67. Ibid.

68. Steven Coll, *Ghost Wars: The Secret History of the CIA, Afghanistan, and bin Laden, from the Soviet Invasion to September 10, 2001* (New York: Penguin, 2005), 230–231.

69. Ibid., 269.

70. S. Sayyid, *A Fundamental Fear: Eurocentrism and the Emergence of Islamism* (London and New York: Zed Books, 2003), xv.

Chapter 4

1. Bernard Lewis, "The Roots of Muslim Rage," *Atlantic Monthly* 266, no. 3 (September 1990): 55–59.

2. Samuel Huntington, *The Clash of Civilizations and the Remaking of the World Order* (New York: Simon & Schuster, 1996), 66.

3. Bernard Lewis, *Islam and the West* (New York: Oxford University Press, 1993), 13.

4. Huntington, *The Clash of Civilizations*, 210.

5. Ibid.

6. Gilles Kepel, *The War for Muslim Minds: Islam and the West* (Cambridge, MA: Belknap Press of Harvard University, 2004), 253.

7. Huntington, *The Clash of Civilizations*.

8. Ron Geaves and Theodore Gabriel, "Introduction," in Ron Geaves, Theodore Gabriel, Yvonne Haddad, and Jane Idleman Smith, eds., *Islam and the West: Post 9/11* (Burlington, VT: Ashgate Publishing, 2004), 4.

9. Huntington, *The Clash of Civilizations*, 28.

10. Ibid.

11. Ibid.

12. Ibid., 51.

13. Ibid., 53–54.

14. Lewis, *Islam and the West*, 4.

15. Huntington, *The Clash of Civilizations*, 210–211.

16. Jytte Klausen, *The Islamic Challenge: Politics and Religion in Western Europe* (Oxford and New York: Oxford University Press, 2005), 2.

17. Ibid., 23.

18. "Muslims in Europe: Confusing and Confused," *The Economist*, October 29, 2005, 87.

19. Haroun Er-Rashid, "Muslims and the West: A Paradigm for Polarization," in *Islam and the West: Critical Perspectives on Modernity*, edited by Michael F. Thompson (Lanham, MD: Rowman and Littlefield, 2003), 10.

20. Olivier Roy, *Globalized Islam: The Search for a New Ummah* (New York: Columbia University Press, 2004), 176.

21. Klausen, *The Islamic Challenge*, 109–110.

22. "Officials Fear Iraq's Lure for Muslims in Europe," *International Herald Tribune*, 2004, p. 4.

23. John R. Stone, *The Routledge Dictionary of Latin Quotations* (New York: Routledge, 2004), 120.

24. Klausen, *The Islamic Challenge*, 56–60.

25. Huntington, *The Clash of Civilizations*, 200.

26. Ibid.

27. Joselyne Cesari, *When Islam and Democracy Meet* (New York: Palgrave/Macmillan, 2004), 31–32.

28. Ibid., 32.

29. Ibid., 40.

30. Dan Eggen, "Alleged Remarks on Islam Prompt an Ashcroft Reply," *Washington Post*, February 14, 2002, A1.

31. Cesari, *When Islam and Democracy Meet*, 33.

32. Ibid.

33. Ibid.

34. Ibid.

35. Ibid., 40.

36. Joel S. Fetzer and Christopher J. Soper, *Muslims and the State in Britain, France, and Germany* (Cambridge, UK: Cambridge University Press, 2005), 104.

37. Roger Karapin, "Major Anti-Minority Riots and National Legislation in Britain and Germany," in *Challenging Immigration and Ethnic Relations Politics*, edited by Ruud Koopmans and Paul Statham (Oxford, UK: Oxford University Press, 2000), 330–335.

38. Dilwar Hussein, "The Impact of 9/11 on British Muslim Identity," in Geaves et al., *Islam and the West*, 125.

39. Ernest Allen, "Identity and Destiny," in *Muslims on the Americanization Path?*, edited by Yvonne Yazbeck Haddad and John L. Esposito (New York: Oxford University Press, 2000), 132–134.

40. Ibid., 138–139.

41. Cesari, *When Islam and Democracy Meet*, 36.

42. Ibid.

43. Huntington, *The Clash of Civilizations*, 201.

44. Judith Miller, "Strangers at the Gate," *New York Times Magazine* (September 15, 1991), 49.

45. Cesari, *When Islam and Democracy Meet*, 2004, 37.

46. Christopher Allen, "Endemically European or a European Epidemic? Islamophobia in a Post-9/11 Europe," in Geaves, *Islam and the West*, 131.

47. Fetzer and Soper, *Muslims and the State in Britain, France, and Germany*, 29.

48. Cesari, *When Islam and Democracy Meet*, 76.

49. Ibid., 75.

50. Klausen, *The Islamic Challenge*, 122.

51. Cesari, *When Islam and Democracy Meet*, 31.

52. Ibid., 75.

53. "Swing Low, Swing Right: The European Elections," *The Economist* (June 13, 2008): 54–55.

54. "Extreme Rightist Eclipses Socialist to Qualify for Runoff in France," *New York Times*, April 22, 2002, p. A1.

55. Liz Fekete, "Issues in the French Presidential Elections," *IRR News* (June 1, 1995), www.irr.org.uk/europebulletin/france/extreme_right_politics/1995/ak000006.html.

56. "Jean-Marie Le Pen renvoyé devant la justice pour ses propos sur l'Occupation," *Le Monde* (July 13, 2006), http://www.lemonde.fr/societe/article/2006/07/13/jean-marie-le-pen-renvoye-devant-la-justice-pour-ses-propos-sur-l-occupation_794895_3224.html#ens_id=776560

57. Klausen, *The Islamic Challenge*, 122.

58. Huntington, *The Clash of Civilizations*, 201.

59. "German Security Laws: Times of Terror," *The Economist* (September 29, 2007): 55.

60. David Gordon Smith, "Schäuble's Terror Plan Shows Complete Insanity," *Spiegel Online International* (July 9, 2007), www.spiegel.de/international/germany/0,1518,493365,00.html.

61. "German Security Laws: Times of Terror," *The Economist* (September 29, 2007).

62. Ibid.

63. Huntington, *The Clash of Civilizations*, 202.

64. Fetzer and Soper, *Muslims and the State in Britain, France, and Germany*, 104.

65. Klausen, *The Islamic Challenge*, 123.

66. "President Bush's State of the Union Address," *Washington Post* (January 31, 2006), http://www.washingtonpost.com/wp-dyn/content/article/2006/01/31/AR2006013101468.html.

67. Huntington, *The Clash of Civilizations*, 202.

68. Ibid., 215.

69. Samuel Huntington, *Who Are We? The Cultural Core of American National Identity* (New York: Simon & Schuster, 2004), 188.

70. Mickelthwaite and Wooldridge, *God Is Back*, 338.

71. Yvonne Yazbeck Haddad, "The Shaping of a Moderate North American Islam: Between 'Mufti' Bush and 'Ayatollah' Ashcroft," in Geaves et al., *Islam and the West*, 98.

72. Yvonne Yazbeck Haddad, "The American Path Option," in Haddad and Esposito, *Muslims on the Americanization Path?*, 24.

73. Ibid., 99–100.

74. Ibid., 100.

75. Ahmed S. Hashim, *Insurgency and Counter-Insurgency in Iraq* (New York: Columbia University Press, 2006), 320.

76. Haddad, "The Shaping of a Moderate North American Islam," 100–101.

77. Ibid., 102.
78. Ibid., 106.
79. Ibid., 108.
80. Ibid., 101–105.
81. Muhommed A. Muqtedar Khan, *American Muslims: Bridging Faith and Freedom* (Portland, OR: Amana, 2002), 95.
82. Haddad, "The Shaping of a Moderate North American Islam," 110.
83. Khan, *American Muslims*, 95.
84. Gershom Gorenberg, *The End of Days: Fundamentalism and the Struggle for the Temple Mount* (New York: Free Press, 2000), 164.
85. Khan, *American Muslims*, 95.
86. Gorenberg, *The End of Days*, 166.
87. Ibid., 167.
88. Khan, *American Muslims*, 96–97.
89. David L. Phillips, *Losing Iraq: Inside the Postwar Reconstruction Fiasco* (Boulder, CO: Westview Press, 2005), 16.
90. Ibid.
91. Ibid.
92. Brian C. Anderson, "Secular Europe, Religious America," *Public Interest* (Spring 2004): 143–156.
93. Benjamin Platt Thomas, *Abraham Lincoln: A Biography* (New York: Knopf, 1960), 359.
94. Brian R. Farmer, *American Conservatism: History, Theory and Practice* (Newcastle, UK: Cambridge Scholars Press, 2005), 173.
95. Ibid.
96. Kevin Phillips, *American Dynasty: Aristocracy, Fortune, and the Politics of Deceit in the House of Bush* (New York: Viking, 2004), 232.
97. Bob Woodward, *Bush at War* (New York: Simon & Schuster, 2002), 67.
98. Phillips, *American Dynasty*, 233.
99. Ibid., 239.
100. Ibid., 223.
101. Ibid., 235.
102. Ibid., 226–227.
103. Daniel Benjamin and Steven Simon, *The Next Attack: The Failure of the War on Terror and a Strategy for Getting It Right* (New York: Henry Holt, 2005), 269.
104. Phillips, *American Dynasty*, 230.
105. Benjamin and Simon, *The Next Attack*, 270.
106. Ibid.
107. Michael Weinstein and Resa Aslan, "Not So Fast, Christian Soldiers," *Los Angeles Times*, August 22, 2007, B17.
108. Olivier Roy, *Globalized Islam*, 80–81.
109. Ibid., 28–29.
110. "Religion and the War Against Evil." *Washington Post*, September 2, 2002, p. A3.
111. Ibid.
112. *Phillips, American Dynasty*, 230.
113. Ibid.
114. John Shepherd, "Self-critical Children of Abraham? Roots of Violence and Extremism in Judaism, Christianity and Islam," in Geaves et al., *Islam and the West*, 34.
115. Jane Lampman, "Mixing Prophecy and Politics," *Christian Science Monitor* (July 7, 2004): 1–2.
116. Phillips, *American Dynasty*, 230.
117. Ibid.
118. Ibid., 230–231.
119. Benjamin and Simon, *The Next Attack*, 269
120. "Evangelicals Flock into Iraq on a Mission of Faith," *Los Angeles Times*, March 18, 2004, p. A1.
121. Ibid.
122. Huntington, *The Clash of Civilizations*, 148.
123. Alec G. Hargreaves, *Immigration, Race and Ethnicity in Contemporary France* (London: Routledge, 1995), 120–121.
124. Fetzer and Soper, *Muslims and the State in Britain, France, and Germany*, 169.
125. Benjamin and Simon, *The Next Attack*, 82.
126. Fetzer and Soper, *Muslims and the State in Britain, France, and Germany*, 67–68.
127. "Focus on Religion," *National Statistics Online*, July 26, 2006, http://www.statistics.gov.uk/cci/nugget.asp?id=954.
128. Benjamin and Simon, *The Next Attack*, 52.
129. Robert Gildea, *France since 1945* (New York and Oxford: Oxford University Press, 1997), 21.
130. Timothy M. Savage, "Europe and Islam: Crescent Waxing, Cultures Clashing," *The Washington Quarterly* (Summer 2004): 31.
131. "Muslims in Britain: Hopes and Challenges," *The Guardian*, November 30, 2004, http://image.guardian.co.uk/sysfiles/Guardian/documents/2004/11/30/Muslims-Novo41.pdf
132. Benjamin and Simon, *The Next Attack*, 84.
133. "A Civil War on Terrorism," *The Economist* (November 25, 2004): 28–29.

Chapter 5

1. Joel S. Fetzer and Christopher J. Soper, *Muslims and the State in Britain, France, and Germany* (Cambridge, UK: Cambridge University Press, 2005), 63.
2. Philip Lewis, *Islamic Britain: Religion, Politics and Identity among British Muslims* (London: I. B. Tauris, 1994), 10–12.
3. Fetzer and Soper, *Muslims and the State in Britain, France, and Germany*, 63.
4. Jytte Klausen, *The Islamic Challenge: Politics and Religion in Western Europe* (Oxford and New York: Oxford University Press, 2005), 5.

5. Alec G. Hargreaves, *Immigration, Race and Ethnicity in Contemporary France* (London: Routledge, 1995), 11–17.

6. Gilles Kepel, *The War for Muslim Minds: Islam and the West* (Cambridge, MA: Belknap Press of Harvard University, 2004), 192–198.

7. Hargreaves, *Race and Ethnicity in Contemporary France*, 19–20.

8. Jorgen S. Nielsen, *Toward a European Islam* (London: Macmillan, 1999), 25–35.

9. Robert Gildea, *France since 1945* (New York and Oxford: Oxford University Press, 1997), 137–138.

10. Fetzer and Soper, *Muslims and the State in Britain, France, and Germany*, 63.

11. John R. Bowen, "Does French Islam Have Borders? Dilemmas of Domestication in a Global Religious Field," *American Anthropologist* 106, no. 4 (2004): 43–55.

12. Klausen, *The Islamic Challenge*, 38.

13. Fetzer and Soper, *Muslims and the State in Britain, France, and Germany*, 189.

14. Kepel, *The War for Muslim Minds*, 244.

15. Fetzer and Soper, *Muslims and the State in Britain, France, and Germany*, 5.

16. Hargreaves, *Race and Ethnicity in Contemporary France*, 201–205.

17. Fetzer and Soper, *Muslims and the State in Britain, France, and Germany*, 69–70.

18. Michael Burleigh, *Earthly Powers: The Clash of Religion and Politics in Europe, from the French Revolution to the Great War* (New York: HarperCollins, 2005), 362.

19. Klausen, *The Islamic Challenge*, 144.

20. Fetzer and Soper, *Muslims and the State in Britain, France, and Germany*, 76.

21. Ibid., 73.

22. Ibid., 74.

23. Kepel, *The War for Muslim Minds*, 244.

24. Joselyne Cesari, *When Islam and Democracy Meet* (New York: Palgrave/Macmillan, 2004), 71.

25. Fetzer and Soper, *Muslims and the State in Britain, France, and Germany*, 74.

26. Cesari, *When Islam and Democracy Meet*, 71.

27. "French Minister Threatens to Expel Extremist Muslims," *New York Times*, September 20, 2003, p. A4.

28. Klausen, *The Islamic Challenge*, 21, 44.

29. Ibid., 114.

30. Dilwar Hussein, "The Impact of 9/11 on British Muslim Identity," in *Islam and the West: Post 9/11*, edited by Ron Geaves, Theodore Gabriel, Yvonne Haddad, and Jane Idleman Smith (Burlington, VT: Ashgate, 2004), 116.

31. Fetzer and Soper, *Muslims and the State in Britain, France, and Germany*, 26.

32. Jessica R. Adolino, *Ethnic Minorities, Electoral Politics and Political Integration in Britain* (London, Pinter Publishers, 1998), 25.

33. Ian R.G. Spencer, *British Immigration Policy since 1939: The Making of a Multi-Racial Britain* (London: Routledge, 1997), 142–143.

34. Fetzer and Soper, *Muslims and the State in Britain, France, and Germany*, 26.

35. Spencer, *British Immigration Policy since 1939*, 152–153.

36. Fetzer and Soper, *Muslims and the State in Britain, France, and Germany*, 4, 30.

37. Ibid., 35.

38. Ibid., 42.

39. Ian Rath, Rinnus Pennix, Kees Groendendijk, and Astrid Meyer, *Western Europe and Its Islam* (Leiden, Netherlands: Brill, 2001), 236.

40. Fetzer and Soper, *Muslims and the State in Britain, France, and Germany*, 30–31.

41. Ibid., 35.

42. Michael Keene and Jan Keene, *Junior Steps in Religious Education, Year 4* (Cheltenham, UK: Stanley Thornes, 1997), 4.

43. Klausen, *The Islamic Challenge*, 143.

44. Cesari, *When Islam and Democracy Meet*, 66–67.

45. Kepel, *The War for Muslim Minds*, 244.

46. Kevin Phillips, *Londonistan* (New York: Encounter Books, 2006), x.

47. Hussein, "The Impact of 9/11 on British Muslim Identity," 125.

48. Stephen V. Monsma and J. Christopher Soper, *The Challenge of Pluralism: Church and State in Five Western Democracies* (Lanham, MD: Rowman and Littlefield, 1997), 176–184.

49. Fetzer and Soper, *Muslims and the State in Britain, France, and Germany*, 112–114.

50. Ibid., 5–6.

51. Cesari, *When Islam and Democracy Meet*, 68.

52. Ibid.

53. Fetzer and Soper, *Muslims and the State in Britain, France, and Germany*, 112–117.

54. Monsma and Soper, *The Challenge of Pluralism*, 164–171.

55. Grace Davie, *Religion in Modern Europe: A Memory Mutates* (Oxford, UK: Oxford University Press, 2000), 5–23.

56. Fetzer and Soper, *Muslims and the State in Britain, France, and Germany*, 108.

57. Ibid., 118–119.

58. Ibid., 99–100.

59. Yasemin Karakasoglu and Gerd Nonneman, "Muslims in Germany, with Special Reference to the Turkish-Islamic Community," in *Muslim Communities in the New Europe*, edited by Gerd Nonneman, Tim Noblock, and Bogdan Szajkowski (Reading, UK: Ithaca Press, 1996), 243.

60. Ulrich Herbert, *A History of Foreign Labor in Germany, 1880–1980* (Ann Arbor: University of Michigan Press, 1990), 203.

61. Fetzer and Soper, *Muslims and the State in Britain, France, and Germany*, 102.

62. Ibid., 103.

63. John L. Esposito, "Muslims in America or American Muslims?" in *Muslims on the Americanization Path?*, edited by Yvonne Yazbeck Haddad and John L. Esposito (New York: Oxford University Press, 2000), 3.

64. Daniel Benjamin and Steven Simon, *The Next Attack. The Failure of the War on Terror and a Strategy for Getting It Right* (New York: Henry Holt, 2005), 289.

65. Ibid., 119.

66. Esposito, "Muslims in America or American Muslims?" 4.

67. Yvonne Yazbeck Haddad, "The American Path Option," in Haddad and Esposito, *Muslims on the Americanization Path?*, 20.

68. Cesari, *When Islam and Democracy Meet*, 11.

69. Muhommed A. Muqtedar Khan, *American Muslims: Bridging Faith and Freedom* (Portland, OR: Amana, 2002), 91–92.

70. Ibid., 92.

71. Yvonne Yazbeck Haddad, "The Shaping of a Moderate North American Islam: Between 'Mufti' Bush and 'Ayatollah' Ashcroft," in Geaves et al., *Islam and the West*, 98.

72. Haddad, "The American Path Option," 22–24.

73. Ibid.

74. Maher Hathout, "Islamic Work in North America: Challenges and Opportunities," in *Islam: A Contemporary Perspective*, edited by Mohammad Ahmadullah Siddiqi (Chicago: NAAMPS, 1994), 62.

75. Mohammad Ahmadullah Siddiqi, "Towards an Islamic Vision and Agenda for the Future," in Siddiqi, *Islam: A Contemporary Perspective*, 25.

76. Hathout, "Islamic Work in North America," 62.

77. Esposito, "Muslims in America or American Muslims?" 5.

78. Haddad, "The American Path Option," 36.

79. National Commission on Terrorist Attacks, *The 9/11 Commission Report: Final Report of the National Commission on Terrorist Attacks Upon the United States* (New York: W.W. Norton, 2004), 215–241.

80. Olivier Roy, *Globalized Islam: The Search for a New Ummah* (New York: Columbia University Press, 2004), 51.

81. Dan Eggen and Julie Tate, "U.S. Campaign Produces Few Convictions on Terrorism Charges; Statistics Often Count Lesser Crimes," *Washington Post*, June 12, 2005, p. A1.

82. Esposito, "Muslims in America or American Muslims?" 7.

83. Ibid., 5–7.

84. Haddad, "The American Path Option," 38.

85. Ernest Allen, "Identity and Destiny," in Haddad and Esposito, *Muslims on the Americanization Path?*, 165.

86. Ibid., 179.

87. Ibid., 164–165.

88. Cesari, *When Islam and Democracy Meet*, 25.

89. Allen, "Identity and Destiny," 163.

90. Cesari, *When Islam and Democracy Meet*, 26.

91. Ibid., 81.

92. Haddad, "The American Path Option," 38.

93. Cesari, *When Islam and Democracy Meet*, 27.

94. Haddad, "The American Path Option," 38.

Chapter 6

1. Olivier Roy, *Globalized Islam: The Search for a New Ummah* (New York: Columbia University Press, 2004), 69.

2. Robin Lustig, Martin Bailey, Simon de Bruxelles, and Ian Mather, "War of the Word," *The Observer*, February 19, 1989.

3. Muhammad Anwar, "Muslims in Britain," in *Muslim Minorities in the West*, edited by Syed A. Abedin and Ziauddin Sardar (London: Grey Seal, 1995), 46.

4. Gilles Kepel, *The Trial of Political Islam* (Cambridge, MA: Harvard University Press, 2003), 188, 201.

5. Dale F. Eckelman and James Piscatori, *Muslim Politics* (Princeton, NJ: Princeton University Press, 1996), 4.

6. Jytte Klausen, *The Islamic Challenge: Politics and Religion in Western Europe* (Oxford and New York: Oxford University Press, 2005), 172, 200.

7. Ibid., 173.

8. Roy, *Globalized Islam*, 192.

9. Klausen, *The Islamic Challenge*, 182.

10. Joel S. Fetzer and Christopher J. Soper, *Muslims and the State in Britain, France, and Germany* (Cambridge, UK: Cambridge University Press, 2005), 115.

11. Kepel, *The Trial of Political Islam*, 198–199.

12. Fetzer and Soper, *Muslims and the State in Britain*, 78.

13. Ibid., 79.

14. Klausen, *The Islamic Challenge*, 174.

15. Ibid., 173, 176.

16. Ibid., 176.

17. Ibid., 177.

18. Ibid., 179.

19. Fetzer and Soper, *Muslims and the State in Britain*, 115.

20. Klausen, *The Islamic Challenge*, 184.

21. *Cooper v. Eugene School District*, 301 Or. 358, 723 P.2d (1986), 298.

22. "Muslims in Europe: Confusing and Confused," *The Economist* (October 29, 2005): 87.

23. *EEOC v. Presbyterian Ministries, Inc.*, 50 Fair Empl. Prac. Cas. BNA (1992), 579.

24. *United States v. Board of Education of School District of Philadelphia*, 911 F .2d 882 3d Cir. (1990).

25. Klausen, *The Islamic Challenge*, 181.

26. Ibid., 91, 171.

27. Carol L. Anway, "American Women Choosing Islam," in *Muslims on the Americanization Path?*, edited by Yvonne Yazbeck Haddad and John L. Esposito (New York: Oxford University Press, 2000), 154.

28. Esmail Shakeri, "Muslim Women in Canada: The Role and Status as Revealed in the Hijab Controversy," in Haddad and Esposito, *Muslims on the Americanization Path?*, 130.

29. Ibid.

30. Amber Nasrulla, "Educators Outside Quebec Mystified by Hijab Ban," *The Globe and Mail*, December 13, 1994, p. A1–4.

31. Chris Sheridan, "Islamophobia," *Mirror*, June 1, 1995, p. 12.

32. Rahat Kurd, "My Hijab Is an Act of Worship — and None of Your Business," *Globe and Mail*, February 15, 1995, p. A20.

33. Shakeri, "Muslim Women in Canada," 130.

34. Klausen, *The Islamic Challenge*, 176.

35. Michele Lemon, "Understanding Does Not Always Lead to Tolerance," *Globe and Mail*, January 31, 1995, p. A2.

36. Catherine Mocks, "The Hijab Has No Place in the Western World," *Globe and Mail*, February 16, 1993, p. A12.

37. Fetzer and Soper, *Muslims and the State in Britain*, 79–81.

38. Klausen, *The Islamic Challenge*, 120.

39. Ibid.

40. Ibid., 118.

41. Ibid.

42. Fetzer and Soper, *Muslims and the State in Britain*, 85.

43. Klausen, *The Islamic Challenge*, 146–147.

44. Ibid., 113.

45. Roy, *Globalized Islam*, 211.

46. Yvonne Yazbeck Haddad, "The Globalization of Islam: The Return of Muslims to the West," in *The Oxford History of Islam*, edited by John L. Esposito (Oxford: Oxford University Press, 1999), 625.

47. Klausen, *The Islamic Challenge*, 15.

48. Ibid.

49. Fetzer and Soper, *Muslims and the State in Britain*, 1.

50. Klausen, *The Islamic Challenge*, 81.

51. Roy, *Globalized Islam*, 162–163.

52. Ibid., 166.

53. Ibid., 162–164.

54. "French Violence Back to Normal," *BBC News*, November 17, 2005, http://news.bbc.co.uk/2/hi/europe/4445428.stm.

55. Fetzer and Soper, *Muslims and the State in Britain*, 4.

56. "Muslims Confront Leadership Void," *Chicago Tribune*, September 14, 2003, p. A1.

57. Ahmed S. Hashim, *Insurgency and Counter-Insurgency* in *Iraq* (New York: Columbia University Press, 2006), 146.

Chapter 7

1. Samuel Huntington, *The Clash of Civilizations and the Remaking of the World Order* (New York: Simon & Schuster, 1996), 129.

2. Ibid., 130.

3. Gordon Thomas, *Gideon's Spies: The Secret History of the Mossad* (New York: Thomas Dunne Books, 1999), 227–231.

4. Ibid., 234–236.

5. Ibid., 247.

6. Ibid.

7. Ibid., 252.

8. Michael Oren, *Power, Faith, and Fantasy: America in the Middle East 1776 to Present* (New York: Norton, 2007), 553.

9. Ibid., 556.

10. Ibid., 557.

11. Thomas, *Gideon's Spies*, 280.

12. Oren, *Power, Faith, and Fantasy*, 557.

13. Gilles Kepel, *The War for Muslim Minds: Islam and the West* (Cambridge, MA: Belknap Press of Harvard University, 2004), 243.

14. Gilles Kepel, *The Trial of Political Islam* (Cambridge, MA: Harvard University Press, 2003), 308.

15. Steven Coll, *Ghost Wars: The Secret History of the CIA, Afghanistan, and bin Laden, from the Soviet Invasion to September 10, 2001* (New York: Penguin, 2005), 275.

16. Ibid.

17. "World Bomb Suspects Alive in France," *BBC News*, June 1, 1999, http://news.bbc.co.uk/1/hi/world/357808.stm.

18. Kepel, *The War for Muslim Minds*, 243.

19. "French Violence Back to Normal," *BBC News*, November 17, 2005, http://news.bbc.co.uk/2/hi/Europe/4407688.stm.

20. "The Week Paris Burned," *The Observer*, November 6, 2005, http://www.guardian.co.uk/world/2005/nov/06/france.focus.

21. "French Violence Rages On," *New York Times*, November 7, 2007, http://nytimes.com/2005/11/07/international/europe/07france.

22. Daniel Benjamin and Steven Simon, *The Next Attack: The Failure of the War on Terror and a Strategy for Getting It Right* (New York: Henry Holt, 2005), 82.

23. Lawrence Wright, *The Looming Tower: Al-Qaeda and the Road to 9/11* (New York: Alfred A. Knopf, 2006), 305.

24. Kepel, *The War for Muslim Minds*, 241–242.

25. Michael Burleigh, *Sacred Causes: The Clash of Religion and Politics, from the Great War to the War on Terror* (New York: HarperCollins, 2007), 452.

26. Ron Suskind, *The One Percent Doctrine: Deep Inside America's Pursuit of Its Enemies Since 9/11* (New York: Simon & Schuster, 2006), 164–165.

27. Wright, *The Looming Tower*, 312.

28. Burleigh, *Sacred Causes*, 452.

29. Ibid.

30. Kepel, *The War for Muslim Minds*, 105–107.

31. Ibid.

32. Ibid.

33. Alison Pargeter, *The New Frontiers of Jihad: Radical Islam in Europe* (Philadelphia: University of Pennsylvania Press, 2008), 146.

34. Ibid., 145.

35. Kepel, *The War for Muslim Minds*, 242.

36. Ibid., 243.

37. Ibid., 148.

38. Pargeter, *The New Frontiers of Jihad*, 158–159.

39. Ibid., 161–162.

40. Ibid., 163–164.

41. Burleigh, *Sacred Causes*, 456–457.

42. Bruce Bawer, *While Europe Slept: How Radical Islam Is Destroying the West from Within* (New York: Doubleday, 2006), 1–2.

43. Burleigh, *Sacred Causes*, 457.

44. Ibid.

45. Jytte Klausen, *The Islamic Challenge: Politics and Religion in Western Europe* (Oxford and New York: Oxford University Press, 2005), 4.

46. Burleigh, *Sacred Causes*, 476.

47. Pargeter, *The New Frontiers of Jihad*, 130.

48. Kepel, *The War for Muslim Minds*, 144–145.

49. Ibid., 145.

50. Pargeter, *The New Frontiers of Jihad*, 115.

51. Kepel, *The War for Muslim Minds*, 242.

52. Ibid., 143.

53. Pargeter, *The New Frontiers of Jihad*, 136–137.

54. Ibid., 125–126.

55. Suskind, *The One Percent Doctrine*, 155–156.

56. Benjamin and Simon, *The Next Attack*, 6.

57. Ibid., 7.

58. Pargeter, *The New Frontiers of Jihad*, 126.

59. Ibid., 127.

60. Ibid., 132–135.

61. Ibid., 132.

62. Kepel, *The War for Muslim Minds*, 240, 245.

63. Ibid., 248.

64. Ibid., 188.

65. Ibid., 188–190.

66. "Special Report: Islam and Free Speech," *The Economist* (February 11, 2006): 24–26.

67. Ibid., 24.

68. Pargeter, *The New Frontiers of Jihad*, 191.

69. Ibid., 192.

70. "Special Report: Islam and Free Speech," 25.

71. Pargeter, *The New Frontiers of Jihad*, 192.

72. "Special Report: Islam and Free Speech," 24–25.

73. Pargeter, *The New Frontiers of Jihad*, 196–197.

74. John Micklethwait and Adrian Wooldridge, *God Is Back: How the Global Revival of Faith Is Changing the World* (New York: Penguin Press, 2009), 344–345.

75. Ibid.

76. Ibid., 345.

77. Ibid.

78. Wright, *The Looming Tower*, 6.

79. Benjamin and Simon, *The Next Attack*, 124.

80. Jerry Markon, "Muslim Lecturer Sentenced to Life; Followers Trained for Armed Jihad," *Washington Post*, July 14, 2005, p. A01.

81. Ibid.

82. Benjamin and Simon, *The Next Attack*, 117.

83. Suskind, *The One Percent Doctrine*, 119.

84. Ibid., 181.

85. Ibid., 157–158.

86. Yvonne Yazbeck Haddad, "The American Path Option," in *Muslims on the Americanization Path?*, edited by Yvonne Yazbeck Haddad and John L. Esposito (New York: Oxford University Press, 2000), 28.

87. Huntington, *The Clash of Civilizations*, 216.

88. Haddad, "The American Path Option," 24–25.

89. Ibid., 31.

90. Huntington, *The Clash of Civilizations*, 216–217.

91. Ibid., 217.

92. Haddad, "The American Path Option," 25.

93. Joselyne Cesari, *When Islam and Democracy Meet* (New York: Palgrave/Macmillan, 2004), 38.

94. "Muslims Get in Touch with Their Faith, Culture," *Chicago Tribune*, September 14, 2003, p. A1.

95. "Jihadist or Victim: Ex Detainee Makes a Case," *New York Times*, July 27, 2005, p. A1.

96. Cesari, *When Islam and Democracy Meet*, 38.

97. Benjamin and Simon, *The Next Attack*, 121.

98. Ibid., 122.

99. Cesari, *When Islam and Democracy Meet*, 39.

100. Ibid.

101. Ibid.

102. Huntington, *The Clash of Civilizations*, 269.

103. Kepel, *The Trial of Political Islam*, 237–250.

104. Olivier Roy, *Globalized Islam: The Search for a New Ummah* (New York: Columbia University Press, 2004), 314.

105. Ibid., 61–64.

106. Kepel, *The Trial of Political Islam*, 251.

107. Huntington, *The Clash of Civilizations*, 270.

108. Ibid., 126, 270.

109. Ibid., 271.

110. Ibid., 268.

111. Roy, *Globalized Islam*, 314.

112. Richard A. Clarke, Glen P. Aga, Roger W. Cressey, Stephen E. Flyn, Blake W. Mobley, Eric Rosenbach, Steven Simon, William F. Wechsler, and Lee S. Wolosky, *Defeating the Jihadists: A Blueprint for Action* (New York: Century Foundation Press, 2004), 45–46.

113. Benjamin and Simon, *The Next Attack*, 20.

114. Ibid., 46.

Chapter 8

1. Steven D. Levitt and Stephen J. Dubner, *Super Freakonomics* (New York: HarperCollins, 2009), 93.

2. Samuel Huntington, *The Clash of Civilizations and the Remaking of the World Order* (New York: Simon & Schuster, 1996), 59.

3. Ibid., 112–113.

4. Gilles Kepel, *Muslim Extremism in Egypt: The Prophet and the Pharaoh* (Berkeley: University of California Press, 1993), 220.

5. Jeff Goodwin and Theda Skocpol, "Explaining Revolutions in the Contemporary Third World," *Politics and Society* 17 (1989): 490.

6. Levitt and Dubner, *Super Freakonomics*, 62–63.

7. Gilles Kepel, *The War for Muslim Minds: Islam and the West* (Cambridge, MA: Belknap Press of Harvard University, 2004), 1–2.

8. Lawrence Wright, *The Looming Tower: Al-Qaeda and the Road to 9/11* (New York: Alfred A. Knopf, 2006), 183.

9. Ibid., 33–34.

10. Ibid., 126.

11. Ibid., 37, 46, 54.

12. Ibid., 183.

13. Kepel, *The War for Muslim Minds*, 89.

14. Wright, *The Looming Tower*, 49.

15. Andrew Higgins and Alan Cullison,

"Terrorist's Odyssey: Saga of Dr. Zawahiri Illuminates Roots of al-Qaeda Terror," *Wall Street Journal*, July 2, 2002, p. A1.

16. Wright, *The Looming Tower*, 249–250.

17. Ibid., 76–80.

18. Ibid., 253.

19. Ibid., 193.

20. Ibid., 253.

21. Ibid., 243–244.

22. Olivier Roy, *Globalized Islam: The Search for a New Ummah* (New York: Columbia University Press, 2004), 306.

23. Wright, *The Looming Tower*, 260.

24. National Commission on Terrorist Attacks, *The 9/11 Commission Report: Final Report of the National Commission on Terrorist Attacks Upon the United States* (New York: W.W. Norton, 2004), 145–146.

25. Ibid.

26. Mark Juergensmeyer, *Global Rebellion: Religious Challenges to the Secular State, from Christian Militias to Al Qaeda* (Berkeley: University of California Press, 2008), 203.

27. National Commission on Terrorist Attacks, *The 9/11 Commission Report*, 147.

28. Ibid., 149.

29. Wright, *The Looming Tower*, 235–236.

30. Jane Mayer, *The Dark Side: The Inside Story of How the War on Terror Turned into a War on American Ideals* (New York: Doubleday, 2008), 272–274.

31. Wright, *The Looming Tower*, 180–182.

32. Ibid., 182.

33. Mark Juergensmeyer, *Terror in the Mind of God: The Global Rise of Religious Violence* (Berkeley: University of California Press, 2003), 59.

34. Wright, *The Looming Tower*, 81.

35. Ibid., 182.

36. Peter Finn, "A Fanatic's Path to Terror," *Washington Post*, September 22, 2001, p. A1.

37. Alison Pargeter, *The New Frontiers of Jihad: Radical Islam in Europe* (Philadelphia: University of Pennsylvania Press, 2008), 111–112.

38. Michael Burleigh, *Sacred Causes: The Clash of Religion and Politics, from the Great War to the War on Terror* (New York: HarperCollins, 2007), 451.

39. Kepel, *The War for Muslim Minds*, 105–107.

40. John Crewdson, "From Kind Teacher to Murderous Zealot," *Chicago Tribune*, September 11, 2004, p. A1.

41. Wright, *The Looming Tower*, 307.

42. Ibid.

43. Burleigh, *Sacred Causes*, 451.

44. Pargeter, *The New Frontiers of Jihad*, 107.

45. National Commission on Terrorist Attacks, *The 9/11 Commission Report*, 165.

46. Wright, *The Looming Tower*, 306.

47. "Imam at German Mosque Preached

Hate to 9/11 Pilots," *New York Times*, July 16, 2002, p. A8.

48. Burleigh, *Sacred Causes*, 451–452.

49. *Mohammad Atta: 9/11 Terrorist Ringleader*, 2005, www.discoverthenetworks.org/individualProfile.asp?indid=757.

50. National Commission on Terrorist Attacks, *The 9/11 Commission Report*, 161.

51. Burleigh, *Sacred Causes*, 452.

52. Ron Suskind, *The One Percent Doctrine: Deep Inside America's Pursuit of Its Enemies Since 9/11* (New York: Simon & Schuster, 2006), 164–165.

53. National Commission on Terrorist Attacks, *The 9/11 Commission Report*, 162.

54. Ibid.

55. Ibid.

56. Ibid., 164.

57. Ibid., 163.

58. Ibid., 165–166.

59. Ibid., 164.

60. *Said Bahaji: Hamburg Cell Member*, January 11, 2006, www.globalsecurity.org/security/profiles/said_bahaji.htm.

61. "Profile, Mounir al-Motassadek," *BBC News*, December 4, 2006, http://news.bbc.co.uk/2/hi/europe/2223152.stm

62. National Commission on Terrorist Attacks, *The 9/11 Commission Report*, 165.

63. Ibid.

64. "Profile, Mounir al-Motassadek," *BBC News*, December 4, 2006, http://news.bbc.co.uk/2/hi/europe/2223152.stm.

65. Ibid.

66. National Commission on Terrorist Attacks, *The 9/11 Commission Report*, 165.

67. Ibid.

68. "Profile, Mounir al-Motassadek," *BBC News*.

69. "My Brother Zac," *The Guardian*, April 19, 2003, www.guardian.co.uk/september11/story/0,11209,939701,00.html.

70. Jane Corbin, *Al Qaeda: Inside the Terror Network That Threatens the World* (New York: Avalon, 2002), 276.

71. *United States of America v. Zacarias Moussaoui*. December 2001, www.usdoj.gov/ag/moussaouiindictment.htm.

72. Kepel, *The War for Muslim Minds*, 146.

73. Wright, *The Looming Tower*, 106, 179.

74. Ibid., 106.

75. Tony Rizzo, "KC Man Linked to Early Al Qaeda Call to Jihad Led Student to Follow Bin Laden," *The Kansas City Star*, September 9, 2006, p. A1.

76. Wright, *The Looming Tower*, 110.

77. Ibid.

78. Rizzo, "KC Man Linked to Early Al Qaeda Call," A1.

79. Wright, *The Looming Tower*, 110.

80. Rizzo, "KC Man Linked to Early Al Qaeda Call," A1.

81. Pargeter, *The New Frontiers of Jihad*, 125–126.

82. Ibid.

83. National Commission on Terrorist Attacks, *The 9/11 Commission Report*, 175.

84. Ibid.

85. Kepel, *The War for Muslim Minds*, 156.

86. Kepel, *The Trial of Political Islam*, 300–301.

87. Evan F. Kohlmann, *Al-Qaida's Jihad in Europe: The Afghan-Bosnian Network* (Oxford: Berg, 2004), 26.

88. Ibid.

89. Wright, *The Looming Tower*, 177.

90. Daniel Benjamin and Steven Simon, *The Age of Sacred Terror* (New York: Random House, 2002), 12.

91. Wright, *The Looming Tower*, 178.

92. Ibid.

93. Benjamin and Simon, *The Age of Sacred Terror*, 12.

94. Wright, *The Looming Tower*, 178.

95. Steve Coll, *Ghost Wars: The Secret History of the CIA, Afghanistan, and bin Laden, from the Soviet Invasion to September 10, 2001* (New York: Penguin, 2005), 249–250.

96. Ibid., 278.

97. Ibid., 273.

98. Quintan Wictorowicz, *Radical Islam Rising* (Lanham, MD: Rowman and Littlefield, 2005), 7–8.

99. Ibid., 8–9.

100. Ibid., 9.

101. Ibid., 10.

102. "J7 Profile: Mohammad Sidique Khan," *The July 7th Truth Campaign*, www.julyseventh.co.uk/7-7-profile-mohammad-sidique-khan.html.

103. Ibid.

104. Ibid.

105. Ibid.

106. Ibid.

107. Pargeter, *The New Frontiers of Jihad*, 148–149.

108. Ibid., 154.

109. Suskind, *The One Percent Doctrine*, 201–203.

110. Pargeter, *The New Frontiers of Jihad*, 167.

111. "Profile: Abu Doha." *History Commons*. 2006, http://www.historycommons.org/entity.jsp?entity=abu_doha

112. "Killer Jailed Over Poison Plot," *BBC News*, April 13, 2005, http://news.bbc.co.uk/2/hi/uk_news/4433709.stm.

113. Suskind, *The One Percent Doctrine*, 325–327.

114. Ibid.

115. Mayer, *The Dark Side*, 89.

116. Ibid.

117. Ibid., 90.

118. Ibid., 90–92.

119. Ibid., 90–91.

120. Ibid., 91.

121. Ibid., 92.

122. Wright, *The Looming Tower*, 298.

123. Hal Bernton, Mike Carter, David Heath and James Neff, "The Terrorist Within," *The Seattle Times*, July 7, 2002, http://seattle times.nwsource.com/news/nation-world/terror istwithin.

124. Ibid.

125. Ibid.

126. Ibid.

127. Ibid.

128. Ibid.

129. Ibid.

130. Ibid.

131. Ibid.

132. Ibid.

133. John Micklethwait and Adrian Wooldridge, *God Is Back. How the Global Revival of Faith Is Changing the World* (New York: Penguin Press, 2009), 24.

134. Efraim Karsh, *Islamic Imperialism: A History* (New Haven, CT: Yale University Press, 2006), 231.

135. Sebastian Rotella, "Before Maryrdom Plan, Belgian Woman's Faith Turned Radical," *Los Angeles Times*, December 2, 2005, p. A1.

136. Pargeter, *The New Frontiers of Jihad*, 166–167.

137. Daniel Pipes, "Converts to Terrorism," *New York Sun*, December 6, 2005, p. A1.

138. Roy, *Globalized Islam*, 48–49.

139. Pargeter, *The New Frontiers of Jihad*, 166–167.

140. Ibid., 181.

141. Ibid., 180.

142. "Bomber Influenced by Preacher," *BBC News*, May 11, 2006, http://news.bbc.co.uk/1/hi/uk/4762123.stm.

143. Pargeter, *The New Frontiers of Jihad*, 183.

144. Ibid., 177.

145. Ibid.

146. Ibid.

147. Roy, *Globalized Islam*, 51.

148. Ibid., 176–177.

149. Ibid.

150. Reuvan Paz, "Middle East Islamism in the European Arena," *Middle East Review of International Affairs* (September 2002): 66–67.

151. Wictorowicz, *Radical Islam Rising*, 3.

152. Ibid., 1–2.

153. Pargeter, *The New Frontiers of Jihad*, 169.

154. Wictorowicz, *Radical Islam Rising*, 3.

155. Pargeter, *The New Frontiers of Jihad*, 167.

156. Ibid., 174.

157. Bernton, et al., "The Terrorist Within."

158. Wictorowicz, *Radical Islam Rising*, 1–2.

159. Ibid.

160. Mayer, *The Dark Side*, 73.

161. Ibid., 73–74.

162. Ibid.

163. Ibid., 75.

164. Ibid., 77.

165. Chris Francescani and Ellen Davis, "John Walker Lindh's Family Seeks Reduced Prison Sentence for Son," *ABC News Law and Justice Unit*, April 4, 2007.

166. Marcia Hermansen, "The Evolution of American Muslim Responses," in *Islam and the West: Post 9/11*, edited by Ron Geaves, Theodore Gabriel, Yvonne Haddad, and Jane Idleman Smith (Burlington, VT: Ashgate, 2004), 89.

167. Mayer, *The Dark Side*, 197–198.

168. Ibid., 198.

169. Joseph Margulies, *Guantanamo and the Abuse of Presidential Power* (New York: Simon & Schuster, 2006), 102–103.

170. Ibid.

171. "Who Is Richard Reid," *BBC News*, December 28, 2001, http://news.bbc.co.uk/1/hi/uk/1731568.stm.

172. Pam Belluck, "Threats and Responses: The Bomb Plot: Unrepentant Shoe Bomber Is Given a Life Sentence," *New York Times*, January 31, 2003, http://www.nytimes.com/2003/01/31/us/threats-responses-bomb-plot-unrepentant-shoe-bomber-given-life-sentence-for.html?page wanted=1.

173. National Commission on Terrorist Attacks, *The 9/11 Commission Report*, 175.

174. Richard Engel, "Inside Al Qaeda: A Window into the World of Militant Islam and the Afghani Alumni," *Jane's*, September 28, 2001, http://www.janes.com/security/internatio nal_security/news/misc/janes010928_1_n.shtml.

175. "Gunman Kills 12, Wounds 31 at Fort Hood," *MSNBC*, November 5, 2009, www.msn bc.msn.com/id/33678801/ns/us_news-cr ime_and_courts/.

176. Ibid.

177. Ibid.

178. "Fort Hood Suspect Asked Military to Give Muslims an Out," *CNN*, November 11, 2009, http://edition.cnn.com/2009/CRIME/11/10/fort.hood.shooting/index.html.

179. "Gunman Kills 12, Wounds 31 at Fort Hood," *MSNBC*.

180. "Fort Hood Suspect Asked Military to Give Muslims an Out," *CNN*.

181. Wright, *The Looming Tower*, 164.

182. Martin Kramer, "Islam vs. Democracy," *Commentary* (January 1993): 38–39.

183. Wright, *The Looming Tower*, 164.

184. Ibid.

185. Ibid., 164–165.

186. Ibid., 165.

187. Lawrence Freedman, *A Choice of Enemies: America Confronts the Middle East* (New York: Public Affairs, 2008), 495.

188. Suskind, *The One Percent Doctrine*, 44.

189. Ron Suskind, "The Tyrant Who Came In from the Cold," *Washington Monthly*, December 27, 2006, www.washingtonmonthly.com/features/2006/0610.suskind.html.

190. Ibid.

191. Suskind, *The One Percent Doctrine*, 76.

192. Steve Coll, *Ghost Wars*, 246–247.

193. Ibid., 374–375.

194. Suskind, *The One Percent Doctrine*, 250–251.

195. Roy, *Globalized Islam*, 311.

Chapter 9

1. Michael Burleigh, *Sacred Causes: The Clash of Religion and Politics, from the Great War to the War on Terror* (New York: HarperCollins, 2007), 476.

2. Efraim Karsh, *Islamic Imperialism: A History* (New Haven, CT: Yale University Press, 2006), 224.

3. Lawrence Wright, *The Looming Tower: Al-Qaeda and the Road to 9/11* (New York: Alfred A. Knopf, 2006), 196.

4. Gilles Kepel, *The Trial of Political Islam* (Cambridge, MA: Harvard University Press, 2003), 303–304.

5. Burleigh, *Sacred Causes*, 476.

6. Gilles Kepel, *The War for Muslim Minds: Islam and the West* (Cambridge, MA: Belknap Press of Harvard University, 2004), 245.

7. Al Gore, *The Assault on Reason* (New York: Penguin Press, 2007), 133.

8. Ibid., 134.

9. Ibid., 135–137.

10. Harold Hogju Koh, "Rights to Remember," *The Economist* (November 1, 2003): 25.

11. Ibid., 147.

12. "Declaration of James Reynolds," *Center for National Security Studies v. U.S. Department of Justice*, 2005, www.cnss.org/dojreynoldsdeclaration.htm.

13. Neil A. Lewis, "Red Cross Finds Detainee Abuse in Guantanamo," *New York Times*, November 30, 2004, p. A1.

14. Joseph Margulies, *Guantanamo and the Abuse of Presidential Power* (New York: Simon & Schuster, 2006), 71.

15. Ibid., 26–27.

16. Tim Weiner, *Legacy of Ashes: The History of the CIA* (New York: Doubleday, 2007), 481.

17. Ibid.

18. Ibid., 482.

19. Ibid., 485.

20. "Bush Vetoes Anti-Torture Bill," *Amarillo Globe News*, March 10, 2008, p. A1.

21. Melissa Jamison, "Detention of Juvenile Enemy Combatants at Guantanamo Bay: The Special Concerns of Children," *University of California at Davis Journal of Juvenile Justice Law and Policy* 9, no. 127 (2005): 127.

22. Tim Golden, "Administration Officials Split over Stalled Military Tribunals," *New York Times*, October 25, 2004, p. A1.

23. Seymour Hersh, *Chain of Command: The Road from 9/11 to Abu Ghraib* (New York: HarperCollins, 2004), 8.

24. Golden, "Administration Officials Split over Stalled Military Tribunals," p. A1.

25. Margulies, *Guantanamo and the Abuse of Presidential Power*, 65–68.

26. Bob Drogin, "No Leaders of Al Qaeda Found at Guantanamo Bay," *Los Angeles Times*, August 18, 2002, p. A1.

27. Margulies, *Guantanamo and the Abuse of Presidential Power*, 69.

28. Golden, "Administration Officials Split over Stalled Military Tribunals," p. A1.

29. Margulies, *Guantanamo and the Abuse of Presidential Power*, 70.

30. "Study by Muslim Group Says Bias Crimes Up 50% in 2004," *New York Times*, May 21, 2005, B5.

31. Gore, *The Assault on Reason*, 156.

32. Margulies, *Guantanamo and the Abuse of Presidential Power*, 33.

33. Ibid., 72.

34. Ibid.

35. Ibid., 55.

36. Ibid.

37. Leon Friedman, ed., *The Law of War: A Documentary History* (New York: Random House, 1972), 819.

38. Arnold Krammer, *Nazi Prisoners of War in America* (New York: Stein and Day, 1979), 27.

39. Margulies, *Guantanamo and the Abuse of Presidential Power*, 77.

40. Ibid., 78–79.

41. Ibid., 90–94.

42. *Intelligence Interrogation*, U.S. Army Field Manual, September 28, 1992, www.fas.org/irp/doddir/army/fm34-52.pdf.

43. Ibid.

44. Ibid.

45. Margulies, *Guantanamo and the Abuse of Presidential Power*, 76.

46. Ibid., 96.

47. Ibid., 97.

48. Ibid., 99.

49. Ibid., 98.

50. Charlie Savage, "Abuse Led Navy to Consider Pulling Cuba Interrogators," *Boston Globe*, March 16, 2005, p. A1.

51. American Civil Liberties Union, *New*

Documents Provide Further Evidence That Senior Officials Approved Abuse of Prisoners at Guantanamo, 2004, www.aclu.org/torturefoia/released/FBI_4622_4624.pdf.

52. Ibid.

53. "TIME Exclusive: Inside the Wire at Gitmo," *TIME*, June 12, 2005, www.time.com/time/press_releases/article/0,8599,1071230.html.

54. Human Rights First, "Command's Responsibility: Detainee Deaths in U.S. Custody in Iraq and Afghanistan," January 6, 2005, http://www.humanrightsfirst.org/us_law/etn/dic/exec-sum.aspx.

55. Daniel Benjamin and Steven Simon, *The Next Attack. The Failure of the War on Terror and a Strategy for Getting It Right* (New York: Henry Holt, 2005), 122.

56. Margulies, *Guantanamo and the Abuse of Presidential Power*, 104.

57. Ibid., 105.

58. Lewis, "Red Cross finds Detainee Abuse in Guantanamo," p. A1.

59. Gore, *The Assault on Reason*, 153–154.

60. Margulies, *Guantanamo and the Abuse of Presidential Power*, 58.

61. Ibid., 106.

62. Ibid.

63. Ibid., 25.

64. Koh, "Rights to Remember," 25.

65. Ibid.

66. Ibid.

67. Weiner, *Legacy of Ashes*, 509.

68. Molly Ivins and Lou Dubose, *Shrub: The Short but Happy Political Life of George W. Bush* (New York: Random House, 2002), xxxi.

69. Weiner, *Legacy of Ashes*, 483.

70. Ron Suskind, *The One Percent Doctrine: Deep Inside America's Pursuit of Its Enemies Since 9/11* (New York: Simon & Schuster, 2006), 232.

71. Ibid.

72. Ivins and Dubose, *Shrub*, 29.

73. *Bowen v. Johnston*, 306 U.S. 19, 26 (1939).

74. Margulies, *Guantanamo and the Abuse of Presidential Power*, 46.

75. Ibid., 47–48.

76. Weiner, *Legacy of Ashes*, 483.

77. Margulies, *Guantanamo and the Abuse of Presidential Power*, 95.

78. Ben Franklin, *Memoirs of Benjamin Franklin* (San Romano, Italy: Nabu Press, 2010), 270.

79. Bernard Lewis, "The Roots of Muslim Rage," *Atlantic Monthly* 266, no. 3 (September 1990): 47–60.

80. Ibid., 60.

81. Weiner, *Legacy of Ashes*, 487.

82. Suskind, *The One Percent Doctrine*, 235.

83. Weiner, *Legacy of Ashes*, 492.

84. *National Counterterrorism Center*, "Statistical Overviews and Resources: Victim's Rights," 2005, www.wits.nctc.gov/reports/crot2005nctcannexfinal.pdf.

85. Weiner, *Legacy of Ashes*, 484.

86. Mark Juergensmeyer, *Global Rebellion: Religious Challenges to the Secular State, from Christian Militias to Al Qaeda* (Berkeley: University of California Press, 2008), 206.

87. "Study Cites Seeds of Terror in Iraq," *Boston Globe*, July 17, 2005.

88. Ibid.

89. Jason Burke, *Al Qaeda: The True Story of Islamic Terror* (London: I.B. Tauris, 2004), 135.

90. Ahmed Hashim, *Insurgency and Counter-Insurgency in Iraq* (New York: Columbia University Press, 2006), 144.

91. Ibid., 144–145.

92. Juergensmeyer, *Global Rebellion*, 210.

93. "Lexington: A House Divided," *The Economist* (May 8, 2004): 34.

94. Philip Gourevitch and Errol Morris, *Standard Operating Procedures* (New York: Penguin, 2008), 300–304.

95. "Europe's Boys of Jihad," *Los Angeles Times*, April 2, 2005, p. A1.

Chapter 10

1. *Calvin: Minds in the Making*, "German Propaganda Archive," www.calvin.edu/academic/cas/gpa/goeb56.htm. (Accessed Online, March 11, 2010).

2. Lawrence Freedman, *A Choice of Enemies: America Confronts the Middle East* (New York: Public Affairs, 2008), 495.

3. *Economist*, "Briefing Internet Jihad: A World Wide Web of Terror" (July 14, 2007), 30.

4. Ibid., 29.

5. Ibid., 29–30.

6. Gilles Kepel, *The War for Muslim Minds: Islam and the West* (Cambridge, MA: Belknap Press of Harvard University, 2004), 99.

7. Ibid., 8.

8. Ibid., 90.

9. *Economist*, "Briefing Internet Jihad," 2007, 29.

10. Tariq Ramadan, *Western Muslims and the Future of Islam* (New York: Oxford University Press, 2004), 225.

11. *Economist*, "Briefing Internet Jihad," 2007, 29.

12. Ahmed S. Hashim, *Insurgency and Counter-Insurgency in Iraq* (New York: Columbia University Press, 2006), 168.

13. *Economist*, "Briefing Internet Jihad," 2007, 29.

14. Ibid.

15. Ibid.

16. Ibid.

17. Daniel Benjamin and Steven Simon, *The Next Attack. The Failure of the War on Terror and*

a Strategy for Getting It Right (New York: Henry Holt, 2005), 60.

18. Kepel, *The War for Muslim Minds*, 2004.

19. Benjamin and Simon, *The Next Attack*, 2005, 60.

20. *Global Issues Report*, "Website Offers Instructions for Crossing Syrian-Iraqi Border: 'This Is the Road to Iraq'" (June 9, 2005).

21. *Economist*, "Briefing Internet Jihad," 2007, 29–30.

22. *Global Issues Report*. "Hostile Website Provides Instructions to Make IEDs and Car Bombs." May 20, 2005.

23. *Global Issues Report*. "Hostile Arabic Website Continues Militant Training Encyclopedia." March 22, 2005.

24. Benjamin and Simon, *The Next Attack*, 2005, 76.

25. *Economist*, "Briefing Internet Jihad," 2007, 29–30.

26. Ibid., 28.

27. Ibid.

28. *Washington Post*, "Terrorist 007 Exposed" (March 26, 2006), p.B01.

29. Abigail Cutler, "Web of Terror," *The Atlantic* (June 2006), www.theatlantic.com/doc/200606u/labi-interview. (Accessed Online, March 10, 2010).

30. Ibid.

31. *The Jawa Report*, "Internet Jihadi #1 *Irhabi 007* Captured, Name Revealed" (February 28, 2006), http://mypetjawa.mu.nu/archives/160985.php. (Accessed Online, March 11, 2010).

32. *Washington Post*, "Terrorist 007 Exposed" (March 26, 2006), B01.

33. *Economist*, "Briefing Internet Jihad," 2007, 29–30.

34. Ibid., 29.

35. Ibid., 29.

36. Ibid., 30.

37. Ibid.

Chapter 11

1. Tariq Ramadan, *Western Muslims and the Future of Islam* (New York: Oxford University Press, 2004), 101.

2. Gilles Kepel, *The War for Muslim Minds: Islam and the West* (Cambridge, MA: Belknap Press of Harvard University, 2004), 158.

3. Olivier Roy, *Globalized Islam: The Search for a New Ummah* (New York: Columbia University Press, 2004), 33.

4. Joselyne Cesari, *When Islam and Democracy Meet* (New York: Palgrave/Macmillan, 2004), 84.

5. Roy, *Globalized Islam*, 271.

6. Cesari, *When Islam and Democracy Meet*, 85.

7. Roy, *Globalized Islam*, 33, 35.

8. Steven Coll, *The Bin Ladens: An Arabian Family in an American Century* (New York: Penguin, 2008), 503.

9. Samuel Huntington, *The Clash of Civilizations and the Remaking of the World Order* (New York: Simon & Schuster, 1996), 131.

10. Ibid., 57.

11. Roy, *Globalized Islam*, 116–117.

12. Carol L. Anway, "American Women Choosing Islam," in *Muslims on the Americanization Path?*, edited by Yvonne Yazbeck Haddad and John L. Esposito (New York: Oxford University Press, 2000), 154.

13. Roy, *Globalized Islam*, 40.

14. Thomas Jefferson, in Andrew Lipscomb, ed., *The Writings of Thomas Jefferson* (Washington, DC: Thomas Jefferson Memorial Association, 1901), 270.

15. Ali A. Allawi, *The Crisis of Islamic Civilization* (New Haven and London: Yale University Press, 2009), 35.

16. Ibid., 35–36.

17. Ibid., 49.

18. Ibid.

19. Khaled Abou El Fadl, "Striking a Balance: Islamic Legal Discourse on Muslim Minorities" in Haddad and Esposito, *Muslims on the Americanization Path?*, 48–49.

20. Ibid., 54–58.

21. Yusuf Talal Delorenzo, "The Fiqh Councilor in North America," in Haddad and Esposito, *Muslims on the Americanization Path?*, 67.

22. Ibid., 69–71.

23. John Micklethwait, and Adrian Wooldridge, *God Is Back: How the Global Revival of Faith Is Changing the World* (New York: Penguin Press, 2009), 91.

24. Roy, *Globalized Islam*, 149.

25. Ibid., 179–181.

26. Ibid., 210–211.

27. Ibid., 224–225.

28. Ibid., 235.

29. Ibid., 211–214.

30. "University of Houston Muslim Students Association." *MSA@UH Forum*. July 12, 2007, http://www.uh.edu/campus/msa/home.php.

31. Roy, *Globalized Islam*, 122.

32. Huntington, *The Clash of Civilizations*, 96–101.

33. Marcia Hermansen, "The Evolution of American Muslim Responses" in *Islam and the West: Post 9/11*, edited by Ron Geaves, Theodore Gabriel, Yvonne Haddad, and Jane Idleman Smith (Burlington, VT: Ashgate, 2004), 80.

34. Daniel Pipes, *In the Path of God: Islam and Political Power* (New York: Basic Books, 1983), 107.

35. Robert Altemeyer, *The Authoritarian Specter* (Cambridge, MA: Harvard University Press, 1996), 93.

36. Ibid., 85.

37. John Shepherd, "Self-critical Children of Abraham? Roots of Violence and Extremism in Judaism, Christianity and Islam," in Geaves et al., *Islam and the West: Post 9/11*, 41.

38. Hermansen, "The Evolution of American Muslim Responses," 84–85.

39. Ibid., 86–87.

40. Mohammad Fathi Osman, "Towards a Vision and an Agenda for the Future of Muslim Ummah," in *Islam: A Contemporary Perspective*, edited by Mohammad Ahmadullah Siddiqi (Chicago: NAAMPS, 1994), 13.

41. Lawrence Freedman, *A Choice of Enemies: America Confronts the Middle East* (New York: Public Affairs, 2008), 496–497.

42. Micklethwait and Wooldridge, *God Is Back*, 292.

43. Ibid., 294, 324.

44. Mark Juergensmeyer, *Global Rebellion: Religious Challenges to the Secular State, from Christian Militias to Al Qaeda* (Berkeley: University of California Press, 2008), 173.

45. Michael Wolfe, ed., *Taking Back Islam: American Muslims Reclaim Their Faith* (Emmaus, PA: Rodale Press, 2002).

46. Hermansen, "The Evolution of American Muslim Responses," 80.

47. *Los Angeles Times*, "A Memo to American Muslims," *Los Angeles Times*, October 10, 2001, p. B12.

48. Hermansen, "The Evolution of American Muslim Responses," 86.

49. Walter Lippmann, *Liberty and the News* (New York: Harcourt, Brace, and Howe, 1920), 64.

50. Micklethwait and Wooldridge, *God Is Back*, 343.

Bibliography

Abedin, Syed Z., and Saleha M. Abedin. "Muslim Minorities in Non-Muslim Societies." In *Oxford Encyclopaedia of the Modern Islamic World*. Oxford, UK: Oxford University Press, 1994.

Abu-Rabi, Ibrahim M. *Intellectual Origins of Islamic Resurgence in the Modern Arab World*. Albany: State University of New York Press, 1996.

Adolino, Jessica R. *Ethnic Minorities, Electoral Politics and Political Integration in Britain*. London: Pinter, 1998.

Adorno, Theodore, Daniel Jay Levinson, R. Nevitt Sanford, and Else Frenkel Brunswick. *The Authoritarian Personality*. New York: W.W. Norton, 1993.

"Afghanistan: The Illusion of Empire Lite." *Economist* (June 24, 2006): 13–14.

Ahmad, Jalal Al-e. *Gharbzadegi*. Translated by John Green and Ahmad Alizadeh. Costa Mesa, CA: Mazda Publishers, 1982.

Aiken, Henry D. *The Age of Ideology: The Nineteenth Century Philosophers*. New York: Mentor, 1956.

Ajami, Fouad. *The Arab Predicament*. Cambridge, UK: Cambridge University Press, 1981.

_____. "The Moor's Last Laugh: Radical Islam Finds a Haven in Europe." *Wall Street Journal*. March 22, 2004, p. A18.

Al-Bab, "Abu Hamza and the Supporters of Shariah." *Abu Hamza and the Islamic Army*. March 7, 1999. http://www.al-bab.com/yemen/hamza/hamza1.htm.

"Al-Muhajiroun in the UK: An Interview with Sheikh Omar Bakri Mohammed." *Jamestown Foundation*. www.jamestown.org/terrorism/news/article.php?search=1&articleid=23622.

Allawi, Ali A. *The Crisis of Islamic Civilization*. New Haven and London: Yale University Press, 2009.

Allen, Christopher. "Endemically European or a European Epidemic? Islamophobia in a Post-9/11 Europe." In *Islam and the West: Post 9/11*, edited by Ron Geaves, Theodore Gabriel, Yvonne Haddad, and Jane Idleman Smith, 130–145. Burlington, VT: Ashgate, 2004.

Allen, Ernest. "Identity and Destiny." In *Muslims on the Americanization Path?*, edited by Yvonne Yazbeck Haddad and John L. Esposito, 163–214. New York: Oxford University Press, 2000.

Al-Marayati, Salam. "Formulating an Agenda of Political Actions for North American Muslims." In *Islam: A Contemporary Perspective*, edited by Mohammad Ahmadullah Siddiqi, 67–72. Chicago, IL: NAAMPS, 1994.

Altemeyer, Robert. *The Authoritarian Specter*. Cambridge, MA: Harvard University Press, 1996.

_____. "Highly Dominating, Highly Authoritarian Personalities." *Journal of Social Psychology* 144, no. 4 (2004).

_____. *Enemies of Freedom*. San Francisco: Jossey-Bass, 1988.

American Civil Liberties Union. *New Documents Provide Further Evidence that Senior Officials Approved Abuse of Prisoners at Guantanamo*. 2004. www.aclu.org/tortrefoia/released/FBI_4622_4624.pdf.

Anderson, Brian C. "Secular Europe, Religious America." *Public Interest* (Spring 2004): 143–156.

Anwar, Muhammad. "Muslims in Britain." In *Muslim Minorities in the West*, edited by Syed A. Abedin and Ziauddin Sardar, 31–46. London: Grey Seal, 1995.

Anway, Carol L. "American Women Choosing Islam." In *Muslims on the American-ization Path?*, edited by Yvonne Yazbeck Haddad and John L. Esposito, 145–163. New York: Oxford University Press, 2000.

Armstrong, Karen. "Was it Inevitable?— Islam through History." In *How Did This Happen? Terrorism and the New War*, edited by James F. Hoge, Jr., and Gideon Rose, 53–70. New York: Public Affairs, 2001.

_____. *Islam: A Short History*. New York: Random House, 2000.

Atlanta Journal-Constitution. "Secular No More, Saddam Adopts Radicalized Islam." January 3, 2003, p. 1.

Auster, Bruce B. "The Recruiter for Hate." *U.S. News and World Report*. August 31, 1998, p. 49.

Baer, Robert. *See No Evil*. New York: Three Rivers Press, 2002.

_____. *Sleeping with the Devil*. New York: Crown, 2003.

Bakewell, Joan. "The Believers Who Despise Our Ways." *New Statesman*. May 29, 2000. www.newstatesman.com/2000052 90011.

Bandura, Albert. *Aggression: A Social Learning Analysis*. Upper Saddle River, NJ: Prentice Hall, 1973.

Baumgarten, Gerald. *Paranoia as Patriotism: Far-Right Influences on the Militia Movement*. New York: Anti-Defamation League, 1995.

Bawer, Bruce. *While Europe Slept: How Radical Islam Is Destroying the West from Within*. New York: Doubleday, 2006.

Bearden, Milton. "Afghanistan, Graveyard of Empires." In *Terrorism and 9/11: A Reader*, edited by Fredrik Lovegall, 38–49. Boston, MA: Houghton Mifflin, 2001.

Belcher, Rosemary. "Europe's Malcolm X." *New Humanist* (July/August 2004): 8–12.

Belien, Paul. "Meet the Mayor of Brussels: She's a Muslim." *The Brussels Journal* (16 January 2006). www.brusselsjournal.com/node/671.

Belluck, Pam. "Threats and Responses: The Bomb Plot: Unrepentant Shoe Bomber Is Given a Life Sentence." *New York Times* (31 January 2003). http://www.nytimes.com/2003/01/31/us/threats-responses-bomb-plot-unrepentant-shoe-bomber-given-life-sentence-for.html?pagewanted=1.

Benjamin, Daniel, and Steven Simon. *The Age of Sacred Terror*. New York: Random House, 2002.

_____. *The Next Attack: The Failure of the War on Terror and a Strategy for Getting It Right*. New York: Henry Holt, 2005.

Bernton, Hal, Mike Carter, David Heath, and James Neff. "The Terrorist Within." *The Seattle Times*. July 7, 2002. http://seat tletimes.nwsource.com/news/nation-wo rld/terroristwithin.

Bergen, Peter L. *Inside the Secret World of Osama bin Laden*. London: Weidenfeld and Nicolson, 2001.

Berlet, Chip. "Dances with Devils." *Political Research Associates*. 1998. www.publiceye. org/Apocalyptic/Dances_with_Devils_1. html; http://www.publiceye.org/Apocaly ptic/Dances_with_Devils_2htm.

Berlet, Chip, and John Salvi. *Abortion Clinic Violence and Catholic Right Conspiracism*. Somerville, MA: Political Research Associates, 1996.

Berlin, Isaiah. "The Bent Twig: A Note on Nationalism." *Foreign Affairs* 1 (1972): 1–28.

Bickerton, Ian J., and Carla L. Klausner. *A Concise History of the Arab-Israeli Conflict*, 4th ed. Upper Saddle River, NJ: Pearson Prentice Hall, 2005.

"Blair Defends the War in Iraq as Part of a Historic Struggle." *New York Times*. April 10, 2004, p. A7.

"Bloodshed in Iraq." *Economist* (April 10, 2004): 21–23.

"A Bloody New Year in Iraq." *Economist* (January 1, 2005): 31–32.

Bloom, Mia. *Dying to Kill: The Allure of Suicide Terror*. New York: Columbia University Press, 2005.

Bright, Martin. "Radical Links of UK's 'Moderate' Muslim Group." *The Observer*. August 14, 2005, http://observer.guardian. co.uk/uk_news/story/0,6903,1548786,00. html.

"Briefing Internet Jihad: A World Wide Web of Terror." *Economist* (July 14, 2007): 28–30.

"Bomber Influenced by Preacher." *BBC News*. May 11, 2006, http://news.bbc.co. uk/1/hi/uk/4762123.stm.

Borisov, Sergey. "Osama Baby Boom in Nigeria." *Pravda*. 2002, http://english.pravda. ru/main/2002/01/08/25036.html.

Bowen, John R. "Does French Islam Have Borders? Dilemmas of Domestication in a Global Religious Field." *American Anthropologist* 106, no. 4 (2004): 43–55.

Bradford, William. *Of Plymouth Plantation, 1620–1647*. New York: Random House, 1981.

Bradley, John R. *Saudi Arabia Exposed: Inside a Kingdom in Crisis*. New York: Palgrave Macmillan, 2005.

Bradshaw, Michael, George W. White, and Joseph P. Dymond. *Contemporary World Regional Geography*. Boston, MA: Mc-Graw-Hill, 2004.

Burke, Jason. *Al Qaeda: The True Story of Islamic Terror*. London: I.B. Tauris, 2004.

Burleigh, Michael. *Earthly Powers: The Clash of Religion and Politics in Europe, from the French Revolution to the Great War*. New York: HarperCollins, 2005.

_____. *Sacred Causes: The Clash of Religion and Politics, from the Great War to the War on Terror*. New York: HarperCollins, 2007.

"Bush Vetoes Anti-Torture Bill." *Amarillo Globe News*. March 10, 2008, p. A1.

"Cartoon Wars." *Economist* (February 11, 2006): 9.

Cesari, Joselyne. *When Islam and Democracy Meet*. New York: Palgrave/Macmillan, 2004.

Chadwick, Owen. *The Victorian Church: Part II*. Oxford, UK: Oxford University Press, 1970.

"CIA Warns Iraq Invasion Could Breed More Terrorists." *Washington Post*. September 9, 2003, p. A3.

"A Civil War on Terrorism." *Economist* (November 25, 2004): 28–29.

Clarke, Richard A., Glen P. Aga, Roger W. Cressey, Stephen E. Flyn, Blake W. Mobley, Eric Rosenbach, Steven Simon, William F. Wechsler, and Lee S. Wolosky. *Defeating the Jihadists: A Blueprint for Action*. New York: Century Foundation Press, 2004.

"Clashes Rise in Southern Iraq." *Washington Post*. April 11, 2004, p. 14.

Cockburn, Andrew, and Patrick Cockburn. *Out of the Ashes: The Resurrection of Saddam Hussein*. New York: Harper-Collins, 1999.

Coll, Steven. *Ghost Wars: The Secret History of the CIA, Afghanistan, and bin Laden, from the Soviet Invasion to September 10, 2001*. New York: Penguin, 2005.

_____. *The Bin Ladens: An Arabian Family in an American Century*. New York: Penguin, 2008.

"The Conflict in Iraq: Intelligence; A New CIA Report Casts Doubt on a Key Terrorist's Tie to Iraq." *New York Times*. October 10, 2004, p. A13.

Cook, David. *Understanding Jihad*. Berkeley: University of California Press, 2003.

Corbin, Jane. *Al Qaeda: Inside the Terror Network that Threatens the World*. New York: Avalon, 2002.

Cox, Caroline, and John Marks. *The West, Islam, and Islamism*. London: Civitas, 2003.

Crewdson, John. "From Kind Teacher to Murderous Zealot." *Chicago Tribune*, September 11, 2004, p. A1.

Cutler, Abigail. "Web of Terror." *The Atlantic* (June 2006), www.theatlantic.com/doc/200606u/labi-interview.

Davie, Grace. *Religion in Modern Europe: A Memory Mutates*. Oxford, UK: Oxford University Press, 2000.

De Blij, Henry, and Peter Muller. *Geography: Realms, Regions, and Concepts*, 10th ed. New York: John Wiley, 2002.

"Declaration of James Reynolds." *Center for National Security Studies v. U.S. Department of Justice*. 2005, www.cnss.org/dojreynoldsdeclaration.htm.

Dees, Morris. *Gathering Storm: America's Militia Threat*. New York: HarperCollins, 1996.

DeLorenzo, Yusuf Talal. "The Fiqh Councilor in North America." In *Muslims on the Americanization Path?*, edited by Yvonne Yazbeck Haddad and John L. Esposito, 65–87. New York: Oxford University Press, 2000.

Diamond, Jared. *Guns, Germs and Steel: The Fates of Human Societies*. New York: W.W. Norton, 1999.

Diamond, Larry. *Squandered Victory: The American Occupation and Bungled Effort to Bring Democracy to Iraq*. New York: Henry Holt, 2005.

"Dozens Killed in Iraq Violence." *Washington Post*. July 17, 2005, p. A1.

Drogin, Bob. "No Leaders of Al Qaeda Found at Guantanamo Bay." *Los Angeles Times*. August 18, 2002, p. A1.

Dunn, Charles W., and J. David Woodard. *American Conservatism from Burke to Bush: An Introduction*. Lanham, MD: Madison Books, 1991.

Eatwell, Roger. "The Nature of the Right, 2: The Right as a Variety of Styles of Thought." In *The Nature of the Right:*

American and European Politics and Political Thought since 1789, edited by Roger Eatwell and Noel O'Sullivan, 62–78. Boston, MA: Twayne, 1989.

Eckelman, Dale F., and James Piscatori. *Muslim Politics*. Princeton, NJ: Princeton University Press, 1996.

Eggen, Dan. "Alleged Remarks on Islam Prompt an Ashcroft Reply. *Washington Post*. February 14, 2002.

Eggen, Dan, and Julie Tate. "U.S. Campaign Produces Few Convictions on Terrorism Charges; Statistics Often Count Lesser Crimes." *Washington Post*. June 12, 2005.

El Fadl, Khaled Abou. "Striking a Balance: Islamic Legal Discourse on Muslim Minorities." In *Muslims on the Americanization Path?*, edited by Yvonne Yazbeck Haddad and John L. Esposito, 47–64. New York: Oxford University Press, 2000.

Emerson, Steven. *American Jihad: The Terrorists Living Among Us*. New York: Simon & Schuster, 2003.

Engel, Richard. "Inside Al Qaeda: A Window into the World of Militant Islam and the Afghani Alumni." *Jane's Security*. September 28, 2001, http://www.janes.com/security/international_security/news/misc/janes010928_1_n.shtml.

Er-Rashid, Haroun. "Muslims and the West: A Paradigm for Polarization." In *Islam and the West: Critical Perspectives on Modernity*, edited by Michael F. Thompson, 5–20. Lanham, MD: Rowman and Littlefield, 2003.

Esposito, John L. *Voices of Resurgent Islam*. Oxford: Oxford University Press, 1983.

_____. "Muslims in America or American Muslims?" In *Muslims on the Americanization Path?*, edited by Yvonne Yazbeck Haddad and John L. Esposito, 3–18. New York: Oxford University Press, 2000.

"Extreme Rightist Eclipses Socialist to Qualify for Runoff in France." *New York Times*. April 22, 2002, p. A1.

"Failure Begins to Look Possible." *Economist* (November 1, 2003): 14–15.

Falwell, Jerry. "Mohammed 'a Demon-Possessed Pedophile'?" *WorldNetDaily*. June 15, 2002, http://www.worldnetdaily.com/news/article.asp?ARTICLE_ID=27975.

Farmer, Brian R. *American Conservatism: History, Theory and Practice*. Newcastle, UK: Cambridge Scholars Press, 2005.

Fekete, Liz. "Issues in the French Presidential Elections." *IRR News*. June 1, 1995, www.irr.org.uk/europebulletin/france/extreme_right_politics/1995/ak000006.html.

Feldman, Stanley. "Enforcing Social Conformity: A Theory of Authoritarianism." *Political Psychology* 24, no. 1 (2003).

Fetzer, Joel S., and Christopher J. Soper. *Muslims and the State in Britain, France, and Germany*. Cambridge, UK: Cambridge University Press, 2004.

Finn, Peter. "A Fanatic's Path to Terror." *Washington Post*. September 22, 2001, A1.

"Focus on Religion." *National Statistics Online*. July 26, 2006, http://www.statistics.gov.uk/cci/nugget.asp?id=954.

"For Some in Iraq's Sunni Minority, A Growing Sense of Alienation." *New York Times*. May 8, 2005, p. 23.

Ford, Peter. "Europe Cringes at Bush 'Crusade' Against Terrorists." *Christian Science Monitor*, September 19, 2001.

"Fort Hood Suspect Asked Military to Give Muslims an Out." *CNN*. November 11, 2009, http://edition.cnn.com/2009/CRIME/11/10/fort.hood.shooting/index.html.

Francescani, Chris, and Ellen Davis. "John Walker Lindh's Family Seeks Reduced Prison Sentene for Son." *ABC News Law and Justice Unit*. April 4, 2007.

Franklin, Ben. *Memoirs of Benjamin Franklin*. San Romano, Italy: Naba Press, 2010.

"Free of Hussein's Rule, Sunnis in North Flaunt A Long-Hidden Piety." *New York Times*. April 23, 2003, p. A13.

Freeden, Michael. *Ideology: A Very Short Introduction*. Oxford and New York: Oxford University Press, 2003.

Freedman, Lawrence. *A Choice of Enemies: America Confronts the Middle East*. New York: Public Affairs, 2008.

"French Violence Back to Normal." *BBC News*. November 17, 2005. http://news.bbc.co.uk/2/hi/europe/4445428.stm.

"French Violence Rages On." *New York Times*. November 7, 2007, http://nytimes.com/2005/11/07/international/europe/07france.

Friedman, Leon, ed. *The Law of War: A Documentary History*. New York: Random House, 1972.

Gabriel, Mark. *Islam and Terrorism*. Lake Mary, FL: Strang Communications, 2002.

Geaves, Ron, and Theodore Gabriel. "Introduction." In *Islam and the West: Post 9/11*, edited by Ron Geaves, Theodore Gabriel,

Yvonne Haddad, and Jane Idleman Smith, 1–12. Burlington, VT: Ashgate Publishing, 2004.

Gergez, Fawaz. *The Far Enemy: Why Jihad Went Global.* New York: Cambridge University Press, 2005.

"German Security Laws: Times of Terror." *Economist* (September 29, 2007): 55.

Gildea, Robert. *France since 1945.* New York and Oxford: Oxford University Press, 1997.

Goebbels, Joseph. "The Radio as the Eight Great Power." *Calvin: Minds in the Making. German Propaganda Archive.* www.calvin.edu/academic/cas/gpa/goeb56.htm.

Golden, Tim. "Administration Officials Split over Stalled Military Tribunals." *New York Times.* October 25, 2004, p. A1.

Goodwin, Jan. "Buried Alive: Afghan Women Under the Taliban." In *Terrorism and 9/11: A Reader,* edited by Fredrik Logevall, 73–84. Boston, MA: Houghton Mifflin, 2002.

Goodwin, Jeff, and Theda Skocpol. "Explaining Revolutions in the Contemporary Third World." *Politics and Society* 17 (1989): 490.

Gordon, Michael R., and Bernard E. Trainor. *Cobra II: The Inside Story of the Invasion and Occupation of Iraq.* New York: Pantheon, 2006.

Gore, Al. *The Assault on Reason.* New York: Penguin Press, 2007.

Gorenberg, Gershom. *The End of Days: Fundamentalism and the Struggle for the Temple Mount.* New York: Free Press, 2000.

Gourevitch, Philip, and Errol Morris. *Standard Operating Procedures.* New York: Penguin, 2008.

Gunaratna, Rohan. *Inside Al Qaeda: Global Network of Terror.* New York: Columbia University Press, 2002.

"Gunman Kills 12, Wounds 31 at Fort Hood." *MSNBC.* November 5, 2009, www.msnbc.msn.com/id/33678801/ns/us_news-crime_and_courts/.

Haas, Ben. *KKK: The Hooded Face of Vengeance.* Evanston, IL: Regency, 1963.

Haddad, Yvonne Yazbeck. "The Globalization of Islam: The Return of Muslims to the West." In *The Oxford History of Islam,* edited by John L. Esposito, 601–642. Oxford: Oxford University Press, 1999.

_____. "The American Path Option." In *Muslims on the Americanization Path?,* edited by Yvonne Yazbeck Haddad and John

L. Esposito, 19–46. New York: Oxford University Press, 2000.

_____. "The Shaping of a Moderate North American Islam: Between 'Mufti' Bush and 'Ayatollah' Ashcroft." In *Islam and the West: Post 9/11,* edited by Ron Geaves, Theodore Gabriel, Yvonne Haddad, and Jane Idleman Smith, 97–114. Burlington, VT: Ashgate, 2004.

Halliday, Fred. *Two Hours that Shook the World, September 11, 2001: Causes and Consequences.* London: Saqi Books, 2002.

Hargreaves, Alec G. *Immigration, Race and Ethnicity in Contemporary France.* London: Routledge, 1995.

Hashim, Ahmed S. *Insurgency and Counter-Insurgency in Iraq.* New York: Columbia University Press, 2006.

Hassan, Nasra. "An Arsenal of Believers: Talking to the 'Human Bombs.'" *New Yorker* (November 19, 2001).

Hathout, Maher. "Islamic Work in North America: Challenges and Opportunities." In *Islam: A Contemporary Perspective,* edited by Mohammad Ahmadullah Siddiqi, 61–66. Chicago: NAAMPS, 1994.

Herbert, Ulrich. *A History of Foreign Labor in Germany, 1880–1980.* Ann Arbor: University of Michigan Press, 1990.

Hermansen, Marcia. "The Evolution of American Muslim Responses." In *Islam and the West: Post 9/11,* edited by Ron Geaves, Theodore Gabriel, Yvonne Haddad, and Jane Idleman Smith, 77–96. Burlington, VT: Ashgate, 2004.

Hersh, Seymour M. "Target Qaddafi." *New York Times Magazine.* February 22, 1987.

_____. *Chain of Command: The Road from 9/11 to Abu Ghraib.* New York: HarperCollins, 2004.

Higgins, Andrew, and Alan Cullison. "Terrorist's Odyssey: Saga of Dr. Zawahiri Illuminates Roots of al-Qaeda Terror. *Wall Street Journal.* July 2, 2002, p. A1.

Hiro, Dilip. *Iraq: In the Eye of the Storm.* New York: Nation Books, 2002.

Hoffman, Bruce. "Holy Terror: The Implications of Terrorism Motivated by a Religious Imperative." *Studies in Conflict and Terrorism* 18 (1995): 271–284.

"Honor Laws." *Economist* (June 21, 2003): 48.

Hoover, Kenneth. *Ideology and Political Life,* 2nd ed. Belmont, CA: Wadsworth, 1994.

"Hostile Arabic Website Continues Militant

Training Encyclopedia." *Global Issues Report*, March 22, 2005.

"Hostile Website Provides Instructions to Make IEDs and Car Bombs." *Global Issues Report*, May 20, 2005.

Huff, Toby. *The Rise of Early Modern Science: China, Islam, and the West.* Cambridge, UK: Cambridge University Press, 2003.

Human Rights First, "Command's Responsibility: Detainee Deaths in U.S. Custody in Iraq and Afghanistan," January 6, 2005, http://www.humanrightsfirst.org/us_law/etn/dic/exec-sum.aspx.

"Human Rights in Saudi Arabia: A Deafening Silence." *Human Rights Watch.* December 2001, www.hrw.org/backgrounder/mena/saudi

Hume, David. *Dialogues and Natural History of Religion*, ed. J.C.A. Gaskin. Oxford, UK: Oxford University Press, 1998.

Hunter, Shireen T. *The Future of Islam and the West: Clash of Civilizations or Peaceful Coexistence?* Westport, CT: Praeger, 1998.

Huntington, Samuel. "Conservatism as an Ideology." *American Political Science Review* 51 (1957): 454–473.

_____. "The Clash of Civilizations?" *Foreign Affairs* 72 (1993): 22–49.

_____. The *Clash of Civilizations and the Remaking of World Order.* New York: Simon & Schuster, 1996.

_____. *Who are We? The Cultural Core of American National Identity.* New York: Simon & Schuster, 2004.

Hussein, Dilwar. "The Impact of 9/11 on British Muslim Identity." In *Islam and the West: Post 9/11*, edited by Ron Geaves, Theodore Gabriel, Yvonne Haddad, and Jane Idleman Smith, 115–129. Burlington, VT: Ashgate, 2004.

"Imam at German Mosque Preached Hate to 9/11 Pilots." *New York Times.* July 16, 2002, p. A8.

"In Sunni Triangle, Loss of Privilege Breeds Bitterness." *Washington Post.* January 13, 2004, p. A1.

"Inequality: For Richer, for Poorer." *Economist* (November 5, 1994): 19–21.

Ingersoll, David E., Richard K. Matthews, and Andrew Davison. *The Philosophic Roots of Modern Ideology.* Upper Saddle River, NJ: Prentice Hall, 2001.

Insight Team. "Focus: Undercover in the Academy of Hatred." *Times Online.* August

7, 2005, www.timesonline.co.uk/tol/news/uk/article552687.ece.

Intelligence Interrogation. U.S. Army Field Manual. September 28, 1992, www.fas.org/irp/doddir/army/fm34-52.pdf.

International Center for Counter Terrorism. "Spotlight: Hilafet Devleti." January 28, 2004, www.ict.org.il/spotlight/det.cfm?id=245.

International Herald Tribune, "Officials Fear Iraq's Lure for Muslims in Europe." October 23–24, 2004, p. 4.

"Iraq After Ayatollah Hakim's Murder." *Economist* (September 6, 2003): 39.

"Iraq: The Struggle for Order." *Economist* (September 25, 2004): 57–58.

"Iraq's Anxious Sunnis Seek Security in the New Order." *New York Times.* August 10, 2003, p. A8.

"Iraq's Christians: Less Safe than Before." *Economist* (August 7, 2004): 39.

"Iraqi Resistance Strikes a Chord with Locals on Mideast Street." *Wall Street Journal.* March 26, 2003, p. 1.

"Iraqis Oppose New Governing Council." *USA Today.* December 4, 2003, p. 1.

"Iraqis Skeptical of U.S. Motives." *Washington Post.* November 12, 2003, p. A3.

Ishaque, Khalid. "The Islamic Approach to Economic Development." In *Voices of Resurgent Islam*, edited by John Esposito, New York: Oxford University Press, 1983, 268–276.

Ismail, Sacha. "What is the Muslim Association of Britain?" *Worker's Liberty.* March 15, 2007, www.workersliberty.org/node/3026.

Ivins, Molly, and Lou Dubose. *Shrub: The Short but Happy Political Life of George W. Bush.* New York: Random House, 2002.

"J7 Profile: Mohammad Sidique Khan." *July 7th Truth Campaign.* www.julyseventh.co.uk/7-7-profile-mohammad-sidique-khan.html.

Jamison, Melissa. "Detention of Juvenile Enemy Combatants at Guantanamo Bay: The Special Concerns of Children." *University of California at Davis Journal of Juvenile Justice Law and Policy* 9, no. 127 (2005): 126–136.

Jawa Report. "Internet Jihadi #1 *Irhabi 007* Captured, Name Revealed." February 28, 2006, http://mypetjawa.mu.nu/archives/160985.php.

Jefferson, Thomas. *The Writings of Thomas*

Jefferson, edited by Andrew Lipscomb. Washington, DC: Thomas Jefferson Memorial Association, 1901.

Jeffrey, Arthur. *Islam: Muhammad and his Religion*. New York: Macmillan, 1958.

"Jihadist or Victim: Ex Detainee Makes a Case." *New York Times*. July 27, 2005, p. A1.

Johnstone, Ronald L. *Religion in Society: A Sociology of Religion*, 4th ed. Englewood Cliffs, NJ: Prentice Hall, 1992.

Jones, Howard. *Quest for Security: A History of U.S. Foreign Relations*. New York: McGraw-Hill, 1996.

_____. *Crucible of Power: A History of American Foreign Relations from 1897*. Wilmington, DE: SR Books, 2001.

Jost, John T., Jack Glaser, Arie W. Kruglanski, and Frank J. Sulloway. "Political Conservatism as Motivated Social Cognition." *Psychological Bulletin* 129, no. 3 (2003): 339–375.

Juergensmeyer, Mark. *Terror in the Mind of God: The Global Rise of Religious Violence*. Berkeley: University of California Press, 2003.

_____. *Global Rebellion: Religious Challenges to the Secular State, From Christian Militias to Al Qaeda*. Berkeley: University of California Press, 2008.

Karakasoglu, Yasemin, and Gerd Nonneman. "Muslims in Germany, with Special Reference to the Turkish-Islamic Community." In *Muslim Communities in the New Europe*, edited by Gerd Nonneman, Tim Noblock, and Bogdan Szajkowski, 241–268. Reading, UK: Ithaca Press, 1996.

Karapin, Roger. "Major Anti-Minority Riots and National Legislation in Britain and Germany." In *Challenging Immigration and Ethnic Relations Politics: Comparative European Perspectives*, edited by Ruud Koopmans and Paul Statham, 312–347. Oxford, UK: Oxford University Press, 2000.

Karsh, Efraim. *Islamic Imperialism: A History*. New Haven, CT: Yale University Press, 2006.

Keddie, Nikki. *Middle East and Beyond*. London, UK: Taylor and Francis, 1988.

Keene, Michael, and Jan Keene. *Junior Steps in Religious Education, Year 4*. Cheltenham, UK: Stanley Thornes, 1997.

Kepel, Gilles. *Muslim Extremism in Egypt: The Prophet and the Pharaoh*. Berkeley: University of California Press, 1993.

_____. *The Trial of Political Islam*. Cambridge, MA: Harvard University Press, 2003.

_____. *The War for Muslim Minds: Islam and the West*. Cambridge, MA: Belknap Press of Harvard University, 2004.

Khan, Muhommed A. Muqtedar, *American Muslims: Bridging Faith and Freedom*. Portland, OR: Amana, 2002.

Khomeini, Imam. *Islam and Revolution: Writings and Declarations of Imam Khomeini*. Berkeley, CA: Mizan Press, 1981.

Kifner, John. "Suspect in Kahane Case Is Muslim Born in Egypt." *New York Times*. November 7, 1990, p. B13.

"Killer Jailed Over Poison Plot." *BBC News*. April 13, 2005, http://news.bbc.co.uk/2/hi/uk_news/4433709.stm.

Kirk, Russell. "Libertarians: Chirping Sectaries." *The Heritage Lectures: Proclaiming a Patrimony*. Washington, DC: Heritage Foundation, 1982.

Klausen, Jytte. *The Islamic Challenge: Politics and Religion in Western Europe*. Oxford and New York: Oxford University Press, 2005.

Koh, Harold Hongju. "Rights to Remember." *The Economist*. November 1, 2003, pp. 24–26.

Kohlmann, Evan F. *Al-Qaida's Jihad in Europe: The Afghan-Bosnian Network*. Oxford: Berg, 2004.

Kramer, Martin. "Islam vs. Democracy." *Commentary* (January 1993).

_____. *Arab Awakening and Islamic Revival: The Politics of Ideas in the Middle East*. Piscataway, NJ: Transaction, 1996.

Krammer, Arnold. *Nazi Prisoners of War in America*. New York: Stein and Day, 1979.

Kristol, Irving. *Two Cheers for Capitalism*. New York: New American Library, 1983.

Kurd, Rahat. "My Hijab Is an Act of Worship — and None of Your Business." *Globe and Mail*. February 15, 1995, p. A20.

Lampman, Jane. "Mixing Prophecy and Politics." *Christian Science Monitor*. July 7, 2004.

Lapidus, Ira M. "State and Religion in Islamic Societies." *Past and Present* 151 (May 1996).

LeDoux, Joseph. *The Emotional Brain*. New York: Simon & Schuster, 1996.

Lemon, Michele. "Understanding Does Not Always Lead to Tolerance." *Globe and Mail*. January 31, 1995, p. A2.

"Letter to Editor." *Amarillo Globe News*. June 28, 2004, p. 8a.

Levitt, Steven D., and Stephen J. Dubner.

Super Freakonomics. New York: Harper-Collins, 2009.

Lewis, Anthony. "Un-American Activities." *The New York Review of Books* 50 (2003): 16.

Lewis, Bernard. *The Assassins: A Radical Sect in Islam*. New York: Basic Books, 2001.

_____. *The Political Language of Islam*. Chicago: University of Chicago Press, 1988.

_____. *The Muslim Discovery of Europe*. New York: Norton, 1982.

_____. "The Roots of Muslim Rage." *Atlantic Monthly* 266, no. 3 (September 1990): 47–60.

_____. *Islam and the West*. New York: Oxford University Press, 1993.

Lewis, Neil A. "Red Cross Finds Detainee Abuse in Guantanamo." *New York Times*. November 30, 2004, p. A1.

Lewis, Philip. *Islamic Britain: Religion, Politics and Identity among Britism Muslims*. London: I.B. Tauris, 1994.

"Lexington: A House Divided." *Economist* (May 8, 2004): 34.

Lia, Brynar, and Thomas Hegghammer. "Jihadi Strategic Studies: The Alleged Al Qaida Policy Study Preceding the Madrid Bombings." *Studies in Conflict and Terrorism* 27 (2004): 355–375.

Lippman, Walter. *Liberty and the News*. New York: Harcourt, Brace, and Howe, 1920.

Loconte, Joe. "I'll Stand Bayou." *Policy Review* (May/June 1998).

Los Angeles Times. "Moderate Islam's Message." October 10, 2001, p. B12.

_____. "Response to Terror: Words Are a Key Weapon in the Taliban's Arsenal." November 4, 2001, p. A1.

_____. "Iran: 100 Pilgrims Headed for Iraq Have Died in Efford." August 11, 2003, p. A1.

_____. "Religious Groups Want Outspoken General Punished." October 17, 2003, p. B17.

_____. "Iraqis See the Enemy Next Door." December 10, 2003, p. 1.

_____. "Coalition Gains Insight into Iraq's Foreign Insurgents." February 9, 2004, p. 1.

_____. "Evangelicals Flock into Iraq on a Mission of Faith." March 18, 2004, p. A1.

_____. "Iraqi City on Edge of Chaos." September 28, 2004, p. A1.

_____. "Europe's Boys of Jihad." April 2, 2005, p. A1.

Lustig, Robin, Martin Bailey, Simon de Bruxelles, and Ian Mather, "War of the Word," *The Observer* (February 19, 1989).

Manchester, William. *The Last Lion: Winston Spencer Churchill*. Boston, MA: Little, Brown, 1983.

Margulies, Joseph. *Guantanamo and the Abuse of Presidential Power*. New York: Simon & Schuster, 2006.

Markon, Jerry. "Muslim Lecturer Sentenced to Life; Followers Trained for Armed Jihad." *Washington Post*. July 14, 2005, p. A01.

"A Matter of Trust." *Economist* (April 3, 2004): 24–28.

Mayer, Ann Elizabeth. *Islam and Human Rights: Tradition and Politics*. Boulder, CO: Westview Press, 1991.

Mayer, Jane. *The Dark Side: The Inside Story of How the War on Terror Turned into a War on American Ideals*. New York: Doubleday, 2008.

Meckes, Catherine. "Wearing a Uniform of Oppression." *Globe and Mail*. July 5, 1993, p. A12.

"A Memo to American Muslims." *Los Angeles Times*. October 10, 2001, p. B12.

Micklethwait, John, and Adrian Wooldridge. *The Right Nation: Conservative Power in America*. New York: Penguin Press, 2004.

_____. *God Is Back: How the Global Revival of Faith Is Changing the World*. New York: Penguin Press, 2009.

Middle East Forum. "We Will Dominate You." December 1999, http://www.meforum.org/448/we-will-dominate-you (accessed May 13, 2010).

Milgram, Stanley. *Obedience to Authority: An Experimental View*. New York: Harper Perennial, 1969.

Miller, Judith. "Strangers at the Gate." *New York Times Magazine* (September 15, 1991): 49.

Mocks, Catherine, "The Hijab Has No Place in the Western World," *Globe and Mail*. February 16, 1993, p. A12.

Mohammad Atta: 9/11 Terrorist Ringleader. 2005, www.discoverthenetworks.org/individualProfile.asp?indid=757.

Monsma, Stephen V., and J. Christopher Soper. *The Challenge of Pluralism: Church and State in Five Western Democracies*. Lanham, MD: Rowman and Littlefield, 1997.

Morgan, Adrian. "UK Islamist Guilty of Soliciting Murder." *Spero News*. January 8,

2007, www.speroforum.com/site/article. asp?id=7364.

"Mosque Bombing Incites Sectarian Strife." *Philadelphia Inquirer.* December 12, 2004, p. 1

Moynihan, Brian. "Hardline Holland." *The Sunday Times.* February 27, 2005, pp. 34–42.

Muller, Jerry Z. *The Other God That Failed: Hans Freyer and the Deradicalization of German Conservatism.* Princeton, NJ: Princeton University Press, 1987.

_____. *Conservatism: An Anthology of Social and Political Thought from David Hume to the Present.* Princeton, NJ: Princeton University Press, 1997.

Murad, Khuram. *The Islamic Movement in the West: Reflections on Some Issues.* Leicester, UK: Islamic Foundation, 1981.

Murphy, John F., Jr. *Sword of Islam: Muslim Extremism from the Arab Conquests to the Attack on America.* New York: Prometheus, 2002.

"Muslims Get in Touch with Their Faith, Culture." *Chicago Tribune.* September 14, 2003, p. A1.

"Muslims in Britain: Hopes and Challenges." *Guardian.* November 30, 2004, http://image.guardian.co.uk/sysfiles/Guardian/documents/2004/11/30/Muslims-Novo41.pdf.

"Muslims in Europe: Confusing and Confused." *Economist* (October 29, 2005): 87.

"My Brother Zac." *Guardian.* April 19, 2003, www.guardian.co.uk/september11/story/0,11209,939701,00.html.

Nash, Gary B., Julie Roy Jeffrey, John R. Howe, Peter J. Frederick, Allen F. Davis, and Allan M. Winkler. *The American People: Creating a Nation and a Society.* New York: Harper and Row, 1979.

Nasrulla, Amber. "Educators Outside Quebec Mystified by Hijab Ban." *The Globe and Mail.* December 13, 1994, pp. A1–4.

"A Nation Sagging under the Weight of Sanctions: Caught in a Spiral of Poverty and Death." *Seattle Post-Intelligencer.* May 11, 1999, p. 1.

National Commission on Terrorist Attacks. *The 9/11 Commission Report: Final Report of the National Commission on Terrorist Attacks Upon the United States.* New York: W.W. Norton, 2004.

"New Fuel for the Culture Wars." *Economist* (March 5, 2004): 11.

"A New Splurge of Torture Papers." *Economist* (June 26, 2004): 23.

New York Times. "French Minister Threatens to Expel Extremist Muslims." September 20, 2003, p. A4.

Niebuhr, Reinhold. *Moral Man and Immoral Society.* New York: Scribner's, 1932.

Nielsen, Jorgen S. *Toward a European Islam.* London: Macmillan, 1999.

North, Gary. *Backward Christian Soldiers? An Action Manual for Christian Reconstruction.* Tyler, TX: Institute for Christian Economics, 1984.

Nursi, Bediuzzaman Said. "Twenty-ninth Letter — Sixth Section, Which Is the Sixth Treatise." In *Letters, 1928–1932*, edited by Bediuzzaman Said Nursi. Istanbul, Turkey: Sozler Nesriyat A.S., 1997.

Ochsenwald, William, and Sydney Nettleton Fisher. *The Middle East: A History,* 6th ed. New York: McGraw-Hill, 2004.

Oren, Michael. *Power, Faith, and Fantasy: America in the Middle East, 1776 to Present.* New York: Norton, 2007.

"Osama Baby Craze Hits Nigeria." *BBC News.* January 3, 2002, http://news.bbc.co.uk/2/hi/africa/1741171.stm.

Osman, Mohammad Fathi. "Towards a Vision and an Agenda for the Future of Muslim Ummah." In *Islam: A Contemporary Perspective,* edited by Mohammad Ahmadullah Siddiqi, 13–24. Chicago: NAAMPS, 1994.

Packer, George. *The Assassin's Gate: America in Iraq.* New York: Farrar, Straus, and Giroux, 2005.

Pape, Robert. *Dying to Win: The Strategic Logic of Suicide Terror.* New York: Random House, 2005.

Pargeter, Alison. *The New Frontiers of Jihad: Radical Islam in Europe.* Philadelphia: University of Pennsylvania Press, 2008.

Paz, Reuvan. "Middle East Islamism in the European Arena." *Middle East Review of International Affairs* (September 2002): 66–67.

Phillips, David L. *Losing Iraq: Inside the Postwar Reconstruction Fiasco.* Boulder, CO: Westview Press, 2005.

Phillips, Kevin. *American Dynasty: Aristocracy, Fortune, and the Politics of Deceit in the House of Bush.* New York: Viking, 2004.

_____. *Londonistan.* New York: Encounter Books, 2006.

_____. "Converts to Terrorism," *New York Sun*. December 6, 2005, p. A1.

Podhoretz, Norman. "Oslo: The Peacemongers Return." *Commentary* (October 2001).

"President Bush's State of the Union Address." *Washington Post*. January 31, 2006, http://www.washingtonpost.com/wp-dyn/content/article/2006/01/31/AR2006013101468.html.

"Profile: Abu Doha." *History Commons*. 2006, http://www.historycommons.org/entity.jsp?entity=abu_doha.

"Profile, Mounir al-Motassadek." *BBC News*. December 4, 2006, http://news.bbc.co.uk/2/hi/europe/2223152.stm.

"Profile, the Caliph of Cologne." *BBC News*. May 27, 2004, http://news.bbc.co.uk/2/hi/europe/1705886.stm.

Radi, Nuha al. *Baghdad Diaries*. London: Saqi Books, 1998.

"Radical Shiite Cleric Urges Revolt." *New York Times*. April 26, 2003, p. A1.

Ramadan, Tariq. *Western Muslims and the Future of Islam*. New York: Oxford University Press, 2004.

Rashid, Ahmed. "Osama Bin Laden: How the U.S. Helped Midwife a Terrorist." In *Terrorism and 9/11: A Reader*, edited by Fredrik Logevall, 110–125. Boston, MA: Houghton Mifflin, 2002.

_____. *Taliban: Militant Islam, Oil, and Fundamentalism in Central Asia*. New Haven, CT: Yale University Press, 2001.

Rath, Jan, Rinnus Pennix, Kees Groendendijk, and Astrid Meyer. *Western Europe and Its Islam*. Leiden, Netherlands: Brill, 2001.

"Rebuilding Iraq." *Economist* (September 13, 2003): 21–23.

"Religion and the War Against Evil." *Washington Post*. September 2, 2002, p. A3.

Rippin, Arthur. *Muslims: Their Religious Beliefs and Practices*, vol. 1. London and New York: Routledge, 1991.

_____. "Literary Analysis of Koran, Tafsir, and Sira: The Methodologies of John Wansbrough." In *The Origins of the Koran: Classic Essays on Islam's Holy Book*, edited by Ibn Warraq, 351–364. New York: Prometheus, 1998.

Rizzo, Tony. "KC Man Linked to Early Al Qaeda Call to Jihad Led Student to Follow Bin Laden." *The Kansas City Star*. September 9, 2006, p. A1.

"Robertson: Stroke Was God's Wrath." *Amarillo Globe News*. January 7, 2006, p. 4A.

Rokeach, Milton. *The Open and Closed Mind: Investigations into the Nature of Belief Systems and Personality Systems*. New York: Basic Books, 1972.

Rossiter, Clinton. *Conservatism in America*, 2nd ed. Cambridge, MA: Harvard University Press, 1982.

Rotella, Sebastian. "Before Maryrdom Plan, Belgian Woman's Faith Turned Radical." *Los Angeles Times*. December 2, 2005, p. A1.

Rothbard, Murray. *America's Great Depression*. New York: New York University Press, 1975.

Roy, Olivier. *The Failure of Political Islam*. Cambridge, MA: Harvard University Press, 1994.

_____. *Globalized Islam: The Search for a New Ummah*. New York: Columbia University Press, 2004.

Rushdoony, Rousas John. *Institutes of Biblical Law*. Nutley, NJ: Craig Press, 1973.

Sachar, Howard M. *A History of Israel: From the Rise of Zionism to Our Time*. New York: Random House, 1996.

Said, Edward W. *Orientalism*. New York: Vintage Books, 1979.

Sankari, Jamal. *Fadlallah: The Making of a Radical Shiite Leader*. London: Saqi Books, 2005.

Sargent, Lyman Tower. *Contemporary Political Ideologies: A Comparative Analysis*, 9th ed. Belmont, CA: Wadsworth, 1993.

Savage, Charlie. "Abuse Led Navy to Consider Pulling Cuba Interrogators." *Boston Globe*. March 16, 2005, p. A1.

Savage, Timothy M. "Europe and Islam: Crescent Waxing, Cultures Clashing." *The Washington Quarterly* (Summer 2004): 25–50.

Sayyid, S. *A Fundamental Fear: Eurocentrism and the Emergence of Islamism*. London and New York: Zed Books, 2003.

Schumaker, Paul, Dwight C. Kiel, and Thomas Heilke. *Great Ideas/Grand Scheme*. New York: McGraw-Hill, 1996.

_____. *Ideological Voices: An Anthology in Modern Political Ideas*. New York: McGraw-Hill, 1997.

Shadid, Anthony. *Night Draws Near: Americans In Iraq*. New York: Henry Holt, 2005.

Shakeri, Esmail. "Muslim Women in Canada: The Role and Status as Revealed in the Hijab Controversy." In *Muslims on the Americanization Path?*, edited by Yvonne Yazbeck Haddad and John L. Esposito, 129–144. New York: Oxford University Press, 2000.

Shepherd, John. "Self-critical Children of Abraham? Roots of Violence and Extremism in Judaism, Christianity and Islam." In *Islam and the West: Post 9/11*, edited by Ron Geaves, Theodore Gabriel, Yvonne Haddad, and Jane Idleman Smith, 27–51. Burlington, VT: Ashgate, 2004.

Sheridan, Chris. "Islamophobia." *Mirror.* June 1, 1995, p. 12.

"Shiites Target of Attacks in Iraq." *Baltimore Sun.* January 22, 2005, p. 1.

Siddiqi, Mohammad Ahmadullah. "Towards an Islamic Vision and Agenda for the Future." In *Islam: A Contemporary Perspective*, edited by Mohammad Ahmadullah Siddiqi, 25–32. Chicago: NAAMPS, 1994.

Sivan, Emmanuel. *Radical Islam: Medieval Theology and Modern Politics.* New Haven: Yale University Press, 1985.

Skidmore, Max. *Ideologies: Politics in Action*, 2nd ed. Fort Worth, TX: Harcourt Brace, 1993.

Smith, B.D., and J.J. Vetter. *Theoretical Approaches to Personality.* Englewood Cliffs, NJ: Prentice Hall, 1982.

Smith, David Gordon. "Schäuble's Terror Plan Shows Complete Insanity." *Spiegel Online International*, July 9, 2007, www.spiegel.de/international/germany/0,1518,4 93365,00.html.

Smith, Huston. *The World's Religions.* New York: HarperCollins, 1991.

Smith, Wilfred Cantwell. *Islam in Modern History.* New York: Mentor Books, 1957.

"Some European Media Not Bullish on Bush: Liberal Newspapers Don't Hide Their Feelings." *MSNBC.* November 4, 2004, msnbc.msn.com/id/6409042/.

"Special Report: Afghanistan." *Economist* (October 9, 2004): 21–23.

"Special Report: Iraq." *Economist* (May 7, 2005): 21.

"Special Report: Islam and Free Speech." *Economist* (February 11, 2006): 24–26.

Spencer, Ian R.G. *British Immigration Policy Since 1939: The Making of a Multi-Racial Britain.* London: Routledge, 1997.

"Statistical Overviews and Resources: Victim's Rights," *National Counterterrorism Center*, 2005, www.wits.nctc.gov/reports/crot2005nctcannexfinal.pdf.

Stone, John R. *The Routledge Dictionary of Latin Quotations.* New York: Routledge, 2004.

"Study Cites Seeds of Terror in Iraq." *Boston Globe*, July 17, 2005.

Suha Taji-Farouki. *A Fundamental Quest: Hizh ut-Tahrir and the Search for the Islamic Caliphate.* London: Grey Seal, 1996.

"A Survey of Retirement: Forever Young." *Economist* (March 27, 2004): 3–4.

Suskind, Ron. *The Price of Loyalty: George W. Bush, the White House, and the Education of Paul O'Neill.* New York: Simon & Schuster, 2004.

_____. *The One Percent Doctrine: Deep Inside America's Pursuit of its Enemies Since 9/11.* New York: Simon & Schuster, 2006.

_____. "The Tyrant Who Came in from the Cold." *Washington Monthly.* 2006, www.washingtonmonthly.com/features/2006/0610.suskind.html.

"Study by Muslim Group Says Bias Crimes Up 50% in 2004." *New York Times.* May 21, 2005, p. B5.

"Swing Low, Swing Right: The European Elections." *Economist* (June 13, 2008): 54–55.

Syal, Rajeev. "Cleric Supports Targeting Children." *Sunday Telegraph.* September 5, 2004.

Taeharah, Pasha Mohamed Ali. *An Introduction to Islamism.* Bloomington, IN: AuthorHouse, 2005.

Taher, Abul. "Banned Extremists Regroup." *The Sunday Times.* October 29, 2006, www.timesonline.co.uk/tol/news/uk/article 616692.ece.

Taji-Farouki, Suha. *Muslim Identity and the Balkan State.* New York: New York University Press, 1996.

Talbot, David. "Terror's Server." *Technology Review.* February 2005.

"Tape in the Name of Leading Insurgent Declares All-Out War on Iraq Elections and Democracy." *New York Times.* January 24, 2005, p. A10.

Territo, Leonard, James Halstead, and Max Bromley. *Crime and Justice in America.* St. Paul, MN: West, 1989.

"Terrorism Deaths Increase." *Amarillo Globe News.* July 10, 2005, p. 1.

"Terrorist 007 Exposed." *Washington Post.* March 26, 2006, p. B01.

Thomas, Benjamin Platt. *Abraham Lincoln: A Biography*. New York: Knopf, 1960.

Thomas, Gordon. *Gideon's Spies: The Secret History of the Mossad*. New York: Thomas Dunne Books, 1999.

"TIME Exclusive: Inside the Wire at Gitmo." *TIME*. June 12, 2005, www.time.com/time/press_releases/article/0,8599,1071230.html.

Trevor, Joan. "Anti-Bans, Anti-Hijab." *Worker's Liberty*. 12 August 2004, www.workersliberty.org/node/2320.

United States of America v. Zacarias Moussaoui. December 2001, www.usdoj.gov/ag/moussaouiindictment.htm.

"University of Houston Muslim Students Association." *MSA@UH Forum*. July 12, 2007, http://www.uh.edu/campus/msa/home.php.

"U.S. Hopes to Divide Insurgency." *Washington Post*. October 13, 2004, p. 1.

Wansbrough, John. *Quranic Studies: Sources and Methods of Scriptural Interpretations*. New York and Oxford: Oxford University Press, 1977.

"War Strategy: Dramatic Failures Require Drastic Changes." *Saint Louis Post-Dispatch*. December 19, 2004, p. A1.

"Website Offers Instructions for Crossing Syrian-Iraqi Border: 'This Is the Road to Iraq.'" *Global Issues Report*, June 9, 2005.

"The Week Paris Burned." *Observer*. November 6, 2005, http://www.guardian.co.uk/world/2005/nov/06/france.focus.

Weiner, Tim. *Legacy of Ashes: The History of the CIA*. New York: Doubleday, 2007.

Weinstein, Michael, and Resa Aslan. "Not So Fast, Christian Soldiers." *Los Angeles Times*. August 22, 2007, B17.

Whine, Michael. "Al-Muhajiroun: The Portal for Britain's Suicide Terrorists." *International Policy Institute for Counter Terrorism*, pp. 1–8. May 21, 2003, www.ict.org.il/articles/articledet.cfm?articleid=484.

White, Jonathan. *Terrorism: An Introduction*. Belmont, CA: Wadsworth, 2002.

"Who Is Richard Reid?" *BBC News*. December 28, 2001, http://news.bbc.co.uk/1/hi/uk/1731568.stm.

Wictorowicz, Quintan. *Radical Islam Rising*. Lanham, MD: Rowman and Littlefield, 2005.

Wolfe, Michael, ed. *Taking Back Islam: American Muslims Reclaim their Faith*. Emmaeus, PA: Rodale, 2002.

Woods, Roger. "The Radical Right: The Conservative Revolutionaries in Germany." In *The Nature of the Right: American and European Politics and Political Thought since 1789*, edited by Roger Eatwell and Noel O'Sullivan, 124–145. Boston, MA: Twayne, 1989.

Woodward, Bob. *Bush at War*. New York: Simon & Schuster, 2002.

World Bank. *World Development Indicators*. Washington, DC: World Bank, 1998.

"World Bomb Suspects Alive in France." *BBC News*. June 1, 1999, http://news.bbc.co.uk/1/hi/world/357808.stm.

"The World This Week." *Economist* (January 29, 2005): 7.

Wolfe, Michael ed. *Taking Back Islam: American Muslims Reclaim their Faith*. Emmaus, PA: Rodale Press, 2002.

Wright, Lawrence. *The Looming Tower: Al-Qaeda and the Road to 9/11*. New York: Alfred A. Knopf, 2006.

Wurmser, David. *Tyranny's Ally: America's Failure to Defeat Saddam Hussein*. Washington, DC: AEI Press, 1999.

"Zarqawi's Journey: From Dropout to Prisoner to Insurgent Leader." *New York Times*. July 13, 2004, p. A8.

Zucchino, David. *Thunder Run: Three Days in the Battle for Baghdad*. London: Atlantic Books, 2004.

Index

American immigration policy 125–126
American Jihadists 120–126
American Muslim alienation 61–63
American Muslim Associations 46–48; and jihad in Afghanistan 48
American Muslim diversity 86
American Muslim immigration 86
American Vision 65
Amir, Yigal 62
Anatolian Federated Islamic State and Kalifasstaat 42
Ansar al-Islam 157
Aquille Lauro 108
Arab-American Anti-Discrimination Committee 123
Arab European League 46
Arab Islamic Conference 164
Arab League 118
Arabia 209
Arkansas Highway and Transportation Department 193
Armey, Dick 66
Armstrong, Herbert 23
Aryan Nations 23
Ashcroft, John 53, 65–66, 125, 170
Asia Exclusion Act 1965 86
Asiedu, Manfo Kwaku 113
asylum 58, 76; in Britain 81
Ataturk, Kemal 211
Atta, Mohamed 28, 31, 111–112, 116, 136–138, 140, 141, 207
authoritarian personality 2, 20, 24–32; and morality 31; and punishment 31; and rights 31; and self-righteousness 32
Azhar University 147
Aziz, Abu Abdul 126
Aznar, Jose Maria 115
Azzam, Abdullah 134, 143–144

Baccus, Brig. Gen. Rick 177
Badawi, Jamal 105
Baizid, Mohammed Loay 143–144
Bajaji, Said 140
Balfour, Sarah 149
Baluchistan University 165
Bandura, Albert 26–27
Battle Hymn of the Republic 64
Bechari, Mohamed 37–38
Begum, Shabina 98
Bektasevic, Mirsad 192
Belgian General Islamic Assembly 81
Benevolence International Foundation 125, 145
Benjamin, Daniel 66, 116, 191
Benna, Zyed 110
Bensaid, Ben Ali Boualem 151–152
Benyettou, Farid 186
Berg, Nicholas 193
Berg, Lt. Col. Thomas 173
Bernardi, Giuseppe 18
Berrea, Heribert 54

Beslan siege 128
Biffi, Cardinal 54
Bilal, Mohamed 112–113, 157
Bilal Mosque 151
Bin al-Shibh, Ramzi 111, 116
Bin Attash, Tawfiq 122
Bin Laden, Mohammed 132
Bin Laden, Osama 3, 10, 12, 16, 21–22, 24, 26, 30–31, 39, 44, 48, 108–109, 116, 118, 120–22, 130–146, 152, 160, 162, 164, 184, 204, 206; and Canadian Islamists 154; and Hamburg cell 138–142; and John Walker Lindh 159; and Richard Reid 161; and Western freedoms 167
Bin Laden, Saad 122
Bin Laden, Um Hamza 133
Bin Laden, Umm Abdullah 133
Bin Laden, Umm Khaled 133
Bin Muhammad, Mahathir 201
Bin Williams Rakan 155
Black September 107
Blair, Tony 39, 149
Bonaparte, Napoleon 77
bones of contention 92–106
book burnings 92–93
Boualem, Yousfi 152–153
Boubakeur, Sheikh Hamza 105
Bouchar, Abdelmajid 117
Bourgass, Kamel 150–151
Bouyeri, Mohammed 114
Boykin, William 53, 66
Boys of al-Qaedand 9/11 130–145
Bradford Council of Mosques 92
Brame, J. Robert, III 65
Bray, Michael 22
British Blasphemy Laws 93
British Muslim Association 36
British National Party 56, 80
British Nationality Act 79
British Shariah Council 52
Brixton Mosque 161
Buchanan, Pat 211
Bundesamt fur Verfassungschutz 46
Bunglawala, Inayat 36–37
burial disputes 52
burqa 98
Bush, George H.W. 176
Bush, George W. 50–51, 57–58, 61, 69, 115, 119–120, 122, 150, 190, 198–199, 212; and Abu Ghraib 186–187; and American Muslims 61–63, 124–126; and civil rights 168–187; and "crusade" 63; and Danish cartoons 119–120; and Geneva Conventions 174–176; and Iraq War 183–187; and Jose Padilla 160; and Muslim resentment 172; and Providence 65; and the religious right 64–65; and right to counsel 171; and searches and seizures 169–170; and secrecy 170; and torture 171–172; and War on Terror 124–126, 165, 168–187